RUSSIAN IDENTITIES

RUSSIAN IDENTITIES

A Historical Survey

Nicholas V. Riasanovsky

OXFORD
UNIVERSITY PRESS
2005

OXFORD
UNIVERSITY PRESS

Oxford University Press, Inc., publishes works that further
Oxford University's objective of excellence
in research, scholarship, and education.

Oxford   New York
Auckland   Cape Town   Dar es Salaam   Hong Kong   Karachi
Kuala Lumpur   Madrid   Melbourne   Mexico City   Nairobi
New Delhi   Shanghai   Taipei   Toronto

With offices in
Argentina Austria   Brazil   Chile   Czech Republic   France   Greece
Guatemala   Hungary   Italy   Japan   Poland   Portugal   Singapore
South Korea   Switzerland   Thailand   Turkey   Ukraine   Vietnam

Copyright © 2005 by Oxford University Press

Published by Oxford University Press, Inc.
198 Madison Avenue, New York, New York 10016

www.oup.com

Oxford is a registered trademark of Oxford University Press

Library of Congress Cataloging-in-Publication Data
Riasanovsky, Nicholas Valentine, 1923–
Russian identities: a historical survey / Nicholas V. Riasanovsky.
p. cm.
Includes bibliographical references and index.
ISBN-13 978-0-19-515650-8
ISBN 0-19-515650-1
1. Russians—Ethnic identity.   2. National characteristics, Russian.   3. Russia—Civilization—Philosophy.
4. Slavs, Eastern—History—Philosophy.   5. Nationalism—Russia—History.   I. Title.
DK33.R53 2005
947—dc22   2004065447

1 3 5 7 9 8 6 4 2
Printed in the United States of America
on acid-free paper

In memory of departed colleagues and friends

Acknowledgments

Taking into account the scope of this work and the fact that parts of it were at the center of my scholarly interest for decades, I find no effective way to make full acknowledgments. I am thinking especially of numerous teachers and colleagues, now dead, to whom the work is dedicated. At this point I am limiting myself to listing the names of those specialists who read and criticized all or some of the manuscript itself: professors Victoria Bonnell, George Breslauer, John Connelly, the late Ernest Haas, the late Martin Malia, Robert Middlekauff, Iuri Slezkine, the late Alexander Vucinich, the late Reginald Zelnik, and Victor Zhivov. I could expatiate on profiting from, among other topics, Zhivov's magnificent knowledge of Russian history, Breslauer's relentless tracking of Soviet leaders, or Connelly's precision about relevant developments in eastern Europe; but all my readers and critics published their own books and do not need my accolades. Obviously, however, they should not be held responsible for the remaining mistakes and weaknesses in my work. I received expert help also from my successive research assistants, Ilya Vinkovetsky and Leonid Kil, both very promising young scholars. Thomas Livingston performed excellently the task of preparing and typing the manuscript for publication as well as compiling the index. And I must thank Oxford University Press, helpful in everything as always, and in particular my editor, Susan Ferber, and production editor, Linda Donnelly (not to forget the two anonymous readers for the Press).

Last and first I want to thank my wife, Arlene.

Contents

Introduction   3

1. Prehistory   7

2. Kievan Russia   18

3. Appanage and Muscovite Russia   33

4. The Reign of Peter the Great   74

5. The Eighteenth Century in Russia after the Death of
   Peter the Great   88

6. The Reign of Alexander I, 1801–1825   111

7. The Reign of Nicholas I, 1825–1855, and
   the New Intellectual Climate   130

8. Russia from the Death of Nicholas I to the Abdication of
   Nicholas II, 1855–1917   167

9. Soviet Russia, 1917–1991   211

   Conclusion   231

   Notes   237

   Index   258

RUSSIAN IDENTITIES

Introduction

When I asked an eminent political scientist during the question period that followed his lecture on nationalism what he thought of the influence of the Hundred
Years' War on the nationalisms of England and France, he first ascertained that I was
speaking of the war that had been fought from 1337 to 1453 A.D. and after that
dismissed my question in two words: "Forget it."[1] However, he explained later that
he had responded as he had not because that war could not have any appreciable
impact on those nationalisms but because the present state of scholarship offered
no way to establish or trace such an impact reliably. The explanation has its point,
and it becomes more convincing as we go further back in time.

There is an enormous and ever-growing literature on nationalism as a modern
phenomenon, linked usually to the French Revolution, or to the Industrial Revolution, or to German Idealistic philosophy and Romanticism as a whole, or to general
education and "the rise of the masses," or to any combination of these and still other
major recent historical developments. To cite one leading writer on the subject,
Ernest Gellner argues roughly as follows: modern economy develops dynamically
and irreversibly, the only alternative being collapse, and at a certain stage in its
development it needs critical elements of support. These include sufficient size,
centralization, discipline, an educated population, and an ideology to tie closely
together and inspire all components of the economic unit. Nationalism supplies or
helps to supply all these needs; and teachers, publicists, writers, professors, philosophers, and intellectuals in general serve as its natural and effective agents. Gellner's
scheme, like many others, aims not only to explain nationalism but also to deter-
mine its course and pace.[2]

Predicating nationalism on major recent historical developments has led to
another principal characteristic of contemporary scholarship on that subject,
namely the emphasis on the artificiality, the constructed nature, of nationalism. Far
from being treated as immemorial, if not eternal, and based forever on ethnicity or
on some transcendent mission, nationalism has been described as a device applied,

both by believers in the nation and by cynics, to bolster capitalism, mobilize society for war, or serve other interests of rulers and ruling classes. From one point of view, it is a leading present-day example of false consciousness. Benedict Anderson's *Imagined Communities* captures in its very title this phenomenon.[3] And indeed, much thorough and convincing scholarship has gone into demonstrating how intellectuals have built, or at least helped to build, modern nations and nationalism. In my case, I got to see the process of nationalism in the making through my friend the late Dr. Sulo Haltsonen, who was secretary of the Finnish Literary Society, the society that, in a sense, made Finland. It was fascinating to observe the still-continuing process of the shaping of the national language itself, from several dialects, and the relationship that Finno-Ugric linguistics established between the Finns and other peoples from Lapland to Hungary and Siberia. One could easily think of similar developments among certain nationalities of the Hapsburg empire or some Balkan peoples a century or so earlier. While the constructed nature of modern nationalism can be seen most clearly in the case of new countries, such as Finland or Latvia, the process of construction is, of course, by no means limited to them. Thus, Eugen Weber in his splendid book, *Peasants into Frenchman: The Modernization of Rural France, 1870–1914*,[4] gives a striking presentation of the workings of that process in France, especially by means of general education, compulsory military service, and improvement of transportation and communication.

Recent scholarship has done much to elucidate nationalism; but some serious problems remain. The most important and troublesome of them, in my opinion, is the relationship between nationalism and the "prenationalist" past. There is no satisfactory terminology. "Prenationalist," or "protonationalist," has a teleological direction, which is not really warranted. Instead I shall often refer to "identity," but that is a general and flexible term, which can also be applied to nationalism itself. Even if we accept in the main the modern view of nationalism, we have to recognize that nationalism in each case descended upon not a tabula rasa, but a society with a past. Moreover, the descent usually took many years, decades, even centuries, with most of the people in question still belonging most of the time to the old world.

But it is not only continuity and completeness that urge attention to the prenationalist past. Substantively, too, what happened long ago can be significant, even decisive, today. For example, if I were to name the single historical event most significant for Russian identity and Russian nationalism, I would propose not Napoleon's invasion of Russia in 1812, not Stalin's turn to a limited and strictly controlled nationalism in the late 1930s, not even the emancipation of the serfs in 1861, but the so-called baptism of the Rus in 988. Without that baptism, Russia (and Ukraine and Belarus too) might have been at present a Muslim state, with an entirely different history, identity, and nationalism. With the baptism, Orthodoxy became a central element in Russian history and culture, whether in the days of the Kievan princes, of the quasi-medieval appanage Russia, of the Orthodox tsardom of Muscovy, of the Orthodox empire of the Romanovs, or even, as the enemy, during the communist regime, which tried desperately but failed to eradicate it. Indeed, one must keep both the old and the new history in mind for a full understanding of nationalism. If, at one extreme, France today, with its rich historical past, can nevertheless be interpreted by Weber and numerous other specialists largely in strikingly modern terms, at the other extreme, Finland, which appeared as a state as late as 1917, remains inconceivable without the Finnish language; and language is old and never a tabula rasa.

The obstacles and difficulties in studying Russian identity and Russian nationalism are many. Prehistory is essentially an area of speculation, with no clear structure, few reliable sources, and grave dangers lurking in arguments by interpolation or analogy. Even such a monumental factor as the struggle with the steppe peoples escapes precise evaluation. The baptism of the Rus in 988 did provide a new Christian identity and brought the Rus into the mainstream of Christian religion and culture. Yet it remains an open question how many Rus, how quickly, and how fully, joined that mainstream or even its rivulets. In Russia, as in the West, for centuries monks served as the main and usually only informers. Whereas the appanage period after the fall of Kiev reminds one of the inchoate early European Middle Ages, a greater organization and cohesion were achieved around Moscow in the fifteenth, sixteenth, and seventeenth centuries. Indeed, some scholars write of the integrated society and organic culture of the Muscovite tsardom. But this integration was broken by the separation of the Old Believers from the official church in 1666, and at the end of the century by the beginning of Peter the Great's reforms. After the relative success of these reforms and the Russian turn westward in general, the society came to be divided sharply into a small, gradually Westernizing educated class and the overwhelmingly peasant masses. The educated proceeded to participate, often creatively, in the entire range of cultural and intellectual life of Europe, including the increasingly prominent issue of nationalism. The ignorant remained offstage. As the empire of the Romanovs expanded, more and more non-Russians became subjects of the tsar. When World War I broke out in the summer of 1914, Russians proper, that is, Great Russians, formed only about half of the population of the state, with another quarter belonging to the Ukrainian or Belarus ethnicities. Still, Russian nationalism was growing, and it was finally acquiring some mass support. The emancipation of the serfs in 1861 and the other "great reforms" of Alexander II certainly contributed to the process. The factors that Weber analyzed in France were also operating in Russia. Most important was perhaps the increase in general education, already considerable in reality and sweeping in prospect. The revolution of 1905 was followed by a constitutional, or a quasi-constitutional, period. If Russia entered World War I as still essentially an old regime, it was not likely to remain in that condition for long. But events took a different turn. The empire collapsed in 1917 and ceded its place not to a modern national state, but, in short order if not immediately, to a communist entity that eventually adopted the name of the Union of Soviet Socialist Republics. Although there is no agreement on the subject, it is safe to say, to put it mildly, that the seventy-five years of communist rule represented a departure and a deviation in the history of Russian identity and nationalism. Since 1991, the earlier orientation has been able to resume its course. But what it is at present and where it will lead is highly controversial and unpredictable. Observers seem to agree only on the assertion that this is a transitional period.

This study is not meant simply as an introduction to modern Russian nationalism but rather constitutes an attempt to depict the different meanings of being Russian in terms of their nature and significance in their own time and place. In much of my narrative, I relied on my history of Russia and occasionally on my other books, such as those on the Slavophiles, on Official Nationality, or on the image of Peter the Great in Russian history and thought. All of them have bibliographies.[5]

Why write this book? History is about the past, a thousand years ago or yesterday, but not about tomorrow. The past has a value in itself for all human beings interested in humanity and human destiny. Yet it also exists, and sometimes very prominently, as part of the present-day world. The question of Rus, Russia, the Russian identity is a fascinating example of that continuous and changeable historical existence, for it covers a huge territory, many centuries, and different political, social, and economic structures. I have tried to present my account broadly, emphasizing such main features as the struggle against the steppe peoples, Orthodox Christianity, autocratic monarchy, westernization, and the Soviet era and its collapse. I even included prehistory, where my information is entirely secondhand and where I am skeptical of speculation. But this area of study attracts some scholars determined to pursue the issue of identity as far back as possible and who, perhaps, may serve as a counterbalance to other searchers who start, say, with the French Revolution. I stop only with today, when all of us should attempt ourselves to understand Russia. After a lifetime of study of different aspects and periods of Russian identity, I am now trying to obtain a complete, if summary, picture.

Prehistory

The history of the Medes is dark and unknown.
—Dmitri Ivanovich Ilovaisky

How far back in time can one trace group identity? Most of our classifications of prehistoric peoples are based on linguistics and on archaeology.[1] In linguistic terms, the Russians are identified as East Slavs, that is, speakers of East Slavic, which eventually evolved into three distinct languages: Great Russian, often called simply Russian; Ukrainian; and White Russian, or Belorussian (Belarus). Other branches of the Slavic languages are the West Slavic, including Polish and Czech, and the South Slavic, represented, for instance, by Serbo-Croatian and Bulgarian. The Slavic languages, in turn, form a subdivision of the Indo-European language family that includes most of the tongues spoken today in Europe and some used in Asia.

To explain the relatedness of the languages within a family and the much closer relationship of the languages of the same subfamily, scholars have postulated an original language and homeland for each family and later languages and homelands for different linguistic subfamilies before further separation and differentiation. The Slavs, who became distinct from other Indo-European speakers around the middle of the second millennium B.C., were usually assigned a common homeland in the general area of the valley of the Vistula and the northern slopes of the Carpathians. The split among the Slavs has been dated, by A. A. Shakhmatov and others, to the sixth century A.D., and the settlement by the East Slavs of the great plain of European Russia to the seventh, eighth, and ninth centuries.

Recent scholarship has subjected the theory of original languages and homelands to a searching criticism. At present, few scholars speak with any confidence about the historical homeland of the Indo-Europeans, and some reject it even as a theoretical concept. The location and the chronology of the Slavic homeland have also been thoroughly questioned. The reevaluation has been largely instigated by discoveries of the presence of the Slavs at a much earlier time and over a much larger area in Russia than had been traditionally supposed. In light of new evidence, certain scholars have redefined the original Slavic homeland, and even the original Indo-European homeland, as including parts of Russia. Others have postulated an earlier dispersal of the Slavs, some suggesting that it proceeded in several waves—to explain both their ancient presence on the Russian plain and their migration thither. Thus a leading authority in the field, B. A. Rybakov, taking a characteristically inclusive approach to the Slavic past, asserted that only two views of the original Slavic homeland now deserve scholarly attention: one placing it between the Western Bug and the Vistula eastward to the Dnieper, and the other placing it between the Western Bug and the Vistula westward to the Oder. Then he combined the two locations to endow the Slavs with a huge homeland, from the Oder to the Dnieper and beyond, and from the Baltic north to the Scythian south, where Slavs might have formed the bulk of the population of the Scythian state.[2] Rybakov's and other such schemes gain in variety and historical possibilities what they lose in simplicity and neatness.

It is of utmost importance to realize, at this point and throughout this book, that these kinds of identifications—mentioned here and throughout the volume—are linguistic, not racial, and do not necessarily correspond to any physical traits. Although it may be argued that a common language and a common location indicate a genetic connection, the argument cannot be reliably sustained. Intermarriage, conquest, and imitation, as well as some other factors, have repeatedly changed the number and composition of those speaking a given language. Today, for instance, English is the native tongue of African Americans as well as of Yorkshiremen.[3] An entire people can lose a language and adopt a new one. Invaders have often been absorbed by the indigenous population, as in the case of the Turkic Bulgars in the Balkans. Other invaders have been able to overwhelm and incorporate native peoples.

To begin with Indo-Europeans and present one standard account:

Recent research has made it clear that 'proto'-Indo-Europeans embarked on an enormous expansion into Europe and the Near East from the steppes of Eurasia. The differentiation of the more or less homogeneous proto-culture and proto-language proceeded gradually as the tribes dispersed and distances between their areas of settlement increased. The first movement from South Russia to the Ukraine and the Lower Danube basin occurred some time before 4000 BC and the repeated migrations and devastation of the Aegean, Mediterranean and Anatolian lands took place in the period around 2300 BC.

The 'proto'-Indo-Europeans were semi-nomadic pastoralists having a patrilinear and patriarchal social system. They were horse breeders and possibly used horses as mounts and possessed vehicles as early as the third millennium BC. This explains their mobility. It took them less than a millennium to conquer and/or assimilate a number of Balkan and Central European food-producing cultures as well as convert some North European hunters and fishers to their way of life. Wherever the Indo-European groups spread, Central or Northern Europe, the Balkan Peninsula or the Near East, they brought with them specifically Indo-European elements recognizable archaeologically in different social, economic and habitation patterns, religious symbols, burial rites and art traditions.

The infiltration of Europe by the Indo-Europeans initiated a new era. Great civilizations of the fifth and fourth millennia in the Balkan Peninsula, the Black Sea coasts and the Aegean area disintegrated.[4]

In fact, the Indo-European takeover of the European continent was eventually so widespread and thorough that only a few of the mysterious pre-Indo-European languages survived until historic time, and of these only Basque is still spoken today. Mobile warriors organized into military bands prevailed over ancient civilizations of "peaceful farmers."

However, it is not clear to what extent this conventional heroic description of Indo-Europeans helps to illuminate the Slavic past. Gimbutas herself wrote of the Slavs as follows.

> The story of the Slavs as deciphered from archaeological, historical, linguistic and folkloristic sources reveals the vital ingredient of tenacity as the attribute that kindled the Slavic phenomenon. Initially an insignificant, repeatedly subjugated Indo-European group living north of the Carpathian mountains and the middle Dnieper river area, the Slavic farmers through their persistence managed to survive and ultimately succeeded in occupying a vast territory in Central and Eastern Europe and Balkan Peninsula. Their expansion was not episodic like that of the Huns and Avars, it was a colonization. Scholars have brilliantly deduced the existence of a Proto-Slavic parent language from the linguistic evidence.
>
> Today there are about 200 million Slavonic-speaking peoples in the world. Their thirteen separate languages, grouped into western, southern and eastern blocs, emerged from what appears to have been a single language until the ninth century ad.[5]

Even those scholars who claim vast and diverse territories for proto-Slavs or pre-Slavs often consider the area north of the Carpathian mountains as the site for the rise of Slavdom. In the more traditional view, the Slavs were largely confined to that area before they burst out of it in the second half of the first millennium A.D. The Slavic homeland experienced strong influences from all sides, perhaps especially from central Europe and from the eastern steppe. Indeed, at times it appeared submerged by Germanic or Sarmatian invaders. Still, the basic proto-Slavic or Slavic population survived and maintained its mode of existence. "For almost two millennia we can trace a cultural continuity, evident in their burial rites, farming, economy, habitation pattern, architecture and artifacts."[6] In fact, the Slavic area advanced northward at the expense of the Baltic-speakers.

The period of Slavic migrations and of the great and rather sudden expansion of the Slavic zone in Europe does raise serious problems. Gimbutas explained the developments as follows, with special reference to the Balkan Peninsula.

> Thus neither Bulgars nor Avars colonized the Balkan Peninsula in the fifth and sixth centuries; after storming Thrace, Illyria and Greece they went back to their territory north of the Danube. It was the Slavs who did the colonizing; travelling on foot in vast numbers, entire families or even whole tribes infiltrated the devastated lands. As an agricultural people, they constantly sought an outlet for their population surplus. Suppressed for over a millennium by the foreign rule of Scythians, Sarmatians, and Goths, they had been restricted to a small territory; now the barriers were down and they poured out.[7]

But, to cite a different, even opposite, opinion, that of Johanna Nichols:

> Ethnic spreads can involve either the spread of a language to speakers of other languages or the spread of a population. Massive population spread or demographic replacement has probably been a rarity in human history, at least until colonial times; the only good examples would appear to be spreads into previously uninhabited territory (such as the colonization of Polynesia). Since there is neither archeological nor historical evidence for large-scale depopulation of central and eastern Europe in the early centuries a.d., and since in their physical anthropology the various modern Slavic populations resemble their respective non-Slavic neighbors more than all Slavs resemble each other, there is no reason to assume the Slavic expansion was primarily a demographic event. Some migration took place, but the most parsimonious assumption is that the Slavic expansion was primarily a linguistic spread.[8]

Unfortunately, although Nichols provides in her article a fascinating linguistic analysis and model of the territory in question, she does not explain why at that particular time various non-Slavic speaking peoples adopted Slavic speech.

In any case, the newly expanded Slavdom soon entered history in a major and sustained manner. Its new role, or roles, were indicated best by the appearance of important Slavic states, notably those of Great Moravia and Kievan Rus in the ninth century and of Poland in the tenth, and also by the conversion of the Slavs to Christianity: Moravia by 863, Bulgaria in 885, Poland in 966, and Russia in 988.

By the ninth century a.d., the East Slavs were widely established in agriculture. Their other significant occupations included fishing, hunting, apiculture, cattle-raising, weaving, and pottery-making, as well as other arts and crafts, such as carpentry. The East Slavs had used iron for centuries. They had also been engaging in varied and far-flung commerce. They possessed a remarkable number of towns. Even M. N. Tikhomirov's extensive count of them is not complete.[9] Certain of these towns, such as Novgorod, Smolensk, and Kiev, a town belonging to the tribe of the Poliane, would have long and important histories.

What can be said about Indo-European religion, especially as it applies to proto-Slavs and, later, Slavs? That religion has been linked to light and fire, to war, to various phenomena and forces reflected in many pagan religions. The most prominent recent scholar of the subject, Georges Dumézil, has constructed a remarkable tripartite theory of Indo-European social and religious structure.[10] Unfortunately, Dumézil's brilliant reconstruction of the deep Indo-European past is both highly speculative and based on material other than Slavic or proto-Slavic, which is only beginning to be investigated along the lines he suggested. The Slavic pantheon and religious ritual, while linked to the Indo-European in many ways, with some striking specific parallels to the material found in the Rig-Veda and other cognate Indo-European sources, also included non-Indo-European gods and associated practices.[11]

Although pagan Slavdom produced no written literature, descriptions and comments of outsiders, archaeology, oral tradition, and folklore, everything from the celebrated Kievan epic cycle to designs on peasants' towels, together with a general effort to project the historic Slavic peasant society and its mentality into the past, have been used to reconstruct the beliefs and concerns of pagan Slavs, East Slavs included. To illustrate the above I shall refer only to some of the great effort at reconstruction mounted by a leading historian and archeologist, the already-mentioned B. A. Rybakov. The conclusion to Rybakov's *The Paganism of Ancient Slavs* contains twenty-four disparate summary points. The first two points dealt with the scope of the work and the fact that the roots of pagan concepts went to the prehistoric primitive age.

Third, the analysis of the depth of popular memory led to an important conclusion: it turned out that the evolution of religious conceptions proceeded not by a replacement of one set of forms by another, but by layering of the new upon the old. The determination of the span of time between the emergence of a certain phenomenon and a recording of its survivals, a span perhaps tens of thousands of years in duration, enables us to extrapolate that phenomenon for the entire span.

Thus, as Rybakov set out in his fourth point:

4. A whole series of elements of the East Slavic folklore goes back to the primeval hunters of the paleolithic and the mesolithic periods: conjurations of the forces of nature, conjurations against evil (the vampires), the image of a "trunk-possessing" monster (the mammoth?) surrounded by fire, the cult of a bear's paw, the legendary bogatyr [mighty warrior] Bear's Ear, halfman-halfbear, bogatyrs dressed in hides—all these are echoes of the stone age.[12]

Rybakov continued with his points, paraphrased below:

5. Originally the bear god of Stone Age hunters, "god of the dead animal," Volos, or Veles, became—in the Bronze Age of pastoral migrations—the god of livestock and eventually, in Kievan Rus, the god of wealth.

6. A Russian writer of the early twelfth century gave a most interesting and essentially correct periodization of ancient paganism: first, people sacrificed to "vampires and protective deities"; during the second stage, they worshiped Fertility

and goddesses of fertility.[13] Unfortunately, the entire scholarly literature avoided discussing the fertility cult. In fact, there were two goddesses of fertility, and their matriarchal cult preceded the patriarchal cult of Fertility itself.

7. The cult of the two goddesses of fertility, the guarantors of fecundity and fruitfulness, went through two stages: the hunting and the agricultural. The heavenly Mistresses of the World were conceived of as half woman, half moose (or half elk). They resided in the sky and were identified with the great constellations of Ursa Major (ancient Russian, the Elk) and Ursa Minor, the two originally called She-Elk and her calf. The Mistresses of the World, mother and daughter, gave birth to all animals, birds, and fish needed by humanity. At that later stage of the hunting age, the universe was no longer conceptualized on a single, earthly plane, but instead was divided into three levels: the lower one, underground and underwater; the middle, the earth; and the upper, the sky and the stars.

8. Conceptualizations of the two Heavenly Mistresses are richly documented in the art of Indo-European farmers of the Aeneolithic Period, some of whom were linguistic ancestors of the Slavs. Sometimes the goddesses retain their archaic appearance of elk or moose, as if floating in the sky in a torrent of rain; on other occasions they appear as enormous faces covering the universe from the earth to "upper sky." Most often they are represented by four female breasts, inseparably linked to the symbolism of a nourishing liquid, that is, again, rain.

9. Together with the concept of the two goddesses of fertility, the early agriculturists also inherited, perhaps all the way from Paleolithic "Venuses," the image of one Great Mother. She came to be considered, on the one hand, cosmogonically, as the Progenitor of the World, the mother of the gods and all beings, and on the other hand as Mother-Earth, Mother-Moist-Earth, the protectress of harvest. In Russia she appeared as the goddess Makosh, the only female deity to be included by Prince Vladimir in his pagan pantheon.

Although neglected by scholars:

10. The cult of the goddesses of fertility among the Russians is documented, first, by a large number of written medieval sources, and, second, by such a mass source as peasant embroidery of the eighteenth and nineteenth centuries in the Russian North. . . .

The embroideries represent the goddesses of fertility as they were described in the myths of hunting tribes: women with branching elk or deer horns, sometimes with a four-nippled udder. The anthropomorphic is intertwined with the zoomorphic. The goddesses of fertility were usually represented in the position of giving birth, with separated legs bent at the knees. Sometimes there were embroidered next to them the small heads of the newborn "little deer."[14]

Not surprisingly, the Church was scandalized by the cult of fertility and struggled for centuries to suppress it. In response, embroideries appeared increasingly with their meaning masked, as the goddesses took the form of crosses, trees with spread-out branches, and the like.

11. Folklore materials enabled scholars to establish the names of the two Slavic goddesses of fertility: the mother, Lada ("Great Lada"), and her daughter, Lelia. Ritualistic embroidery provided remarkable compositions on their subject, associated usually with spring and the beginning of the agricultural year or with the rapid growth of grain in midsummer. "The oldest prototype of the embroideries on pre-Slavic territory, depicting a woman with her arms raised toward the sky (the sun) and also surrounded by birds, as on the embroideries, has been dated to the seventh century B.C."

12. The Slavic and Baltic Lada corresponds to the Greek Leto (Cretan-Mycenaean Lato) and the Italic Latona. Lada was the mother of Lelia; Leto was the mother of Artemis and Apollo. Leto, or Lato, was in the fifteenth century B.C. the dominant deity on the island of Crete.

> Greek Leto had been born in the land of the Hyperboreans. The connection between Leto-Lato and northern Lada is beyond doubt. Probably that was an ancient Indo-European variant of the cult of the two goddesses of fertility, which had undergone different changes in the Greco-Italian south and in the Slavic-Baltic north. [15]

13. An important break in human orientation occurred with the transition from an appropriating to a producing economy, from hunting to agriculture. Farming depended on weather, on rains and droughts; and thus there arose the perception of threatening and almighty yet capricious heavenly deities deciding the fate of people.

14. The farmers of the Aeneolithic Period, the fourth and the third millennia B.C., developed the new conception of the universe and passed it to later times:

Earth, ploughed and seeded, was likened to a woman (or a maiden) "who had conceived in her womb." Rain was represented by the breast of a woman or by a grass-snake that crawls out when it rains. The sky, the earth and the rain were ruled as yet not by one god, but by the two fertility goddesses inherited from the mesolithic period. On vessels for seeding grain, artists of the Tripolye culture drew pictures of their understanding of the universe: below, the earth (the soil, without an underground world) with seeds in it and plants on it; higher up, the sky with the sun shown in motion, in an unbroken alternation of sunrises and sunsets and with strips of rain. Above it all, at the very neck of the vessel, there were painted (as a wavy line or as zigzags) the reserves of heavenly water, which guaranteed rainfall. This picture of the universe corresponds completely to the one reflected in the Rig-Veda: 1. The earth. 2. "The middle sky" with the sun and the stars. 3. "The upper sky" with reserves of water. [16]

15. The not very long period of the spreading of pastoral tribes in Europe in the Bronze Age brought further changes in human consciousness. Funeral mounds appeared. The stars and the motions of the sun and the moon were studied, and calendaric calculations began, with a requisite attention to the four phases of the sun. The cult of the sun gained momentum. "One of the most interesting discoveries of

the human mind, it might well be said, was the geocentric theory, which held its ground until Copernicus: in daytime the sun moves in the sky (propelled by horses or by swans); at night it moves on the underground ocean, pulled by swans or other water fowl."[17]

16. The Slavs can be considered distinct from the general Indo-European milieu from about the middle of the second millennium b.c. They retained the considerable earlier religious development already discussed. Spread on a huge territory from the Dnieper to the Oder, they proceeded to participate in new cultural units. In particular, they must be considered part of what has been presented as simply the Scythian world, as in fact was observed by Herodotus, who distinguished royal Scythians and Scythians-ploughmen—if not by his countrymen.

17. At the very beginning of the first millennium b.c., striking changes in the Slavic religious and intellectual orientation appeared. The curled embryo-like position of buried corpses was replaced by the extended position of sleep or rest. The first position, linked to totemism, indicated reincarnation as an animal or a bird; the second asserted that a human being will remain a human being even beyond death.

18. Cremation of the dead also developed. That implied the belief in the human soul, rising to the sky with the smoke of the bonfire and more durable than the human body. In connection with the concepts of the sky, the lord of the sky, and the sun, the Slavs lighted huge bonfires, especially at the time of the vernal equinox and the summer solstice, sacrificing dogs and horses, while pictures of swans were cut into the soil.

20. Most unfortunately, scholars continued to neglect or conceal the cult of Fertility (Rod) or to treat Fertility as a minor family and home spirit who would lap up milk left for him near the stove. In fact, Fertility was depicted in medieval Russian sources as God in heaven, ruling the clouds and breathing life into everything that lives, comparable to the Egyptian Osiris, the biblical Baal, and the Christian Sabaoth, god creator and ruler of the world.

21. The time of the establishment of the concept of a supreme god of the Universe, Nature, and humankind can be determined only approximately:

> in the agricultural aeneolithic period only the goddesses of fertility were present; male deities began to appear only at the end of the Tripolye culture, but they occupied a secondary position. For the triumph of the idea of a male god as Ruler of the World, a complete victory of the patriarchate was necessary. Sometime in the bronze age (perhaps at the end of it, when the role of agriculture had become more prominent) in all probability, there was established the new-in-principle cult of the god of the Universe—Fertility (*Rod*), a cult which followed logically from the world view of farmers.[18]

22. Dazhbog, son of Svarog, as Apollo was son of Zeus, became an important figure in the Slavic mythology in the sixth to fourth centuries b.c. Like his Greek counterpart, he was the luminous god of sun and light, a bestower of benefits.

23. The first millennium b.c. was the time of the flourishing of the pre-Slavic patriarchal paganism. The ancient cults of female deities continued their existence, but social development, the growth in the power of the leaders, the appearance of elements of statehood—all that gave birth to new religious conceptions and contributed to the creation of a Slavic Olympus with male deities at the top.[19]

24. And it was in that first millennium b.c. that there appeared in its original form the heroic epic of the bogatyrs, the mighty defenders of the Slavic land from the steppe invaders. "The struggle against the Cimmerians at the beginning of the millennium, the struggle against the Scythians (the protection[20] of one's land) in the middle of the millennium and the unequal struggle against the Sarmatians at the end of that period—all this found reflection in myths and epic narratives, which were to reach us in the nineteenth and the twentieth centuries already in the greatly changed form of magical tales and legends."[21]

Rybakov's imaginative and controversial reconstructions of the pre-Slavic and Slavic past—whether of the hunts for the mammoth, on the basis of folktales, or of the fertility cult, as depicted in the embroidery of the Russian North—deserve more than passing mention. But I shall focus here, and briefly at that, on only one item, namely Rybakov's depiction of the struggle between the forest and the steppe, a subject that many specialists consider a leitmotif, even the leitmotif, of Russian history.

Rybakov wrote:

> Oral folklore, passed from generation to generation, brought to us the memories of the raids of southern steppe peoples in different periods of the history of East Slavdom. But the sameness of the basic situation in the course of two thousand years (mounted hordes, burned villages, captives driven away) smoothed and leveled individual signs of particular invasions; they all merged into a single image of a suddenly attacking flying serpent.[23]

Still, references to the first smiths, heroes of very ancient legends, and their forging of iron, and the building of the original defensive line against the serpent echo the struggle against the Cimmerians in the tenth to the eighth centuries b.c. Similarly, stories of "serpent sisters" and a kingdom of maidens suggest Sarmatians and can be dated to the third or the second century b.c. Most difficult to clarify are the intervening centuries, complex in ethnic and social structure and poor in folkloric sources, when the Scythians invaded and came to rule the southern steppes.

Rybakov believes that whereas the new nomadic invaders and conquerors were Iranian-speaking Scythians, the bulk of the basic sedentary agricultural population of the area was Slavic. In a sense, a new amalgam emerged. Yet the struggle between the steppe and the forest continued, both in terms of the original Scythian invasion and of the persistent warfare along the shifting boundary between the Scythian steppe empire and the Slavs further north. To demonstrate his point, Rybakov turned to archeology and, in particular, to applied art in the celebrated Scythian "animal style."

Los, the great European elk, or moose, was central to the argument. Elks never lived in the steppe, but always in the forest, in thickets, near swamps, lakes, and rivers. In the south they could be found in large forested areas within the transitional forest-steppe zone, but not in the open grass steppe. Outside the nomadic territory proper, they inhabited the northern Slavic borderland, and that is where their representations were found, done in "Scythian" style. Stylized elks appeared on banners, badges, horse harnesses, and so on. They have been considered part of Scythian animal art and given no special attention. Yet, properly analyzed, they could tell us much.

Take the four plates, produced in the seventh or sixth century b.c., that were used to decorate a horse harness and found in mound number 2 near Zhabotin. Two of them had flying vultures and two elks as their subject. Put together as a united composition rather than random depictions of animals and birds, the plates told their story clearly and quickly:

> The meaning of the entire composition can be easily established: a flock of steppe birds of prey, similar to vultures with enormous hypertrophied beaks, is attacking a herd (a family) of elks at the time female elks are giving birth, when the predators still have the hope of carrying away the expected booty—newborn little elks. The herd of elks is positioned exactly as it must position itself in the moment of danger; in the middle stands the female elk with a young elk; near her behind is the newborn (shown upside down, almost as at the moment of birth), who is shielded from the birds by a young elk, perhaps two years old, with small horns. On the right elk plate there is depicted one more young elk, covering with his snout the other newborn elk, who is hanging upside down. As a rule a female elk gives birth to twins; and they are both shown here. At the right edge of the flock there is engraved the leader-elk, the only adult male elk in the entire group. With a jump he is driving off one of the vultures, forcing it to return to its flock.[23]

Rybakov insisted that the creator of the plates was a Slav, not a Scythian, both because of his excellent knowledge of elks and because he was obviously on their side rather than on that of the vultures. But the determined scholar also made a much larger claim:

> Analyzing the symbolic meaning of the composition, we have the right to think, that in the historical conditions of the seventh century or the sixth century b.c., when the Scythians, having defeated the Cimmerians, invaded the steppes in the Dnieper area, and became the immediate neighbors of the pre-Slavs, such an image of a family of elks under attack by steppe predators wholly corresponded to the historical situation and expressed the idea of the defense of the northern, "elk" land from the steppe peoples.[24]

Reproductions of birds of prey with exaggerated curved beaks, Rybakov continued, frequently decorated Scythian banners to be eventually buried in Scythian mounds, whereas north of the divide it was the image of the elk that topped the banners, sometimes of an elk crushing a foot of a bird. The perfect realism of the Zhabotin tablets in content, composition, place, and time was thus matched by their perfect symbolism. Having utilized the animal style in art to obtain historical information, Rybakov turned next to Herodotus and Scythian legends, seeking again to uncover their relevance for Slavdom, and, after that, to Great Russian, Ukrainian, and Belorussian fairy tales with their enormously rich, though difficult to interpret, material about the deep past.

Rybakov's creative reconstruction of the beliefs and mentality of pagan pre-Slavs and Slavs illustrates well some of the efforts and difficulties of scholars in the intractable field of prehistoric paganism. And it provoked considerable criticism. In particular, the historian's emphasis on antiquity and ethnic continuity of his proto-Slavs and Slavs emerging out of them has been questioned for absence of evidence in an area and time of mixed population and insufficient sources. Still, Rybakov's work helped to demonstrate, as one rich example, how particular intellectual and psychological structures had a hold on human beings for decades, centuries, and even millennia. To be sure, these structures also changed, sometimes to the extent that people practiced rituals or embroidered designs without any idea of what they meant and why; and the structures could and did disappear apparently entirely. Yet it would be rash to state at what point, if ever, their influence had been completely outlived.

In terms of self-definition, identity, the dominant view in scholarship postulates common language and even living together—for such living is inextricably con-nected to languages, their distribution, and their proliferation—as substantive links. And indeed, the linguistic definition was as clearly present, understood, and operative at the time of the missionary work of the apostles to the Slavs, in the ninth century, which resulted in a Slavic form of Christianity, as it is often today. Pagan religion is more difficult to evaluate in that connection. Of course, some and not other people gathered at particular holy places, prayed and made sacrifices to cer-tain gods, or observed specific rituals and traditions. Yet, on the whole, paganism tended to be flexible and eclectic. More specific and exclusive, one surmises, were self-definitions in terms of one's family, extended family (which existed in the Slavic world and reached modern times in Yugoslavia), clan, or tribe, as well as, perhaps, locality. Slavic politics seem undeveloped, although there were some princes; and such activities as building a line of defense against the steppe invaders indicate mass effort. The issue of self-definition or identity of the East Slavs, as well as so much else, became richer and more complicated through the agency of the two events that brought them from prehistory into history: the creation of a major East Slav state, and the conversion of East Slavs to Christianity.

Kievan Russia

In that city, in the city of Kiev. . . .

Although it has had its critics, Kievan Russia (more exactly Kievan Rus) has been generally presented as the brilliant and glorious initial period of Russian history. Out of an indistinct and largely unknown past there emerged, rather suddenly, a new historic state, spreading from the Carpathians to the Urals and from the Baltic to the approaches to the Black Sea. Indeed, its activities, based on the celebrated waterway "from the Varangians to the Greeks," quickly extended beyond its boundaries, to Byzantium and the Balkans, as is attested by a series of raids on and treaties with Byzantium from the ninth to the eleventh centuries, Prince Sviatoslav's Balkan campaigns in the mid–tenth century, and much other evidence. This state was ruled originally by princes of apparently Scandinavian origin, who, according to the *Primary Chronicle*, the main early twelfth-century source of ancient Russian history, were invited in 862 A.D. to govern Novgorod and the surrounding area, and who in 882 occupied Kiev. The new state underwent three stages: that of growth and consolidation, including the abandonment of Sviatoslav's Balkan enterprise; that of highest development, prosperity, and success, associated with the reigns of two remarkable princes, Saint Vladimir (978–1015) and Iaroslav the Wise (1019–1054); and that of decline and fall in civil wars and foreign invasions in the two centuries that followed Iaroslav's death. The Mongol utter destruction of Kiev in 1240 may be considered the ultimate end of the Kievan period.

To be sure, the Kievan state was never centralized or otherwise effectively organized. A few scholars even challenge the use of the word "state" itself. Perhaps Kievan history can be better understood as a series of extraordinary performances by a number of able princes, with the rest of the time devoted mainly to civil wars. One specialist calculated that 80 of the 170 years following the death of Iaroslav the Wise witnessed such internecine struggle. A regular system of succession did not exist, or it was based on a peculiar passing of authority from brother to brother, with the resulting battle for that authority pitting nephews against uncles. Yet other aspects of the Kievan political system appear more attractive. The system was certainly plu-

ralistic and to an extent even populist and democratic. The power of the prince typically depended on a great personal effort, and it was circumscribed not only by the
need to satisfy his associates and retainers, the *druzhina*, but also by the older and
well-established town administrations and institutions, as well as, after 988, by the
vast jurisdiction and authority of the Church and its hierarchy. The populist and
democratic element in the Kievan system found important expression in the *veche*,
or town meeting, similar to the assemblies of freemen in the barbarian kingdoms of
the West. All heads of households could participate in these gatherings, held usually
in the marketplace and called to decide such basic issues as war and peace, emergency legislation, and conflict with the prince or between princes. The frequently
unruly *veche* practice of decision by unanimity can be described as an application of
direct democracy, without representation or majority rule. In the Kievan period, the
veche in Kiev itself played an especially significant role, but there were others in
action all over Russia. Just as in the cases of politics and administration, justice in
Kievan Russia contained numerous different, at times disparate, elements, including
trial by jury.

The political development of the Kievan state was sustained by its rich and varied economy. Traditionally considered a trading state, founded on the waterway
from the Baltic Sea to Constantinople, and profiting from numerous other commercial connections, such as the Volga route to the Orient, the Kievan land also possessed prosperous agriculture based on centuries of prehistoric development. Some
specialists stressed that the original importance of trade was gradually superseded
by landholding and the cultivation of land; others wrote of a military and commercial upper class ruling over millions of peasants. Still other variants of Kievan history and social structure were also offered. In any case, Kievan Russia was favorably
located for trade and for agriculture, and prospered from both. Other occupations
of its people included cattle raising, hunting for furs, hides and meat, fishing, apiculture, pottery, metalwork, furriery, tanning, carpentry and woodwork of every
kind, stone masonry, and still other crafts. Although Kievan Russia possessed a
highly developed agriculture and although most of its people were peasants, it also
had many towns and a more prominent middle class than its counterparts in other
European countries at the time or in Russia in later periods.

The baptism of Russia, that is, the conversion of the Rus to Christianity in 988
A.D., is often ascribed to Prince Vladimir's desire to obtain a strong religion to
match and support his powerful state, after his initial effort to revive East Slavic
paganism failed to satisfy him. At about the same time, similar conversions were
taking place among some of the Baltic Slavs and in Poland, Hungary, Denmark, and
Norway. Christendom in effect was spreading rapidly across all of Europe, with only
a few remote peoples, such as the Lithuanians, holding out. Nevertheless, Vladimir's
decision represented a real and extremely significant choice. The legendary account
of how the Russians selected their religion, spurning Islam because it prohibited
alcohol—for "drink is the joy of the Russian"—and Judaism because it expressed

the beliefs of a defeated people without a state, and opting instead for Byzantine liturgy and faith, contains a larger meaning: Russia did lie at a cultural crossroads, and had contacts not only with Byzantium and other Christian neighbors but also with the Muslim state of the Volga Bulgars and other more distant Muslims to the southeast, as well as with the Jewish Khazars. In other words, Vladimir and his associates chose to become the eastern flank of Christendom rather than an extension into Europe of non-Christian civilizations. The most obvious result of the conversion was the appearance in Kievan Russia of the Christian Church itself. But Christianity extended beyond the Church proper to permeate Kievan society and culture, and eventually the societies and cultures of Ukraine, Russia, and Belarus. Politically it gave the Kievan prince and state a stronger ideological basis, urging the unity of the country and at the same time emphasizing its links with Byzantium and with the Christian world as a whole. To put it differently, Christianity quickly became part of Russian identity, and later of Russian nationalism.

Significantly, Christianity came to Russia from Byzantium, not from Rome. Although at the time this distinction did not have its later importance, and the break between the Eastern and the Western Churches in 1054 at first seemed to be just another quarrel between Rome and Constantinople, not a historic divide, the Russian allegiance to Byzantium helped to determine much of the subsequent history of the country. It meant that Russia remained outside the Roman Catholic Church, which contributed in a major way to the relative isolation of Russia from the rest of Europe and its Latin civilization. Notably, it helped to inspire Russian suspicions of the West and the tragic enmity between the Russians and the Poles. But at the time, Vladimir's turn to Constantinople represented the richest and most rewarding spiritual, cultural, and political choice he could make. Even the absence of Latinism had its advantages: it brought religion, in the form of an understandable Slavic rite, close to the people and gave a powerful impetus to the development of a national culture. In addition to being remembered as a mighty and successful ruler, Vladimir was canonized by the Church as the baptizer of the Russians, "equal to the apostles."

The conversion of the Rus to the Greek form of Christianity brought with it the highly developed Byzantine culture. Kievan literature, art, law, manners, and customs all experienced a fundamental impact of Byzantium. Great new areas of cultural activity and creativity emerged. Whereas East Slavs possessed a very rich oral folk literature, written literature and writing itself came essentially with the conversion. Similarly, building in stone, based especially on Greek ecclesiastical models, joined the age-old Slavic wooden architecture. The success was uneven, but there was much success. To mention only two developments, beautiful buildings—particularly cathedrals, churches, and monasteries—came to adorn Kiev, Novgorod, and other towns of the Russian land, while late in the Kievan period a strikingly splendid architecture arose in the Vladimir-Suzdal area of the Russian east. The Kievan period also witnessed the establishment of icon-painting in Russia, the field that, in the opinion of many specialists, was to offer unsurpassed expression to Russian artistic genius.[1]

Some specialists are too exclusive in their definition of Kievan Russia, which they prefer to regard as strictly Ukrainian. To be sure, Kiev is located in Ukraine, and, much more broadly speaking, Kievan Russia deserves full consideration as a very impressive initial period of the rather fragmented and tragic Ukrainian history. But not only Ukrainian. The Kievan state encompassed the ancestors of the Russians (more precisely, Great Russians) and of the Belarus as well as of the Ukrainians. The way "from the Varangians to the Greeks" ran through northern as well as southern Russia. According to the *Primary Chronicle*, the linkage between Novgorod and Kiev marked the very origin of the new state. The same princely family ruled the entire vast realm, with individual princes changing their particular seats—because of the fortunes of constant civil wars, the support or lack of support of their subjects, or the unusual rules of succession, but not out of considerations of ethnicity. The "baptism of Rus" in 988 meant that Christianity spread to Great Russia and Belarus together with Ukraine, and no other general date of conversion to Christianity is known in the whole East Slavic world. The new Church was one for the entire state, and, at least after 1037 (before that there is a gap in our sources, giving rise to much controversy), it was subordinate to the patriarch of Constantinople and headed by a metropolitan in Kiev, although Novgorod and some other towns also became religious centers. Literature and ecclesiastical architecture and art flourished in an urban environment, whether in Ukraine or in Great Russia, in Kiev and Chernigov, or in Novgorod, Pskov, and Smolensk. In the last century preceding the Mongol invasion, the political gravity in the state shifted to the Great Russian northeast, where at the same time, in Rostov, Suzdal, and Vladimir, architecture and arts developed with exquisite brilliance. It is worth noting that oral, folk literature also testifies to a certain unity of Kievan culture. In particular, the celebrated epic cycle of the deeds of the famous Russian warriors, the *byliny* and their heroes, the *bogatyri*, linked very strongly to Kiev and especially to Prince Vladimir, have been preserved in the popular memory only in the Great Russian far north, which had been fortunate enough to escape the invasions and the wars of the south. Earlier specialists postulated massive migrations from the tormented south during and after its breakdown to the northeast and thus, so to speak, a physical continuity of population from the southern steppe to Archangel; more recent historians have deemphasized migration, but that only stresses the power and the unity of Kievan culture. In sum, as one studies written and other evidence from the Kievan period, it becomes clear that the tripartite ethnic differentiation within East Slavdom, incipient or otherwise, was not an issue at that time. In fact, it usually escapes detection altogether, except, perhaps, in retrospect.

There is another reason why a historian of Russia must object to the monopolization of the Kievan state for Ukraine. An inevitable result of that monopoly is a postponement of Russian history to an inchoate emergence of some northeastern principalities, possibly Finnic or Turkic as much as Slavic, to the Mongol invasion, and, especially, to the rise and dominion of Moscow. The mistake is not in the heavy emphasis on the northeastern princes and eventually Muscovite tsars, but in considering their rule as the initial period of Russian history. Yet all these princes descended from those of Kiev, with the ultimately victorious Muscovite line stemming from the last highly effective Kievan grand prince, Vladimir Monomakh (1113–1125). The religion and the Church were the ones we encountered in Kiev, with the metropolitan and the metropolitanate moving to Moscow in 1326 or 1328. Kievan culture belonged to the entire domain, and, in fact, on the eve of the Mongol invasion it flourished especially in the northeast. Moreover, the connection between the northeast and its Kievan past was recognized by all concerned, although, to be sure, there existed other rightful heirs to the Kievan inheritance. Interestingly, certain characteristics, such as limits on the power of the prince and popular participation in government, sometimes cited as typically Kievan and Ukrainian, as opposed to Russian despotism, were even more developed in the Great Russian Novgorodian north and in particular in such Novgorodian centers as Novgorod itself, Pskov, and Viatka, than in Ukraine. In Viatka, the historic Khlynov, the people lived for a long time, ill or well, without any prince at all.

The Kievan state was the state of the East Slavs. It was also a European state. That followed not only from its location in Europe, but also from its entire nature and orientation. In addition to the Scandinavian connection, to which some specialists attach vast importance, the country on the great Russian plain had numerous ties to its other counterparts to the west. More commercial than Russia was to be for centuries to come, Kievan society both traded on a large scale and welcomed traders. As Christianity spread throughout Europe, religion became another major unifying link. One result of the new closeness were the very numerous, sometimes quite remarkable, marriages of Kievan princes and princesses with members of other European ruling houses. During the reign of Iaroslav the Wise (1019–1054), himself the husband of a Swedish princess, the Kievan ruler obtained the hands of three European princesses for three of his sons and married his three daughters to the kings of France, Hungary, and Norway; one of his sisters became the wife of the Polish king, another the wife of a Byzantine prince. Iaroslav also offered asylum to exiled European rulers and princes, such as the princes who fled from England and Hungary, and Saint Olaf, the king of Norway, with his son, and his cousin Harold Hardrada. While such links with the rest of Europe were particularly numerous in the reign of Iaroslav, they were a rather common occurrence in Kievan Russia. Following Baumgarten, Vernadsky calculated, for instance, that six Kievan matrimonial alliances were established with Hungary, five with Bohemia, some fifteen with Poland, and at least eleven with Germany, or, to be more precise on the last point, at least six Russian princes had German wives, while "two German marquises, one count, one landgrave, and one emperor had Russian wives."[2] The emperor was Henry IV, a central and dramatic figure in the European affairs of the time. Some Kievan princes knew foreign languages well. Thus Vladimir Monomakh mentioned proudly that his father, Grand Prince Vsevolod, learned five languages. Perhaps especially noteworthy is the fact that throughout the rich and varied intercourse between Kievan Russia and other European countries, the newcomers from the west, whether princesses, merchants, artisans, or monks from Regensburg soliciting funds for their abbey, apparently felt at least reasonably comfortable in the land of their arrival, which they saw as a recognizable part of Christendom. European views of Russia as something very strange and utterly different belong entirely to a later age.

Of course, for most purposes Byzantium was the foreign country of greatest importance for Kievan Russia. Although never part of the Byzantine empire (in spite of some ambitious Byzantine claims, based in particular on the status of the Church in Russia as a diocese of the patriarchate of Constantinople), ancient Russia experienced a tremendous Byzantine impact. Originally the magnetic terminal of the "way from the Varangians to the Greeks," Byzantium became after the conversion of 988 the supreme teacher and ideal of Kievan religion and culture. Less directly, it proceeded to exercise an influence on the Kievan social development, politics, and economics. For some seventy-five years, Soviet specialists minimized the Byzantine influence for two important reasons: the centrality of religion in that influence and the fact that it placed Russians in the position of beginning students and debtors. The last point also affected a number of Russian émigré intellectuals, who developed an extremely high regard for religion and culture in Kievan Russia and were eager to assert its originality, often even its superiority to the original Greek models. In the words of George Fedotov:

> Yet, Kievan Russia, like the golden days of childhood, was never dimmed in the memory of the Russian nation. In the pure fountain of her literary works anyone who wills can quench his religious thirst; in her venerable authors he can find his guide through the complexities of the modern world. Kievan Christianity has the same value for the Russian religious mind as Pushkin for the Russian artistic sense: that of a standard, a golden measure, a royal way.[3]

Yet the opposite view has had its strong representatives. For instance, Michael T. Florinsky wrote in his history of Russia:

> Old customs and beliefs have left but the slightest trace in the documents of the earlier period, and no systematic attempt to record the national epic was made until the middle of the nineteenth century. Moreover, it is generally admitted that the survival of folklore has suffered important modifications in the course of time. Under these conditions any attempt to present a comprehensive survey of Russian cultural developments previous to the seventeenth century meets with insurmountable obstacles and is necessarily incomplete and one-sided. The sources have preserved merely the Christian literature, while the bulk of the national epic has been irretrievably lost.

In the official Church literature Byzantine influence was supreme. . . .
The early literary efforts of native origin were hardly more than slavish imitations of the Byzantine patterns.[4]

In some important areas Kievan Christianity not only could not surpass that of Byzantium but in effect failed to produce anything of its own. Thus there was no Kievan theology, philosophy, or, perhaps more surprisingly, mysticism, which developed in subsequent centuries. The absence of independent creative theology and philosophy has generally been considered a historic weakness of the Russian Church, all the more glaring because of the overwhelming Greek performance. Yet it is precisely the overwhelming nature of the Byzantine performance that has also been cited as the reason for the Russian failure. It has been argued that the Russians were mesmerized by the glory and the beauty of Byzantine Christianity to the point of not being able to think on their own. The issue of "de-Byzantinization" is still present in Russian, and more generally Orthodox, Christianity today. Nor was the Russian relationship to the Greek Church really comparable to that of Catholic countries to the Roman. The great difference resided in the Latinism of the Roman Catholic Church as against the Orthodox reliance on local languages. Whereas most metropolitans heading the Russian Church were Greek (only two Russians, both very prominent figures, have been identified in that position, Hilarion in the eleventh century and Clement in the twelfth), as were perhaps half of its bishops, there were otherwise relatively few Greeks in Russia and little Greek language, by contrast with the massive Latinism in the West.

Kievan Christianity has been described by its admirers, often in glowing terms, as peculiarly associated with a certain joyousness and affirmation of man and his works; as possessing a powerful cosmic sense and emphasizing the transfiguration of the entire universe, possibly under the influence of the closeness to nature of the pagan East Slavs; or as expressing in particular the kenotic element in Christianity, that is, the belief in the humble Christ and his sacrifice, in contrast to the Byzantine stress on God the Father, the ruler of heaven and earth. It has been stressed repeatedly that the joyous and enthusiastic Kievan stance toward Christianity was at least in part based on the fact that Christianity came not as a foreign imposition after a defeat but as the result of a victorious settlement with what was, for the Kievan Russians, the most impressive power on earth. Again, it is necessary to discriminate. Most suspicious is the contrasting pairing of Kievan Christianity with Christ and of Byzantine Christianity with God the Father. All Christianity has to be centered on Christ. Besides, the Christology of the entire Christian world is almost exclusively Greek. Yet—on a more modest level—Russian iconography, as it developed, did tend to become less rigid, more flexible, more humane than its Byzantine prototypes. Quite naturally, Russian Christianity grew increasingly on its own. It represented, after all, the religion of an entire newly baptized people with its special attitudes, demands, and ethical and esthetic traditions. This Russification, so to speak, of Byzantine Christianity became gradually apparent in the emergence of Kievan saints, in the creative growth of church architecture and art, in the daily life of the Kievan Orthodox Church, and in its total influence on Russian society and culture.[5]

Kievan saints (who, it might be added, were sometimes canonized with considerable delay and over pronounced opposition from Byzantium, which was apparently unwilling to accord too much luster to the young Russian Church) included, of course, Vladimir the baptizer of Russia, Olga the first Christian ruler of Kiev, and certain princes and religious leaders. Of these princes, Boris and Gleb deserve special notice, as reflecting both Kievan politics and, in a sense—in their lives and canonization—Kievan mentality. The brothers, sons of Saint Vladimir and his Bulgarian wife, were murdered, allegedly, by their half-brother Sviatopolk, in the fratricidal struggle preceding Iaroslav the Wise's accession to power. They were elevated to sainthood as innocent victims of civil war, but also, at least in the case of Boris, because they preferred death to active participation in the deplorable conflict. Saint Anthony, who lived from approximately 982 to 1073, and Saint Theodosius, who died in 1074, stand out among the canonized churchmen. Both were monks associated with the establishment of monasticism in Russia and with the creation and organization of the Monastery of the Caves near Kiev. Yet they possessed unlike personalities, represented dissimilar religious types, and left different impacts on Russian Christianity. Anthony, who took his monastic vows on Mount Athos and whose very name recalled that of the founder of all monasticism, Saint Anthony the Great, followed the classic path of asceticism and struggle for the salvation of one's soul. His disciple, Theodosius, while extremely ascetic in his own life, made his major contribution in developing the monastic community and in stressing the social ideal of service to the needy, be they princes who required advice or the hungry poor. Following the lead and the organizational pattern of the Monastery of the Caves near Kiev, monasteries spread throughout the land, although in Kievan Russia, in contrast to later periods of Russian history, they clustered in and near towns.

At the end of the Kievan period, the Russian Church, headed by the metropolitan in Kiev, encompassed sixteen dioceses, a doubling of Saint Vladimir's original eight. Two of them had the status of archbishoprics. The Russian metropolitan and Church remained under the jurisdiction of the patriarch of Constantinople. The link with Byzantium contributed to the strength and independence of the Russian Church in its relations with the state. But in general the period witnessed a remarkable cooperation, rather than conflict, between Church and state. As in the West, the Church in Kievan Russia obtained vast holdings of land and preempted such fields as charity, healing the sick, and sheltering travelers, in addition to its specifically religious functions. Canon law extended not only to those connected with the ecclesiastical establishment but also, especially on issues of morality and proper religious observance, to the people at large. Orthodox priests and various clerical assistants marry and raise families; it is only at the episcopal level that the clergy is exclusively monastic. The result was a rapid growth of a clerical estate. The Church came to occupy a central position in Kievan education, literature, architecture, and the arts.

The language of the Russians too was affected by their conversion to Christianity. The emergence among the Russians of a written language, using the Cyrillic alphabet, has been associated with the baptism of the country, the writing itself having been originally devised by Saint Cyril and Saint Methodius, the apostles to the Slavs, in the second half of the ninth century, for the benefit of the Moravians. The dominant view today is that Saint Cyril invented the older Glagolithic alphabet and that Cyrillic was a somewhat later development carried out by one of his disciples, probably in Bulgaria. While there exists some evidence, notably in the early treaties with Byzantium and in the fact that these treaties were translated into Slavic, that the Russians had been acquainted with writing before 988, the conversion firmly and permanently established the written language in Russia. The liturgy itself, as well as the lesser services of the Church and its other activities, was conducted in Church Slavonic, understandable to the people, not in Greek, nor in Latin as in the West. A written literature based on the religious observances grew quickly and before long embraced other fields as well.

The language of Kievan written literature has been generally considered to be the same as Church Slavonic, a literary language based on an eastern South Slavic dialect that became the tongue of Slavic Christianity. A few Soviet scholars, however, emphasized the popular element in it and even concluded that the basic written, as well as spoken, language of Kievan society had been and remained essentially Russian, although it experienced strong Church Slavonic influences. Perhaps it would be best to say that many written works of the Kievan period were written in Church Slavonic, others in Russian—Old Church Slavonic and Old Russian, to be more exact—and still others in a mixture or blend of both. The issue of the differentiation between Ukrainian and Great Russian (and Belarus or Belorussian) represents another aspect of the problem. In any case, the Kievan Russians possessed a rather rich and well-developed literary language; one comparison of an eleventh-century Russian translation with the original Byzantine chronicle indicates that the Russian version had the exact equivalent of 80 percent of the Greek vocabulary. The conversion to Christianity meant not only an influx of Greek terms, but also certain borrowings from the Balkan Slavs, notably the Bulgarians, who had accepted Christianity earlier and who helped its dissemination in Russia. Indeed, the Bulgarians, and the South Slavs in general, can be considered to have been, at that time and even during the centuries that followed, teachers of the Russians second in importance only to the Greeks.

Kievan religious literature included Church service books; collections of Old Testament narratives, canonical and apocryphal, known as *Palaea* after the Greek word for Old Testament; sermons and other didactic works; hymns; and lives of saints. Among the more prominent pieces, one might mention the hymns composed by Saint Cyril of Turov; a collection of the lives of the saints of the Monastery of the Caves near Kiev, known as the *Paterikon*; and the writings of Hilarion, the aforementioned Russian head of the Russian Church and a leading Kievan intellectual, whom Fedotov described as "the best theologian and preacher of all ancient Russia, the Muscovite period included."[6] Hilarion's best-known work, the sermon *On Law and Grace*, begins with a skillful comparison of the law of Moses and the grace of Christ, the Old and the New Testaments, and proceeds to a rhetorical account of the baptism of Russia and a paean of praise to Saint Vladimir, the baptizer. It has often been cited as a fine expression of the joyously affirmative spirit of Kievan Christianity.

A consideration of the architecture and the arts of Kievan Russia again indicates an enormous Byzantine influence, as well as influences coming from other countries throughout the Byzantine cultural world and still other countries beyond that world, whether in the East or in central Europe. Moreover, Kievan architects and artists not only learned, like Kievan writers, from Byzantium, but also displayed a great original creativity. That at least seems to be the testimony of such marvelous buildings in northeastern Russia of the twelfth and the first half of the thirteenth century as the two cathedrals in Vladimir, that of the Assumption of Our Lady, which later became the prototype for the cathedral by the same name in the Moscow Kremlin, and that of Saint Dmitri; the Cathedral of Saint George in Iuriev Polsky, with its marked native characteristics; and the Church of the Intercession of Our Lady on the Nerl river, near Vladimir, which has often been cited as the highest achievement of ancient Russian architecture. In a sense, Russian allegiance to Christianity, and in particular the Byzantine form of Christianity, could not be more effectively affirmed.

That Christian identity of Kievan Russia and Kievan Russians was, of course, fully explicit. From the victorious and glorious account of the conversion of the Rus in the *Primary Chronicle* to Hilarion's sermons and Vladimir Monomakh's admonitions to his children, Christianity stood out as the truth, the light, and the one sure guide for Russia and the Russian people. This fundamental view would not officially change from 988 to 1917. Yet we need also to consider the nature of the sources for the Kievan period and the nature of the audience these sources addressed.

Not unlike the contemporary West, all of Kievan written sources, with but a few important exceptions, such as Vladimir Monomakh's *Testament* and the unique and controversial *Lay of the Host of Igor*, were produced by clerics, more precisely by monks. The original view of these monks as simple scribes recording faithfully the events of their time did not last long. It became apparent, as critical approaches became increasingly promninent in the nineteenth century, that their historical narrative supported a particular point of view and at times even served special interests. Thus, for example, the vaunted peaceful, joyous, and enthusiastic conversion of the Russian people to Christianity needs to be treated with caution. Although obviously not to be compared to the missionary work of the Teutonic Knights, the Christianization of Russia had some violent aspects, which break into the optimistic account, while for a long time to come chronicles were occasionally to report popular riots, usually led by some "magician" or "sorcerer."

In addition to the ever-present religious allegiance, there were frequently political agendas, with the chroniclers backing a particular prince or princely family with whom they or their monasteries were associated. The most famous and controversial issue in question is the story of the origin of the Kievan state itself, and its peculiar link to Riurik and Novgorod, that appeared first, to our knowledge, in the *Primary Chronicle*. Very possibly intended to connect the Russian south with the Russian north, it is strange and even contradictory in its particulars, suggesting different aims and redactions and allowing great play to the ingenuity of inquiring specialists. Associated with the Church and often involved in princely politics, the writers of Kievan Russia represented the rest of the Russian people in only a very general sense.

The readership for Kievan written literature was quite limited, in the first place by illiteracy. Although the Kievan state had many towns and an active commercial, civic, and cultural urban life, comparable favorably to corresponding developments in many other contemporary European countries, or in Russia in subsequent centuries, the bulk of its population remained uneducated peasants.[7] Once again, this underscores the importance of the conversion to Christianity, which was meant to reach all inhabitants of Kievan Russia, the illiterate as well as the literate.

How successful was it in accomplishing that aim? The crucial issue is that of *dvoeverie*, or "double faith," a term associated with Saint Theodosius of the Monastery of the Caves near Kiev, although apparently in a special sense.[8] It came to mean the double religion of the people, paganism together with Christianity, or, more generally, the great staying power of paganism in Russia. Specialists have differed widely regarding *dvoeverie*. At one extreme, Academician Likhachev saw no problem at all. In Russia, he repeatedly averred, *dvoeverie* never existed. The upper level of paganism, the worship of the pagan gods, was easily swept away, while the lower level, the morals and customs of the people, was marvelously suitable for Christianity and naturally grew into it. The argument was supported by the usual references to the relatively easy victory of Christianity in Russia and by the less common emphasis on the gradual adaptation of such earlier practices as joint labor in villages to the Christian help to the needy. Not very convincing, and careful to avoid any contrary evidence, the argument was clinched by the following logic: "So this is *dvoeverie*? No, it is not *dvoeverie* either! In general there cannot be any *dvoeverie*: either there is one faith, or there is no faith."[9] And once more: "The conversion to Christianity did not repeal the lower level of paganism just as higher mathematics did not repeal elementary mathematics. There are no two mathematics, and there was no *dvoeverie* among the peasants."[10] The Orthodox Church in Russia, from Kievan times to the present, did not share Likhachev's optimism and has been struggling against paganism, or at least remnants of paganism, to this day. From a different vantage point, many Soviet scholars also searched for and emphasized the presence and strength of paganism in Old Russia but considered it a healthy traditional popular reaction against the religion and exploitation promoted by the oppressive Church. Numerous other commentators, not identified with the Church or with Marxism-Leninism, readily included *dvoeverie* as part of the ignorance and the superstitiousness of the Russian masses throughout history.

Dvoeverie is an extremely difficult issue. Ideally, its resolution would imply the knowledge over centuries of the inner worlds of many millions of human beings, who usually left no historical record at all. Moreover, what was religion for one investigator could easily be superstition for another. Still, it may be possible to proceed somewhat beyond the simple recognition that there has been much religion as well as much superstition among the Russian people. Christianity in Russia kept spreading structurally as well as geographically, embracing more and more believers. Its impact could be seen not only in written literature, but also in daily life, notably in the change in burial customs. Except perhaps in the beginning, paganism presented no united ideology or front in opposition to the new faith. As a rule, the superstitious masses considered themselves Christian, and the clerics were exasperated not by their denial of Christianity, but by their peculiar ability to retain incompatible pagan elements in their new Christian existence. When the one major break in the history of the Russian Church finally came in the second half of the seventeenth century, the Old Believers rose against the establishment not in the name of paganism or of any other kind of a different faith, but in defense of what they regarded as the authentic Russian Church. True Orthodox Christianity was basic to the self-definition and identity of both parties in the tragic conflict.

Yet Rus or Russia could never be simply equated with Christianity or with Orthodoxy, perhaps least of all in the Kievan period, when the Russian Church stayed under the jurisdiction of the patriarch of Constantinople, and the Holy Land remained, as ever, in the Near East. Kievan Russians always knew that they were not Greeks, or even Bulgarians. As elsewhere in Christendom, one Christian state fought another. For instance, the last campaign of the Rus against Byzantium was mounted by Iaroslav the Wise in 1043, with the peace settlement being reached in 1046, while Novgorod continued to battle its Christian, as well as its non-Christian, neighbors throughout its history. Yet it was the Christian part of their identity that gave the converted Rus not only their religion, but also, broadly speaking, their view of the world and of their place in the world.

What of the other part or parts? The Rus were a people, a state, and a country, and this implied corresponding functions, obligations, and problems, which clutter the sources of the period. But the one subject that recurred with a special insistence and force was the never-ending deadly struggle of Kievan Russians with the invading nomadic peoples of the steppe. Interestingly, although the chronicles and other Kievan sources also devote much attention to internecine civil wars, which were even more frequent at the time than invasions from the southeast, these wars are usually presented as mistakes, aberrations, results of sinful acts, something that should have never occurred. The constant plea is for an unattainable unity among the princes. By contrast, warfare in the steppe stands out as a primary obligation of the Kievan rulers, their associates, and their armies.

Unhappily, reality corresponded rather well to this Kievan self-image of a murderous struggle against the steppe peoples as virtually a part of Kievan identity. The Pechenegs replaced the Khazars, the Polovtsy the Pechenegs, and the Mongols the Polovtsy, but the fighting continued. Numerous specialists believed that the Kievan Russians and the Polovtsy virtually knocked each other out, so that it remained for the Mongols merely to give the *coup de grâce*.

Heroic fighting in defense of one's country and one's people applied especially to the Kievan princes, their retainers, and their armies, but there are reasons to believe that their performance, image and reality, also had a broad popular appeal. For one thing, contrary to the evolution of warfare in central and western Europe, Kievan princes continued to resort, especially on their open southern and eastern frontiers, to large-scale military operations and armies of very considerable size, thus involving many Russians directly or indirectly in combat. Other Russians became involved, because the invasions and raids of the steppe peoples devastated their land and often carried them or their relatives and neighbors into slavery. In surviving oral literature, several hundred epic poems—the famous *byliny*, produced over centuries—tell us of the struggle of the Russians against the steppe, although the Khazars, with their Hebrew faith, may appear in the guise of the legendary Zhidovin, the Jew, or Tugor Khan of the Polovtsy may become the serpent Tugarin. The epic poems express heroism and victory but also tragedy. Thus the tale about the destruction of the Russian land tells of the *bogatyri*, the mighty warriors of Kievan Russia, meeting the invaders head on. The *bogatyri* fought very hard; indeed, they split their foes in two with the blows of their swords. But then each half would become whole, and the enemies kept pressing in ever-increasing numbers until finally they overwhelmed the Russians.[11]

Religion and war did much to shape the Kievan mentality, and their combined impact found a strange, almost caricatured, expression in Vladimir Monomakh's famous *Testament* to his children, which referred to the Kievan prince's eighty-three campaigns and the slaughter of hundreds of Polovsty, together with injunctions to fear God, abhor the sin of pride, give alms, and never resort to capital punishment. In fact, Vladimir Monomakh merely reacted to the problem that early Christian thought had bequeathed to Byzantium and, after the conversion, to Kievan Russia: opposition to military service and even state service of any kind. When Byzantium became a great Christian empire, major adjustments were made, but even these adjustments had significant qualifications. Thus, under the threat of deposition, the clergy was never to engage in any kind of violence. (The Orthodox Church never had any military orders, such as that of the Teutonic Knights). Orthodox laymen were allowed to fight and kill, if necessary, but the killing itself was to be always regarded as an evil, justified only by the greater evils it would prevent. There is evidence that soldiers had to do penance for the sin of killing and until doing so were barred from Holy Communion. What was praised was their sacrifice of their own lives, not their taking the lives of others. For example, princes Boris and Gleb were canonized largely because they refused to fight and kill. Even in the case of Saint Alexander Nevsky, the victor over the Swedes and the Germans, his cult emphasized not his military prowess and achievements but his "suffering" for the Russian land and, in particular, his humble submission to the Mongol khan. Like so much else acquired in Kievan times, this attitude became a part of the dominant Russian culture until 1917.[12]

The issue of war leads to the broader problem of the value of human life in Kievan Russia. Some historians have even argued that capital punishment was unknown in the Kievan state. Strictly speaking, the argument is incorrect, and a famous piece of evidence produced in support of it, namely Vladimir Monomakh's injunction cited in the preceding paragraph, indicated, rather, the opposite. For why should one prohibit execution, if it did not exist? Moreover, in the very next sentence Vladimir Monomakh made it clear that his injunction extended to those who would be subject to the death penalty (ashche kto budet povinen smerti).[13] There is also other evidence for the presence of capital punishment in Kievan Russia. In broader terms, however, Vladimir Monomakh's instructions to his children certainly do express a high regard for human life in Kievan Russia. And the same regard is reflected in the entire Kievan legal system, with its emphasis on fines rather than on torture, maiming, or death. This mildness has been ascribed to the nature and traditions of the East Slavs and their customary law, to their understanding of Christianity (as in the often-repeated and apposite, even if apocryphal, story of the Greek clergy having to explain to Saint Vladimir that sometimes capital punishment was appropriate), or to Christianity itself, but, whatever the case, it distinguished Kievan Russia favorably from many other societies. Regard for human life, of course, was not limited to Kievan princes or Kiev proper. It can also be found, for instance, by a careful reading of the chronicle of Novgorod, which sometimes refers to the death of several human beings as a disaster.

Kievan society was pluralistic and to a large extent free. The slaves, to be sure, occupied the bottom of the social pyramid, going back to prehistoric times and constant wars. But the bulk of the population, the peasants, or *smerdy*, seem to have been free men at the dawn of Kievan history; and free peasantry remained an important element throughout the evolution of the Kievan state, although bondage gradually increased. Soviet historians emphasized that process and considered the evolution of Kievan society in terms of the establishment of a full-fledged feudalism. But the prevalence of a money economy in Kievan Russia, the importance of towns and trade, the unrestricted rather than feudal attitude to landed property, the limited and delegated authority of the local magnates, and certain other factors indicate that any serious discussion of feudalism in Russia must refer to a later period of Russian history.

Rus, russkaia zemlia, Russia, apparently held the allegiance of many inhabitants of the Kievan state. Glorified by Hilarion, whose prayer for his nation "remained for centuries the national prayer of the Russian Church on the day of the New Year,"[14] and other writers, and fought over as well as defended by princes, it incorporated numerous humbler folk, linked to their leaders by religion, war, and daily life. Of course, in considering Kievan Russia, as on other occasions, ideals must be distinguished from reality, particularly when they are far apart. In the age that followed, the gap between the two widened rather than narrowed, and the ideals themselves underwent certain changes, and also dimmed.

Appanage and Muscovite Russia

The Kievan legacy stood the Russians in good stead. It brought them a uniform religion, a common language and literature, and, with numerous regional and local modifications, common arts and culture. It embraced a similarly rich heritage in the economic, social, and political fields. While the metropolitan in Kiev headed the Church of the entire realm, the grand prince, also in Kiev, occupied the seat of the temporal power of the state. Both offices outlived by centuries the society that had created them, and both remained of major significance in Russian history, in spite of a shift in their locale and competition for preference among different branches of the huge princely clan. The concept of one common "Russian land," so dear to Kievan writers and preachers, stayed in the Russian consciousness. These bonds of unity proved to be of decisive importance in the age of division and defeat that followed the collapse of the Kievan state, in particular during the dark first hundred years following the Mongol conquest, approximately from the middle of the thirteenth to the middle of the fourteenth century. They ensured the survival of the Russians as a major people, even though the powerful Moscow state that finally emerged on the east European plain looked, and often was, strikingly different from its Kievan predecessor. Yet Muscovite Russia remained linked to Kievan Russia in many essential as well as less essential ways and affirmed and treasured at least a part of its Kievan inheritance.

The twin terrors of Kievan Russia, internal division and invasion from abroad, prevailed in the age that followed the collapse of the Kievan state. The new period has been named after the *udel*, or appanage, the separate holding of an individual prince; such holdings proliferated at that time. Typically, in his will a ruler would divide his principality among his sons, thus creating after his death several new political entities. Subdivision followed upon subdivision, destroying the tenuous political unity of the land. As legal historians have emphasized, private law came to the fore at the expense of public law.

The parceling of Russia in the appanage period combined with population shifts, a political, social, and economic regrouping, and even the emergence of new peoples. These processes began long before the final fall of Kiev, on the whole developing gradually. But their total impact on Russian history may well be considered revolutionary. As the struggle against the inhabitants of the steppe became more exhausting and as the fortunes of Kiev declined, migrants moved from the south to the southwest, the west, the north, and especially the northeast. The final terrible Mongol devastation of Kiev itself and southern Russia only helped to emphasize the ongoing process. The areas that gained in relative importance included Galicia and Volynia in the southwest, the Smolensk and Polotsk territories in the west, Novgorod with its huge holdings in the north, as well as the principalities in the northeast, notably Rostov, Suzdal, Vladimir, and eventually Moscow. Population movements led to a colonization of vast lands in the north and northeast of European Russia, although there too the continuity with the Kievan period persisted, for the new expansion radiated from such old Kievan centers as Novgorod, Rostov, and Suzdal.

Of special significance was the linguistic and ethnic differentiation of the Kievan Russians into three peoples: the Great Russians, usually referred to simply as Russians; the Ukrainians; and the Belorussians, or White Russians. While certain differences among these groups go far back, the ultimate split was in part caused by the collapse of the Kievan state and the subsequent history of its population, and in particular by the fact that southwestern and western Russia, where the Ukrainian and the White Russian nationalities grew, experienced Lithuanian and, notably, Polish rule and influences, whereas virtually the entire territory of the Great Russians remained out of their reach.

Appanage Russia was characterized not only by internal division and differentiation but also by external weakness and, indeed, conquest. The Mongol domination over the Russians lasted from 1240 to 1380, or even 1480, if the period of more or less nominal Mongol rule is included. But divided Russia became subject to aggression from numerous other quarters as well. The western and southwestern parts of the country fell to the Lithuanians—whose state, because of the size and significance of its East Slavic component, represented in a sense a successor state to that of Kiev— and eventually fell to the Poles. Novgorod to the north had to fight constant wars against the German Knights, the Swedes, and the Norwegians, in addition to the Lithuanians. In general, in contrast to the earlier history of the country, a relative isolation from the rest of Europe became characteristic of appanage Russia, cut off from many former outside contacts and immersed in local problems and feuds. Isolation, together with political, social, and economic parochialism, led to stagnation and even regression, which can be seen in the political thought, the law, and most, though not all, the fields of culture of the period.

The equilibrium of appanage Russia proved to be unstable. Russian economy would not permanently remain at the dead level of local agriculture. Politically, the weak appanage principalities constituted easy prey for the outside aggressor or even for the more able and ambitious in their own midst. Thus Lithuania and Poland obtained the western part of the country. In the rest, several states contended for leadership until the final victory of Moscow over its rivals. The successful Muscovite "gathering of the Russian land" marked the end of the appanage period and the dawn of a new age. Together with political unification came economic revival and steady, if slow, cultural progress, the entire development reversing the basic trends of the preceding centuries. The terminal date of the appanage period has been variously set by specialists at the accession to the Muscovite throne of Ivan III in 1462, or Basil III in 1505, or Ivan IV, the Terrible, in 1533.

The rise of Moscow was a major historical process, which began in obscurity and ended in triumph. The name Moscow first appears in a chronicle under the year 1147, when Prince Iury Dolgoruky of Suzdal sent an invitation to his ally Prince Sviatoslav of the eastern Ukrainian principality of Novgorod-Seversk: "Come to me, brother, to Moscow." And in Moscow, Iury feasted Sviatoslav. Under the year 1156, the chronicle notes that Grand Prince Iury Dolgoruky "laid the foundations of the town of Moscow," meaning—as on other such occasions—that he built the city wall. Moscow as a town is mentioned next under 1177, when Gleb, prince of Riazan, "came upon Moscow and burned the entire town and the villages." Moscow was located in Suzdal territory, close to the borders of the principalities of Novgorod-Seversk and Riazan. Under Daniel, the youngest son of Alexander Nevsky, who became the ruler of Moscow in the second half of the thirteenth century, Moscow acquired a separate family of princes who stayed in their appanage and devoted themselves to its development.

The epochal rise of Muscovy from little or nothing to the status of a powerful east European tsardom, and eventually to that of the Russian Empire and even the Union of Soviet Socialist Republics, deservedly has attracted much attention and led to many explanations. The argument in terms of a geographical causation, developed early by the great historian S. Soloviev and generally strong in Russian historiography, emphasized the advantages of the location of Moscow: at the crossing of three important roads; on a bend of the Moscow river, which flows into the Oka, which flows in turn into the Volga; and near the headwaters of four major rivers of European Russia, the Oka, the Volga, the Don, and the Dnieper, thus offering marvelous opportunities for expansion across the rolling plain, with no mountains or other natural obstacles anywhere nearby. Moscow stood in the midst of the Great Russian people, its "natural" future subjects, in the opinion of many commentators, while its central location also cushioned it to some extent from foreign invaders— thus it was Novgorod that had to absorb blows from the northwest, whereas some invaders from the southeast devastated Riazan but never reached Moscow (notably the invincible Tamerlane in 1395).

The economic argument is linked in part to the geographic. The Moscow river served as an important trade artery, and as the Muscovite principality expanded along its waterways it profited by and in turn helped to promote increasing economic intercourse. Soviet historians in particular treated the expansion of Moscow largely in terms of the growth of a common market. Another economic approach emphasizes the success of the Muscovite princes in developing agriculture in their domains and supporting colonization. These princes, it is asserted, clearly outdistanced their rivals in obtaining peasants to settle on their lands, their energetic activities ranging from various inducements to free farmers to the purchase of prisoners from the Mongols. As a further advantage, they managed to maintain in their realm a relative peace and security that was highly beneficial to economic life. If the dauntless warrior Vladimir Monomakh provided the classical image of a Kievan prince, his counterpart in Muscovy was Ivan I Kalita (1328–1341), better remembered for his financial and organizational abilities. It was Ivan Kalita who obtained the commission of gathering tribute for the khan from other Russian princes.

But Muscovite princes and their policies made a major contribution to the rise of Moscow in a variety of ways. There was an important element of sheer luck: for several generations the princes of Moscow, like the Capetian kings who united France, had the advantage of a continuous male succession unchallenged. When the classic struggle between "the uncles" and "the nephews" finally erupted in the reign of Basil II, direct succession from father to son possessed sufficient standing and support in the principality of Moscow to overcome the challenge. To be sure, Muscovite rulers, like other Russian appanage princes, divided their principality among their sons, but the Muscovite practice, unlike that of their competitors, was that the eldest son of a grand prince received a comparatively larger share of the inheritance, and his share grew relatively, as well as absolutely, with time. Thus, Dmitri Donskoi left his eldest son one-third of his total possessions, Basil II left his eldest one-half, and Ivan III left his eldest three-fourths. The eldest son became, of course, grand prince and thus had a stronger position in relation to his brothers than was the case with other appanage rulers. Gradually the right to coin money and to negotiate with foreign powers came to be restricted to the grand prince.

The celebrated "gathering of the Russian land" by the princes of Moscow was itself a remarkably continuous, determined, and many-sided process, although hardly a heroic one. The most famous historian of Muscovy, Kliuchevsky, distinguished five main Muscovite methods of obtaining territory: purchase, armed seizure, diplomatic seizure with the aid of the Golden Horde, service agreements with appanage princes, and the settlement by Muscovite population of the lands beyond the Volga.[1] The relative prosperity, good government, peace, and order prevalent in the Muscovite principality attracted increasingly not only peasants, but also boyars and members of still other classes to the growing grand princedom. In addition to outperforming and defeating many princely rivals, notably the princes of Tver, the Muscovite rulers were remarkably successful in dealing with two other disparate powers, the Mongols and the Church. In the case of the Golden Horde, they even managed to eat the proverbial cake and have it too. The key to success lay in timing. For a long period, the princes of Moscow cooperated with the khans, and they became firmly established as grand princes after helping the Mongols to devastate the more heroic and impatient Tver and some other Russian lands. In addition, as already mentioned, they came to collect tribute for the Mongols, thus acquiring some financial and, indirectly, judicial authority over other Russian princes. Yet, as the power of the Golden Horde declined and that of Moscow rose, it was Dmitri Donskoi of Moscow who in 1380 destroyed the Mongol army in the great battle of Kulikovo, and Ivan III of Moscow who in 1480 threw off the Mongol yoke in Russia.

Still another major factor in the rise of Moscow was the role of the Church. To estimate its significance one should bear in mind the religious character of the age, similar to the Middle Ages in the West. Moscow became the seat of the metropolitan and thus the religious capital of Russia in 1326 or 1328, long before it could claim any effective political domination over most of the country. It became, further, the city of St. Alexis and especially of St. Sergius, whose monastery, the Holy Trinity—St. Sergius Monastery, some forty miles north of Moscow, was the fountainhead of a broad monastic movement and quickly became a most important religious center, rivaled in all Russian history only by the Monastery of the Caves near Kiev. Religious leadership, very valuable in itself, also affected politics. St. Alexis acted as one of the most important statesmen of the princedom of Moscow in the mid-fourteenth century, and the metropolitans in general, linked to Moscow and at least broadly conscious of the larger Russian interests, favored the Muscovite "gathering of Russia." Their greatest service to this cause consisted probably in their frequent intervention in princely quarrels and struggles, through advice, admonition, and occasionally even excommunication; this intervention was usually in favor of Moscow.

Whatever the connection between Kievan Russia and Muscovy, the two entities were also very different. The new tsardom had a novel geographical focus and different boundaries. It possessed a simpler economy and society than its predecessor, and a strikingly dissimilar political structure. The former easy relationship with other European countries was replaced by suspicion and a relative isolation. Even the Russian perception of Byzantium changed in the course of centuries and catastrophes. Such events as the collapse of the Kievan world, the Mongol yoke, and the successful "gathering of the Russian land" by the Moscow princes were bound to affect the history, life, and self-perception of the Russians. But before I turn to the complicated and speculative issue of the self-definition and identity of the Russians in new circumstances, it may be best to refer briefly to the two centuries or so that followed the appanage period and gave expression to Muscovite Russia in full bloom. For one thing, they often witnessed the development and even the culmination of earlier trends, in self-perception as in much else.

Ivan III, also known as Ivan the Great, who ruled from 1462 to 1505, largely completed "the gathering" of Russian principalities by Moscow. In particular, he annexed his two main rivals, the principality of Tver and Novgorod with its huge northern lands. Ivan's son, Basil III (1505–1533), picked up the few remaining

appanages. Former Kievan lands came to be divided between only two political entities: Muscovy and the Lithuanian, or Lithuanian-Russian, state.

The reign of Basil III (1505–1533) was followed by that of Ivan IV, the Terrible
(1533–1584). Actually the new ruler's appellation, Groznyi, would probably be better
translated as "the Terrifying" rather than "the Terrible" and even as "the Mighty" or
"the Great," perhaps given as a result of the capture of Kazan and other successes
early in his reign. His name and appellation, however, became indelibly linked to the
horrible repression of the boyars and others, such as the entire population of Novgorod, in the second half of his rule. Indeed, Ivan the Terrible remains the classic
Russian tyrant, in spite of such successors as Peter the Great, Paul I, and Nicholas I.
He himself believed in and did all he could to enhance the majesty of his position.
Thus he was the first Muscovite ruler to be crowned tsar, to have this action
approved by the Eastern patriarchs, and to use the title regularly and officially both
in governing his land and in conducting foreign relations.

Ever since the celebrated correspondence between Ivan IV and his associate (and
subsequent escapee) Prince Andrew Kurbsky, Ivan the Terrible's reign has been
divided into two parts, the good and the bad, with the year 1564 as the turning point.
And although most historians do not treat the subject quite so simply, arguing in
particular about the nature and significance of the "bad" part, there is no denying
that the two halves of the reign were different. It should be added that the "good"
half was especially welcome to many in Russia, because the years following his succession to the Muscovite throne at the age of three until he became an active ruler at
age sixteen or seventeen were marked by a bitter struggle around the throne, with
imprisonments, exiles, executions, and murders proliferating to the point of a
breakdown of effective government authority.

In 1547, at the age of sixteen, Ivan IV had himself crowned tsar, and the same year
he married Anastasia of the popular Romanov boyar family, resulting in a happy
union until Anastasia's sudden death in 1560. Also in 1547, a great fire, followed by a
riot, swept Moscow. As the city burned, and even the belfry of Ivan the Great in the
Kremlin collapsed, crazed mobs killed an uncle of the tsar and imperiled the tsar's
own life before being dispersed. The tsar himself experienced one of the psychological crises that periodically marked his explosive and unpredictable rule. He apparently believed the disaster to be a punishment for his sins: he repented publicly in
Red Square and promised to govern in the interests of the people.

The young tsar worked with a small group of able and enlightened advisers, the
Chosen Council, which included Metropolitan Macarius, a priest named Sylvester,
and a court official of relatively low origin, Alexis Adashev. In 1549 he called together
the first full *zemskii sobor*, an institution similar to a gathering of the representatives
of estates in other European countries. While our knowledge of the assembly of 1549
remains fragmentary, it seems that Ivan IV solicited and received its approval for his
projected reforms, notably for a new code of law and for changes in local government, and that he also used that occasion to hear complaints and learn opinions of

his subjects concerning various matters. In 1551 a great Church council, known as the Council of a Hundred Chapters, took place. Its decrees did much to regulate the position of the Church in relation to the state and society, as well as to regulate ecclesiastical affairs proper. And in general, Metropolitan Macarius and his associates accomplished a great deal in tightening and perfecting the organization of the Church in the sprawling, but now firmly united, Russian state. One interesting aspect of this process was their incorporation of different regional Russian saints—with a number of new canonizations in 1547 and 1549—into a single Church calendar. The celebrated designation *sviataia Rus*, that is, Holy Rus, might have emerged as a byproduct of that work (by an association of the words *sviatye Rusi*, meaning the saints of Russia, *sviataia Rus*, and other possible variants). Some Russian nationalists in the nineteenth century and later were to glory in the facts that while the accepted designation for England was Merry England, and for France *la belle France*, for Russia it was *sviataia Rus*.

Ivan the Terrible also presented to the Church council his new legal code, the Sudebnik of 1550, and the project of local government reform, and received its approval. Both measures became law. The local government reform, involving popular participation, was a promising attempt to deal with that perennially difficult matter; but it did not survive the Time of Troubles at the beginning of the seventeenth century. In 1556, Ivan IV established general regulations for the military service of the gentry. While this service had existed for a long time, it remained without comprehensive organization or standardization, until the new rules set a definite relationship between the size of the estate and the number of warriors and horses the landlord had to produce on demand. It should be noted that by the middle of the sixteenth century, the distinction between the hereditary *votchina* and the *pomestie*, granted for service, had largely disappeared: in particular, it had become impossible to remain a landlord, hereditary or otherwise, without owing service to the tsar. In 1550 and thereabout, Ivan the Terrible and his advisers also engaged in an army reform, which included a new emphasis on artillery and engineering, as well as development of the southern defense line. Moreover, the first permanent, regular regiments, known because of their chief weapon as the *streltsy*, or musketeers, were added to the Russian army.

Although the Golden Horde dissolved by about 1500, Muscovy remained subject to constant large-scale raids by its successor states, notably by the khanates of Kazan, Astrakhan, and the Crimea, the last-named increasingly a vassal to and supported by Turkey. These repeated invasions in search of booty and slaves cost Muscovy dearly, because of the havoc and devastation they wrought and the immense burden of guarding the huge southeastern frontier. Yet the Muscovite power was clearly on the rise. In 1552, in a great campaign against the khanate of Kazan, the tsar's troops surrounded the capital city itself by land and water, and after a siege of six weeks stormed it successfully, using powder to blow up some of its fortifications. Following the conquest of Kazan on the middle Volga, the Russians turned their attention to the mouth of the river, to Astrakhan. They seized it first in 1554 and installed their candidate there as khan. After this vassal khan established contacts with the Crimea, the Russians seized Astrakhan once more in 1556, at which time the khanate was annexed to the Muscovite state. The new major annexations of Kazan and Astrakhan, however, could no longer be readily called "the gathering of Russia": the population of the two territories was mainly Turkic and Muslim rather than East Slavic and Orthodox, and the former allegiance of the area to the Kievan state was questionable at best.

Another major war was waged at the opposite end of the Russian state, in the northwest, against the Livonian Order. It started in 1558 over the issue of Russian access and expansion to the Baltic beyond the small hold on the coastline at the mouth of the Neva. The first phase of this war, to 1563, brought striking successes to the Muscovite armies. In 1558 alone they captured some twenty Livonian strongholds, including the greatest of them, the town of Dorpat (Estonian Tartu), originally built by Iaroslav the Wise and named Iuriev. In 1561 the Livonian Order was disbanded, its territories were secularized, and its last master, Gotthard Kettler, became the hereditary duke of Courland and a vassal of the Polish king. Yet the resulting Polish-Lithuanian offensive failed, and Russian forces seized Polotsk from Lithuania in 1563.

Ivan IV and his assistants tried to mitigate the relative isolation of Muscovy that was characteristic of the appanage period and the resulting deficiency in knowledge and skills compared to other European countries. As early as 1547, the Muscovite government sent an agent, the Saxon Slitte, to central and western Europe to invite specialists to serve the tsar. Eventually over 120 doctors, teachers, artists, and different technicians and craftsmen from Germany accepted the Russian invitation. But when they reached Lubeck, authorities of the Hanseatic League and of the Livonian Order refused to let them through, with the result that only a few of their number ultimately came to Russia on their own. More successful and lasting was the creation of a direct contact with England. In 1553 an English captain, Richard Chancellor, in search of a new route to the East through the Arctic Ocean, reached the Russian White Sea shore near the mouth of the Northern Dvina. He went on to visit Moscow and establish direct relations between England and Russia. The agreement of 1555 gave the English great commercial advantages in the Muscovite state, for they were to pay no dues and could maintain a separate organization under the jurisdiction of their own chief factor. Arkhangelsk—Archangel in English—on the Northern Dvina became their port of entry. Ivan IV valued his English connection highly. Characteristically, the first Russian mission to England returned with some specialists in medicine and mining.

But, in spite of its many successes, the "good" part of the reign came to an end in a jerky and abrupt manner typical of Ivan IV's rule. Several events led to the change. There were the reluctance of some boyars, even some of the closest associates of the tsar, to swear allegiance to his infant son Dmitri at the time of the tsar's grave illness in 1553; the tensions over the Livonian War, which Sylvester and Adashev opposed in favor of an assault on the Crimean Tartars; and in 1560 the sudden death of Ivan the Terrible's young and beloved wife, perhaps poisoned. Convinced that Sylvester and Adashev were involved in her death, the tsar had them condemned in extraordinary judicial proceedings, during which they were not even allowed to state their case. The priest was apparently exiled to a distant monastery; the layman was thrown into jail, where he died. Adashev's and Sylvester's relatives, associates, and friends perished without trial. Before long Ivan the Terrible's wrath descended upon everyone connected with the Chosen Council. Two princes lost their lives merely because they expressed disapproval of the tsar's behavior. At this turn of events, a number of boyars fled to Lithuania. The escapees included a hero of the capture of Kazan and a close associate of the tsar, Prince Andrew Kurbsky, who spent the rest of his life organizing forces and coalitions against his former sovereign, and who in 1564–1579 exchanged remarkable letters with him. Finally, in late 1564 Ivan IV suddenly abandoned Moscow for the small town of Alexandrov, some sixty miles away. A month later he sent two letters, addressed to the metropolitan. In them he expressed his desire to retire from the throne and denounced the boyars and the clergy. In the letter to be read to the masses, he emphasized that he had no complaints against the common folk. In confusion and consternation, the boyars and the people of Moscow begged the tsar to return and rule over them.

Ivan the Terrible did return in February 1565, after his two conditions had been accepted: the creation of a special institution and subdivision in the Muscovite state, known as the *oprichnina*—from the word *oprich*, that is, "apart," "beside"—to be managed entirely at the tsar's own discretion; and an endorsement of the tsar's right to punish evildoers and traitors as he would see fit, executing them when necessary and confiscating their possessions. After the tsar returned to Moscow, it became apparent to those who knew him that he had experienced another shattering psychological crisis, for his eyes were dim and his hair and beard almost gone. The *oprichnina* acquired more than one meaning. It came to stand for a separate jurisdiction within Russia that consisted originally of some twenty towns with their countryside, several special sections scattered throughout the state, and a part of Moscow where Ivan the Terrible built a new palace. Eventually it extended to well over a third of the Muscovite realm. The tsar set up a separate state administration for the *oprichnina*, paralleling the existing one for the rest of the country, now known as the *zemshchina*. (Later, and not in connection with the *oprichnina* reform, Ivan the Terrible even established a new and nominal ruler of Russia, a baptized Tartar, Prince Simeon, to whom for two years, 1574–1576, he pretended to render homage.) Our knowledge of the structure and functioning of the *oprichnina* remains fairly limited. It has been suggested that after the reform of 1564 the state had actually one set of institutions but two sets of officials. In any case, new men under the direct control of Ivan the Terrible ran the *oprichnina*, whereas the *zemshchina* stayed within the purview of the boyar *duma* and old officialdom. Many landlords in the territory of the *oprichnina* were transferred elsewhere, while their lands were granted to the new servitors of the tsar. The term *oprichnina* also came to designate especially the new corps of servants to Ivan the Terrible—called *oprichniki*—who are described sometimes today as gendarmes or political police. The *oprichniki*, dressed in black and riding black horses, numbered at first one thousand and later as many as six thousand. Their purpose was to destroy those whom the tsar considered to be his enemies.

A reign of terror followed. Boyars and other people linked to Prince Kurbsky fell first. The tsar's cousin, Prince Vladimir of Staritsa, once a rival to the infant Dmitri, perished next, along with his relatives, friends, and associates. The circle of suspects and victims kept widening: not only more and more boyars, but also their families, relatives, friends, and even servants and peasants were swept away in the purge. The estates of the victims and the villages of their peasants were confiscated by the state, and often plundered or simply burned. Metropolitan Philip, who dared remonstrate with the tsar, was thrown into jail and killed there by the *oprichniki*. Entire towns, such as Torzhok, Klin, and, especially, in 1570, Novgorod, suffered utter devastation and ruin. The wave of extermination engulfed some of the *oprichniki* themselves. In 1572, Ivan the Terrible declared the *oprichnina* abolished, although the division of the state into two parts lasted at least until 1575.

Following the death of his first wife, Ivan the Terrible appeared to have lost his emotional balance entirely. His six subsequent wives never exercised the same beneficial influence on him as had Anastasia. The tsar was increasingly given to feelings of persecution and outbreaks of wild rage. He saw traitors everywhere. With Maliuta Skuratov and other *oprichniki*, the sovereign personally participated in the investigations and the horrible tortures and executions. Weirdly he alternated dissolution and utmost cruelty with repentance, and blasphemy with prayer. Some contemporary accounts of the events defy imagination. In 1581, in a fit of violence, Ivan the Terrible struck his son and heir Ivan with a pointed staff and mortally wounded him. It has been said that from that time on he knew no peace at all. The tsar died in March 1584; a Soviet autopsy of his body indicated poisoning.[2]

While the *oprichnina* was raging inside Russia, enemies pressed from the outside. Although the Crimean Tartars failed to take Astrakhan in 1569, in 1571 Khan Davlet-Geray led them to Moscow itself. Unable to seize the Kremlin, they burned much of the city, laid waste to a large area, and captured an enormous booty and 100,000 prisoners. Famine and plague added to the horror of the Tartar devastation. The Livonian war also began to go against the Russians. After the Union of Lublin of 1569 connecting Lithuania to Poland, Russia had to fight their joint forces, as well as Sweden. In particular, in 1578, led by their recently elected king and fine general, the Hungarian Prince of Transylvania Stephen Bathory, the Poles started an offensive in southern Livonia. The following year they captured Polotsk and Velikie Luki, although, in exceptionally bitter combat, they failed to take Pskov. On their side, in 1578, the Swedes smashed a Russian army at Wenden. By the treaties of 1582 with

Poland and 1583 with Sweden, Russia had to renounce all it had gained during the first part of the war and even cede several additional towns to Sweden. Thus, after some twenty-five years of fighting, Ivan the Terrible's move to the Baltic failed dismally. The Muscovite state lay prostrate from the internal ravages of the *oprichnina* and continuous foreign war.

How to explain the policies of Ivan IV's reign, and especially of its strange second part? Faced with this question, specialists divided into two main groups. The first stressed the personal element of Ivan the Terrible's violence and even madness— "the madness of a genius," according to one British historian—apparent to them even in the briefest possible summary of the facts of the reign, such as the one just sketched. The second group, however, proceeded to find, or at least to look for, fundamental historical reasons for these facts. S. F. Platonov argued that the real issue was the creation of a centralized Russian monarchy out of an appanage past. The Chosen Council belonged to that past, and the *oprichnina* reform represented a masterful effort to break boyar power once and for all. The *oprichniki* formed the necessary new corps of servitors for that historic struggle. Even for the cruelty of the process ready parallels were found in other European countries, notably in Louis XI's somewhat earlier campaign to centralize and unify France. Most Soviet historians engaged in a similar class analysis, arguing, for example, that the turn in 1564 meant a shift from boyar control of the government to an alliance between the crown and the service gentry and merchants; and they endorsed a positive view of the reign. Nonetheless, its horror is difficult to forget. Moreover, even if we accept the basic social interpretation, it is not at all clear that drastic measures were needed, because the opposition was apparently divided and weak: the *oprichnina* is a story of civil massacre, not civil war. What looms largest is the superhuman image of the tsar Ivan the Terrible recognizing no limits to his will or action.

The reign of Ivan IV's son Theodore, or Fedor (1584–1598), gave the county a certain respite. It was followed, however, by some of the most catastrophic years in Russian experience. The Time of Troubles (Smutnoe Vremia, in Russian) refers to the particularly turbulent, confusing, and painful segment of Russian history at the beginning of the seventeenth century or, roughly, from Boris Godunov's accession to the Muscovite throne in 1598 to the election of Michael as tsar and the establishment of the Romanov dynasty in Russia in 1613. Following the analysis of S. F. Platonov, it has become customary to subdivide those years into three consecutive parts on the basis of paramount issues at stake: the dynastic, the social, and the national. The dynastic aspect stemmed from the fact that with the passing of Tsar Theodore, the Muscovite ruling family died out. The problem of succession was exacerbated because there existed no law of succession in the Muscovite state, because a number of claimants appeared, because Russians looked in different directions for a new ruler, and because, apparently, they placed a very high premium on some link with the extinct dynasty, which opened the way to fantastic intrigues and impersonations.

But it was the social disorganization, strife, and virtual collapse that made the dynastic issue so critical, as well as opening the Muscovite state to foreign intrigues and invasion. The Time of Troubles can be understood only as the end product of the rise of the Muscovite state, with its attendant dislocations and tensions. The extremely strenuous process of "the gathering of Russia" affected directly or indirectly every Russian, but it relied especially on the continuous efforts of two classes, the service gentry and the peasants, who constituted the great bulk of the people and whose labor supported the gentry. While the gentry complained about the crushing burden of service and, indeed, during the Time of Troubles often joined all kinds of rebellious movements, the peasants experienced an even more general deterioration of their position, and in the first place the strengthening and the further spread of serfdom. Serfdom had been present on a large scale in Russia at least from the late Kievan period, but during the sixteenth century the government, in its concern for gentry service and while granting more and more land and peasants to the gentry through the *pomestie* system, introduced some specific legislation in support of serfdom in Muscovy. That legislation included the institution of so-called forbidden years, when serfs could not leave their master at the customary time after the autumn harvest, even if they had settled their accounts with him (more realistically, could not be purchased by rich boyars, for serfs were generally in no position to settle accounts on their own), as well as extension of the number of years during which fugitive serfs could be returned to their master (the statute of limitation disappeared altogether in the legal code of 1649) and increased punishment for those harboring them. Serfs, nevertheless, continued to flee, especially to the borderlands. The shattering impact of the *oprichnina* also stimulated the growth of that restless, dislocated, and dissatisfied lower-class element that played such a significant role during the Time of Troubles. Moreover, some fugitive peasants became cossacks. First mentioned in the chronicles in 1444, the cossacks represented free or virtually free societies of warlike adventurers that began to emerge along distant borders and in areas of overlapping jurisdictions and uncertain control. Combining military organization and skill, the spirit of adventure, and a hatred of the Muscovite political and social system, and linked socially to the broad masses, the cossacks were to act as another major and explosive element in the Time of Troubles.

Finally, the national aspect that dominated the third and last part of the Time of Troubles resulted largely from the centuries-old Russian struggle in the west and in the northwest. Poland, and to a lesser extent, Sweden, felt compelled to take advantage of a sudden Russian weakness. The complex involvement of Poland, especially, in the Time of Troubles reflected some of the key issues and possibilities in the history of eastern Europe. It should be added that conditions and problems varied in the different areas of the huge Muscovite state, and that the Time of Troubles included local as much as national developments. The Russian north, for example, had no problem of defense and very few gentry or serfs.

The dynastic phase of the Time of Troubles is connected particularly with a series of brief reigns—those of Boris Godunov (1598–1605), who died suddenly in April 1605; his young son Theodore, who succeeded him, only to be murdered, with his mother, in June 1605; and the extraordinary outsider, the False Dmitri, who at that point ascended the Russian throne, which he held for a little less than a year before being overthrown and killed. Basil Shuisky then became tsar and occupied that office until 1610.

Boris Godunov had risen to the highest prominence in the reign of the weak Tsar Theodore, who was also his brother-in-law; he ascended the throne after being elected by a specially convened *zemskii sobor* and appeals being made by the patriarch (Russia had a patriarch from 1589), the clergy, and the people. False Dmitri, by contrast, came from nowhere; his identity is not clear to this day, nor is his own conviction or lack of conviction that he was in fact Ivan the Terrible's son and Tsar Theodore's half-brother Dmitri, who had died under mysterious circumstances in Uglich in 1591. He was supported by some Polish and Lithuanian aristocrats and adventurers, although not by the Polish government as such; by the Jesuits; and by the restless social elements that were increasingly prominent after several years of a frightful famine and the general upheaval late in Godunov's reign. False Dmitri's forces, originally only about fifteen hundred men, could not match the Muscovite army, but neither could they be wiped out; and then, following Boris Godunov's death, Muscovite resistance collapsed, with the commander going over to False Dmitri's side.

Acclaimed as the divinely preserved, rightful tsar, False Dmitri lasted only eleven months on the Russian throne. Although evidence is lacking, many specialists have been convinced that the entire False Dmitri episode was essentially a boyar intrigue to destroy the Godunovs, and, once that had been accomplished, the new ruler was to be eliminated in turn. False Dmitri contributed to the sentiment against him with his brash and, to the Muscovites, strange behavior on the throne, and especially by the provocative attitude of his hated Polish following, both the original Poles who came with him and the new group that arrived with the tsar's fiancée, the Pole Marina Mniszech, for a wedding early in May 1606. Having prepared the ground, Prince Basil Shuisky, apparently the chief plotter, who had investigated the death of Prince Dmitri in Uglich and later hailed the False Dmitri, and other boyars led a large military detachment on the night of May 26 into Moscow. Their coup began under the slogan of saving the tsar from the Poles, but as it progressed, the tsar himself was denounced as an impostor. False Dmitri tried to escape, but was handed over to the rebels and death by a guard of the *streltsy*, after they had been persuaded by the mother of Prince Dmitri of Uglich, who had earlier recognized False Dmitri as her child, that their tsar was indeed a usurper. Two or three thousand of his followers, Poles and Russians, were also massacred. Basil Shuisky became tsar.

An amazing intriguer, Basil Shuisky was also a member of one of the oldest princely families of Russia, and his reign, 1606–1610, has been generally considered a victory for the reactionary boyar elements. That victory proved ineffective, however, while the troubles spread quickly and overwhelmingly much beyond the issue of exactly who occupied the throne in Moscow. The social phase of the Time of Troubles swept over Russia. Opposition to the government and outright rebellion took many forms. An enemy of Basil Shuisky, Prince Gregory Shakhovskoi, and others roused southern Russian cities against the tsar. Disorder swept towns on the Volga, and in Astrakhan in the far southeast, the governor, Prince Ivan Khvorostinin, turned against Basil Shuisky. Similarly in other places, local authorities refused to obey the new ruler. The political picture in the Muscovite state became one of extreme disorganization, with countless local variations and complications. Rumors persisted that False Dmitri had escaped death, and people rallied to his mere name. Serfs and slaves started numerous and often large uprisings against their landlords and the state. On occasion they joined with native tribes, such as the Finnic-speaking Mordva, who also sought to overturn the oppressive political and social system of Muscovite Russia. The rebellion in the south, led by Shakhovskoi and by Bolotnikov, presented the gravest threat to the government and in fact to the entire established order. Ivan Bolotnikov, a slave and a captive of the Tartars and the Turks, from whom he escaped, rallied the lower classes—the serfs, peasants, slaves, fugitives, and vagabonds—in a war against authority and property. Bolotnikov's manifestoes appealed to the masses to fight for their own interests, not for those of the boyars. In October 1606, the southern armies came to the gates of Moscow, where, however, they were checked by government forces, commanded by the tsar's brilliant young nephew, Prince Michael Skopin-Shuisky. Perhaps inevitably, the rebels split. The gentry armies of Riazan and Tula broke with the social rebel Bolotnikov and even in large part went over to Basil Shuisky's side. The tsar also received reinforcements. In 1607 a huge government army invested the rebels in Tula and, after a bitter four-month siege and a partial flooding of the town, forced them to surrender. Shakhovskoi was exiled to the north; Bolotnikov was also exiled and, shortly afterward, dispatched.

It should be noted that Shakhovskoi and Bolotnikov claimed to act in the name of Tsar Dmitri, although they had no such personage in their camp. Later they did acquire a different pretender, False Peter, who claimed to be Tsar Theodore's son, born allegedly in 1592, although this son never existed. False Peter was hanged after the capture of Tula. As order collapsed and disorganization spread, more and more pretenders appeared. The cossacks in particular produced them in large numbers and with different names, claiming in that strange manner, it would seem, a certain legal sanction for their bands and movements. But it was another False Dmitri, the second, who became a national figure. Although he emerged in August 1607, shortly before the fall of Tula, and thus too late to join Shakhovskoi and Bolotnikov, he soon became a center of attraction in his own right. The new False Dmitri, who claimed to be Prince Dmitri of Uglich and also the Tsar Dmitri who defeated the Godunovs and was deposed by a conspiracy of the boyars, resembled neither. In contrast to the first pretender, he certainly realized that he was an impostor, and his lieutenants also had no illusions on that score. Nothing is known for certain about the second False Dmitri's identity and background. The earliest mention in the sources locates him in a Lithuanian border town, in jail. Yet, in spite of these unpromising beginnings, the new pretender quickly gathered many supporters. After the defeat of Shak-hovskoi and Bolotnikov, he became the focal point for forces of social discontent and unrest. He attracted a very large following of cossacks, soldiers of fortune, and adventurers, especially from Poland and Lithuania, including several famous Polish commanders. Marina Mniszech recognized him as her husband and later bore him a son; the mother of Prince Dmitri of Uglich declared him her child.

In the spring of 1608, the second False Dmitri defeated a government army under the command of one of the tsar's brothers, Prince Dmitri Shuisky, and approached Moscow. He established his headquarters in a nearby large village called Tushino—hence his historic appellation the Felon of Tushino. Prince Michael Skopin-Shuisky again prevented the capture of the capital, but he could not defeat or dislodge the pretender. A peculiar situation arose: in Tushino the second False Dmitri organized his own court, a boyar *duma*, and an administration, parallel to those in Moscow; he collected taxes, granted lands, titles, and other rewards, judged, and punished. Southern Russia and a number of cities in the north recognized his authority. The second False Dmitri suffered a setback, however, when his forces tried to capture the well-fortified Holy Trinity—St. Sergius Monastery, one of the gateways to northern Russia. A garrison of fifteen hundred men, reinforced later by another nine hun-dred, withstood for sixteen months the siege of a force numbering up to thirty thousand troops. In addition, the Felon of Tushino's rule in those northern Russian cities that had recognized his authority proved to be ephemeral, once they had a taste of his agents and measures.

In his desperate plight, Basil Shuisky finally, in February 1609, made an agree-ment with Sweden, obtaining the aid of a detachment of Swedish troops six thou-sand strong in return for abandoning all claims to Livonia, ceding a border district, and promising eternal alliance against Poland. Throughout the rest of the year and early in 1610, Prince Michael Skopin-Shuisky, assisted by the Swedes, cleared north-ern Russia of the Felon of Tushino's troops and bands, lifted the siege of the Holy Trinity–St. Sergius Monastery, and finally relieved Moscow of its rival Tushino neighbor. The pretender and a part of his following fled to Kaluga. After his depar-ture, and before the entire camp disbanded, the Russian gentry in Tushino asked King Sigismund III of Poland to let his son Wladyslaw, a youth of about fifteen, become the Russian tsar on certain conditions. Sigismund III granted the request and signed an agreement in February 1610 with Russian emissaries from Tushino, who by that time had ceased to represent any organized body in Russia. The Polish king had become deeply involved in Russian affairs in the autumn of 1609, when he declared war on the Muscovite state on the ground of its anti-Polish alliance with Sweden. His advance into Russia, however, had been checked by a heroic defense of

Smolensk. It would seem that from the beginning of his intervention, Sigismund III intended to play for high stakes and obtain the most from the disintegration of Russia: his main goal was to become himself ruler of Russia as well as Poland. The invitation to Wladyslaw, however, gave him an added opportunity to participate in Muscovite affairs.

In March 1610 the successful and popular Prince Michael Skopin-Shuisky triumphantly entered Moscow at the head of his army, only to die suddenly at the age of about twenty-four two months later. (Rumor had it that he was poisoned by Dmitri Shuisky's wife, who wanted to assure the throne to her husband after the death of childless Tsar Basil.) Defeats at the hands of the Poles followed. Even the Felon of Tushino reappeared near the capital. In July 1610, Basil Shuisky finally lost his throne: he was deposed by an assembly of Muscovite clergy, boyars, gentry, and common people, and forced to become a monk. The boyar *duma,* in the persons of seven boyars, with Prince Theodore Mstislavsky as the senior member, took over the government, or what there was left of it. The interregnum was to last from 1610 to 1613.

The national aspect of the Time of Troubles, which became so prominent during those years, resulted from the Swedish and especially the Polish involvements in Russian affairs. After much debate and for a number of reasons, not the least of which was the need to obtain an effective leader against the Thief of Tushino, the dominant political and social circles of Moscow, meeting in an assembly, invited Prince Wladyslaw of Poland to rule Russia on certain conditions, in the first place provided that he become Orthodox. A great embassy went to Sigismund III, only to be unexpectedly rebuffed and, indeed, arrested: the Polish king apparently decided to play for higher stakes, that is, no conditions and his own rule over Russia. What followed in the midst of a continuing disintegration and multiple strife in the country were two patriotic rallies, greatly inspired and promoted by the Church; first, to liberate Moscow from the Poles (who had occupied it following the abortive Russian invitation to Wladyslaw to rule), and second, to defeat them and the Swedes and restore order in the land. Characteristically, the first liberation movement collapsed, mainly because of the split between the service gentry and the cossacks, together with other more radical elements. But the second effort succeeded in recapturing Moscow and in making a new Russian government in the country possible. The specially called *zemskii sobor* to elect a tsar that met in the beginning of 1613 consisted of five hundred to perhaps seven hundred members, although only 277 signatures have come down to us on the final document. It included the clergy, the boyars, the gentry, the townspeople, and even some representatives of peasants, almost certainly of the state peasants of northern Russia rather than of serfs. After deciding not to invite any foreigner, the assembly considered a number of Russian candidates. It selected the sixteen-year-old Michael Romanov to be tsar; his family would rule Russia for over three hundred years.

The seventeenth century witnessed both the full flowering and culmination of Muscovy and the appearance of trends and developments in Russia indicating the arrival of a new age. Three Romanov tsars ruled the country before the appearance of Peter the Great: Michael (1613–1645), Alexis (1645–1676), and Theodore (1676–1682). On the whole, their reigns constituted another period of hardship in Russian history, although one that was different from either the government of Ivan the Terrible or the Time of Troubles. Although Russia seemed to have come back together almost miraculously in 1612 and 1613, the heavy legacy of the preceding years remained. More wars with Poland and Sweden had to be fought before effective settlements could be reached, while the Crimean Tartars and the Turks threatened in the south. It was no less difficult to maintain peace within the country itself. Even after the pretenders and rebels of the Time of Troubles were destroyed or driven into the borderlands and beyond—and that took time—the Muscovite social system, apparently, created new ones, and of different kinds. The protests included the huge "copper coin riot" of 1662, a reaction to the debasing of silver coinage with copper, and the massive and major rebellion led by Stepan Razin in 1670–1671, which was highly reminiscent of Bolotnikov's uprising. The restoration of "order" in Russia meant a reaffirmation and even a further strengthening of serfdom.

Once reestablished, Muscovite autocracy flourished in the seventeenth century, although, interestingly enough, the *zemskie sobory*, or estates general, played their greatest role in Russian history in the first half of the seventeenth century, beginning with the *sobor* that elected Michael Romanov to rule Russia. A *zemskii sobor* was influential in the creation and promulgation of a new legal code for the entire land, the Ulozhenie of 1649. Other major events near midcentury included the extension of the tsar's suzerainty over left-bank Ukraine and Kiev in 1654, and the development of a great split in the Russian Orthodox Church, culminating in the break between the established Church and the so-called Old Believers in 1666 and 1667. Less tangible, but no less real, was the continuous change of the intellectual and cultural climate, with the great iconography and some other products of medieval Russia coming to the end of their creative development, and new influences and impulses arriving from Poland and the West. In fact, certain specialists believe that the seventeenth century itself, or at least its second half, already marks the arrival of a new period of Russian history.

What can a historian affirm about Russian identity, Russian self-definition, during some five hundred years between the decline and fall of the Kievan state and the accession to the throne of Peter the Great? The topic is immense, even if limited only to the Great Russians, all of them eventually Muscovites, leaving aside closely related yet strikingly distinct identities of the inhabitants of Ukraine and Belarus. The sources are one-sided and fragmented rather than balanced and comprehensive. What is mainly missing, as earlier and indeed also as later, is the direct and explicit evidence of the beliefs of the bulk of the population, especially the so-called common people. Yet, as in the days of Kiev, some elements of Russian identity can be readily found, displaying both a great continuity and certain significant, at times puzzling, changes in the views the Russians held of themselves and of their world.

Orthodox Christianity remained basic to the Russian identity, not unlike Roman Catholicism in medieval western and central Europe. Faith and dogma, the Church as an institution, and its role in society and culture were essentially the same as in the reign of Iaroslav the Wise or Vladimir Monomakh.

There took place, to be sure, many secondary adjustments, as the Church expanded and responded to the historical evolution of the country. After the destruction of Kiev and a period of unsettled location, the head of the Russian Church, the metropolitan, moved to Moscow, which thus became the ecclesiastical capital of Russia long before it acquired the dominant political position. The first head of the Church to come to Moscow (and die there), Metropolitan Peter, was canonized, as was Metropolitan Alexis, referred to earlier as a leading Russian statesman in the reign of Ivan the Meek (1353–1359) and the minority of Ivan's son and successor Grand Prince Dmitri. Before very long, Moscow could gather luster from a whole series of saints. The one who made the strongest impression on the Russian religious consciousness was St. Sergius of Radonezh. St. Sergius, who died in 1392 at the age of about seventy-eight, began as a monk in a forest wilderness and ended as the recognized spiritual and moral head of the Russian Church. Although he declined the office of metropolitan, his word could on occasion stop princely quarrels, and many considered his blessing of Grand Prince Dmitri and the Russian army essential for the victory of Kulikovo. The monastery St. Sergius founded north of Moscow, which came to be known as the Holy Trinity—St. Sergius Monastery, became one of the greatest religious and cultural centers of the country and the fountainhead of a powerful monastic movement. For centuries after the death of St. Sergius, and even throughout the Soviet period, tens and hundreds of thousands of pilgrims continued to come annually from all over Russia to his burial place in one of the churches of the monastery. They still come. As in the case of many other saints, the chief explanation of the influence of St. Sergius lies in his ability to give a certain reality to the concepts of humility, kindness, brotherhood, and love that remain both beliefs and hopes of Christians.

The disciples of St. Sergius spread the Christian religion to vast areas in northern Russia. Thus St. Stephen of Perm, the most distinguished of the associates of St. Sergius, brought Christianity to the Finnic-speaking tribes of the Zyriane: he learned their tongue and created a written language for them, utilizing their decorative designs as a basis for letters. In this manner, following the Orthodox tradition, the Zyriane could worship God in their native language. Whereas in the Kievan period Russian monasteries were established typically in or near towns, in subsequent centuries they appeared frequently in the wilderness—a hermit would move into the forest for solitude and prayer, to be followed by a few disciples, and after that a larger group of people forming a community, at which point that same hermit or another would move deeper into the forest for more solitude and better prayer, to be pursued by an increasing number of eager newcomers, thus repeating the process. Some of the greatest Russian monasteries rose in the far north.

The relationship of the Russian Church to the Greek also changed. Long a dutiful diocese of the partriarchate of Constantinople, the Russian Church acquired an independent standing following the Russian repudiation of the Council of Florence of 1439 and the deposition of the Greek head of the Russian Church, Metropolitan Isidore, who had signed the Union of Florence. The Greeks themselves soon renounced the Union with Rome, but the administrative allegiance of the Russian Church to the Byzantine was never restored. The "gathering of Russia" by Moscow led to an expansion, consolidation, and coordination of Church administration and practice, illustrated especially well by the formulation of the all-Russian calendar of saints and other ecclesiastical reforms of the mid-sixteenth century. Then, in 1589, the head of the Russian Church became a patriarch, thus ascending to the highest position possible in Orthodox Christianity. A logical step in itself, because by that time Russia contained the largest Orthodox community in the world, in the only major Orthodox state, as well as enjoying six hundred years of Orthodox development, with many saints of its own and other signs of divine blessing, it nevertheless had to be skillfully promoted by Boris Godunov's diplomacy, even trickery, to overcome the reservations of other patriarchs. The new importance of the Russian Church led to an upgrading and enlargement of its hierarchy through the appointment of a number of new metropolitans, archbishops, and bishops. While the Russian Church kept increasing in size, strength, and significance, it could not preserve indefinitely the ecclesiastical unity of Kievan times. The growing division of the land and the people between Moscow and Lithuania resulted in the establishment, in Kiev, of a separate Orthodox metropolitanate for the Lithuanian state, with the final break with Moscow coming in 1458.

On the whole, the Russian Church helped mightily the "gathering of Russia" by Moscow. In addition to providing the basic religious, intellectual, and cultural setting for Muscovy, its contributions ranged from Metropolitan Alexis's statesmanship to the pioneering lives and labors of uncounted hermits, monks, and their followers who led the penetration and colonization of the huge northeastern frontier. The Time of Troubles, and especially its successful resolution, must have only enhanced the standing and significance of the Church. The national rally that finally prevailed was greatly inspired by Patriarch Hermogen, who died a prisoner of the Poles, Abbot Dionysus of the Holy Trinity–St. Sergius Monastery, and other clerics. It even bore certain characteristics of a religious crusade, because the Poles were Catholics and after the establishment in 1596 of the Uniate Church were especially well equipped to bring the Orthodox under the jurisdiction of the pope by allowing them to retain the Eastern ritual and the Slavonic language in religious services, as well as their other practices and customs. The seventeenth century thus became in many ways the apogee of the Russian Church, the victorious and long-unchallenged center of Russian ideology, culture, society, and life, an immensely rich landowner, especially through its monasteries, and an institution with enormous prestige and some remarkable leadership—although the century was to end on a great split and struggle between the Old Believers and the religious establishment, to be followed by the reforms of Peter the Great.

Indeed, two of the patriarchs also carried the title Great Sovereign, that is, co-ruler with the tsar. However, on closer examination, these strange relationships appear more to be remarkable curiosities than important indications of the nature of the Russian Church or of its attitude toward the state. Patriarch Filaret was the father of Tsar Michael Romanov and was said to be a much more powerful personality than his young son. An associate and even leading rival of Boris Godunov, he was forced to abandon politics in 1601 and become a monk when Godunov purged the Romanov party. He was made metropolitan of Rostov by the False Dmitri in 1605, and patriarch of All Russia first by the Thief of Tushino in 1609 and after that, more properly, by a Church council in 1619, when a settlement with Poland enabled him to return to Moscow from Polish arrest. Patriarch Filaret proved to be an able and severe Church administrator, determined to defend strict Orthodoxy, as he understood it (not always well, because of his lack of theological education), and especially interested in typography and producing appropriate literature. He remained a co-ruler and the second, when not the first, person in the state until his death in 1633 at the age of about eighty.

Unlike Filaret, Patriarch Nikon, a key figure in the great schism, was born a peasant. He became a monk after a family tragedy. Intelligent and possessing an extremely strong and domineering character, Nikon attracted the favorable attention of young Tsar Alexis, distinguished himself in his usual combative manner as metropolitan in Novgorod, and, in 1652, became patriarch. The strong-willed cleric proceeded to exercise a powerful personal influence on the much younger and softer monarch, who even bestowed on him the title of Great Sovereign, which Nikon held until his break with the tsar in 1658. Patriarch Nikon championed the view common in the Catholic West, but not in the Orthodox world, that the Church was superior to the state, like the sun to the moon, and he endeavored to assert his own authority over the tsar's in a variety of matters. Charged with papism, he answered characteristically that one had to respect the pope for that which was good. Nikon pushed his position and power too far, and Alexis had to rebel against his exacting colleague and mentor (although he could never forget Nikon personally and, as he was dying, asked Nikon's pardon both through a messenger and in his will and testament). Finally the Church council of 1666–1667, in which Eastern patriarchs participated, deposed Nikon as patriarch and defrocked him, on the basis of his improper claims and interference in state affairs. Yet the Council approved Nikon's stand against the Old Believers. The former Great Sovereign ended his days in exile in a distant monastery. The view of Church superiority over the state even in secular affairs found no support in Orthodoxy. It may well be correct to emphasize that Muscovy in full bloom had two supreme leaders, the patriarch and the tsar, but they were supreme in different spheres.

In medieval Russia, as in medieval Europe as a whole, intellectual life centered on religious problems, although their ramifications often encompassed other areas of human activity. While in the main, Russia stayed outside the rationalist and reforming currents which developed in western Christendom, it did not remain totally unaffected by them. Significantly, Russian religious movements stressing rationalism and radical reform emerged in western parts of the country and especially in Novgorod. They never acquired considerable popular support. As early as 1311, a Church council condemned the heresy of a certain Novgorodian priest who denounced monasticism. In the second half of the fourteenth century, in Novgorod, the teaching of the radical sectarians known as the *strigolniki* acquired prominence. Quite similar to the evangelical Christians in the West, they denied the authority of the Church and its hierarchy, as well as all sacraments except baptism, and wanted to return to the time of the apostles; an extreme faction within the movement even renounced Christ and wanted to limit religion to prayer to God the Father. It might be noted that the protest began apparently over the issue of fees for the sacraments, and that the dissidents came rapidly to adhere to increasingly radical views. All persuasion failed, but violent repression by the population and authorities in Novgorod and Pskov, together with disagreement among the *strigolniki*, led to the disappearance of the sect in the early fifteenth century. Later in the century, new heretics, known as the Judaizers, appeared. Their radical religious movement has been linked to the arrival in Novgorod in 1470 of a Jew named Zechariah, or Skharia, and to the spread of his doctrines. The Judaizers in effect accepted the Old Testament but rejected the New, considering Christ a prophet rather than the Messiah. Consequently, they also denounced the Church. Through the transfer of two Novgorodian priests to Moscow, the movement obtained a foothold in the court circles of the capital. Joseph of Volok, an abbot of Volokolamsk, led the ecclesiastical attack on the heretics. They were condemned by the Church council of 1504, and Ivan III, finally ceding to the wishes of the dominant Church party, cruelly suppressed the Judaizers and had their leaders burned at the stake.

Whereas after the break between Constantinople and Rome in 1054 and the fall of the Kievan state, Muscovy—and later, Russia—found itself largely isolated from the religious developments in the West, it remained, of course, part of the Orthodox ecclesiastical and spiritual world. One example, major but complicated, of Russian participation in the life of that world is Hesychasm. This difficult term refers to such overlapping phenomena as the "prayer of the mind" or "the prayer of the heart"; the psychosomatic techniques that sometimes accompanied such "Jesus prayer" and were designed to aid spiritual concentration; the theology of St. Gregory Palamas, archbishop of Thessalonica in the fourteenth century; and even the cultural, social, and political programs of a succession of ecumenical patriarchs who belonged to the Hesychast movement. Hesychasm arose in the monasteries on Mount Athos and in Constantinople in the fourteenth century to become a prominent feature of the Orthodox Church. In particular, it established a creative spiritual bond among Greek, Balkan Slavic, and Rumanian monks and hierarchs. And in Russia it apparently found a strong abode in the Holy Trinity–St. Sergius Monastery, where St. Sergius emphasized *bezmolvie* or *molchanie* (that is, "silence," to concentrate on inner prayer) and had personal links to the Hesychast patriarchs Philotheos and Kallistos, while the monastery library came to contain Slavonic translations of many of the classics of Hesychast spirituality. Hesychasm flourished again in Russia in the second half of the fifteenth century, revived by St. Nil Sorsky, whom I shall soon discuss in a different connection. Indeed, Hesychast monastic practices spread with the spread of monasticism in Russia; in 1429, one of the monks from the great Beloozero (White Lake) Monastery "settled on an island in the White Sea, laying the foundation of the monastery of Solovki: East Christian monasticism, still inspired by the Hesychast tradition, had reached the confines of the Arctic Ocean." The first coming of Hesychasm to Russia was also linked, through St. Sergius and the Holy Trinity–St. Sergius Monastery, to Andrew Rublev, generally considered the greatest icon painter in world history and strongly associated with the monastery. He lived approximately from 1370 to 1430. His so-called Old Testament Holy Trinity and other works, as well as the icons by his disciples and followers, testify to the presence of a remarkable light in that usually very dark and difficult age.

If Hesychasm was a quintessentially spiritual movement, other trends and disputes within the Russian Church had more obvious political and economic implications. The most important and celebrated controversy of the age pitted the "possessors" against the "nonpossessors," with Joseph of Volok occupying a central position as the outstanding leader of the first-named faction. Joseph of Volok and the possessors believed in a close union of an autocratic ruler with a rich and powerful Church. The prince, or tsar, was the natural protector of the Church, with all its lands and privileges. In return, he deserved full ecclesiastical support, his authority extending not only to all secular matters but also to Church administration. The possessors emphasized, too, a formal and ritualistic approach to religion, the sanctity of Church services, rituals, practices, and teachings, and a complete, if need be violent, suppression of all dissent. The nonpossessors, who because of their origin in the monasteries of the northeast, have sometimes been called the "elders from beyond the Volga," had as their chief spokesman Nil Sorsky, a man of striking spiritual qualities. The nonpossessors, as their name indicates, objected to ecclesiastical wealth and in particular to monastic landholding. They insisted that the monks should in fact carry out their vows, be poor, work for their living, and remain truly "dead to the world." The Church and the state should be independent of each other; most especially, the state, which belonged to a lower order of reality, had no right to interfere in religious matters. The nonpossessors stressed contemplation and the inner spiritual light, together with a striving for moral perfection, as against ecclesiastical formalism and ritualism. By contrast with the possessors, they differentiated in the teaching of the Church among Holy Writ, tradition, and human custom, considering only Holy Writ—God's commandments—as completely binding. The rest could be criticized and changed. But even those who challenged the foundations of the Church were to be met with persuasion, never with force. The Church council of 1503 decided in favor of the possessors. Joseph of Volok and his associates cited Byzantine examples in support of their position and also argued, in practical terms, the necessity for the Church to have a large and rich establishment in order to perform its different functions, including the exercise of charity on a large scale. Their views, especially on relations of Church and state, suited on the whole the rising absolutism of Moscow, although it seems plausible that Ivan III sympathized with the nonpossessors in the hope of acquiring monastic lands. After Joseph of Volok died in 1515, subsequently to be proclaimed a saint, other high clerics continued his work, notably Daniel, who became metropolitan in 1521. At the councils of 1524 and 1531, and even as late as 1554–1555, some of Nil Sorsky's chief followers were declared to be heretics. Nil Sorsky himself, however, was canonized.

In explaining the controversy between the possessors and the nonpossessors, many scholars have emphasized that the possessors championed the rise of the authority of the Muscovite rulers, while the nonpossessors, with their high social connections, reflected the aristocratic opposition to centralization. In a different context, that of the history of the Orthodox Church, the nonpossessors may be considered to have derived from the mystical and contemplative tradition of Eastern monasticism, whereas the possessors championed a more practical religious approach. However, in a still broader sense, the possessors and the nonpossessors expressed two recurrent attitudes that devoted Christians have taken toward things of this world, burdened as they have been by an incompatibility between the temporal and the eternal standards and goals of behavior. The nonpossessors thus resemble the Franciscans in the West, as well as other religious groups that have tried hard to be in, yet not of, this world. And even after all the sixteenth-century councils, they remained an important part of the Russian Church as an attitude and a point of view.

While the seventeenth century marked in many respects the zenith of the Russian Orthodox Church, it also witnessed one of its greatest tragedies. And, as in a true classical Greek tragedy, the catastrophe was essentially self-inflicted, even after one makes all the allowances for the international setting and outside influences. Whether the critical flaw resided in pride, ignorance, or, probably, both together, the result was disaster at the time and for centuries to come. The *raskol*, the only major split in the history of the Orthodox Church in Russia, and one still unhealed, began with the correction of religious texts. The much-needed corrections were attempted as early as the first quarter of the sixteenth century, but the rectification proceeded in brief and ineffective bursts, which sometimes introduced as many new errors as those that had been eliminated. The situation changed when Nikon became patriarch in 1652 and when left-bank Ukraine and Kiev joined Muscovy in 1654. As a result, the sway of the Russian Orthodox Church was extended to the Ukrainian lands, and it was made all the more glorious by the crucial role Orthodoxy played in making Ukraine turn to Moscow. Better educated than the Russians and more experienced in religious debate, for they had opposed the Union and the Uniates since 1596 and had at times themselves attended Catholic schools, Ukrainian, especially Kievan, monks became readily available to support Nikon's reforms and, indeed, later Petrine religious reforms as well. The Ukrainian element also quickly evoked suspicion, hostility, and accusations of Uniate tendencies and Latinism from many Muscovites. The conflict was played out against the background of Western, most particularly Polish, influences sweeping across Russia in the seventeenth century and producing a nativist reaction.

Determined and direct, Nikon turned to church reform as soon as he became patriarch. The reign of Tsar Alexis was witnessing a religious and moral revival in the Church, an effort to improve the performance of the clergy and to attach a higher spiritual tone and greater decorum to various ecclesiastical functions. Yet, once Nikon introduced the issue of corrections, many leaders of this revival, such as Stephen Vonifatiev, Ivan Neronov, and the celebrated Archpriest Avvakum, or Habakkuk, turned against him and in 1653 accused him of heresy. To defeat the opposition, the patriarch proceeded to obtain the highest possible authority and support for his reforms: in 1654, a Russian Church council endorsed the verification of all religious texts; next, in response to inquiries from the Russian Church, the patriarch of Constantinople called a council that added its sanction to Nikon's reforms; a monk was sent to bring five hundred religious texts from Mount Athos and the Orthodox East, while many other texts arrived from the patriarchs of Antioch and Alexandria; a committee of learned Kievan monks and Greeks was set up to do the collating and correcting; another Russian Church council in 1656 also supported Nikon's undertaking. Nikon widened the scope of the reform to include the ritual in addition to texts, introducing in particular the sign of the cross in the Greek manner with three rather than two fingers, the older practice still prevailing in Russia (two fingers stood for the two natures of Christ, and three fingers for the later dogma of the Holy Trinity). But the patriarch's opponents refused to accept all the high authorities brought to bear against them and stood simply on the Muscovite precedent—to keep everything as their fathers and grandfathers had it. They found encouragement in Nikon's break with the tsar in 1658 and in the ineffectiveness of the cleric who replaced him at the head of the Church. To settle matters once and for all, a Russian Church council was held in 1666, and another Church council, attended by the patriarchs of Alexandria and Antioch, convened later that year and continued in 1667, in Moscow. This great council, which deposed Nikon for his bid for supreme political power, considered the issue of his reforms, listened to the dissenters, and in the end completely endorsed the changes. The opponents had to submit or defy the Church openly.

It is remarkable that, although no dogmatic or doctrinal differences were involved, priests and laymen in considerable numbers refused to obey ecclesiastical authorities, even though the latter received the full support of the state. The *raskol* began in earnest. The Old Believers, or Old Ritualists—*starovery* or *staroobriadtsy*—rejected the new sign of the cross, the corrected spelling of the name of Jesus, the tripling instead of doubling of the "Hallelujah," and other similar emendations, hence rejected the Church. Persecution of the Old Believers was soon widespread. Avvakum himself—whose stunning autobiography represents the greatest document of Old Belief and one of the great documents of human faith—perished at the stake in 1682. The Solovetsky Monastery in the far north had to be captured by a siege that lasted from 1668 to 1676. Apocalyptic views prevailed among the early Old Believers, who saw in Church reform the end of the world and in Nikon the Antichrist or at least the forerunner of the Antichrist. It has been estimated that between 1672 and 1691, over twenty thousand of them burned themselves alive in twenty-seven known communal conflagrations—to escape the Antichrist and attain what many Old Believers considered to be the equal of martyrdom for the true faith.

Yet, surprisingly, the Old Belief survived. Reorganized in the eighteenth century by a number of able leaders, especially the Denisov brothers, Andrew and Simeon, it claimed the allegiance of millions of Russians up to the Revolution of 1917 and after. It exists today. With no canonical foundation and no independent theology to speak of,[4] the Old Belief divided again and again, usually in the direction of an ever-greater religious radicalism, but it never disappeared. The main cleavage came to be between the *popovtsy* and the *bespopovtsy*, those who had priests and those who had none. Although the Old Believers refused to change a tittle in the texts or the least detail in the ritual, they soon found themselves without priests and thus without the liturgy, without most of the sacraments, and in general without the very core of traditional religious life: bishops were required for elevation to the priesthood, and no bishops joined the Old Belief. Some dissenters, the *popovtsy*, bent all their efforts to obtain priests by every possible means, for instance, by enticing them away from the established Church. The priestless, on the other hand, accepted the catastrophic logic of their situation and tried to organize their religious life along different lines. It is from the priestless Old Believers that most Russian sects derive.

The *raskol* constituted the only major schism in the history of the Orthodox Church in Russia. It was in an important sense the opposite of the Reformation: in the West, Christians turned against their ecclesiastical authorities because they wanted changes; in Russia, believers revolted because they refused to accept even minor modifications to traditional religious practices. Many scholars have tried to explain the strange phenomenon of the *raskol*. Thus A. P. Schapov and numerous others have stressed the social composition of the Old Believers and the social and economic reasons for their rebellion. The dissenters were originally and continued to be mostly well-established peasants and traders. Their action could, therefore, be interpreted as a protest against gentry domination and the entire oppressive Muscovite system. More immediately, they reacted against the increased ecclesiastical centralization under Nikon that led to the appointment of priests—formerly they had been elected in northern parishes—and to the loss of parish autonomy and democracy. In addition to being democrats—so certain historians have claimed— the Old Believers expressed the entrepreneurial and business acumen of the Russian people. Over a period of time they made a remarkable record for themselves in commerce. Some parallels have even been drawn with the Calvinists in the West. As to the other side, the drive for reform has been ascribed, in addition to the obvious reason of correcting mistakes, to the influence of the more learned Ukrainian clergy, and to the desire of the Muscovite Church to play effectively a larger role among the peoples of Ukraine and Belarus and perhaps even some other Orthodox peoples beyond.

Even more rewarding as an explanation of the *raskol* has been the emphasis on the ritualism and formalism of Muscovite culture. The Old Believers were, characteristically, Great Russians, that is, Muscovite Russians, and not, for example, Ukrainians. To them, the perfectly correct form and the untainted traditions of the Muscovite church could not be compromised, and this goes a long ways toward explaining the rebellion. The reformers exhibited a similar formalism. In spite of the advice of such high authorities as the patriarch of Constantinople, Nikon and his followers refused to allow any local practice or insignificant variation to remain, thus also confusing the letter with the spirit. The Russian Church had developed especially in the direction of religious ceremony, ritualism, and formalism, which for the believers served as a great unifying bond and a tangible basis for their daily life. It has been estimated, for instance, that the tsar often spent five hours or more a day in church. Even visiting Orthodox hierarchs complained of the length of Russian services. The appearance of the Old Belief, as well as the excessively narrow and violent reaction to it, indicated that in Muscovy, religious content in certain respects lagged behind religious form. The *raskol* can thus be considered a tribute to the hold that Muscovite culture had on the people, and, as time made apparent, to its staying power. It also marked the dead end of that culture.

The *raskol* throws a dazzling light, yet one that is difficult to analyze and assess, on the religious beliefs of the Russian people. Russian Orthodoxy certainly grew in strength and spread over a huge area between the fall of the Kievan state and Nikon's reforms. It remained the faith of the country, the framework for the activities of the Church and the cultural elite, and, increasingly, part of the warp and woof of the daily life of all Russians. The tragedy of the split was that it divided that body of believers and led to the persecution of one part of it. The religious separation was soon followed by a cultural one resulting from Petrine reforms, creating a break between Muscovy and imperial Russia. P. N. Miliukov and others have argued that, because of the split, the Russian Church lost its most devoted and active members and, in effect, its vitality: the courageous joined the Old Belief; the cowardly and the listless stayed put. Even if we allow for the obvious exaggeration implicit in this view (enough determined people stayed in the Orthodox Church to carry its work during some two centuries of imperial Russia, and even through seventy-five years of Soviet persecution, often described as the greatest religious persecution in world history) and note further that many of the most ignorant and fanatical must also have joined the dissenters, the loss remained major. It certainly made it easier for Peter the Great to treat the Church in a high-handed manner.

What were the leading characteristics of the Orthodox religion in Russia and of its reception by the people in the appanage and Muscovite periods? Reference has already been made to ritualism, formalism, long church services, and, in general, it should be added, the very strong monastic element in Russian Christianity. Monasticism included asceticism as one of its principal vehicles, and asceticism was admired by many more in pre-Petrine Russia than those who practiced it. But, in the overall sense, too much stress has been laid on the "peculiarities" of Russian Christianity, such as the canonization of certain "holy fools," and not enough on its basic beliefs and message. To be sure, in conditions of overwhelming illiteracy and for certain other reasons, individual reading of the Bible did not become as widespread in Russia as in many other countries in Europe, especially Protestant lands. Still, the message of the Russian Church was that of the evangelists and the apostles, emphasized in every church service, and it was supported in that visual age by the development of the greatest iconography in the world.

Perhaps all history is a story of hardship, but in any case, life was extremely difficult in Russia in the period or periods under consideration. The first hundred years after the collapse of the Kievan state and the arrival of the Mongols, that is, the time roughly from the mid-thirteenth to the mid-fourteenth centuries, has been generally considered the nadir for Russia. It was followed by the burdensome and exacting "gathering of the Russian land" by Moscow (burdensome and exacting on the Muscovite side, thoroughly destructive for Novgorod or Pskov), by the wars and terror in the reign of Ivan the Terrible, by the Time of Troubles, and by new trials and disasters in the seventeenth century. Through it all the institution of serfdom kept growing, to have its complete development assumed, and in a sense confirmed, by the legal code of 1649. The dissatisfied and the oppressed staged uncounted rebellions in the Time of Troubles or fought in Stenka Razin's great uprising, but they could not change the basic course of Muscovite history. No wonder that the tone in religion became more pessimistic; "punishment for our sins" kept recurring as the historical explanation, and the élan of the Kievan period was largely gone.[5] Yet the hold of religion remained and perhaps grew. After all, the most frequent Christian prayer is "Lord, have mercy!"

Warfare and, in particular, the struggle against the peoples of the steppe continued to be a central aspect of Russian self-definition and identity through the long centuries following the fall of Kiev. This period began with the Mongol invasion of 1237–1240 and ended with Prince Basil Golitsyn's disastrous campaigns against the

Crimean Tartars in 1687 and 1689. (Nor was that the end of the historical struggle; great wars against Turkey followed, with Crimea itself annexed to Russia only in 1783—indeed, as late as the Balkan wars of the 1870s, common Russian people volunteered to defend Orthodox Christians, that is, Bulgarians and Serbians, against "pagans" or "infidels," i. e., Muslim Turks.) Of course, the Mongol invasion and the Mongol yoke, which continued in some form for almost two and a half centuries, were major events in Russian history. So were Dmitri Donskoi's great victory of Kulikovo and Ivan III's final abolition of Mongol domination. In fact, the entire history of the rise of Moscow cannot be separated from the clever policy of the Muscovite princes in regard to the Mongols. Warfare continued with the successor states to the Golden Horde. The annexation of Kazan in 1552 (followed by the annexation of Astrakhan in 1556) has been regarded by some historians as the beginning of the Russian empire, with the Russians moving decisively into non-Russian lands. Nor was there any respite in the seventeenth century. Major raids of the Crimean Tartars and large-scale warfare persisted, involving, as in the days of Kiev, not only direct combatants, but also common Russian people, who were pillaged and driven by the invaders into slavery. Estimates of those kidnapped during parts of the seventeenth century have been as high as ten and even twenty thousand a year. Increasingly during the century artillery developed in Russia, and *streltsy*, infantry musketeers, appeared, as well as foreign mercenaries, in particular officers. Eventually the musketeers were replaced by infantry recruited from the peasants, using flintlocks and led by foreign officers.[6] Peter the Great profited from earlier changes but was still left with the daunting task of catching up militarily with the West, most especially with Sweden during the course of the Great Northern War, and this task has often been considered both the raison d'être and the leitmotif of his reign.

It is probable, then, that warfare, and in particular the struggle against the steppe peoples, persisted as part of the Russian identity after the fall of the Kievan state as before that fall. Even the nature and technology of the fighting on the huge southern and southeastern frontier remained essentially the same, except perhaps for the last part of the period under consideration, and that fighting continued to involve many Russians, noncombatants as well as combatants. Yet contrasts also emerged, and they can be felt in the generally pessimistic, sparse, and restrained tone of the sources. The utterly devastating Mongol invasion, followed by the Mongol yoke, represented a uniquely catastrophic experience in Russian history, different in the length of time and import from such earlier events as Vladimir Monomakh's constant campaigns against the Polovtsy. Some specialists, including such a leading figure as Alexander Presniakov (Aleksandr Evgenievich Presniakov) even concluded that the Russian chroniclers suppressed or at least abbreviated the Mongol issue as too painful to bear, while one recent historian went so far as to claim that the Russian sources refused to recognize the very fact of the Mongol yoke, admitting only to Mongol raids and pillaging. Later, of course, there were great victories, such as Dmitri Donskoi's destruction of Mamai's army on the field of Kulikovo and Ivan the Terrible's capture of

Kazan, and they were effectively recorded in the Russian sources. But on the whole, the spirit of gloom prevailed, perhaps because the Mongols returned from their defeat to burn down much of Moscow, while Ivan the Terrible's successes in Kazan and Astrakhan were followed by the terror of the *oprichnina*. Yet one is tempted to suggest that it was not only the "objective reality" of the events narrated, and not only the nature of the particular sources we possess for different periods of Russian history, but also the increasing problems of Muscovite society that account for the restrained and even negative tone. The growth and consolidation of serfdom and the uncounted popular rebellions come first to mind. That increasing social division was followed by the religious split occasioned by the phenomenon of Old Belief in the second half of the seventeenth century and by the growing cultural separation promoted powerfully by Peter the Great's reforms.

What did Russians fight for in the time span from the fall of the Kievan state to the reign of Peter the Great? Constant wars pitting Russians against Russians aside, and these were as common in the appanage as in the Kievan period and even extended in part to the great struggle of Moscow with Lithuania, they were defending themselves, their families, their homes, and their fields from outside invaders, most notably so on the huge steppe frontier. Because the invaders kept pillaging, burning, destroying, capturing booty, and, especially, carrying off droves of human beings into slavery, there was no doubt in the Russian mind who were the defenders and who were the aggressors, even when Russian armies counterattacked deep into the steppe or, for that matter, seized Kazan and Astrakhan. Russians also regarded themselves as defenders of Orthodoxy, although the Mongols, first pagans and later Muslims, were not hostile after the original devastation to the Russian Orthodox Church and even granted it certain advantages and privileges, notably an exemption from the tribute levied on the conquered Russians. Dmitri Donskoi's successful campaign against the Mongols bore certain marks of a crusade. Defense of Orthodoxy again played a part in the ultimate defeat of the Catholic Poles during the Time of Troubles and—this time with Ukrainians, not Great Russians, as the main actors—in Ukraine turning to Muscovy in 1654. Russians also fought for their country, Rus, Russia, or the Russian land, which, in the course of centuries, became coterminous with Muscovy. All these elements, family and home, Orthodoxy, motherland, for which one was to live and die, went back at least to 988 or beyond that date. However, during the period under discussion a new element did appear: the tsar. Step by historical step, Kievan princes did become Muscovite tsars. But while the steps connected, the end product was stunningly different. Ivan IV, or Ivan III for that matter, if we prefer to assign Ivan IV mainly to pathology, bore no resemblance to such Kievan grand princes as Vladimir Monomakh or (at the end of the Kievan period) Alexander Nevsky. And, together with the change in the rulers, the entire pluralistic, participatory, mobile, and unstable Kievan political system turned into a rigid Muscovite autocracy. Moreover, it is my impression that the transformation in the popular image of the ruler was even more extraordinary than the actual historical facts warranted.

It was largely this drastic difference between the Kievan and the Muscovite polit-ical systems that influenced some historians and other specialists to deny any organic connection between the two and to derive the state of Muscovy from other sources. At one extreme, certain scholars and publicists declared the Muscovite tsars to be successors not of the Kievan princes but of the khans of the Golden Horde. To be sure, the Mongol invasion and yoke and the impact of the Mongols on the Rus-sians is a major historical issue. Russian historiography offers three very different approaches to it. A large body of scholars paid minimal attention to the subject; paradoxical as this attitude may seem, it finds strong support in such fields as Rus-sian religious, legal, cultural, and perhaps even economic and social history, where the Mongol presence, at least direct presence, is virtually invisible. Many other com-mentators, however, emphasized a major negative impact of the Mongols on Russia: the horrible devastation of the original invasion, followed by numerous later incur-sions; the heavy burden of an annual tribute the Russians had to pay precisely when their impoverished and dislocated economy was least prepared to bear it (and pun-ishment when the payment was not forthcoming); the relative isolation of Russia from Byzantium and from the West; and the general decline of cultural, educa-tional, and moral standards. Certain writers went to the extent of claiming that it was because of the Mongols that Russia did not experience the Renaissance and the Reformation or that in general the development of the country was retarded by the invaders by some 150 or 200 years. Finally, and more recently, from 1921 to be exact, a group of intellectuals, calling themselves Eurasians, reconsidered the Mongol impact on Russia as positive and creative, in fact as an essential element in the evo-lution of the organic entity of Eurasia, to which the future belonged.[7] The Eurasians derived Muscovy from the Golden Horde and gave a strikingly new interpretation to Muscovite tsardom. Their views are well represented in English, because the lead-ing and most prolific Eurasian historian, George Vernadsky (Georgy Vladimirovich Vernadsky), wrote and taught for many years at Yale. Interestingly, Eurasian views have had a confused revival since the fall of the Soviet Union, as Russian intellectu-als search for Russian identity (see the concluding remarks to this study). I find Eurasianism highly imaginative, informative, and even impressive in certain details, and on the whole utterly unconvincing.

Vernadsky wrote:

> A convenient method of gauging the extent of Mongol influence on Russia is to compare the Russian state and society of the pre-Mongol period with those of the post-Mongol era, and in particular to contrast the spirit and institutions of Muscovite Russia with those of Russia of the Kievan age. . . . The picture changed completely after the Mongol period.[8]

However, on second look, as Vernadsky admitted, not everything changed, but much remained. Moreover, many important changes could not be readily related to the Mongol impact. In fact, in such major areas as social evolution and spiritual and cultural life, the Mongol influence was of necessity "less drastic." And, indeed, we might ask, how could Muscovite serfdom or Muscovite Christianity be credited to the Mongols? The hub of the matter resided in government and in administration, in the political succession of Muscovy to the Golden Horde (and the accompanying political psychology and ethos). Of course, the Mongols did not establish their own dynasty in Russia, as they did in China or in Iran, and they brought no new system of government to the Russian lands. Russian appanage and grand princes continued to rule and struggle as before, although the Mongols influenced at times that struggle, a situation that was put to good use by Moscow. The important point, Vernadsky insisted, was that Moscow princes went beyond local victories to become, as their fortunes rose, tsars in succession to the khans of the Golden Horde:

> And indeed it was but natural for the Muscovite ruler to take the title of his former suzerain. Moreover, when the Russian counterattack started and the Russians conquered the Khanates of Kazan and Astrakhan (in 1552 and 1556 respectively), the Russian tsar could claim to have become heir to at least two of the Golden Horde succession states. The implications of the conquest were emphasized by the Moscow government in its effort to obtain for its ruler recognition of the title of tsar from the king of Poland. A Russian note handed to the Polish and Lithuanian ambassadors in 1556 stated in addition to the Byzantine argument, along the lines of the two stories above [the crownings of Saint Vladimir and of Vladimir Monomakh], that besides the Russian land God gave Ivan IV the tsardoms of Kazan and Astrakhan, "and the throne of Kazan and Astrakhan has been a tsar's see from the origins." It may be added that a seventeeth-century Muscovite writer, Gregory Kotoshikhin, who was thoroughly familiar with his country's institutions and traditions, also considered the conquest of Kazan and Astrakhan the historical foundation of the Tsardom of Moscow.[9]

How to evaluate Vernadsky's argument? It seems best to discuss the issue of the Muscovite tsar (and tsardom) in some detail, both to place that argument in its proper context and, more broadly, to pay attention to an important new phenomenon in the Russian identity.

The title of "tsar" derives from the Roman-Byzantine title "caesar." Originally this title belonged to the heir to the throne, sometimes a co-ruler. Next to the emperor stood the caesar. Later, the emperor himself came to be called caesar. From Byzantium the title spread to the Slavs. Of the Slavic neighbors of Byzantium, it was first borrowed by the Bulgarians. Already, their ruler Simeon, who died in 927 and had aimed to conquer Byzantium, adopted the title of caesar and was styled by Bulgarian writers as the tsar of Bulgarians and Greeks (or, more formally, of the Romans and the Bulgars—the pope recognized the title). The Bulgarian ruler Samuel, reigning from 976 to 1014, also used the title of tsar. The Serbs followed the Bulgarians, and their remarkable ruler Stephan Dushan was even crowned in 1355 as the tsar of Serbs and Greeks. Indeed, in the fourteenth century, South Slavic scribes promoted the capture of Constantinople and the creation of a great empire: Bulgarians with Alexander of Tyrnovo (whom they called "God-anointed," "autocrat," and "Tsar of Bulgarians and Greeks," and his capital of Tyrnovo "the new Constantinople") at its head, and Serbs with Stephan Dushan. The conquest of both Bulgaria and Serbia by the Turks at the end of the fourteenth century put an end to such projects of Bulgarian or Serbian victorious leadership in the formation of a great empire, but not to the corresponding ambitions of South Slav ideologists. For a time they looked to kings of Poland and Hungary for help, but already in the first half of the fifteenth century, and especially after the fall of Constantinople to the Turks in 1453, they turned their attention to the increasingly successful rulers of Muscovy, who had become the only Orthodox rulers in the world, and bestowed on them their hopes, together with the titles "tsar," "autocrat," and other attributes of majesty. Even the wording of the prophesy of Methodius of Patara and Leo the Wise, to the effect that a certain *rusyi* clan will defeat Ismael and capture the city of seven hills (Constantinople), had *rusyi* changed to *russkii*—*rusyi* means a certain kind of blond or fair color as applied to hair, *russkii* means Russian.

The Russians, for their part, had long been calling the Byzantine emperor tsar, and his capital, Constantinople, Tsargrad, that is, the city of the tsar. Moreover, in the Kievan period, many Russian princes applied to themselves high Byzantine court titles (although never the two highest, those of emperor and caesar) and dressed accordingly.[10] It will also be remembered that most of the Kievan metropolitans, as well as some other clerics of the Russian Church, were Greeks. In other words, the Russian ruling circles and ecclesiastical intelligentsia were well aware of the Byzantine court, hierarchy, ritualism, and symbolism. They knew, too, that South Slav writers bestowed the title of tsar on their own successful rulers, and they were thus, given favorable circumstances, prepared to follow that example. The catalyst was probably the great victory of Kulikovo in 1380, in which Dmitri Donskoi represented Russia, or at least much of Russia, rather than simply Muscovy.[11] The raising of the position of the Moscow grand prince to that of the Russian tsar by native authors corresponded admirably to the appeal to him of South Slav intellectuals as the last and best hope of the Orthodox world. Even before the fall of Constantinople to the Turks in 1453, they called the Muscovite ruler "tsar" and "autocrat," and after the fall, the only Orthodox tsar in the universe, while Moscow was named the new Constantinople or the new Tsargrad. Together the South Slavs and the Russians did not limit themselves to bestowing impressive titles on the Muscovite prince, but created a history, or rather pseudohistory, of the Russian tsar and tsardom with their special aspects and attributes. A key figure in this process was Pakhomi Logofet, a Serbian monk from Mount Athos who arrived in Moscow in 1440 and in 1442 composed a "chronograph," in which he gave a brief survey of South Slavic history in connection with the Byzantine and Russian histories, including the prophecy of the "Russian" clan that was to rule in Constantinople. Pakhomi called the Muscovite grand prince "Orthodox tsar and autocrat" and provided a foundation for that title: he based it on its acceptance on the eve of the Council of Florence of 1439 by the Byzantine Emperor John VIII Palaeologus. Pakhomi styled Moscow "the new Tsargrad." The influence of the chronograph can be seen in such sources of the Muscovite period as Metropolitan Zosima's "Paschalia" (calculation of the dates of Easter in the eighth millennium from the creation of the world) of 1492, and Abbot Philotheus's (or Filofei's) letters in the early sixteenth century, which will be discussed later.

As we know, the Muscovite rulers themselves contributed mightily to the rise in the standing of their principality and their own standing. Most important, of course, was their successful "gathering of the Russian land," which transformed a minor appanage into the largest state in Europe. But the Muscovite grand princes were also concerned with the titles, rituals, and symbols confirming their new authority and power. To repeat, in 1472 Ivan III married (his second marriage) Sophia, or Zoe, Palaeologus, a niece of the last Byzantine emperor. Later he combined the Byzantine two-headed eagle with his own emblem, St. George vanquishing the dragon (apparently originally simply a rider of no known provenance), to create the new Russian coat of arms. Deeply worried by the Turkish advance and engaged in different kinds of political planning in that connection, foreign powers and authorities were more than sympathetic to the new Muscovite possibilities and vistas. It was the Republic of Venice that pointed out to Ivan III in 1473 that through his marriage to Sophia he could have certain rights of succession to the Byzantine throne. Moreover, the holder of those rights, Sophia's brother Andrew, twice tried to sell them to the Russian grand prince "at bargain price." The Holy Roman Emperor (more exactly, Roman Emperor elect) Maximilian I offered Ivan III a kingship, if he would join the alliance against Turkey. The papacy also displayed great interest in Muscovy. Ivan III rejected all these dangerous offers and plans, which were predicated on a major struggle against the Ottoman Empire, and instead proceeded with a policy of his own. In 1480 he ended any kind of Russian submission to the Golden Horde. He continued on a sweeping scale "the gathering of the Russian land," acquiring notably the crucial principalities of Tver and Novgorod. And he made it clear that he considered himself the rightful heir of the entire Kievan legacy, the sovereign (*gosudar*) of All Russia, which referred in particular to the former Kievan lands that had become part of the Lithuanian state. *Samoderzhets* (autocrat) after he rejected his Mongol overlord, *gosudar* (sovereign) of Russian lands, and grand prince of Moscow and all Russia, Ivan III apparently aspired also to the title of tsar. That title, as I have shown, had already been used by some Bulgarian and Serbian rulers, and, closer to home, it had been applied by some Russian writers to Dmitri Donskoi and by Pakhomi Logofet to Ivan's father, Basil II. Beginning approximately in 1484, Ivan III proceeded to introduce the title of tsar in his correspondence with secondary European states, such as that of the Livonian Order of Knights. More than that, he made an attempt to assure that title officially for his successor. Around

1500 he appointed as his successor his minor grandson Dmitri (son of Ivan's deceased eldest son from his first marriage) and had him crowned according to the Byzantine ritual; however, in 1502 he turned against Dmitri's mother and sent her and Dmitri to prison, where the grandson later died. Ivan III designated as his new successor his and Sophia's son Basil, who in 1505, upon his father's death, became grand prince.

Basil III continued the policies of Ivan III, picking up the few remaining appanage principalities and contesting western Russian lands with Lithuania. Like his father, he refused to be involved in coalitions against Turkey, in particular even when the pope offered, in return for his participation, to crown him and to recognize his right to the Byzantine inheritance. But he held on to the title of tsar and expanded its use, styling himself tsar in all foreign relations, west or east. Moscow writers cooperated with their princes by providing a new derivation for that title, again Byzantine but not, as in the case of Pakhomi Logofet, from John VIII Palaeologus. John VIII was under a cloud in Russia because of his acceptance of the brief Union of Florence with the Catholic Church. The new derivation was unexceptionably Orthodox. Known as the tale of the Vladimir princes, it asserted that the Kievan grand prince Vladimir Monomakh received from his grandfather on the maternal side, the Byzantine Emperor Constantine Monomakh, a tsar's crown (the so-called hat of Monomakh), precious shoulder dress, a gold chain, a chalice, and some other items, with the instruction that the Russian grand prince, crowned with this crown, must be called "the God-crowned tsar of great Rus." The tale noted that from that time on the Vladimir grand princes (descendants of Vladimir Monomakh's son Iury) have been crowned by that crown and, therefore, have the right to the title of tsar. Still more grandly, the Muscovite literati even connected their rulers to the Roman emperors. According to the new genealogy, Emperor Augustus, a sovereign of Rome and the world, in his old age divided his possessions among his relatives, placing his brother Prus as ruler on the banks of the Vistula. Riurik was a fourteenth-generation descendant of this Prus, St. Vladimir a fourth-generation descendant of Riurik, and Vladimir Monomakh a fourth-generation descendant of St. Vladimir. Concurrently with the revision of the genealogy of the princes of Moscow, Christianity in Russia was antedated, and St. Andrew the apostle was proclaimed its true originator. It is worth noting that the two imaginative constructions just mentioned bypassed Byzantium. The culmination came with the extremely impressive and elaborate (trying to improve even on the Byzantine precedent) coronation of Ivan IV as tsar of Moscow and All Russia in 1547. It was sanctioned by the patriarch of Constantinople in 1561.

What, then, of Vernadsky's argument that the Russian tsar and tsardom rose as successors to the Golden Horde? Even a brief look at the subject indicates how much it is related to Byzantine, South Slavic, and Russian political and ecclesiastical history and ideology, and how little to the Mongols. In addition, an orientation to the Mongols leads to constant chronological confusion. If tsar and tsardom emerged from the collapse of the Golden Horde, what about the prior history of those terms and institutions? If, on the other hand, one wants to pay attention to the full long-term affirmation of tsar and tsardom in Russia in Ivan IV's coronation of 1547, then why did it take Russians decades to formalize their succession to the overthrown overlord? And how can the conquests of Kazan in 1552 and Astrakhan in 1556 be "the historical foundation of the Tsardom of Moscow" if it already had been established in 1547? These queries can be multiplied. Besides, Muscovite princes could not obtain the title of tsar from the rulers of the Golden Horde, because those rulers never carried that title. Their title was *khan*. But no Russian princes claimed to be khans. Russian references to some rulers of the Golden Horde, as well as to some other rulers, as tsars—Russians also referred to Mongol rulers as khans or great khans, as the occasion demanded—cannot change the basic situation. The theory of succession to the Byzantine title of caesar-tsar through the khans of the Golden Horde, who themselves never carried that title, seems artificial to say the least.

Although a new title of a ruler can at times have a considerable historical significance, the actual nature and operation of the governing system itself is generally and rightly considered to be of greater importance. In that respect, the Eurasians emphasized that the Muscovite tsardom was essentially a Mongol creation and heir, radically different from Kievan Russia. Centralization replaced diffusion, order superceded disarray, discipline supplanted disobedience, power emerged where formally weakness prevailed. And indeed, a number of Mongolian words in the fields of administration and finance have entered the Russian language, indicating a degree of influence. For example, the term *iarlyk*, which means in modern Russian a trademark or a customs stamp, comes from a Mongol word signifying a written order of the khan, especially the khan's grant of privileges; similarly, the Russian words *denga*, meaning coin, and *dengi*, money, derive from Mongolian. The Mongols did take a census of the Russian population. They have also been credited with affecting the evolution of Russian military forces and tactics, notably as applied to the cavalry. The financial measures of the Mongols, together with the census and the Mongol insistence on building roads and establishing a kind of postal service, added something to the process of centralization in Russia. Yet even these restricted Mongol influences have to be qualified. In matters of finance, the invaders had as their aim to exact the greatest possible tribute from the conquered Russians, and their policies proved to be neither beneficial to the people nor lasting. They replaced the old "smoke" and "plough" taxes with the cruder and simpler head tax, which did not at all take into account one's ability to pay. This innovation disappeared when Russian princes, as intermediaries, took over from the Mongol tax collectors. As to frequently cited military matters, where the invaders did excel, the fact remains that Russian armies and tactics of the appanage period, based on foot soldiers, evolved directly from those of Kiev, not from the Mongol cavalry, although that cavalry influenced later Muscovite gentry horse formations. Similarly, a real postal system came to Russia as late as the seventeenth century, and from the West; the Mongols merely resorted to the Kievan practice of obligating the local population to supply horses, carriages, boats, and other aids to communication for the use of officials, although they did implement this practice widely and bequeathed several words in the field of transportation to the Russians.

As to government and administration, Vernadsky and certain other scholars greatly exaggerate the Mongol presence and influence in Russia. To be sure, the Mongol khan, at first the great khan in Karakorum and from 1259 the khan of the Golden Horde in Sarai, was recognized as the overlord or suzerain over the Russian princes, his vassals. He invested or confirmed them as rulers of their principalities, acted as the judge over them, occasionally obtained military help from them, and, of course, he collected tribute from the conquered Russians. Vernadsky, however, also writes loosely about a direct Mongol military administration in Russia, which was true only of some areas briefly after the invasion, and even of a long-term double administration, or two administrations, Mongolian and Russian, throughout the country. The Mongolian administration, he asserts, was concerned primarily with military and financial affairs. In regard to the military side, there is no evidence of any such administration. Scholars have discovered three or four auxiliary Russian units serving with Mongol armies, and even if there existed in fact several times that number, this would not argue for the presence for a century or two centuries of a regular Mongol military conscription system inside Russia. Apparently, separate Russian units were very occasionally sent by Russian princes to help the Mongols. In addition, there is no record of any Mongol military administration in Russia, officers or officials, in connection with the numerous wars the Russians waged during that period with their western neighbors or in other Russian military undertakings. The financial issue, was, of course, real and central, although it may be better described simply as collecting tribute, for the Mongols were not a party to numerous other financial affairs of the Russians. Originally performed by Mongols themselves, that activity was leased to "Saracen" (probably Arab) entrepreneurs and, after further trouble and in particular the rebellion of 1290, assigned to Russian princes, with the princes of Moscow, as already mentioned, playing a crucial role. Matters of money and tribute represented throughout one of the important connections between the Russians and the Mongols, although on that subject, too, caution is necessary and precision desirable.

Of special interest is the census, which the Mongols introduced to raise tribute from the conquered Russians, and which probably represented their most effective and far-reaching penetration into Russian administrative and generally internal affairs. Scholars have differed as to whether the count in the census was based on households or on individuals, with chronicles providing some evidence for both points of view, but most of them have been willing to accept individual registration. The problem has been the huge scope of such a registration of a population of about ten million, even allowing for the fact that it was conducted in four stages (in 1245 in southern Russia, in 1258–1259 in central and northern, in 1260 in southwestern, and in 1274–1275 in eastern Russia and in the Smolensk area). If registration centers were established for every ten thousand adult males, they numbered no less than fifty; if for every thousand, five hundred. The centers needed such specialists as copyists, translators, supervisors, and probably, already, collectors of tribute. All this must have exceeded the resources of the Mongols. The solution was most probably found in letting the Russians themselves do the counting and the registering, with the Mongols acting as supervisors and perhaps doing some checking. It should be noted that the counting was done by the conventional decimal system used by the Russians, without the intermediate units of twenty (*horin*) and forty (*döcin*) known to the Mongols.[12] The innovation was the new unit of ten thousand, introduced by, or at the order of, the Mongols—the *tma* of the Russian sources, *tumen* in Mongolian.

Yet *tma*, like *iarlyk* and other specific Mongolian contributions to Russian history, does little or nothing to support the Eurasians' claims of the Mongol provenance of the tsardom of Muscovy. As already mentioned, the Mongols kept apart from the Russians, limiting their interest in their unwilling subjects to a few items, notably the exaction of tribute. Religion posed a formidable barrier between the two peoples, both at first when the Mongols were still pagan and later when the Golden Horde became Muslim. The Mongols were perfectly willing to leave the Russians to their own ways; indeed, they patronized the Orthodox Church.

Perhaps a still greater significance attaches to the fact that the Mongol and the Russian societies bore little resemblance to each other. The Mongols remained nomads in the clan stage of development. Their institutions and laws could in no wise be adopted by a much more complex agricultural society. A comparison of Mongol law, the code of Jenghiz Khan, to the Pskov Sudebnik, an example of Russian law of the appanage age, makes the difference abundantly clear. The Mongol influence on Russia could not parallel the impact of the Arabs on the West, because, to quote Pushkin, the Mongols were "Arabs without Aristotle and algebra"—or other cultural assets. Even the increasing harshness of Russian criminal law of the period should probably be attributed to the conditions of the time rather than to borrowing from the Mongols. Perhaps ironically, such dreaded instruments of punishment and torture as the notorious knout came to Russia from the West, more exactly from Germany and the north, not from the Mongols.

The Eurasian argument also tends to misrepresent the nature of the Mongol states. Far from having been particularly well organized, efficient, or lasting, they turned out to be relatively unstable and short-lived. Thus, in 1260 Kublai Khan built Peking and in 1280 he completed the conquest of southern China, but in 1368 the Mongol dynasty was driven out of China; the Mongol dynasty in Persia lasted only from 1256 to 1344; and the Mongol Central Asiatic state with its capital in Bukhara existed from 1242 until its destruction by Tamerlane in 1370. In the Russian case, the dates are rather similar, but the Mongols never established their own dynasty in the country, acting instead merely as overlords of Russian princes. While the Mongol states lasted, they continued on the whole to be rent by dissension and wars and to suffer from arbitrariness, corruption, and misrule in general. Not only did the Mongols fail to contribute a superior statecraft, but they had to borrow virtually everything, from alphabets to advisers, from the conquered peoples to enable their states to exist. As one of these advisers remarked, an empire could be won on horseback, but not ruled from the saddle. True, cruelty, lawlessness, and at times anarchy, in that period, also characterized the life of many peoples other than the Mongols, the Russians included. But at least most of these peoples managed eventually to surmount their difficulties and organize effective and lasting states. Not so the Mongols, who, after their sudden and stunning performance on the world scene, receded to the steppe, clan life, and the internecine warfare of Mongolia.

When the Muscovite state emerged, its leaders looked to Byzantium for their high model, and to Kievan Russia for their historical and still meaningful heritage. As to the Mongols, a single attitude toward them pervades all Russian literature: they were a scourge of God sent upon the Russians as dreadful punishment for their sins. Historians too, whether they studied the growth of serfdom, the rise of the gentry, or the nature of princely power in Muscovite Russia, established significant connections with the Russian past and Russian conditions, not with Mongolia. Even for purposes of analogy, European countries stood much closer to Russia than Mongol states. In fact, from the Atlantic to the Urals absolute monarchies were in the process of replacing the feudal or quasi-feudal division. Therefore, Vernadsky's affirming the importance of the Mongol impact by contrasting Muscovite with Kievan Russia appears to miss the point. There existed many other reasons for changes in Russia; and, needless to say, other countries changed during those centuries without contact with the Mongols.

The search for Mongol roots of Muscovite tsars, tsardom, and identity has been essentially illusory. The role of Byzantium in that respect is much more complicated. I have already repeatedly emphasized, perhaps even overemphasized, the impact of Byzantium on Russia, especially after the conversion of the Rus to Christianity in 988. A discussion of the possible Mongol antecedents of and influences on the Muscovite tsar became instead an exegesis into Byzantine history and into that of "the Byzantine commonwealth." Kievan princes already used Byzantine dress and ranks, and, following a long process, with Ivan IV's coronation of 1547, the Byzantine title of tsar itself was fully, even extravagantly, established in "Moscow and all Russia." Yet it would be wrong to call Muscovite and Russian rulers successors to Byzantine emperors. For one thing, none of them ever made that claim. Whereas certain Bulgarian and Serbian monarchs, as already described, declared themselves to be tsars of Bulgarians and Greeks or Serbians and Greeks ("Greeks" sometimes came out as "romei," "Romans," that is, citizens of the Roman Empire, the capital of which had been transferred from Rome to Constantinople by Emperor Constantine), no Russian ruler followed suit. In fact, Ivan III and, again, Basil II explicitly rejected the Byzantine succession, when it was offered to them by others. Muscovite grand princes indeed coveted and obtained the title of tsar as an affirmation of a new and higher level of majesty and power for themselves and their state, but they thought of that title in terms of the conditions and prospects in Russia, not in Byzantium.

Among numerous ideological connections between Byzantium and the tsardom of Muscovy, the most controversial and—according to some interpretations—the most far-reaching has been the so-called doctrine of Moscow, the Third Rome. Its originator, an abbot from Pskov named Philotheus or Filofei, wrote a letter to Basil III describing three Romes: the Church of Old Rome, which fell because of a heresy, the Church of Constantinople, brought down by the infidels shortly after the capitulation to the pope at the Council of Florence, and finally the Church in Basil III's own tsardom, which, like the sun, was to illumine the entire world—furthermore, after two Romes had fallen, Moscow, the Third Rome, would stand permanently, for there was to be no fourth. Little noticed at the time and for some centuries following, and obviously irrelevant to the actual policies of Muscovite rulers, the doctrine had a strange revival in the nineteenth and especially the twentieth centuries, when it was interpreted politically: to explain to some writers the Soviet expansion and alleged aim to conquer the world, to serve as a slogan for certain ideologists, particularly on the Russian Right, and, worst of all, to be taken as a basic programmatic document of Russian history by a number of serious scholars, who have not themselves studied the subject. Therefore, it bears emphasizing that Philotheus thought, in the first place, of churches, not states, and that he was concerned with the preservation of the true faith, not political expansion. He was painfully worried by a corruption of monastic morals and other transgressions in what was the last Orthodox state in the world.[13]

Not the Mongol khan and not the Byzantine emperor, what was the real nature of the Muscovite tsar? Most important, what was the basis of the apotheosis of the tsar by his people? To be sure, Muscovite tsars descended directly from Kievan princes, but the change they and their images underwent were fundamental. Numerous, eventually very numerous, Kievan princes constituted the ruling stratum of Kievan Russia, but they drastically lacked the majesty and authority of Muscovite tsars. They quarreled and bargained not only among themselves but also with their retainers and with town officials and town *vecha*. In the case of Novgorod, they remind a modern observer more of salaried city managers or, for a closer analogy, of the *podestà* of the Italian Renaissance than of mighty kings and emperors. They assumed at times Byzantine ranks and dress, but never those of the highest Byzantine levels. The title of the grand prince itself apparently applies only to the late stages of Kievan history and after, and it might have been used less by its contemporaries than by later scholars. The so-called hat of Monomakh, eventually the Russian crown, though properly classified among ancient and beautiful regalia, certainly postdates the Byzantine Emperor Constantine Monomakh and the Kievan Grand Prince Vladimir Monomakh, who were incorrectly linked to it by the Muscovite tradition. There were never False Vladimirs or False Iaroslavs in Kievan days to match False Dmitris, False Peters, and many other such false claimants to the throne by different names in later Russian history.[14]

It was in the late appanage or early Muscovite period, when Muscovite grand princes were becoming Russian tsars, that a new, overwhelming, in a sense magical concept of the all-powerful, just, and benevolent true monarch laid hold of the popular psyche and imagination to find extraordinary expression in the Time of Troubles and beyond.

Although greatly exaggerated, the new popular image did correspond to some extent to reality. Muscovy did become big and strong, and its rulers played a major role in the process. In addition, as I have shown, some commentators have tried to explain the new orientation and ethos in Muscovy by the legacy of Jenghiz Khan and some by the transfer of the empire from the Second Rome to the Third. The religious, or quasi-religious, nature of the Muscovite tsar and tsardom have frequently been stressed. But that approach can also create more problems than it solves. If one writes that the tsar was regarded in Muscovy as God or as the chief servant of God, one should realize that there is an immeasurable distance between the two identities. And the first is impossible in Christianity, in particular Orthodox Christianity. Even Ivan the Terrible apparently repented almost as much as he blasphemed, and there was no other candidate for divinization in Muscovy. No Muscovite hierarch could preach that tsar was God; no Muscovite government could decree it. Later, too, the outstanding Russian autocrat Peter the Great ordered his subjects not to take off their headdress as they passed his residence, because such reverence was appropriate only in regard to God, not in regard to the monarch; another notorious despot, Nicholas I, was especially concerned that no element of the ruler's divinization appear in print, not even allusively, poetically, figuratively, or in any other form.[15] What then of the popular belief in the tsar? The best explanation seems to me to be A. V. Kartashev's reference to the propensity of Russian Orthodoxy to emphasize the sacredness on this earth of everything associated with the divine, which he postulated as the foundation of Old Belief. Insignificant practices and even outright errors thus became sacralized and would not be abandoned by the Old Believers, even when repudiated by the Church itself. The tsar also became so sacralized in Muscovy, and indeed his links with religion, that is, with the divine, were many and important: the coronation, the constant prayers for the tsar, the great deference accorded him in religious services and ceremonies, and in general by the hierarchs and the entire Church, and so on. Russians in the Muscovite period (and later) did not consider the tsar divine, and most of them probably lacked theological clarity to face the issue squarely. But enough sacral elements clung in one way or another to the popular image of the tsar to speak of an apotheosis.[16] Sacralization of rulers, distinct in each particular case, was prominent in medieval Europe, as was the affirmation of a new Rome.[17]

Much has been written about the isolation of appanage and Muscovite Russia, and some aspects of Muscovite society and culture, such as suspicion of foreigners and an arrogant and ignorant preference for their own ways, have been closely related to it. The first century after the Mongol invasion probably represented the nadir for Russia, in terms of isolation as well as in many other respects. The rise of Moscow, however, reversed the situation. A large influx of foreigners came in the reign of Ivan III in connection with the great building going on in the Kremlin and for other reasons. At the end of the sixteenth century, foreigners in Muscovite service could be counted in hundreds and even thousands, if we include Poles, Lithuanians, and Ukrainians. After a setback during the Time of Troubles, foreigners again greatly increased in numbers, and foreign influences, especially Polish or other European influences mediated by Poland, swept through Russia. Many scholars consider the seventeenth century as a transition between old Russia and new, and a few include it already in the new age. Yet it was only with Peter the Great and his successors that the turn to the West became comprehensive government policy, and before long also part of the identity of educated Russians.

The Reign of Peter the Great

If we consider the matter thoroughly, then,
in justice, we must be called not Russians,
but Petrovians. . . . Russia should be
called Petrovia, and we Petrovians.

—Kankrin

Was the momentous reign of Peter the Great (1682–1725) a fundamental divide in Russian history?[1] The controversial issue of the Petrine impact and influence has been central to Russian intellectual life and culture.[2] The division of opinion among specialists has resulted in large part from differences in approach and concentration on one or another aspect of the reign. The evolution of Russian society experienced no turning point around the years 1700 or 1725. To be sure, the determined autocrat judged his servitors by their work and thus opened the road to talent, or at least some talent. But his motley and often unusual associates, both foreign and domestic, either disappeared, having performed their function, or were absorbed with their families into the Russian traditional aristocracy or gentry.[3] Serfdom remained and was even strengthened by the legislation amalgamating (for financial purposes) various bonded and marginal groups into the single category of serfs. In the economic field, too, the reign of the first emperor marked no startling new departure, although the monarch's frantic activity added considerable energy to the economic development of the country—in particular to manufacturing—and bequeathed some valuable beginnings to the future. No wonder that Marxists, as well as other economic and social determinists, do not consider Peter the Great's reign epoch-making.

Diplomatic historians share a different perspective. While fully aware of the continuous nature of Petrine foreign policy, for it represented in effect a new round or rounds of the long-term engagement of Muscovy with Sweden, Poland, and Turkey, they have been understandably impressed by its results. The decisive victory over Sweden, confirmed by the Treaty of Nystadt in 1721, projected Russia into the position of a great European and, before long, world power, which had to be considered in all important matters on the continent. Nor could the process of the Russian rise be reversed. And in the course of the Petrine wars, Russia created an impressive navy, a true first and almost a creation out of nothing, and thoroughly transformed its antiquated army into a mighty and up-to-date force.

The import of the Petrine reforms for the government of Russia, for its institutions and administration, proved to be especially controversial and difficult to evaluate. Of course, Peter the Great changed wholesale the government institutions and the entire administrative apparatus of Muscovite Russia, including the transfer of the capital from Moscow to St. Petersburg, just being built. Efforts to delimit clearly the authority of every agency, to separate powers and functions, to standardize procedure, and to spell out each detail could well be considered revolutionary from the Muscovite point of view. And this revolutionary quality was emphasized by the ruler himself, who hated the old order, which he identified with backwardness and stagnation, as well as with the lethal intrigue and conspiracy that had surrounded him in his early years. On the surface, the new system seemed to bear a greater resemblance to Sweden and the German states than to the realm of the reformer's father, the good Tsar Alexis. Content, however, did not necessarily agree with form. While statutes, prescriptions, and precise regulations looked good on paper, many scholars have argued that in actuality, in the main cities and especially in the enormous expanses of provincial Russia, everything depended as of old on the initiative, ability, and behavior of officials—on their personal and arbitrary rule. Yet, as those holding to the middle ground have stressed, a totally negative judgment may well miss the mark. A beginning at westernization was made, and there could be no return to the Muscovite past and Muscovite isolation. Even German ranks and Swedish regulations had in that sense a progressive role to play in Russia.

By contrast, almost all students of Russian intellectual life and Russian culture assign a major importance to the reign of Peter the Great. The reformer himself has been praised for consciously and willfully leading Russia to its true destiny, for westernizing Russia, or at least for making a fundamental and irreversible contribution to that westernization, for moving Russia out of the Middle Ages and into the modern—or, more exactly, early modern—world, and for enabling Catherine the Great later in the century to write in her *Instruction to the Legislative Commission*: "Russia is a European State."[4] Even those few intellectuals, perhaps especially those few, such as the Slavophiles, who opposed the new direction, placed the responsibility for it squarely on Peter the Great.

While much of this is hyperbole, the reign and activities of Peter the Great made their significant and distinctive contribution to modern Russian thought and culture, although in those realms there was no single day like July 8, 1709, when the Russian army destroyed the Swedish forces in the battle at Poltava and gave European international relations a new course. Many scholars stress that whereas earlier westernization had reached Russia mainly through Poland and as part of Polish culture, the reformer grasped directly the West itself through making his own travels, assigning Russians to study abroad, and inviting numerous foreign specialists to Russia. Although individual specialists had been coming down to Muscovy earlier, and on a considerable scale, it was unprecedented to model Russian institutions, administration, and legislation on Sweden, northern German states, and even Great

Britain. Peter the Great earned his membership in the French Academy of Sciences and furthered his shipbuilding skills in Holland and in England. Perhaps even more important was the Petrine emphasis on speed and compulsion. While westernization prior to the reformer had been largely a gradual and voluntary process, with him it became part of government policy. And this policy, whether in culture, in the tragic and costly building of St. Petersburg, or in war, demanded utmost immediate effort from all Russians. Indeed, there was no clear divide between military and civic duties, for schools were a necessity for the new army, navy, and administration, while Peter the Great never had sufficient qualified personnel for all of his undertakings and plans. All in all, one can well understand why his educated contemporaries, as well as so many later Russians, felt that a new age had come to their country with the dauntless reformer.

The dominant European intellectual climate of the "Enlightenment," or "Age of Reason," fit Peter the Great's character, orientation, and ambitions marvelously. The optimistic belief in reason, in the possibility and feasibility of reasonable solutions to human problems, ranging from technical matters of administration, economics, or finance to the broader issues of the nature of a genuine education, or of an ideal society and polity, constituted the leading inspiration of the age. And it was the same concept of reason that, by providing the common measure and link for all men and women and all human societies, was largely responsible for the magnificent cosmopolitanism of the Enlightenment.

Criticism shared the stage with reason. A number of the leading students of the Enlightenment have persuasively presented the thought of their period as above all a critique of the existing order of things in the world. If reason constituted the standard of judgment, the beliefs, institutions, and affairs of human beings left, indeed, very much to be desired. The answer lay, of course, in education, knowledge, *les lumières*. Assisted by Lockean psychology, the field of education proper came to occupy the center of attention and hope, while implicit and very frequently explicit didacticism permeated all literature.

Russia could be considered, at least in theory, an ideal subject for Enlightenment. If an application of reason held promise for England or France, it could be easily regarded as the only and at the same time the most profoundly inspiring hope in the much more backward Russian conditions. If in the West progress suggested compromise with the past, in Russia, in the opinion of Peter the Great and some of his assistants, the past could be simply swept away. If the *philosophes* wanted to reform early modern European societies along certain lines, in Russia such a society had to be formed in the first place. Throughout the eighteenth century much of the educational effort of the government went simply into teaching its subjects European manners and usages. On the whole, from gunnery to the Academy of Sciences, from newspapers and periodicals to vaccination, Peter the Great and, in the second half of the century, Catherine the Great, in their very different ways, spent more time and effort teaching than any other contemporary monarchs. In other respects, too, the thought of the Age of Reason corresponded to Russian aspirations and needs. Cosmopolitanism, and certain proselytizing tendencies, for that matter, proved extremely welcome to a country that wanted to join the European society of states. Even more specific concepts such as the emerging religious tolerance had much to offer the increasingly multireligious and multicultural empire of the Romanovs.

Russian autocracy itself received rich support from the thought and practice of the Age of Reason. A belief in the enlightened ruler as the source of progress permeated that thought. If a society was sunk in ignorance and prejudice and was to be pulled out of its stupor, it required a lever, an outside force to do the pulling. The enlightened despot was to be such a force, and his presence became more imperative as that of God grew more distant.

Peter the Great was a true enlightened despot. That he has not generally been so called is to be explained by the facts that that appellation has been usually reserved for the second half of the eighteenth century, that the Russian history of the period has not been sufficiently studied in the European context, and that the crudity and cruelty of the reformer, as well as the barbarism of his surroundings, have stood in the way of a full recognition of his place among the elect of his age. Yet, if Enlightenment meant bringing light, as understood at the time, into darkness, no other ruler of the period could compete in the scope, decisiveness, and irreversibility of his actions with the Russian emperor. Not only did he perform impressively as an enlightened despot, but he also bequeathed enlightened despotism to his successors. They knew whence the legacy came: "To Peter I, Catherine II."[5]

Peter the Great was an absolute ruler in theory and in practice. He never questioned his inherited position of tsar of Muscovy and Russia; in 1721, after the victorious treaty with Sweden, "Emperor," "Great," and "Father of the Fatherland" also became his titles, with "Emperor," hence "empire" for Russia, becoming the accepted designation, especially in foreign relations, although the title "tsar" was never abolished. More important, he acted like one of the memorable autocrats of history. An uncompromising character and a violent temper accentuated further his decisiveness and the plenitude of his power. Still, important changes from the uncodified principles and the more tangible attitudes and mores of Muscovite tsardom emerged under Peter's rule. Most significant was a drastic separation of the ruler as a person from the state, in fact, a subordination of his private person to the state, and a new utilitarian rationale for the ruler's behavior. N. I. Pavlenko emphasized that the concept of the common good, *obshchee blago*, was first advanced in 1702, in a *ukase* concerned with inviting foreign specialists into Russian service, and that it became increasingly prominent thereafter. Pavlenko said, in particular, that a growing stress on the interests of the country as distinct from those of the person of the ruler can be detected in the recurrent official Russian justification of the Great Northern War.[6] And what the monarch practiced and preached above all was service—service to the state for the common good. Revealingly, when reorganizing the army, he crossed out "the interests of His Tsarist Majesty" as the object of military devotion and substituted "the interests of the state."[7] Or, to quote from Peter the Great's celebrated address to his troops immediately preceding the battle of Poltava: "As to Peter, they should know clearly that his life is not dear to him, provided only that Russia lives, Russian piety, glory, and well-being."[8] Not surprisingly, Peter the Great drew a sharp distinction between his own resources, which he considered limited to the salaries he earned in his various functions, and the possessions of the state. The principle of devoted and selfless service to the state, to Russia, as distinct from the person of the ruler, became one of the legacies of the first emperor to his successors. Some of them, such as Nicholas I, showed a similar zeal, if not an equal ability, in implementing that principle.

In spite of the colossal demands of his self-assigned task, Peter the Great on the whole looked confidently to the future. A part of that confidence stemmed, no doubt, from his own energetic optimism; a part reflected the affirmative and hopeful outlook of the age. The ruler expected reason to accomplish the transformation of Russia. It was reason that made the Russian sovereign prize experts, whether Leibniz or a shipwright, and utilize them as much as possible, for they usually had reason on their side. It was reason that even made him at times, defying his own temperament, listen to dissenting or contrary advice and admit his mistakes. As the monarch jotted down once on a piece of paper: "Thinking is above all virtues, because without reason every virtue is empty."[9] Peter the Great's hectic, disjointed, at times desperate reordering of Russia was nevertheless also meant to be a tribute to reason and to result eventually in its triumph in the entire land.

This point bears repeating, for at the time Russia was confusion worse confounded. Reality rarely corresponds to theory, and in the reign of Peter the Great the disjunction was extreme. Instead of happily leading his people on the path of enlightenment, the monarch had to fight both abroad and at home for the very survival of his state, his new system, and himself.[10] In regard to internal developments in Russia in the Petrine period, scholars have generally taken one of two sharp and opposite approaches. On the one hand, the ruler's reforming of Russia has been presented as a series, or rather a jumble, of disconnected ad hoc measures necessitated by the exigencies of the moment, in particular by the Great Northern War. Contrariwise, the same activity has been depicted as the execution of a comprehensive, radically new, and well-integrated program. In a number of ways the first view seems closer to the facts. Only a single year in Peter the Great's whole reign, 1724, passed entirely without war, while no more than another thirteen peaceful months could be added for the entire period. Connected to the enormous strain of war was the inadequacy of the Muscovite financial system, which had been overburdened and in a state of virtual collapse even before Peter the Great made vastly increased demands upon it. The problem for the state became simply to survive, and survival exacted a heavy price. Under Peter the Great, the population of Russia might have declined. Pavel Nikolaevich Miliukov (Paul Miliukov), a very prominent Russian historian and statesman, who made a brilliant analysis of Petrine fiscal structure and economy,[11] and other scholars of his persuasion have shown how military considerations repeatedly led to financial measures, and in turn to edicts aiming to stimulate Russian commerce and industry; to changes in the administrative system, without the improvement of which these and other edicts had proved ineffective; to attempts to foster education, which a modern administration needed in order to function; and on and on. It has further been argued, on the whole convincingly, that in any case, Peter the Great was not a theoretician or planner, but an intensely energetic and practical man of affairs.

Yet a balanced judgment has to allow something to the opposite point of view as well. Although Peter the Great was preoccupied during most of his reign with the Great Northern War and although he had to sacrifice much else to its successful prosecution, his reforming of Russia was by no means limited to hectic measures to bolster the war effort. In fact, he wanted to Westernize and modernize all of the Russian government, society, life, and culture, and evenf if his efforts fell far short of this stupendous goal, failed to dovetail, and left huge gaps, the basic pattern emerges, nevertheless, with sufficient clarity. Countries of the West served as the emperor's model; but the Russian ruler also tried to adapt a variety of Western institutions to Russian needs and possibilities. While the reformer was no theoretician, he had the makings of a visionary. With characteristic grandeur and optimism, he saw ahead the image of a modern, powerful, prosperous, and educated country, and it was to the realization of that image that he dedicated his life.

Applied to the monarch's subjects, reliance on reason meant explanation and education. It has been noted that, in his all-pervasive, minute regulation of the lives of his people, the sovereign almost invariably supplied the reasons for his legislation. *Ponezhe* or *dlia togo*, that is, "because," became the hallmark of his edicts.[12] To be sure, he also stated appropriate punishment for each transgression, but this only added further point to the didacticism of his efforts. From the first translated book of manners, the so-called *Mirror of Youth*,[13] the new Russian publishing industry devoted special attention to teaching its readers how to behave. Again, the ruler worked feverishly himself, whether simplifying the Russian alphabet, establishing different schools, or organizing the Academy of Sciences. "For learning is good and fundamental and as it were the root, the seed, and first principle of all that is good and useful in church and state."[14]

To review some educational and cultural highlights of the reign, it was in 1700 that the reformer arranged for publication of Russian books by a Dutch press; several years later the publishing was transferred to Russia. Six hundred different books published in Peter's reign have come down to our time. In 1702 the first Russian newspaper, *Vedomosti*, or *News*, began to be published, the monarch himself editing its first issue. Next Peter the Great took part in reforming the alphabet to produce what came to be known as the civil Russian alphabet. Composed of Slavonic, Greek, and Latin letters, the new alphabet represented a considerable simplification of the old Slavonic. The old alphabet was allowed for Church books, but, following a decree in early 1710, all other works had to use the new system. In addition, Peter I introduced Arabic numerals to replace the cumbersome Slavonic ones.

Peter the Great sent hundreds of young Russians to study abroad, and he opened schools of new types in Russia. For example, as early as 1701 he established in Moscow a School of Mathematical and Navigational Sciences. Essentially a secondary school, that institution stressed the teaching of arithmetic, geometry, trigonometry, astronomy, and geography. The number of its students reached five hundred by 1715, and two elementary schools were founded to prepare Russian boys to enter it. In 1715 a naval academy for three hundred pupils opened in St. Petersburg. Moscow, in turn, received an artillery and an engineering academy of the same general pattern. Some other special schools, such as the so-called admiralty and mathematical ones, also appeared in the course of the reign. In 1716, in an attempt to develop a broader educational system, the government opened twelve elementary "cypher" schools in provincial towns. By 1723 their number had increased to forty-two. In 1706 a medical school with a student body of fifty began instruction in Moscow; in 1709 another medical school, this time with thirty students, started functioning in St. Petersburg. Peter I also organized small classes to study special subjects such as Chinese and Japanese and the languages of some non-Russian peoples within the empire. In addition to establishing state schools, the reformer tried to improve and modernize those of the Church. Finally, education in Russia expanded by means of private schools, which began to appear in the course of his reign.

Peter the Great's measures to promote enlightenment in Russia also included the founding of a museum of natural sciences and a large general library in St. Petersburg. Both were opened free to the public. But the reformer's most ambitious cultural undertaking was the creation of the Imperial Academy of Sciences. Although the Academy came into being only some months after his death, it represented the realization of a major project of the reformer's last years. The Academy had three departments, the mathematical, physical, and historical, as well as a special section for the arts. The academicians gave instruction, and a high school was attached to the Academy to prepare students for this advanced education. Although the Academy operated at first on a small scale and consisted of only seventeen specialists, all of them foreigners, before long it became, as intended, the center of science and scholarship in Russia. It still occupies that position. It has been noted repeatedly that Russia obtained an Academy of Sciences before it developed a network of elementary schools—a significant comment on the nature of Peter the Great's reforms and the role of the state in eighteenth-century Russian culture.

Peter the Great's reorganization of the Church in Russia, highly significant and long-lasting, can well be considered a logical and integral part of his tireless efforts to modernize and even Westernize his country. Yet that reform, together with the issue of the monarch's own religious orientation, have produced much controversy among scholars, eliciting numerous and sometimes misleading explications and interpretations. In fact, Peter the Great was, apparently, a sincerely and strongly religious man, who often felt the presence of God in his daily life and reflected on it, especially in connection with the dangers and fortunes of war. I know of no evidence contradicting Feofan Prokopovich's hagiographic depiction of his dying.[15] The sovereign liked very much to attend church services, frequently singing in the choir or reading the epistle. Nor is there any reason to doubt that he identified the God he worshiped in church with the God who saved him in battles, in which, indeed, he was repeatedly lucky to have survived. The difficulty with this assessment of Peter the Great as simply and thoroughly religious is not his struggle against the ecclesiastical establishment and his church reform—reformers can also be religious—nor even his enthusiasm for the secular world and a secularization of Russian life and culture, but his notorious blasphemous debauchery. I find explanations that the blasphemy was meant against the Catholic Church but not the Orthodox, or against superstition but not true religion, insufficient, but I have no clear solution to offer. We might be able to understand the phenomenon in question best, if we think of the concept of carnival, charivari, or Mardi gras, present in a number of civilizations, including the Byzantine and the western European, when values and standards are reversed and the forbidden comes into the open. It is worth noting that, to the best of my knowledge, Peter the Great expressed no remorse or regret in connection with his particular blasphemous episodes.

The change in the organization of the Church paralleled Peter the Great's reform of the government. When the old-fashioned patriarch Hadrian died in 1700, the ruler kept his seat vacant, and the Church was administered for over two decades by a mere *locum tenens*, the very able moderate supporter of reform Metropolitan Stephen Iavorsky. Finally, in 1721, the so-called Spiritual Reglament, apparently written mainly by the chief ideologist and the most influential cleric of the reign, Archbishop Feofan (or Theophanes) Prokopovich, established a new organization of the Church. The Holy Synod, consisting of ten, later twelve, clerics, replaced the patriarch. A lay official, the ober-procurator of the Holy Synod, was appointed to see that that body carried on its work in a perfectly legal and correct manner. Although the new arrangement fell under the conciliar principle widespread in the Orthodox Church and received approval from the Eastern patriarchs, the reform belonged—as much as did Peter the Great's other reforms—to Western, not Muscovite or Byzantine, tradition. In particular, it tried to reproduce the relationship between Church and state in the Lutheran countries of northern Europe. Although it did not make Russia Byzantine as some writers assert, or even caesaropapist—for the emperor did not acquire any authority in questions of faith—it did enable the government to exercise effective control over Church organization, possessions, and policies. If Muscovy had two supreme leaders, the tsar and the patriarch, only the tsar remained in the St. Petersburg era. The Holy Synod and the domination of the Church by the government lasted until 1917. In a sense itself an example of secularization, the ecclesiastical reform made it easier in turn for secularism to spread in Russia. To be sure, Orthodoxy remained in imperial Russia, and it even continued to be linked to the state and to occupy formally a high and honored position. But instead of being central to Russian life and culture, it became, at least as far as the government and the educated public were concerned, a separate and rather neglected compartment.[16]

Peter the Great's view of himself as the drastic enlightened reformer of his country, even as the creator of a new Russia, modern Russia, was promptly picked up by the ideologists of the reign to become a leitmotif of Russian thought and culture. Cascades of glorification and worshipful admiration descended upon the sovereign already in his lifetime and, after his death, during the decades and centuries that followed. (The reformer himself was not given to glorification, let alone worshipful admiration, of his own persona.) One has to pursue repeatedly the image of Peter the Great as one studies the issue of Russian identity and Russian nationalism. But the main pro-Petrine thesis was clearly stated and even richly embellished already in the reformer's own time. To refer again to the archbishop and marvelous preacher Feofan Prokopovich: "Your amazing deeds are your trophies. Entire Russia is your statue, reshaped by your expert skill, as pictured not in vain in your emblem; and the entire world is your poet and the preacher of your glory."[17] And once more:

> It would have been amazing had one sovereign accomplished one thing and another the other: as Romans praise their first two tsars, Romulus and Numa, that one by war and the other by peace strengthened the fatherland, or as in sacred history David by arms and Solomon by politics created a blessed well-being for Israel. But in our case both this and that, and, in addition, in countless and varied circumstances, were achieved by Peter alone. For us he is Romulus, and Numa, and David, and Solomon—Peter alone.[18]

Yet, as when dealing with earlier periods of Russian history, it is appropriate to ask exactly whom did the official ideology, this time the Petrine ideology, faithfully represent. And the answer, of necessity lacking precision, has to be that it represented only a minority of Russians, probably to begin with a very small minority. Peter the Great was not deterred by that fact, because his guiding stars were reason and enlightenment as he understood them, not popular preference or approval. Even the limited Muscovite channels of a more popular participation in politics disappeared in the reformer's reign: no *zemskii sobor* was ever summoned by him or his successors, and the *duma* was left to wither away without any place in the new political structure. Major rebellions, reacting to the continual oppressiveness of the social and economic system—as well as, to some extent, to the reformer's orientation—highlighted the opposition. Thus the rising led by Bulavin was quite similar to the great lower-class rebellions associated with the names of Razin a third of a century earlier, or with that of Bolotnikov during the Time of Troubles, while the revolt in Astrakhan was sparked partly by the rumor that all Astrakhan maidens would be ordered to marry foreigners. To be sure, Peter the Great prevailed over the opposition and even managed in a desperate effort to mobilize the country suffi-

ciently to defeat Sweden and make Russia a major European power. Still, it is doubt-
ful that his beliefs and vision were shared much beyond the group of his immediate
assistants; and even among them, it was likely shared only to a limited extent. Even
if we accept for the reign itself the dichotomy of the subsequent decades between
educated Russians backing the government and the rest of their countrymen, there
will be very few in the former camp. The Church offered fundamental support to
the sovereign, as it had done for centuries, and there were even a few clerics such as
Archbishop Feofan Prokopovich and Bishop Gabriel Buzhinsky, the head chaplain
of the newly created Russian navy, who became the sovereign's ideologues and pro-
pagandists and largely shaped his original image. Ukrainians then and later were
especially prominent in that "progressive" wing of the Church. But the Church as a
whole, while loyal, was, of course, conservative and opposed to westernization and
reform. That, indeed, was the main reason for the Spiritual Reglament and the
reshaping of the Church by the dauntless monarch. The army fought on command,
as it had since time immemorial, and even especially well after the Petrine military
reforms. The general masses, too, responded to most demands. But their fealty, such
as it was, went, surely, more to the tsar of Muscovy and All Russia than to the westernizing innovator.

And it should not be surprising in the Muscovite context that the most far-
reaching attack on the reformer came to be the denial of his legitimacy as tsar.
Already by the year 1700 and the turn of the century, a legend emerged, with the
government trying to extirpate it, that Peter I on the Russian throne was not the true
Peter I but a substitute and, apparently, an un-Russian and evil one. K. V. Chistov[19]
and others, attempting to trace the circumstantial origins of this view, cited the sovereign's early avoidance of state affairs and frequent absences (the tsars were supposed to be in the Moscow Kremlin, except for some pilgrimages); the prominence
of foreigners around him; his blasphemous, quasi-ritualistic debauchery; his constant preference for subordinate roles while leaving center stage to his Swiss favorite
Francis Lefort or other associates, a practice baffling to the popular imagination; the
unprecedented and mystifying voyage abroad, when the monarch was not listed in
his own name in the traveling party and thus, in effect, vanished from the earth,
abandoning his tsardom; his precipitous return and most violent punishment of the
streltsy; and so forth. At least three fundamental versions of the legend, with numerous variants, have been recorded: first, the substitution took place in Peter I's
infancy, in fact, in the usual variant, immediately after birth; second, the substitution occurred "beyond the seas"; and third, the Antichrist substituted himself for
Peter I. In the first version, the ruling monarch was most commonly presented as
Lefort's son, with the elucidation that Tsar Alexis had demanded a son, and when his
wife gave birth to a daughter instead, she exchanged her secretly for a boy born in
the Lefort household—incidentally, an impressive way to explain Lefort's special
position in the new reign. In the second, the emphasis was on the true Peter I's
imprisonment abroad, sometimes in a barrel thrown into the sea, and the substitu-

tion of a foreign prince to rule Russia. In the third version, the Antichrist had different ways of appearing: in some variants, from the beginning, but in others, when the true Peter I, who had been on the throne during the earlier part of the reign, was doing penance for his persecution of Old Believers and other sins while buried in a grave. Whatever the version, Holy Russia was ruled, in effect, either by a heretical foreigner or by the Antichrist himself. Utilizing published sources alone, Chistov found for the years 1700–1722 over thirty separate recordings of the substitution legend, coming from different groups of the Russian population and extending from the far north to the Don and Ukraine and from Pskov to Siberia.[20]

The identification of Peter the Great as the Antichrist had a touch of genius. It fitted the religious and apocalyptic vision of the Old Believers as effectively as the definition of the reformer as the model enlightened despot suited the Russian proponents of the secular Enlightenment, and it was equally ably developed—a remarkable parallel and a wonderful indication of the importance of the point of view. Neither concept, to be sure, was invented for the first Russian emperor, but *mutatis mutandis* he became a brilliant incarnation of each one. The doctrine of Antichrist goes back to the early years of Christianity; it acquired a new significance in Russia with the Old Believer split from the established Church. For the persecuted Old Believers, Patriarch Nikon and Tsar Alexis had already served as Antichrists before Peter I ascended to the throne.[21] In the absence of the reformer, other crowned Antichrists could also probably have been found, but almost certainly not as compelling as the first emperor.

The sovereign's unusual, mighty, and striking appearance, his face twitching, itself suggested evil power. The foreign dress, the smoking, the novel drinking and eating habits, the pointed, clipped whiskers, "like those of a cat," the new uniforms introduced everywhere had something satanic in them. Foreigners were ever present. The cutting of beards—so recently condemned not only by the Old Believers but also by Patriarch Hadrian—was a clear violation of the image of God in man, a catastrophic sacrilege. The magic ruler stole time from God as he changed the calendar and began the year in January; similarly, he introduced a new script instead of the old one in which all Church books had been written. He brought heretical Western learning into Russia. He sent his lawful wife to a convent and lived with a *chukhonka*, a local Finnic inhabitant, without the benefit of church sacrament. He killed his son. Above all, he extended his control to everything, branding his soldiers—an authentic mark of the Beast—and "obtained the number," that is, census data for taxation, from the entire population of Holy Russia. He abolished the patriarchate and took direct command of the Church itself. His pagan classical festivals (with "crowns of thorns," i. e. laurel wreaths, which also appeared as part of the ruler's image on his coins) presented him as a divinity and parodied the true religion, whereas his drunken and debauched rites spoke directly of the devil. The convincing picture was filled in with very rich further factual detail, elucidated, where necessary, with countless calculations of the number of the Antichrist, 666—mainly by adding the numerical values of letters of names and titles connected with the ruler—and with relevant sacred texts. The Old Believers had no difficulty explaining the first emperor's victories on the battlefield and other successes, for the Antichrist, supported by magic and the forces of hell, was indeed bound to prevail until the final climax. And the Antichrist in the main Christian tradition, it must be emphasized, was not an abstract concept or a void or on the other hand simply a savage destructive creature but a very close imitation and caricature of Christ the ruler of the world. His realm was a satanic perversion of the divine order of things. It is this perversion that the Old Believers saw as they looked around and compared Petrine Russia to their idealized image of Muscovy before the time of Peter I or, more precisely, before the time of Nikon—the reformer's blasphemous drunken rites to holy liturgy. The fundamental denunciation of Peter the Great by Old Believers continued through the eighteenth, nineteenth, and even twentieth centuries.[22]

And it should be added that the *Preobrazhenskii prikaz*, the sovereign's police, was preoccupied not only with the Antichrist charge or exclusively with the Old Believers. Obviously, criticism of the reformer and opposition to him had a broader base.[23] Chistov made the interesting point that Peter the Great was never pictured as a peasant tsar, one of those recurrent would-be saviors who were to abolish serfdom and establish justice and well-being in the land. No pretender ever claimed his name; no popular movement or rebellion used it as its banner. By contrast—and indeed in direct opposition to the image of the first emperor—there emerged saviors and pretenders bearing the name of Aleksei Petrovich, that is, Tsarevich Alexis. (Alexis, who totally failed to satisfy his father and even on one occasion escaped abroad, died in unclear circumstances in the summer of 1718 in the fortress of Peter and Paul in the Russian capital following investigation and torture related to the opposition and possibly conspiracy against Peter the Great). The first false Aleksei Petrovich appeared in 1724, still during the reformer's lifetime. There were at least six altogether, active at the time of the first emperor's death and especially in the period from 1731 to 1738.[24]

Still, the popular reaction to Peter the Great was not only or simply negative. Even the remarkable presentation of him as Antichrist was often peculiarly and strikingly ambivalent: doubles appeared and reappeared, the errant tsar kept praying in his grave that his sins be forgiven, or the true Peter was hiding among the Old Believers, waiting for the right moment to reclaim his throne from the usurper. The ambivalence reflected the transitional nature of the age, the change from the old Russia to the new. For instance, some Old Believers professed full allegiance to Peter as tsar but not as emperor (a title specifically connected to Antichrist from the times of Nero and Caligula). Or, to cite a touching prayer by a certain simple woman, Alena Efimova, who begged God, all heavenly powers, and even the entire universe that the persecution of the Old Believers cease and all Russian Christians reunite:

> Hear me, holy catholic church with the entire altar of the cherubim and with the gospel and every holy word in that gospel—all remember our tsar Petr Alekseevich. Hear me, holy, catholic and apostolic church, with all the local icons and honored small images, with all the apostolic books and censers, and with local candles, and the holy shrouds, with stone walls and with iron boards, with different kinds of fruitbearing trees. . . . Oh, I beg you also, beautiful sun, pray to the Heavenly Tsar for Tsar Petr Alekseevich! Oh, young crescent moon with the stars! Oh, the sky with the clouds! Oh, mighty clouds with storms and whirlwinds! Oh, birds of the sky and of the earth! Oh, the blue sea, with rivers and minor springs and small lakes! Start praying to the Heavenly Tsar for Tsar Petr Alekseevich, and the fish of the sea, and the cattle of the field, and the animals of the forest, and the fields, and all that comes out of the earth, start praying to the Heavenly Tsar for Tsar Petr Alekseevich![25]

Interestingly, the author of this prayer was married to an apparently rather extreme Old Believer, who rejected icons, whereas she herself belonged in a sense to both worlds, crossing herself with two rather than three fingers but attending Orthodox church services and trying to promote the praying for Tsar Petr Alekseevich through the Orthodox Church.

Moreover—and now I am turning to the opposite side of the folk perception of Peter the Great—many of the popular sources on the first emperor, far from condemning him or even trying to redeem him and praying for him, take a distinctly approbative view of the ruler and his work. True, no popular positive image emerged to challenge in comprehensiveness and power the figure of the Antichrist. Affirmative depictions of the remarkable tsar were usually limited to some aspect of his activity or even to an incident or a series of incidents. They are no less authentic for all that and should be given their full weight.

One area where Peter the Great stood out as a hero from the beginning and forever after was war:

> The action was at Poltava,
> A glorious action, friends.
> We were then fighting the Swede
> Under Peter's banners.

Not just soldiers' songs but all kinds of popular tales and legends reflected Petrine military events basically in the positive sense.[26] In addition to the usual, and certainly eventual, victory, accounts often stressed the sovereign's personal participation and his closeness to common soldiers. In the "glorious action" of Poltava, "our great emperor" flew "like a hawk in front of the regiments, himself used a soldier's rifle, and himself loaded a cannon."

A related and overlapping, but also distinct, focus of popular approval and appreciation of the first emperor centered on his general closeness to the people, for the sovereign joined ordinary Russians not only on the battlefield. A. F. Nekrylova, a specialist on the popular literature of the Russian north, stressed the persistence and the precision of the Petrine tradition in some of that huge territory, for instance, in connection with a road built at top speed through the wilderness to assail enemy troops from the rear.[27] Popular memory retained the inspiring hard labor of the sovereign himself, his encouragement of other workers, and his punishment of slackers, and also how he met peasants, treated them to a kind of liqueur, and baptized their children; how he gave a caftan as a gift to the owner of the house where he stayed, and so forth. More stylized legends told of a giant stepping out of the forest to aid a peasant or a fisherman, who realized only later that his helper had been the tsar of All the Russias. The ability to work, to help, and to overcome difficulties recurs in the stories. And, at least sometimes, that image must have left a lasting impression. A scholar of Russian folklore informed me of having heard in person an old peasant woman telling a *kolkhoz* chairman that Peter the Great would have straightened him out, had he only been still alive.

However, even popular support, as opposed to popular condemnation, did not imply an understanding of the reformer's vision or sympathy with it. Admiration of courage in battle or of hard work had little to do with reason or Enlightenment. A study of the popular reaction to the first emperor serves to emphasize the vastness of the divide between Peter the Great and his associates on the one hand and his people on the other. The gulf between the two sides was to widen even farther in the decades following his death, when serfdom reached its greatest extent in Russia, while the educated and governing upper layer of society grew in numbers and in distinctiveness from the common people.

The Eighteenth Century in Russia after the Death of Peter the Great

I shall never fail in my respect to those sacred words:
Peter *gave bodies to the Russians,* Catherine *their souls.*
—M. M. Kheraskov, *Numa ili Protsvetaiushchii Rim*

Russian history from the death of Peter the Great to the accession of Catherine the Great has been comparatively neglected.[1] Moreover, the treatments available are often superficial in nature and derisive in tone. Sandwiched between two celebrated reigns, this period—"when lovers ruled Russia," to quote one writer—offers little to impress, dazzle, or inspire. Rather, it appears to be taken up with a continuous struggle of unfit candidates for the crown; the constant rise and fall of their equally deplorable favorites; court intrigues and palace coups of every sort; Biren's police terror, Empress Elizabeth's engrossment in French fashions, and Emperor Peter III's imbecility. The considerable number of those aspiring to the throne, members of the reformer's family or of the family of his half-brother and co-tsar, Ivan V, together with their progeny, as well as the utilitarian first emperor's edict that the ruling monarch was to appoint his successor, proved to be a disaster. In the course of thirty-seven years, Russia had, sardonic commentators remarked, six autocrats: three women, a boy of twelve, an infant, and a mental weakling. (In fact, during the entire eighteenth century, including the reigns of Peter the Great and Catherine the Great, women ruled Russia two-thirds of the time, demonstrating, like men, everything from the incompetence of Empress Anne to the brilliance of Catherine the Great; it was Paul I at the end of the century who restricted the succession to the direct male line.)

But the tragicomedy at the top should not be allowed to obscure important developments that affected the country at large. Westernization continued to spread to more people and broader areas of Russian life. Foreign policy followed the Petrine pattern, bringing Russia into an ever-closer relationship with other European powers. And the gentry, freed from the titanic reformer's control, made a successful bid to escape service and increase their advantages.

The eighteenth century constitutes a distinct period in the history of Russian culture. On one hand it marked a decisive break with the Muscovite past—although that break had been foreshadowed and assisted by earlier influences and trends. Peter the

Great's violent activity was perhaps most revolutionary in the domain of culture. All of a sudden—skipping entire epochs of scholasticism, Renaissance, and Reformation—Russia moved from a parochial, ecclesiastical, quasi-medieval civilization to the Age of Reason. On the other hand, Russian culture of the eighteenth century also differed significantly from the culture of the following periods. From the beginning of Peter the Great's reforms to the death of Catherine the Great, the Russians applied themselves to the huge and fundamental task of learning from the West. By 1800 they had acquired and developed a comprehensive and well-integrated modern culture of their own, which later attracted attention and adaptation abroad. The eighteenth century in Russia was an age of apprenticeship and imitation par excellence. It has been said that Peter the Great, during the first decades of the century, borrowed Western technology, that Empress Elizabeth, in the middle of the period, shifted the main interest to Western fashions and manners, and that Catherine the Great, in the course of the last third of the century, brought Western ideas into Russia. Although it is much too simple, this scheme contains some truth. It gives an indication of the stages in the Russian absorption of Western culture, and it suggests that by 1800 the process had spread to everything from artillery to philosophy.

In addition to the all-pervasive government sponsorship, Enlightenment came to Russia through the educated gentry. After the pioneer years of Peter the Great, with his motley group of foreign and Russian assistants, the gentry increasingly asserted itself to control most phases of the development of the country. Despite some striking individual exceptions, modern Russian culture emerged as gentry culture and maintained that character well into the nineteenth century. It became the civilization of an educated, aristocratic elite, with its salons and its knowledge of French—a civilization that was more preoccupied with an elegant literary style and proper manners than with philosophy or politics. Nonetheless, this culture constituted the first phase of modern Russian intellectual and cultural history and the foundation for its subsequent development.

Not surprisingly, the death of Peter the Great was followed by a certain relaxation and reaction against his rule. Some of the schools established by the tireless reformer could find no students, while intrigue and corruption ran rampant in government and administration. Even the seat of the government returned, briefly, to Moscow. More important, without Peter the Great it quickly became impossible to exact a full measure of service from the gentry, to insist on the principle of position and reward strictly according to merit. So-called gentry emancipation developed into a major trend of the century, culminating in the exemption of the gentry from compulsory state service by Peter III in 1762 and Catherine the Great's special Charter to that estate granted in 1785. But there was no essential change in terms of intellectual orientation and ideology. Peter the Great's chief assistant, Prince Alexander Menshikov, or the princes Dolgorukiis and Golitsyns, who became very prominent in the years following the reformer's death, not to mention the insignificant rulers themselves, with their numerous favorites and hangers-on, had nothing to offer in lieu of the first emperor's direction and vision. In Russia, the only truly alternative view of the world resided among the "dark masses," Old Believers, and Orthodox, and among the unreconstructed monks, priests, and nuns, who had no voice in the councils or destiny of their country.

The authorities, on the other hand, proceeded to invoke loudly, in and out of turn, the name and the example of Peter the Great. Empress Elizabeth, Peter's daughter, who reigned from 1741 to 1761 (or 1762, depending on the calendar used), emphasized especially her absolute devotion to her father, his policies, and his legacy. Indeed, the image of the reformer became, with slight modifications and numerous additions, the banner of modern Russia throughout the eighteenth century and beyond. To select a single example from the flood of praise and fervor, the ode "To Peter the Great," written in 1776 by the best poet of the century, Gabriel Derzhavin:

> Russia, clothed in glory,
> Wherever it turns its gaze,
> Everywhere, with exultant joy,
> Sees Peter's work.
> > Carry the voices to heaven, o wind:
> > You are immortal, great Peter!
>
> He, conquering our ancient darkness,
> Established the sciences in the midnight land;
> Lighting a torch in blackness,
> He also poured into us good morals and manners.
> > Carry the voices to heaven, o wind:
> > You are immortal, great Peter!
>
> Like God, with great foresight,
> He encompassed everything in his gaze,
> Like a slave, with unheard of devotion,
> He executed everything himself.
> > Carry the voices to heaven, o wind:
> > You are immortal, great Peter!

Sixteen more stanzas followed, glorifying Peter the Great for learning abroad to teach in turn his subjects; for engaging personally in every kind of labor ("To this date there reverberate in the world the sounds of his axe striking"); for elevating his childish games to military glory; for serving as a simple warrior and teaching the commanders; for valor against enemies and kindness to prisoners; for giving an accounting of his activities to his servants, in spite of his supreme position; for establishing all kinds of honors and rewards not for himself, but for the merit of others; for being firm in his faith and generous in evil as in good fortune; for returning crowns to monarchs, and writing laws for his subjects; for serving as an example of what they should be doing to millions; for grinding water through mountains and planting cities on swamps; for bringing prosperity to his peoples; for linking the West and the East; for loving truth and preserving justice; for stunning the universe by the greatness of his miracles, to the point of observers asking "Could it be that God came down to us from heaven?"[2]

The Enlightenment image of Peter the Great dominated eighteenth-century Russian thought and literature. True, one may speak instead of a cluster of images. There was Peter the Great the Enlightener, who introduced light into darkness, transforming nonbeing into being. There was Peter the Great the Educator, perhaps the very same personage only seen at closer range, who went himself to study in the West in order to teach his subjects, who sent them there to learn, and who established schools in Russia. There was Peter the Great the Lawgiver, who issued progressive laws and regulations for the development and happiness of his country. There was always Peter the Great the Worker, who did everything himself and who labored every minute of his life, undertaking the most ordinary tasks, such as repairing fishing nets and making shoes. By contrast, Peter the Great the Titan, a godlike avatar of the first emperor, constructed canals to change the river network in Russia and erected cities upon swamps. There was also Peter the Great the dauntless Hero of Poltava, Peter the Great the Founder of the Russian Navy, and, related but by no means identical, Peter the Great the victorious Naval Commander. There were other Peters the Great besides. Yet, united by the sensibility of the Age of Reason and the concept of that age of the ideal ruler, all Peters the Great complemented one another or at least coexisted without getting unduly in one another's way.

About the only thing his eulogists could not claim for Peter the Great was that he was God. They came close. The question raised at the end of Derzhavin's ode and associated ideas recur in the literature of the Russian Enlightenment. For example, some twenty years earlier, the first great Russian scientist, a remarkable poet and writer and a most remarkable polymath, Michael Lomonosov, made virtually the same points as Derzhavin, and more, in his celebrated "Laudatory Oration to Lord Emperor Peter the Great of the Blessed Memory, Pronounced on the Twenty-Sixth Day of April of the Year 1755," which was presented at a public session of the Imperial Academy of Sciences. Longer, more detailed, more precise, and more powerful, if less melodious, than Derzhavin's eulogy, Lomonosov's oration dwelt at length on the enormous and enormously varied achievements of the emperor, who in a single reign and in his own person accomplished "what the Neposes, the Scipios, the Marcelluses, the Reguluses, the Metelluses, the Catos, the Sullas accomplished in two hundred and fifty years," and concluded:

> To whom, then, shall I liken our Hero? I have often thought, what is like He, Who by an almighty wave of His hand rules the sky, the earth, and the sea: His spirit blows—and waters flow; He touches mountains—and they rise. But there is a limit assigned to human thoughts! They can not comprehend

Divinity! Usually He is pictured in human form. Well then, if a man similar to God, according to our understanding, must indeed be found, I know of no other than Peter the Great.

Another one of the most prominent mid-eighteenth-century Russian literati, who, as usual, wrote many times of Peter the Great, Alexander Sumarokov, drew special attention with his combination-prose-and-verse piece entitled "Russian Bethleem." It contained the following lines:

> Russian Bethleem: the Kolomenskoe village,
> Which brought Peter into the World!
> You are the source and the beginning of our happiness;
> In you Russian glory began to shine.[4]

It was also Sumarokov who stated most explicitly the dilemma of Petrine eulogists:

> Do not resound, icy waves,
> Do not storm, northern wind,
> Harken, people of all the lands,
> *Peter* is bringing verses to my mind.
> Planets, what were your positions,
> When you greeted Peter into the World!
> From the beginning of the first age
> Nature never saw
> Such a Man.
>
> It is not appropriate in Christianity
> To revere creatures as Gods;
> But if still during paganism
> Such a Tsar had occurred,
> As soon as his fame had spread
> The entire universe would have been shaken
> By his most marvelous deeds:
> Fame, like an unsilenceable trumpet,
> Would have proclaimed God, not Tsar,
> That Warrior, who ascended the throne.[5]

The problem was, of course, that Russia was a Christian, not a pagan, state.

There is an uncanny resemblance between the flowery and sophisticated image of the enlightened despot of the Russian educated public and the inarticulate belief in the Muscovite tsar of the Russian masses. Both the despot and the tsar were just, benevolent, effective, and virtually all-powerful. Indeed, in both cases their authority was limited only by God, and even that limitation was at times difficult to maintain. The two views supported autocratic monarchy in Russia and disappeared from central prominence only as late as 1917.

Once formulated early in the eighteenth century, the Enlightenment image and cult of Peter the Great displayed incalculably more bombastic rhetoric and repetitiveness than originality. Yet there was one important addition and amendment made in the 1760s, associated, appropriately, with Catherine the Great. The extremely ambitious and vain empress could not accept the postulate that Peter the Great and Peter the Great alone created modern Russia. Whereas other Russian rulers in the course of the century were generally glad to be associated with the reformer in any way possible, Catherine set out to compete with him for the first place in Russian history.

Many factors must be kept carefully in mind in trying to reconstruct Catherine II's image of Peter the Great and her treatment of her illustrious predecessor throughout her long reign. A princess from Anhalt-Zerbst, the most famous Russian empress had originally, in contrast to all other modern Russian rulers, no connection with the reigning Romanov dynasty and, indeed, no connection at all with Russia. Her pietistic references to "Our Most Beloved Grandfather" meant, of course, the grandfather of her husband, Peter III, who was killed in the coup that brought her to power. Free of direct links to Peter the Great and his family, Catherine II was also free, in a much broader sense, of any relationship to Muscovy. She lacked totally the explosive hatred of the old order, which had been so prominent in the life and work of the reformer himself and of his associates and which was still present in such figures as Lomonosov. Yet this absence of a certain kind of personal involvement did not result in a weakening of interest. To the contrary, the first crowned intellectual in modern Russia, Catherine the Great spent a lifetime trying to understand Peter the Great in terms of the Enlightenment to which she entirely belonged, to interpret him, to live with him. Her efforts would deserve notice even if she were not an autocrat imposing her will on a huge empire for a third of a century. Other factors, especially those of character and political style, entered the picture. One was the empress's enormous vanity, which, it would seem, made Peter the Great and his work an immediate and persistent challenge, both in general and in detail, to her sense of her own worth and accomplishment. Other relevant traits included Catherine II's duplicity, hypocrisy, and rare gift for propaganda. On the topic of Peter the Great, as on other significant topics, it is at times difficult to establish what it was that Catherine the Great believed and whether she believed anything at all.

Still, a study and interpretation of the evidence can suggest a complex pattern. First and most important, the empress started from an ardent cult of Peter the Great, and she never explicitly repudiated it. Whatever her shifts of emphasis, reservations, and criticisms, whatever her private comments, or at times her revealing silences, the overwhelming established public image of the reformer continued to dominate the Russian intellectual scene. In fact, Catherine II herself contributed and had others contribute to that image. Nor was the connection between her and the first emperor ignored. Falconet's celebrated statue known as "The Bronze Horseman," with its inscription "To Peter I, Catherine II," unveiled in 1782, is only one illustration of the official ideology. And, according to the Prince de Ligne, the empress allowed no criticism of Peter the Great in her presence.[6] In the true Enlightenment tradition, Catherine II emphasized the role of the reformer as the benefactor of his subjects, the monarch who worked for their well-being, for the common good. But she was also very much impressed by his military successes on land and on water. Not inappropriately, military standards captured from the Turks were brought to Peter the Great's tomb. It was especially during the First Turkish War (1768–1774) that the empress kept referring to her martial predecessor. Beyond that, however, she seemed to be interested in everything Peter the Great had done at all times.

Catherine's close attention to the first emperor also led to criticisms, which, apparently, deepened with the passage of years. Although the empress might have discovered the critical approach early in her favorite Montesquieu, who considered Peter the Great a tyrant, most of her observations were, no doubt, her own, based on her constant rethinking of the role of the reformer, especially after she came to occupy his throne and deal directly with many of his measures and problems. Concerned especially with the ideal of the just legislator, central to the concept of enlightened despotism and even to the political thought of the Age of Reason in general, Catherine II found Peter the Great sadly wanting. His laws, in particular his penal code, were essentially the old, backward, and cruel Ulozhenie of 1649, and he failed to make them more modern and humane. In fact, he tended to emphasize punishment and to rule by fear rather than through love and approbation of his subjects. Although the enlightened German empress approved the direction of the Russian ruler's reforms, his desire that the old world be replaced by the new, he himself, in her perspective, belonged too much to that old world.

Peter the Great was a formidable rival—Catherine the Great's only possible competitor, she came to be convinced, for the honor of being the greatest ruler of Russia. The empress's preoccupation with that rivalry is beyond doubt, although the pertinent evidence has to be analyzed with care. Little can be concluded from the mere fact that Catherine II always promoted herself, that she tended to occupy center stage, to push Peter the Great into the background, to receive the highest praise. That was simply the prerogative, indeed the proper due, of a reigning monarch. Probably more relevant is the argument from silence, from omission. Karen Rasmussen studied carefully the references to Peter the Great in the Catherinian legislation and in other materials connected with the reign to discover periods when Peter the Great did not appear, even when such appearance would have been most appropriate. Deliberate suppression seems likely. Paradoxically—in commonsense logic, not in terms of depth psychology—another relevant line of reasoning points to the frequent and varied references to Peter I by Catherine II. These references were often not simple pairings of the reigning sovereign and a particularly illustrious predecessor in terms of affirmation, continuity, and achievement—a common practice in monarchies, beautifully exemplified by Empress Elizabeth's treatment of her father—but, rather, determined efforts to indicate that Catherine the Great did better than Peter the Great, whether in legislation, culture, or land and sea campaigns and battles. The very last available comment of the empress about the emperor, written in 1796, consisted of the boast that her conquest of Baku had eclipsed his.[7]

Catherine the Great's deliberate pairing of her own image with that of Peter the Great aimed to capitalize on his immense prestige and to underline his importance, for indeed there would have been no Catherinian Russia without him. At the same time it was designed to assign a still higher place in Russian history to the desperately ambitious empress. Its daring classical formulation can be found, for instance, in Ivan Betsky's address to the throne, quite early in the reign: "Peter the Great created men in Russia; Your Highness has given them souls."[8] The formula accounted for Peter the Great and, in fact, assigned an awesome importance to him—for who was he who could create men?—yet it placed Catherine the Great still higher. It even provided an explanation and a justification for the crudity and the harshness of the reformer's measures, natural and unavoidable at the time, although personally distasteful to the philosophic empress and no longer required in her truly enlightened age. With the formula, modern Russian history presented two stages, the Petrine and the Catherinian, the second building on the first but also rising above it. Voltaire, probably the most outstanding Western admirer of Peter the Great, caught on skillfully to what was wanted and wrote to the Russian empress of Peter the Great and Catherine the Greater.[9]

It would be an exaggeration, however, to claim that Catherine II tamed, so to speak, the image of Peter I and made it simply serve her own purposes. Although the remarkable propaganda of the willful empress even achieved some long-range successes, she was the weaker figure in the new coupling. After her death, the image of the first emperor uncoupled itself and continued its progress through Russian history without its would-be companion. Personally, too, the empress could not settle her accounts with her celebrated predecessor. Late in her reign, she underwent another change toward him, this time in the direction of a greater admiration and acceptance. The main reason was her own failure as legislator, certainly earlier with the Legislative Commission, but in effect throughout her rule. It was in relation to the concept of the enlightened legislator that Catherine II had constructed her main criticisms of the reformer and postulated her superiority over him: by the end of her reign she could see that that superiority was largely imaginary. It is quite possible that it was at the time of her death that Catherine the Great had the deepest appreciation of Peter the Great as well as of the obstacles in his path.

It should be emphasized that, in her view of Peter the Great as in everything else, Catherine the Great belonged entirely to the intellectual world of the West. The question raised in connection with Peter the Great as to how a traditional Muscovite milieu could produce such an iconoclast does not occur in the case of his famous successor. Brought up in the modest but cultured surroundings of a princely house in a petty German principality, the future Russian autocrat learned French as a child and proceeded to read avidly the French belles-lettres and later the *philosophes*. The German and the French enlightenments always remained her intellectual ambience. When she arrived in Russia at the age of fifteen, Catherine did her best to become acquainted with the country and to learn and use its language, but she could never write Russian idiomatically. If Catherine the Great did not hesitate to manipulate skillfully her avowed "prayer book," Montesquieu's *Spirit of the Laws*, the fact remains that in a very real sense she had no other.

The Russian empress, of course, subscribed fully to the concept of enlightened despotism, and at times even went beyond the bounds of the concept. Thus in her correspondence with Grimm she liked to refer to herself not only as a great libertarian but even as a republican, and she included "republican sentiments" in the epitaph she composed for herself. On the whole, however, Catherine the Great kept emphasizing the necessity and the virtues of absolute monarchical rule, at least in Russia. As she put the matter in strikingly Age-of-Reason terms in her celebrated *Instruction to the Legislative Commission*, the *Nakaz*:

> 9. The Sovereign is absolute; for there is no other Authority but that which centers in his single Person, that can act with a Vigour proportionate to the Extent of such a vast Dominion.
>
> 10. The Extent of the Dominion requires an absolute Power to be vested in that Person who rules over it. It is expedient so to be, that the quick Dispatch of Affairs, sent from distant Parts, might make ample Amends for the Delay occasioned by the great Distance of the Places.
>
> 11. Every other Form of Government whatsoever would not only have been prejudicial to Russia, but would even have proved its entire Ruin.
>
> 12. Another Reason is; That it is better to be subject to the Laws under one Master, than to be subservient to many.
>
> 13. What is the true End of Monarchy? Not to deprive People of their natural Liberty; but to correct their Actions, in order to attain the *supreme Good*.
>
> 14. The Form of Government therefore, which best attains this End, and at the same Time sets less Bounds than others to natural Liberty, is that which coincides with the Views and Purposes of rational Creatures, and answers the End, upon which we ought to fix a steadfast Eye in the Regulation of civil Polity. [10]

The supreme good, or the common good, embraced "the Glory of the Citizens, of the State, and of the Sovereign,"[11] but it was also frequently defined in a more humane manner. In the words chosen by the empress for her tombstone: "When she had ascended the throne of Russia, she wished to do good, and tried to bring happiness, freedom and prosperity to her subjects."[12] Such goals, including the incongruous one of liberty, kept occurring in the thought, and correspondence, of the empress throughout her life. The autocrat presented herself to Voltaire and others as the protector of freedom in Russia and deplored its decline in Sweden and France. Russian freedom would rest on just and rational laws, which Catherine the Great promised to introduce in her empire. "The Equality of the Citizens consists in this; that they should all be subject to the same laws."[13] Moreover: "Nothing ought to be forbidden by the Laws, but what may be prejudicial, either to every Individual in particular, or to the whole Community in general."[14] The autocrat concluded forcefully:

> 520. All this will never please those Flatterers, who are daily instilling this pernicious Maxim into all the Sovereigns on Earth, *That their People are created for them only.* But *We* think and esteem it *Our* Glory to declare, "That *We* are created for *Our* People"; and, for this Reason, *We* are obliged to Speak of Things just as they ought to be. For God forbid! that, after this Legislation is finished, any Nation on Earth should be more just; and, consequently should flourish more than Russia; otherwise the Intention of *Our* Laws would be totally frustrated; an Unhappiness *which I do not wish to survive.* [15]

Yet, while the empress was preoccupied with the importance of rational law and correct legal procedure, and while she followed Beccaria to promise the most enlightened criminal code for Russia, she remained equally concerned with the economic well-being of her subjects, the substantive, so to speak, as much as the formal elements of happiness. The *Nakaz* itself dwelt on such topics as the importance of agriculture for the prosperity of the country. It contained even the following remarkable article: "346. An Alms bestowed on a Beggar in the Street, can never acquit a State of Obligation it lies under, of affording all its Citizens a certain Support during Life; such as wholesome Food, proper Cloathing, and a Way of Life not prejudicial to Health in general."[16] In her correspondence with the *philosophes,* Catherine II liked to stress that she was waging her wars and embellishing her court without raising new taxes, and that in general her foremost thought was not to burden her subjects. If perfect laws belonged to the future, economic prosperity had, apparently, already been achieved, or so the empress wrote, shamelessly, to Voltaire: "Besides, our taxes are so modest that there is not a peasant in Russia who does not eat a chicken when he wants to; recently there have appeared provinces where turkeys are preferred to chickens."[17]

The vision of the Russian peasant choosing at will between chicken and turkey illustrates the chasm between fancy and fact in eighteenth-century Russia and might put into question the very notion of Enlightenment as applied to the government and society of that country. Still, fairness requires a closer look. Policies of Church control and secularization, notably both those of Peter the Great and of Catherine the Great, certainly corresponded to the injunctions of the Age of Reason. Administrative reforms, inaugurated wholesale by the first emperor, continued throughout the century and included the introduction of a new system of local government by Catherine the Great in 1775. Although Catherine's Legislative Commission failed to produce a code of laws, Russian legislation experienced some influence of the climate of the Enlightenment, as in the case of Empress Elizabeth's celebrated abolition of capital punishment. The government repealed internal tariffs in 1753, built new canals, following the example of Peter the Great, and promoted commerce in various other ways. In fact, the Russian government consistently played a greater role in the economic development of the country than did governments elsewhere. Once again, the concept of enlightened despotism seemed to fit especially well the realm of the tsars. Even the cruel social policy of the Russian rulers that had led, or at least contributed, by the end of the century both to the so-called emancipation of the gentry and to the climax, in nature and extent, of the institution of serfdom, possessed—or, rather, so it has been claimed—its positive side. Peter III's abolition of compulsory gentry service to the state in 1762 and Catherine the Great's Charter to the Gentry in 1785 created, it has been argued, the first essentially independent class in modern Russian history, that necessary initial step on the road of liberalism and progress.

Government efforts in the field of education and culture were especially striking, as well as consonant with the ideas of the Age of Reason. The Academy of Sciences, planned by Peter the Great, opened its doors immediately following his death. In 1755, Russia acquired its first university, the University of Moscow. Although the great scientist and polymath Michael Lomonosov (1711–1765) remained essentially an isolated individual, the eighteenth century was also noteworthy in Russian history for large-scale, organized scientific effort. That effort took the form of expeditions to discover, explore, or study distant areas of the empire and sometimes neighboring seas and territories. Geography, geology, mineralogy, botany, zoology, ethnography, and philology, as well as some other disciplines, all profited from these well-thought-out and at times extremely daring undertakings. Begun by Peter the Great, the expeditions promptly led to important results. Alaska was discovered in 1742. The so-called First Academic Expedition, which lasted from 1733 to 1742 and included 570 participants, successfully undertook the mammoth task of mapping and exploring the northern shore of Siberia. Numerous expeditions, often of great scholarly value, followed later in the century.

Although ordinary Russian schools remained few and far between throughout the period, and indeed long after, Catherine the Great pioneered the education of women, establishing notably the famous Smolny Institute, and she tried to apply the most advanced pedagogical theories of the Enlightenment to the upbringing of her subjects. Russian rulers proved to be remarkable builders. Founded in 1703 by Peter the Great as the capital of the new age of Russian history, St. Petersburg was, by the end of Catherine the Great's reign, well on the way to becoming one of the most magnificent cities in the world. Its glittering court could rival any other. Architects and artists of all sorts, Russian and foreign, profited from imperial patronage. The theater, the opera, and the ballet were among its greatest beneficiaries. Writers of different kinds also had their share. From Peter the Great's reform of the alphabet and his creation of the first Russian newspaper to Catherine the Great's sponsorship of periodicals, Russian monarchs worked hard to bring literacy and literature to their subjects.

The imperial Russian government was brilliantly successful in the eighteenth century in another field or fields: international relations, war, and expansion. From the defeat at Narva at the hands of Charles XII of Sweden in 1700 until the time of Napoleon, Russian troops suffered no major military disaster, and they scored many remarkable victories. Military achievements, together with effective diplomacy, led to the capture of all of southern Ukraine and Russia from Turkey, and to the astounding, if tragic and in a sense self-defeating, partitioning of Poland. While enormous lands fell under the scepter of the Romanovs, Russian soldiers occupied Berlin in the course of the Seven Years' War, and Russian seamen sailed the Mediterranean in their campaigns against the sultan. The once isolated Muscovy had clearly become a major European power, deeply involved in the affairs of the continent. Enlightened or not, the Russian monarchy could certainly claim respect according to the older and more generally accepted criteria of power and success.

And Russia obtained respect. This new appreciation of Russia arose not only among rulers, statesmen, and generals, but also and especially among the *philosophes.* Voltaire, following his admiration for Peter the Great, fell under the spell of "Catherine the Greater." The correspondence between him and the Russian empress is a remarkable literary, psychological, and intellectual document, wherein the most famous writer of the century heaps endless and boundless praise upon the autocrat and her works. Catherine the Great was both "la premiere personne de l'univers, sans contredit"[18] and Voltaire's own "passion dominante."[19] She was a model to the world and a benefactress of mankind. Her legislative work would surpass that of Justinian. It was her destiny to recover Constantinople and restore Greece. Voltaire, on his part, intended "venir achever ma vie,"[20] and actually to die on a pilgrimage[21] to "the North star," "Notre-Dame de Petersbourg."[22] "Te Deum . . . Te Deam! "[23] Diderot's description of the empress, whom he did get to visit in 1773, had a more strictly classical ring: Catherine the Great possessed "the spirit of Brutus in the body of Cleopatra, the courage of the one, and the charms of the other."[23] D'Alembert joined his colleagues of the *Encyclopédie* in unmeasured praise of the autocrat. As Voltaire explained the matter: "We are three, Diderot, d'Alembert and I who are setting up altars to you."[25] Three such priests should have proved sufficient for any cult, but in fact many others joined them in the course of the Enlightenment.

There was an opposition, to be sure. The celebrated names of Catherine II's fawning admirers were contradicted by other illustrious names—Rousseau, Mably, Raynal, or Condillac. To be sure, too, the admirers themselves were not always faithful. Diderot's journey to Russia proved to be a disappointment, and he became much more critical of that state and its ruler. Even Voltaire could express himself in a different manner when he wrote about Catherine the Great rather than to her. There were, of course, extraneous reasons for paying homage to the Russian monarch. In Voltaire's case, they ran the gamut from a burning desire to expel barbarous Turkey from Europe and restore glorious Greece to a need to sell watches produced by his Swiss tenants. And much must be allowed for the style, manner, and amenities of the period. Thus the image of old Voltaire, on his knees, kissing the hands, or feet, of the imperial goddess—while persistently criticizing the Russian habit of kissing the hands of priests—can be largely written off as an epistolary flourish.

And yet, in the last analysis, the admiration of many *philosophes* for Russia was both serious and revealing. As a French scholar put it:

> With Voltaire Europe saw that this immense land, peopled by ignorant and brutish muzhiks, "had given birth to Peter the Great, tsar legislator and reformer," that next it placed at its head a "new Semiramis," Catherine, whose writings and codes were admired by all; the *philosophes* wept as they read these laws, laws so beautiful that it was the duty of all the sovereigns of the world to take them as their example. Within a few decades Russia steps out of its historical and intellectual "non-being," provides for itself "rational, harmonious" laws and becomes for Western intellectuals a kind of model state, which attracts the eyes of all the theoreticians in politics and philosophy. The "Muscovy" of 1700 had transformed itself into an "enlightened" empire, into a country of "Light," into an example.[26]

Diderot and others suggested what was to be repeated so often in later times—namely, that it was the very newness of Russian participation in history and culture that augured so well for the progress and success of that country. Imprisoned by its own past, the Age of Reason looked with hope at the unencumbered giant that was validating and would continue to validate its most cherished beliefs. No wonder that there occurred what its closest student called "the Russian mirage in France in the eighteenth century."[27]

What was the attitude of the Russian educated public when Catherine the Great was bidding for the position of the foremost enlightened despot in the world and when Voltaire, Diderot, and d'Alembert were singing her praises? More broadly, what was the role of the educated public in the evolution of Russia in the eighteenth century, as well as its own perception of that evolution and that role?

The modern Russian educated public was created by the reforms of Peter the Great and his successors. Its very *raison d'être* was the turning of the country toward the West, a process completely dominated by the government. In contrast to Western states, Russia in the eighteenth century lacked an independent caste of lawyers, advanced private education, and a powerful Church balancing the state or competing for the minds of men in the modern world. More fundamentally still, the development of Muscovy, based on the service gentry and serfdom, deprived the country of a middle class of any prominence, of precisely that Third Estate that was crucial to the Western Age of Reason. Russian Enlightenment remains the despair of those who must link that phenomenon to a new stage in the development of a market economy, to a victorious rise of the bourgeoisie, or to a diffusion of literature and learning among broad layers of population. In Russia, the educated public, especially at first but to a large extent even later in the century, remained a small, thin, sectarian layer, conscious at all times of its break with the past and its separation from the masses. Russian government and society shared the herculean task of learning from the West and of implanting the new knowledge in their own country. The obstacles were enormous, and the best efforts of innovators must have often seemed no more than a ripple on the surface of deep waters. Yet educated Russians, like their rulers, found profound encouragement and support in the philosophy of the Enlightenment. After all, they were performing the fundamental work of creating a new, rational world on the debris of the old. If change proved slow, no informed person could mistake its direction. "Man's labor and reason, what is there in the world that they do not overcome!"[28]

On the whole, educated Russians accomplished much. The development of the Russian language is one critical example of their achievement. On the eve of Peter the Great's reforms, Russian linguistic usage was in a state of transition, as everyday Russian began to assert itself in literature at the expense of the archaic, bookish, Slavonicized forms. This basic process continued in the eighteenth century, but it was complicated further by a mass intrusion of foreign words and expressions that came with westernization. The language used by Peter the Great and his associates was in a chaotic state. However, in the course of the century, the basic linguistic issues were resolved, and modern literary Russian emerged. The battle of styles, although not entirely over by 1800, resulted in a definitive victory for the contemporary Russian over the Slavonicized, for the fluent over the formal, for the practical and the natural over the stilted and the artificial. As to foreign words and expressions, they were either rejected or gradually absorbed into the Russian language, leading to a great increase in its vocabulary. The Russian language of 1800 could handle many series of terms and concepts unheard of in Muscovy. That the Russian linguistic evolution of the eighteenth century was remarkably successful can best be seen from the fact that the Golden Age of Russian literature, still the standard of linguistic and literary excellence in modern Russian, followed shortly after. Indeed, Pushkin was born in the last year of the eighteenth century.

The linguistic evolution was linked to a conscious preoccupation with language, to the first Russian grammars, dictionaries, and philological and literary treatises. Lomonosov deserves special recognition for the first effective Russian grammar, published in 1755, which proved highly influential. A rich dictionary prepared by some fifty authors, including almost every writer of note, appeared in six volumes published from 1789 to 1794. Theoretical discussion and experimentation by Basil Trediakovsky, Lomonosov, and others led to the creation of the now established system of modern Russian versification. Similarly, it became the pressing task of educated eighteenth-century Russians to introduce and develop in their homeland such other major forms of Western literary expression as the drama and the novel. The emergence of an original and highly creative Russian literature took time, with the richest work produced in the last decades of the century. Still, the entire pioneering effort of eighteenth-century writers made a great contribution to the establishment and development of modern Russian literature.

Of the early innovators, Antioch Kantemir (1709–1744), a Moldavian prince educated in Russia and employed in the Russian diplomatic service, has been called the originator of modern Russian belles-lettres. He produced original works as well as translations, poetry and prose, satires, songs, lyrical pieces, fables, and essays. Michael Lomonosov (1711–1765), a central figure in the culture of the entire age, is best remembered in literature for his odes, some of which are still considered classics of their kind, in particular when they describe the vastness and glory of the universe. Alexander Sumarokov (1718–1777), a prolific and influential writer, has been honored as the father of Russian drama. In addition to creating tragedies and comedies, as well as satires and poetry, and publishing a periodical, Sumarokov was the first director of a permanent Russian theater and introduced the pseudo-classical drama of the Age of Reason to a Russian audience.

The reign of Catherine the Great witnessed both a considerable improvement in the quality of Russian literature and a remarkable increase in its quantity. The place of honor belonged to the writer of comedies Denis Fonvizin (1745–1792) and the poet Gabriel Derzhavin (1743–1816), whom we already met glorifying Peter the Great.[29] Many other talented and less talented writers made their contributions. Catherine the Great's effort to stimulate journalism in her state produced a ready response—a response, indeed, that, the Soviet commentators insisted, went beyond the intentions of the empress and made her retreat. In any case, in 1769–1774, Russia suddenly acquired a remarkable series of satirical journals. And if these particular periodicals generally did not last, journalism as a whole became firmly established in Russia. From love lyric to classical tragedy to *feuilleton*, Russians came to participate in the European literary development.

The arts joined literature and the sciences. Russians learned, sometimes with conspicuous success, portrait painting, sculpture, and modern music. In 1757 the art section of the Academy of Sciences became an independent Academy of Arts. Architecture flourished in eighteenth-century Russia, with the neoclassical style gradually replacing the earlier baroque. In the reign of Catherine the Great, its leading practitioners came to include, in addition to distinguished foreigners, such outstanding Russians as Bazil Bazhenov and Matthew Kazakov. Although the first native Russian theater became established only in the 1750s, by the end of the century, Russia possessed several public theaters, a theatrical school, and a periodical, the *Russian Theater*. Moreover, great landlords began to organize their own private theaters, some fifteen of them in Moscow alone.

Immersion in the literary, scientific, or artistic culture of the West meant, of course, participation in the intellectual world of the Age of Reason. And indeed, almost all specialists refer, at least for the reign of Catherine the Great, to a Russian Enlightenment, although there is little agreement on its exact nature and significance. To be sure, the celebrated French *philosophes* loomed largest in Russia, as elsewhere. Catherine II's special admiration for Voltaire, whom she considered to be, among his other accomplishments, the best writer in world literature, was shared by many of her educated subjects. Voltairianism has frequently been mentioned as a leading orientation of educated Russians of the Age of Reason. Although Catherine the Great's offer to transfer the publication of the *Encyclopédie* to her empire when it met with difficulties in France produced no results, the subjects of the enlightened empress read avidly the writings of Diderot, d'Alembert, and their associates, as well as those of other *philosophes*. Translations multiplied and appeared more and more promptly. "It can be said that in the second half of the century and more especially in the last third all the texts published in France are almost immediately known in Russia, where some enlightened spirits make it their duty to spread them. . . . From that time on Russia has made up her 'delay.'"[30]

Moreover, many Russians did not need translations to read the *philosophes*. From the reign of Empress Elizabeth in midcentury, French became the favorite language of the Russian aristocracy and the Russian educated public in general. While in preferring French the Russians merely followed the common European taste of the period, their devotion to it proved particularly strong and lasting, as readers of Tolstoy well know. A few figures of the Russian Enlightenment wrote everything, even poetry, only in French, while for generations some Russian aristocrats and intellectuals were more at home writing in the language of Voltaire than in their own tongue. With the rise of national consciousness, persistent attacks on Gallomania paid unwilling tribute to this Russian devotion to French language and culture. But perhaps even more revealing than Fonvizin's resounding sallies in *Brigadier* are such bits as the following passage in Prince P. A. Viazemsky's notebooks: "What is Mikhail Aleksandrovich Saltykov doing in Moscow?—Still sighing over the change in the French language."[31]

In several ways, Germany was even more important for the Russian Enlightenment than France. If Russian literary culture tended to follow the French example, science and scholarship in Russia were dominated, long and heavily, by Germans. Leibniz, from the time of his early contacts with Peter the Great, Christian Wolff, and other Germans rivaled French *philosophes* in their impact on the intellectual emergence and development of modern Russia. It is probable that in the eighteenth century, more Russians attended German universities than all other foreign universities combined. German was second only to French as the language of education and culture in Russia. Moreover, after the Treaty of Nystadt, the empire of the Romanovs acquired Baltic provinces with their German upper classes of landlords and townsmen. Other Germans lived in Russia proper, not only as colonists on the Volga but, more important, as artisans and professionals in St. Petersburg, where they had their own churches, theater, and other institutions. Dynastic and court foreign connections were also overwhelmingly German. In fact, Catherine the Great herself may be considered as a gift of German Enlightenment to Russia.

Great Britain too played a significant, if lesser, role in the Russian Age of Reason. Beginning with such important Petrine assistants as Patrick Gordon and James Bruce, and through increasing contacts in the course of the century, when Russians studied in England or Scotland and British specialists came to serve the Romanovs, Great Britain made its contribution to Russian westernization. Still, on the whole, Great Britain remained much more culturally remote from educated Russians than France or Germany; and it was primarily through the French medium that the fundamental British contributions to the Age of Reason made their impact on Russia. Italy attracted Russians of the period especially because of its art and music, although occasionally they attended such universities as that of Padua, and read, their enlightened empress at their head, such significant authors as Beccaria. Still other countries contributed in a variety of ways to the intellectual and cultural development of former Muscovy. They ranged from Sweden and Holland, so important for Peter the Great, to the North American colonies, later the United States of America, which affected Russian radical thought from Radishchev to the Decembrists and beyond. All in all, Russia gathered a rich heritage. Its varied nature and provenance should not obscure the fact that the Enlightenment was an outspokenly cosmopolitan age with an essentially common ideology.

Several themes dominated the thought and literature of the Russian Enlightenment. As in the West, criticism poured forth. The aforementioned "first modern Russian writer," Antioch Kantemir, proved to be most successful as a satirist, and his nine satires written between 1729 and 1739 were to be highly characteristic of the entire age. Beginning with the first and most important one, *To One's Reason or Against Those Who Deprecate Education*, Kantemir assailed such crucial Russian evils as the superstitiousness, ignorance, and drunkenness of the common people, the poor state of the clergy, the dishonesty of merchants, the uselessness and the vices of the gentry, and the venality of officials. Kantemir's translations included Montesquieu's *Persian Letters* and, in an effort to combat superstition and ignorance, Bernard de Fontenelle's *Plurality of Worlds*. Following Kantemir, satire remained a favorite genre among Russian writers, ranging from Fonvizin's brilliant comedies to the pedestrian efforts of Catherine the Great herself and numerous other aspiring authors. Fables, fed in large part by the same critical and satirical approach to reality, constituted another popular literary form in eighteenth-century Russia to culminate in Ivan Krylov's immortal creations in the nineteenth. The same satire, the same social criticism inspired journalism; in fact, no clear line divided journalism from literature. Both during the remarkable outburst of 1769–1774 and in general throughout the century, Russian writers and publicists inveighed against the backwardness, boorishness, and corruption of their countrymen, without neglecting such newer sins as Gallomania and a craving for luxury. The critical spirit spread everywhere. When in 1789 a periodical, *Conversing Citizen* (*Beseduiushchii Grazhdanin*), decided to translate foreign terms into Russian, it chose as the equivalent of "criticism," *kritika*, the words *zdravoe suzhdenie*, "sensible judgment."[32]

Naturally, there was criticism and criticism. One can well appreciate the attempts of especially Soviet scholars to arrange it meaningfully according to its content and significance, and even their preference for the more over the less concrete. Much Russian eighteenth-century satire and denunciation aimed at general human vices and weaknesses, virtually a critique out of time and place, so to speak. These sallies, however, acquired a much sharper edge when occasionally directed against particular human beings and their specific sins. The propriety of attacking individuals in print was much debated during the period, while some modern specialists have achieved a high expertise in deciphering hints and allusions. Next to the question of the human condition, and intrinsically linked to it, stood the problem of an enormous backward country steeped in superstition and ignorance, against which the Russian writers battled indefatigably, in the best Enlightenment tradition, throughout the century. The deepest belief and inspiration of the Age of Reason found expression in their mighty effort.

Yet this sweeping and essentially cultural general critique failed on the whole to assert itself specifically in the political and the social realms. In politics, as I have already shown, the Russia of the Age of Reason remained under the sign of enlightened despotism. In social matters, serfdom formed the main obstacle to progressive Russian thought and action. That institution, while the very opposite of enlightened, was both so well accepted and so fundamental to Russian life that few in the eighteenth century dared challenge it. The period was, after all, the age of the Russian gentry. Catherine the Great herself, after some vague preliminary wavering, came out entirely on the side of the gentry and its power over the serfs. The fact that the newly created Free Economic Society, patronized by the empress, awarded its first prize to a work advocating the eventual abolition of serfdom remained an isolated incident. Numerous writers proceeded to criticize certain individual excesses of serfdom, such as the cruelty of one master or the wastefulness of another, but they did not assail the system itself. Moreover, painful references to the transgressions of "bad" landlords were usually balanced by appropriate depictions of "good" ones, lifeless though these pictures commonly were. Nicholas Novikov and a very few others went further: their image of serf relations could not be ascribed to individual aberrations, and it cried for reform. Still, it remained to Alexander Radishchev to make the condemnation of serfdom total and unmistakably clear. His attack on serfdom, in particular in his *Journey from Petersburg to Moscow*, published in 1790, marked the high point of the social critique of the Russian Age of Reason and in a sense the culmination of that entire trend.

Education was, of course, the pendant to criticism and the antidote to prejudice and ignorance, and it too constituted a dominant theme in the Russian, as well as the general European, Enlightenment. Kantemir not only entitled his first satire *Against Those Who Deprecate Education*, devoted another satire to education, and kept bringing the subject up on still other occasions, but, in a broader sense, dedicated himself to enlightening Russia. Kantemir's mentality and pattern of literary activity were basic to the age, in Russia as elsewhere. Major and minor figures of the Russian Enlightenment differed in talent and accomplishment, but usually not in orientation or inspiration.

One thinks of Novikov (1744–1818), both as a representative intellectual of the period and the outstanding Russian counterpart of the great Western *philosophes*, those indefatigable teachers of humanity. Thinker, writer, translator, and a uniquely important pioneer publicist and publisher, Novikov made better use than any other individual of the opportunities provided by Catherine the Great to spread enlightenment, only to fall victim to the reaction at the end of her reign.

If Novikov stood for the breadth of the Russian Enlightenment, some others expressed even better than he the depth of its educational message. It was surely a testimony to the centrality of the problem of education in the Age of Reason that it inspired some of its best literature. The entire work of perhaps the greatest Russian creative literary genius of the age, Fonvizin, has been interpreted as a treatment of the crucial issue of education in the setting of his native land:

> Fonvizin's dramatic output is not large: he wrote only two plays, *The Brigadier* (1769) and *The Minor* (1782), and he left three sketches, one of them composed before *The Brigadier* and known as *The First Minor* (Ranny Nedorosl). The other two date from the end of his life, *The Good Teacher* (*Dobryi nastavnik*) around 1784 and *The Choice of a Tutor* (*Vybor guvernera*) around 1790 or 1792.

> But this output possesses the interesting characteristic of being entirely devoted to the same problem, essential in the eyes of "the civilizers," the problem of education. . . . The aim of this study is to demonstrate that ceaseless reflection on the same problem led our author to approach it in different, always richer, ways, that this enrichment of his thought caused a profound transformation of his dramatic conception, and, finally, that this aesthetic discovery of Fonvizin exercised such an influence on the Russian drama that one can see in it one of the deep reasons for the turning of that drama towards realism. . . .

> His essential preoccupation did not change; he dedicated his life to demonstrating to the Russian public the importance of education in a modern state.[33]

Another major trend in the thought of the Russian Enlightenment, as important in its way as criticism of the existing society and promotion of education, was the already-discussed affirmation and glorification of enlightened despotism. As so censorious a commentator as G. V. Plekhanov put it:

> And the most important thing—precisely what I want to point out to the reader—the ode writers were adorers of autocratic power not only from fear but also out of conviction. From it, and from it only they expected the

impulse for progressive development in Russia. How then could they fail to glorify it and sing it in their odes?[34]

The thought and culture discussed in this chapter were those of the rulers and of the small educated class. Earlier, too, it had been very difficult to establish the views of the masses below the governing and ecclesiastical elites. Yet as Muscovy developed and spread, there was some justification in referring to a monolithic country and culture. The Old Believer catastrophe broke the monolith. Next, Westernization produced the deepest ever gulf between the educated few and the masses. By the end of the eighteenth century, the common people were virtually invisible in the world of official Russia and high culture, except as hardy soldiers, nameless tillers of the soil, troublesome Old Believers, or participants in the great Pugachev rebellion of 1773–1774. And that culture was fully and irrevocably part of European thought and civilization. In Russian history, only Orthodoxy and Byzantium had provided a comparably immense outside impact, although in many other respects, the two situations were quite different. Moreover, Russia joined Europe, so to speak, on very favorable terms. The cosmopolitan and rationalistic Enlightenment in many ways welcomed the powerful new giant, so eager to learn, to the extent that Catherine the Great could already pretend to be the summit of European thought and culture, while a little later Alexander I would be acclaimed far and wide as the liberator of Europe from Napoleon, as Agamemnon, the king of kings. On the surface at least, Russia's future in Europe and the world looked stunningly promising.

To be sure, links with the past remained, even among the educated and governing elites, let alone the common people. Orthodoxy continued as the religion of the country, which it had been since 988, in spite of a greater toleration of other denominations and special problems produced by the partition of Poland. Formally, I have never seen Orthodoxy in any position but the first in the documents of the imperial period of Russian history.[35] Historians have probably underestimated the personal importance of Orthodoxy for members of the Russian governing elite, even at the height of the Age of Reason. Catherine the Great was assisted not only by Voltairians and secularists, but also by some notable figures, such as the most important favorite and statesman of her reign, Gregory Potemkin, who were seriously concerned with religion and in a rather old-fashioned manner. Still, the role of the Russian Church had indeed declined. Most significant in this respect was the secularization resulting from Westernization. Institutional and economic arrangements made their contributions. After Peter the Great abolished the patriarchate and established a synodal administration linked to the ruler, in 1764, Catherine took over Church lands—something that the Reformation accomplished in other countries—in exchange for an annual subsidy worth about a third of what those lands had been bringing in. (Only one bishop protested, and he was punished.) With inflation and the subsidy worth less and less, the Russian Church, not very rich to begin with, became very poor and dependent on the usually very poor believers.

Russia, of course, also remained a monarchy. But the transition from Muscovite tsars to eighteenth-century emperors and empresses is difficult to evaluate. It seems reasonable to assume that little or nothing changed for the common people and that for them the sovereign retained the Muscovite mystique and magic, although some of them, and apparently not only Old Believers, were upset by women ruling in their own right. The Church and churchmen also, one surmises, continued on the whole to look at the ruler in the old way. Even some members of the newly Westernized elite must have retained, consciously or subconsciously, certain Muscovite attitudes and beliefs in regard to the monarch. And yet, as we know, beginning with Peter the Great, Russian monarchs based their ideology and their justification squarely on the principles of the Age of Reason. In the case of Catherine the Great, the Enlightenment philosophy was so stark that it threatened to become a caricature of itself. Indeed, such successors of Ivan the Terrible as Catherine the Great and Alexander I declared that they were at heart republicans. (By contrast, Pugachev belonged to the old world and announced as he staged his huge rebellion that he was really Peter III who had escaped death and was now reclaiming his throne.)

The marvelous success, suitability, and adaptability of Russia in the Age of Reason were, nevertheless, linked to serious problems, which increased with the passage of time. Enlightened despotism itself, the very foundation of the Russian state ideology throughout the century, while central to the Age of Reason, by no means exhausted its doctrines and possibilities. In fact, Russia itself had a very brief oligarchic constitutional interlude, when Empress Anne, a daughter of Ivan V, was invited in 1730 to rule Russia under extremely restrictive conditions in favor of the Supreme Secret Council of eight leading figures of the state; Anne accepted the conditions, came to Russia from Courland, and finding the situation there propitious for her, repudiated the conditions in short order. A potentially greater danger resided in the more radical doctrines of the Enlightenment. For Russia, a culminating point was reached when in 1790 Alexander Radishchev published *A Journey from Petersburg to Moscow* and called for making Russia a true republic with full liberties for the individual. The main target of that explosive and seminal work, serfdom, was becoming an increasing embarrassment for the Russian government and society. Whereas at the beginning of the century, serfdom had been widespread in Europe, at the end of it, and in the early nineteenth century, it was centered largely in Russia and Poland. Even Western education, still desperately needed by the state and the country, was beginning to create difficulties.

It is a truism, however, that history does not stand still, in the West any more than in Russia. While the empire of the tsars was following the path and the logic of the European Enlightenment, that Enlightenment itself was changing. Not only was radicalism increasing, a disturbing development for an autocracy such as Russia, but stranger transformations were revealing themselves, as if forces pent up by eighteenth-century reason were finally breaking into the open. Fashionable literature, as much as Rousseau's philosophy—and, of course, the two cannot be entirely separated—oozed with sensitivity and emotion. Pseudoscientific and occult teachings of all sorts were becoming the rage of emancipated minds. In some important ways, the Enlightenment was going full circle.

The Russians trod the same curving line, attuned more than ever to developments in the West. In 1792, Nicholas Karamzin's *Poor Liza* marked the triumph of sentimentalism in Russian literature, with many writers eager to imitate its newly famous author. Tears and sighs bid to replace satire as the order of the day. Many varied, complex, and conflicting trends of the late eighteenth century found particular expression in Russian Freemasonry. Freemasonry came to Russia from Great Britain, Germany, Sweden, and France. Although the first fraternal lodges appeared at the time of Empress Elizabeth, the movement became prominent only in the reign of Catherine the Great. Then it consisted of about one hundred lodges, located in St. Petersburg, Moscow, and some provincial towns, and of approximately twenty-five hundred members, almost entirely from the gentry. In addition to the contribution made by Freemasonry to the life of polite society, specialists distinguish two main trends within that movement in eighteenth-century Russia: the mystical, and the ethical and social. The first concentrated on such elusive and essentially individual goals as contemplation and self-perfection. Rather than simply following reason, its devotees sought "true knowledge," "the awakening of the heart," or "the inner essence of man." The second reached out to the world and thus constituted the active wing of the movement. It was the socially oriented Freemasons, centering around the University of Moscow and led by Nicholas Novikov, who engaged in education and publishing on a large scale, establishing private schools and the first major program of publication in Russia outside of the government. But it is wrong to contrast the two groups too sharply or to argue, for example, that Novikov cleverly utilized his addle-brained colleagues in the interests of the Age of Reason. The genius of the time was to combine, not to separate, the two approaches.

The Bastille was stormed on July 14, 1789. The ensuing French Revolution provided a climax to the Enlightenment such as few ideologies, or periods, could claim. Many theories suddenly became exhilaratingly—or terrifyingly—real. In France itself, the Revolution, practice and theory, became constantly more radical, until the fall of Robespierre and the end of Terror in 1794. Elsewhere, the governments and, gradually, the educated publics, too, began to rally against the French Revolution and everything it stood for.

Educated Russians shared with other Europeans the excitement of the French Revolution. The calling of the Estates General received the approval of Catherine the Great herself, who liked to believe that the French were belatedly following the lead of her *Instruction*. Many of her educated subjects applauded the early developments in Paris. In fact, this Russian support of the Revolution lasted, apparently, for an extensive period of time. It was only the fall of Louis XVI in August 1792, the proclamation of a republic, and the execution of the king on January 21, 1793, that led to an almost uniformly adverse reaction in Russia. Over a sequence of years, some prominent Russian intellectuals, like their counterparts in Germany, England, and elsewhere, experienced under the impact of the French Revolution a major shift of position from the left to the right. Nicholas Karamzin might serve here as the leading, but by no means isolated, example.

The government, for its part, did not wait: Catherine the Great's early sympathetic interest in the developments in France was replaced by worry, fear, and rage. A feeling of betrayal by the spirit of the age probably added to her violent and tangled emotions. After the outbreak of the French Revolution, Radishchev was sentenced to death for his inopportune *Journey from Petersburg to Moscow*, although the sentence was commuted to Siberian exile; Novikov and his fellow Masons also suffered; and edicts against travel and other contacts with the revolutionary West appeared in profusion. Catherine the Great broke diplomatic relations with France after the execution of Louis XVI, and, but for her death, Russia might have joined a military coalition against that revolutionary country. The unexpected death of the empress in November 1796, following a stroke, gave the crown finally to her son Paul I, whom Catherine had for decades successfully kept away from the throne. While Paul too believed in enlightened despotism, represented by such rulers as Peter the Great and Frederick the Great of Prussia, his emphasis was entirely on the power and prerogatives of the autocrat. Moreover, in practice, Paul's reign quickly developed into a devastating, even insupportable, petty tyranny.

It is appropriate to end a chapter on the Russian Enlightenment with the French Revolution having run its tragic course, Paul I occupying the throne of the tsars, Russian armies marching with their allies to restore legitimacy and order in Europe, and the Russian educated public terrified by the French assault on the sovereign and the upper classes alike, in fact on the entire *ancien régime*. Yet the outlook of the Age of Reason had such strength and pertinence in Russia that it was to stage a full comeback, giving the Petrine empire a second Enlightenment, or a post-Enlightenment, if you will, in the reign of Alexander I.

The Reign of Alexander I, 1801–1825

*If, during the two centuries which divide the Russia of Peter the Great
from the Bolshevik revolution, there was any period in which the spell
of the authoritarian past might have been overcome, the forms of the
state liberalized in a constitution and the course of Russian
development merged withthe historic currents of the west, it is the
earlier part of the reign of Alexander I. Or so, for a moment one is
tempted to think.*

—R. D. Charques, *A Short History of Russia*

Alexander I's reign manifested the culmination of the Age of Reason, of the Enlightenment in Russia, inaugurated by Peter the Great and developed for a century.[1] Or, because the historic time was late and because the reign followed the oppressive last years of Catherine the Great's rule and Paul I's tyranny, one can refer to a neo-Enlightenment or a second Enlightenment. In any case, Enlightenment was found wanting in Russia. Many specialists, including Soviet scholars as a group, emphasized the superficiality of the Russian Enlightenment, as well as its unsuitability to the country and the people, and wrote on occasion simply of hypocrisy and mystification. Other historians, however, took the Russian Enlightenment and its possibilities more seriously, a few even to the extent of considering Alexander I's reign a logical turning point in history, when history refused to turn for certain particular, perhaps even adventitious, reasons. A brief discussion should throw some light on the issues involved.

The sudden and unexpected death of Paul I (actually killed in a palace coup, although, of course, the circumstances of his death were not announced) and the accession of Alexander I to the throne struck Russians like a bolt from the blue. The reaction, at least among the educated public, was that of overwhelming joy. As one eyewitness who hurried to his Moscow home at the news testified:

> I ran more than I walked; still, I looked attentively at all the people I came
> across, those in simple peasant coats as well as the well-dressed ones. It was

noticeable that the important news had been carried to all parts of the city and was no longer a secret for the most common people. This is one of those recollections which time can never destroy; mute, general joy illumined by the bright spring sun. Having returned home, I could not at all find out the facts: acquaintances constantly came and went, all talked at the same time, all embraced as on Easter Sunday; not a word about the departed in order not to dim even for a moment the heartfelt joy, which shone in all the eyes; not a word about the past, only about the present and the future.[2]

Thus was inaugurated, to cite Pushkin's winged phrase, "the beautiful beginning of the days of Alexander." One specialist counted over fifty published poems glorifying Alexander I's accession to the throne, declared that "the number of those remaining in manuscript cannot be totalled," and reproduced opinions of contemporaries to the effect that no other inauguration inspired so much poetry. Intoxicated by the event, even people hitherto "entirely foreign to literature" composed poems.[3] Bad poetry and other signs of the joy of the educated public told an important story. They welcomed the return of Enlightenment to Russia. The monolithic unity of the government and the educated public in Russia was probably never stronger, nor the belief in Enlightenment and enlightened despotism firmer, than in the remarkable year 1801.

The fervent belief in the new emperor was to last, it would seem, for many years and to help the Russians survive the Napoleonic wars, including the cataclysmic invasion of 1812. At Borodino and elsewhere, Russian soldiers (and there arose even numerous spontaneous partisan detachments to fight the French, as occurred in Spain but no other European state) proved their steadfastness in defending their country. As to the educated public, the year 1812 left an indelible impression not only on the contemporaries but also on succeeding generations, as they came to consider the nature of Russia and its role in the world.

Perhaps more surprisingly, as the Russian emperor pursued Napoleon across the continent, entered Paris, and, together with his allies, drew up in Vienna a global peace settlement, ecstatic admiration of him spread broadly to the educated classes of other European countries. Perhaps shamefully but understandably, the French led the way. None other than Rouget de Lisle, the creator of the "Marseillaise," eulogized the Russian sovereign, imploring him to "restore to the Bourbons their throne, to the lilies their splendor." At its meeting of April 21, 1814, the Institut de France expressed its warm gratitude to Alexander I for bringing back to France the fruits of civilization, in search of which Peter the Great had once visited their land. There was a proposal to honor the Russian monarch, together with the emperor of Austria and the king of Prussia, on the Colonne Vendôme and on the Arc de Triomphe de l'Étoile, and to transform the Madeleine into a church of Saint Louis and Saint Alexander.[4] For a time, at least, the magic of Alexander I appeared to combine power, order, the restoration of legitimate rulers, and traditional values with magnanimity displayed in the French settlement, liberalism exemplified by the Polish constitution, and Christian peace and brotherhood proclaimed in the Holy Alliance.

But to return to the beginning of the reign, the early measures of the emperor fed general euphoria:

> After all, the new tsar declared that, promoting zealously the "inviolable felicity" of all his subjects, he intended to rule following the guidance of "the action of law alone." After all, in the first days of the reign he freed from prison and returned from exile some 500 human beings who fell victim at the time of Catherine and Paul (A. N. Radishchev was among those fully amnestied), while the total number of persons who[,] according to the ukase of 15 March 1801[,] recovered their service and civil rights, extended to twelve thousand. After all, one after another there appeared the tsar's ukases, from which it could be concluded that the government had taken the liberal road in politics: on 15 March, the escapees hiding abroad were amnestied; on 16 March, the prohibition against importing goods from abroad was lifted; on 19 March, there followed the ukase that the police must not cause "injuries and oppressions"; on 22 March, those travelling into Russia and out of Russia were permitted freely to cross the border; on 31 March, the prohibition against importing books into Russia from abroad was repealed, and it was permitted "to unseal" private printing establishments; on 2 April, the Secret Expedition was abolished, and it was stated in the ukase that "in a well-organized state all crimes must be encompassed, judged and punished by the general power of law'; on 28 May, it was forbidden to announce in the press the sale of human beings without land; on 5 June, the creation of a Commission to formulate laws was proclaimed, and so on.[5]

Alexander I seemed to represent the best of the Enlightenment: twenty-three years old, stunningly handsome, and wondrously charming and brought up on the rhetoric of his grandmother Catherine the Great and the instructions of the prominent Swiss general, statesman, and *philosophe* Frederic-Cesar de LaHarpe. The new ruler stood as the very embodiment of the humaneness, progressiveness, affirmation of human dignity, and freedom that educated Russians fervently desired. In June 1801 he established the so-called Unofficial Committee of young advisers to consider fundamental reform. These advisers, all of whom shared progressive views with their sovereign, were Nicholas Novosiltsev, Count Paul Stroganov, Count Victor Kochubei, and a Polish patriot, Prince Adam Czartoryski. LaHarpe, who returned to Russia and maintained very close relations with the emperor and with his friends, has occasionally been presented as, in effect, another member of the Committee. Novosiltsev and, especially, Stroganov had spent some time in revolutionary Paris and could claim the Jacobin Gilbert Romme as their personal tutor. Czartoryski came from a somewhat different background and invariably concentrated much of his attention on his native land; yet he too responded fully in his own way to the liberal spirit of the age and was to be associated with the Polish constitution of 1815. Less is known about the precise opinions of Kochubei, but apparently he blended naturally with the group. The members of the Unofficial Committee reflected in a striking manner the abstract rationalism and the optimism of the Age of Reason. For years, they had been talking and writing of civil rights and constitutions and of their speedy introduction to transform societies. Enthusiasm ran rampant. The emperor spoke jokingly of his "Committee of Public Safety," a reference to the French Revolution that would have made his predecessors shudder. He met with the Committee informally and frequently, often daily over coffee.

Yet this first liberal period of Alexander I's reign, 1801–1805, brought more disappointment than reform, as did the second, 1807–1812, which was dominated by the figure of Michael Speransky. Both periods were followed by wars with Napoleonic France. As to the second half of the reign, it has been on the whole justly labeled as reactionary, although, characteristically for Alexander I, the reaction too was inconsistent, and possibilities of reform occasionally flared up. It may be best, however, first to consider briefly what was accomplished before turning to how and why fundamental reform failed.

During the first reform period and, to a lesser extent, later in the reign, the best results were achieved in the field of education, a central concern of the Age of Reason. With the creation of the Ministry of Education in 1802, the empire was divided into six educational regions, each headed by a curator. The government plan called for a university in every region, a secondary school in every provincial center, an improved primary school in every district, and at least one parish school for every two parishes. By the end of the reign, the projected expansion of the three upper tiers had been largely completed: Russia then possessed six universities, forty-eight secondary state schools, and 337 improved primary schools. French émigrés escaping the Revolution, as well as the Jesuits, who were active in Russia between 1796 and their expulsion in December 1815, also contributed to the education of the country, through a few select boarding schools, private tutoring, and their influence in polite society. Shortly after his accession to the throne, Alexander I founded universities in Kazan, Kharkov, and St. Petersburg (the last-named, however, first appeared as a pedagogical institute); transformed "the main school," or academy, in Vilna into a university; and revived the German university in Dorpat, which, with the University of Moscow, made a total of six. In addition, a university existed in the newly acquired (1809) Grand Duchy of Finland: originally in Abo (Turku in Finnish) and then, beginning in 1827, in Helsingfors (Helsinki). Following a traditional European pattern, Russian universities enjoyed a broad measure of autonomy. While university enrollments, except for the University of Moscow, numbered usually a few hundred or less each, and while the total of secondary school students had risen to only about fifty-five hundred by 1825, these figures represented undeniable progress for Russia.

Moreover, private philanthropy emerged to supplement government efforts. It played an important part in the creation of the University of Kharkov, and it established two private institutions of higher education that were eventually to become the Demidov Law School in Iaroslavl and the Historico-Philological Institute of Prince Bezborodko in Nezhin. Karamzin's *Vestnik Evropy* (*The Messenger of Europe*) insisted that even modestly situated members of the gentry were to make their contribution to the spreading of education in their native land. They could provide scholarships for impecunious students training in the new institutions of higher learning to become teachers throughout the length and breadth of Russia. "Each would be concerned with his particular protégé and would be proud of his achievement. The support of a student costs about 150 rubles a year: what other pleasure can be purchased so cheaply?"[6]

It is this concern with an encompassing, broad, and popular education introduced by the central government and at the same time championed by at least some of the more liberal segments of the educated public that is especially noteworthy, for it pointed beyond the court, the officialdom, and the upper classes to the peasant masses of Russia, separated more than ever from their "betters" since the days of Nikon and Peter the Great. Here is how the *Messenger of Europe* presented and evaluated, in March 1803, the educational policy of the government:

On January 24, Alexander's august hand signed the immortal ukase concerning the establishment of new schools and the spreading of learning in Russia. This fortunate emperor—for doing good to millions is the greatest blessedness on earth—solemnly called popular education an important part of the state system dear to *his* heart. Many sovereigns had the glory of patronizing learning and talents; but probably no one issued such a thorough all-encompassing plan of popular education as the one of which Russia can now be proud. *Peter* the Great established the first Academy in our fatherland, Elizabeth the first university, the Great *Catherine* town schools, but *Alexander*, multiplying universities and secondary schools, says in addition: *let there be light also in the huts!* A new, great epoch is beginning henceforth in the history of the moral formation of Russia which is the root of state glory and without which the most brilliant reigns represent only the personal glory of the monarchs, not of the fatherland, not of the people. Russia, strong and fortunate in many respects, remained abased by a just envy, seeing the triumph of enlightenment in other countries and its weak, unsteady flicker in the vast Russian lands. Romans, already conquerors of the world, were still despised for their ignorance by Greeks, and not by might, not by victories, but only through learning could they escape at last the name of barbarians.

The name of *Peter* and of *Catherine* will for ever shine at the head of the history of reason and enlightenment in Russia; but what they could not accomplish, that is being done by Alexander, who has the happiness of reigning after them, and in the nineteenth century. Heaven left for *him* the glory and the opportunity of crowning their immortal work. . . .

The establishment of village schools is incomparably more useful than all the secondary schools, for they are true *popular* institutions, the true foundation of the enlightenment of a state. The subject of their study is *the most important one* in the eyes of the philosopher. Between people who can only read and write and the totally illiterate there is a much greater distance than between the uneducated and the leading metaphysicians of the world. *The history of reason* presents *two* main epochs: the invention of the alphabet and of the printing press; all the others were their consequences.[7]

Sadly, it was precisely this lowest level of education that fared worst in the reign of Alexander I. In the words of one historian:

In the first years of Alexander's reign, while his advisers were seriously concerned with the peasant question, educational designs also included the rural masses. Both LaHarpe and Maximilian von Klinger, the director of the cadet corps, urged the extension of enlightenment to the villages. When emancipation of the serfs proved impossible except in several minor ways, state instruction of the peasantry was discarded in favor of private, gentry, communal and ecclesiastical enterprise. This meant its effective abandonment.[8]

The early years of Alexander I's rule saw a remarkable quickening of a many-sided discussion of education in Russia, following a partial freeze under Paul I. During this period, intellectuals such as Alexander Bestuzhev (the father of four Decembrists), Ivan Pnin, Basil Popugaev, Alexander Vostokov, and Ivan Born wrote works on such topics as "Concerning Education," "An Essay on Enlightenment in Relation to Russia," and "On the Wellbeing of Popular Bodies" (Popugaev's treatise included chapters "About the Influence of Enlightenment on Governing," "About Popular Enlightenment and Its Results," "About the Necessary Connection between Laws and Enlightenment," and "About Enlightenment and the Personal Worth of Those Governing") or addressed the newly founded Free Society of Lovers of Literature, the Sciences and the Arts on similar topics. "Enlightenment is the true purpose of our life. In achieving it we learn human worth and grandeur."[9] The discussion of education by Russian intellectuals followed the broad current of the Age of Reason and occasionally, as in Popugaev's insistence on classless, democratic schools, reflected faithfully the more progressive Western trends. Here again the range of thought of the educated public closely paralleled government resources. After all, it was the Jacobin Romme, Stroganov's and Novosiltsev's tutor, who helped Condorcet draft the school bill presented to the French National Assembly in 1792.

Not only was formal schooling increasing in Russia, but the Russian public was also becoming better educated in a broader sense. In particular, it was reading more books. The *Messenger of Europe,* published by Karamzin, himself one of the leading practitioners and promoters of literature of his age, pointed to that development with pride at the same time that it was celebrating Alexander I's educational reforms. The number of Russian bookstores and their turnover grew by leaps and bounds. To be sure, the Russian book trade could not as yet rival those of Germany, France, or England, but its prospects were great. As to the favorite reading matter, translated novels, they too had their uses: "The worst novels contain a certain logic and rhetoric: one who reads them will speak better and in a more connected manner than a total ignoramus, who had not opened a book all his life. Besides, novels today are rich in all kinds of knowledge"[10]—and they exercised, on balance, a moral, rather than an immoral, influence, and nurtured sensitivity and sentiment. "In a word: it is good that our public reads at least novels."[11] Or, according to a modern authority:

> The culture of the beginning of the nineteenth century expressed itself with the greatest force not in supreme creations of the human mind, but in a sharp rise of the average level of spiritual life. . . . That which had still appeared natural and normal to their fathers, began in the early nineteenth century to seem shameful to dozens and hundreds of members of the Russian gentry. [12]

And, if the early years of Alexander I's reign indicated cultural promise, its ending saw already the emergence of Pushkin and the commencement of what is generally known as the Golden Age of Russian literature.

Impressive in the fields of education and culture, the reign of Alexander I also witnessed important developments in the administration and government of the country, although in that area it has usually been judged a failure, for it failed to limit autocracy, produce a constitution, or, to use the language of the epigraph to this chapter, merge the evolution of Russia with the historic currents of the West. Yet the changes actually introduced were of a considerable, if much more limited, significance. During the years of the Unofficial Committee (1801–1805), the Senate was restored, or perhaps promoted, to a very high position in the state: it was to be the supreme judicial and administrative institution in the empire, and its decrees were to carry the authority of those of the sovereign, who alone could stop their execution. Peter the Great's colleges, which had a checkered and generally unhappy history in the eighteenth century, were gradually replaced in 1802 and subsequent years by ministries, with a single minister in charge of each. At first there were eight: the ministries of war, navy, foreign affairs, justice, interior, finance, commerce, and education. Later the Ministry of Commerce was abolished, and the Ministry of Police appeared.

The second period of reform in Alexander I's reign, 1807–1812, corresponded to the French alliance and was dominated by the emperor's most remarkable assistant, Michael Speransky.[13] In contrast to the members of the Unofficial Committee and most other associates of the sovereign, Speransky came not from the aristocracy but from poor village clergy. It was Speransky's intelligence, ability to work, and outstanding administrative capacity that made him for a time Alexander I's prime minister, in fact if not in name, as no such formal office then existed. Brought up through the bureaucracy, Speransky was much more realistic and practical than the dilettanti of the Unofficial Committee. At the same time, proficient in languages and a man of great learning, he absorbed and reflected exceptionally well the theory and practice of government in Napoleonic Europe. In Speransky, the *esprit de système* of the Age of Reason found its best Russian representative.

In the event, only one element of Speransky's grand and comprehensive plan to reform Russia (to be discussed shortly) was translated into practice. In 1810, on the advice of Speransky, Alexander I created the Council of State, modeled on Napoleon's Conseil d'État, with Speransky attached to it as the secretary of state. This body of experts appointed by the sovereign to help him with legislative work in no way limited the principle of autocracy; moreover, the Council tended to be extremely conservative. Still, it clearly reflected the emphasis on legality, competence, and correct procedure so dear to Speransky. In the eulogistic words of a British historian: "But from the time when it was instituted, there was a right and a wrong way of conducting business in Russia; . . . Speransky gave the bureaucracy a conscience, and henceforward it knew when it was not following it."[14]

Speransky also reorganized the ministries and added two special agencies to the executive, one for the supervision of government finance, the other for the development of transport. A system of annual budgets was instituted, and other financial measures were proposed and in part adopted. Perhaps still more important, Speransky strengthened Russian bureaucracy by introducing something in the nature of a civil service examination and tried in other ways to emphasize merit and efficient organization. This remarkable statesman was not alone in his efforts. It is noteworthy, for example, that the former members of the Unofficial Committee proceeded to occupy a whole series of top government positions, frequently reorganizing and improving departments and functions under their jurisdiction.

Of course, secondary changes and improvements could not resolve the primary problems of Russia. Russia chose the road of Enlightenment and advanced upon that road without changing its basic political, social, and economic structure—or, in the simplest of terms, while retaining autocracy and serfdom. To be sure, that seemed to represent much less of a problem at the beginning of the eighteenth century than at its end. At the beginning, one could compare the rule of Peter the Great to that of Louis XIV, whereas at the end, the issue was not how to imitate best the Sun King, but how to react to the execution of Louis XVI and, soon after, how to face the extraordinary new phenomenon of Napoleon. With the passage of time and the historic change in Europe, the Russian political system appeared to some to resemble the sultanate of Turkey more than European states. Serfdom, too, widespread on the continent at the beginning of the century, came to be increasingly restricted to Russia and eastern Europe. When Alexander I ascended the throne, the circumstances for Russia to become a full-fledged member of enlightened Europe were complex and the time late. Yet it is this possibility of an Enlightened transformation that gives the poignancy, and, many would add, the point to Alexander I's reign.

Our information about the work of the Unofficial Committee—which includes Stroganov's notes on the meetings—suggests that at first Alexander I intended to abolish both autocracy and serfdom. That would have been perfectly in keeping with the general orientation of that product of late Enlightenment, who declared himself on occasion a republican and complained throughout his life of the crushing burden of autocratic rule.[15] Moreover, Russia, apparently, was to receive a liberal constitution, not a highly restrictive and oligarchical one adumbrated among some Senators. But the issue of implementation stymied the proceedings. The Committee concentrated on education instead, its meetings became less frequent, and the war of 1805 terminated its activities. Even more limited projects, such as the proclamation of a Russian charter of rights, failed to be translated into practice.

Alexander I requested and received the most thorough and far-reaching project to reshape Russia in 1809 from Speransky.[16] In his customary methodical manner, the statesman divided the Russians into three categories: the gentry; people of "the middle condition," that is, merchants, artisans, and other owners of property of a certain value; and, finally, working people, including serfs, servants, and apprentices. The plan postulated three kinds of rights: general civil rights; special civil rights, namely exemption from regular service and the right to obtain populated estates; and political rights, which depended on a property qualification. The members of the gentry were to enjoy all the rights. Those belonging to the middle group were to receive general civil rights and political rights when they could meet the property requirement. The working people would obtain general civil rights, but they clearly did not own enough to participate in politics.[17] Russia was to be reorganized on four administrative levels: the *volost*, a small unit sometimes translated as "canton" or "township"; the district; the province; and the country at large. On each level, there were to be the following institutions: legislative assemblies, or *dumy*, culminating in the state *duma* for all of Russia; a system of courts, with the Senate at the apex; and administrative boards, leading eventually to the ministries and the central executive power. The state *duma*, the most intriguing part of Speransky's system, showed the statesman's caution, for in addition to the property restriction imposed on its electorate, it depended on a sequence of indirect elections. The assemblies of the *volosti* elected the district assemblymen, who elected the provincial assemblymen, who elected the members of the state *duma*, or national assembly. In addition, the activities of the state *duma* were to be rather narrowly restricted. On the other hand, the state *duma* did provide for popular participation in the legislative process, and thus it would transform an autocracy into a constitutional monarchy. In a sense, Speransky offered a farsighted outline of the Russian future, one that took long to materialize, thus serving—in the opinion of many specialists—as a noteworthy historical example of too little too late. Russia received district and provincial self-government by the so-called *zemstvo* reform of 1864; a national legislature, the *duma*, in 1905–1906; and *volost* self-government in 1917. A mere fragment, the Council of State, appeared in 1810.

The second half of the reign of Alexander I came to be better known for its reaction than for its liberalism, even though some liberal elements could be found even in reactionary policies. Thus the notorious "military settlements," managed by General Alexis Arakcheev, the emperor's most prominent assistant in the last part of his reign, represented not only frightful discipline and minute regulation of soldiers' existence but also an attempt to have those soldiers live with their families, engage in agriculture, and be better integrated in the life of their country. Moreover, Alexander I's benevolent interest in constitutions continued. The Russian sovereign sponsored the French Charter of 1814. In 1815, the Kingdom of Poland received a constitution, a remarkably liberal document for its time. At that point, Alexander I combined in his own person the positions of a Russian emperor and autocrat, a constitutional king of Poland, and a constitutional Grand Duke of Finland (after gaining Finland from Sweden in 1809). In March 1818, in a celebrated address to the Polish Diet, the monarch spoke of extending the benefits of "free institutions" to the other parts of his empire.

Also in 1818, and in the two following years, Nicholas Novosiltsev, a former associate of Alexander in the original Unofficial Committee and a leading statesman, prepared, at Alexander's urging, a constitution for the entire realm, the *Constitutional Charter of the Russian Empire*.[18] Novosiltsev's project bore a strong resemblance to Speransky's in its emphasis on legality and rights, the Rechtsstaat, and its narrowly based and weak legislative assembly. While more conservative than Speransky's, it too provided for a legislature, a *sejm*, with elected members. Novosiltsev differed from Speransky's rigorous centralism in allowing something to the federal principle: he wanted the Russian Empire, including Finland and Russian Poland, to be divided into twelve large groups of provinces, which were to enjoy a certain autonomy. The emperor was characteristically enthusiastic about the new plan. A leading writer and intellectual of the age, Prince Peter Viazemsky, who in his official capacity had helped Novosiltsev draw up the plan, described an audience with the emperor in a palace study in St. Petersburg in 1819:

> after the political education which he had given to Poland he turned to the political reform which he was preparing for Russia. He said that he knew about my participation in the editing of the project of the Russian constitution, that he is satisfied with our work, that he will take it to Warsaw and pass his critical comments to Novosiltsev, that he hopes without fail to bring this matter to a desired conclusion, that at the present time only a shortage of funds, needed for such a state measure, is delaying the realization of a thought which is to him sacred.[19]

Serfdom proved to be no easier to abolish than autocracy, and the two crucial issues evolved along parallel lines. To begin with, the emperor and the Unofficial

Committee, Stroganov in particular, favored outright emancipation. Although this initial impetus bogged down in dangers and difficulties, real or assumed, some social legislation was enacted in the early years of Alexander I's reign. In 1801, the right to own estates was extended from the gentry to other free Russians. In 1803, the so-called law concerning the free agriculturists went into effect. It provided for voluntary emancipation of the serfs by their masters, assuring that the emancipated serfs would be given land and establishing regulations and courts to secure the observance of all provisions. The newly emancipated serfs were to receive in many respects the status of state peasants, but, by contrast with the latter, they were to enjoy stronger property rights, as well as exemption from certain obligations. Few landlords, however, proved eager to free their serfs.

A leading historian of serfdom in Russia, V. I. Semevsky, charitably described the emperor's relationship to serfdom as follows.

> A very favorable circumstance for the solution of the peasant problem was the fact that emperor Alexander himself desired, as we know, the liberation of the serfs. In Paris, at Madame de Staël's, he had given a promise to destroy serfdom. He ordered to pay out from the resources of his chancery 200 *chervontsy* for the making of two medals to be awarded for the best solutions to the problems (concerning the relative advantage of serf and free labor and concerning separating peasants from factory workers) proposed by the Free Economic Society in 1812. He directs Arakcheev and Kankrin to compose projects changing the life of peasants; to him Miloradovich hands N. I. Turgenev's memorandum on that subject; all these projects he carefully gathers later to select everything that is best in them; during his reign the emancipation of the peasants in the Baltic provinces takes place, an emancipation which, although it was to cause much misery to the emancipated, was based on principles which then seemed to many to be just; finally, he with great firmness stops the granting of inhabited estates into hereditary possession, in spite of the fact that even such enlightened men as Mordvinov wanted the parcelling of all state lands to the most eminent Russian families. [20]

Unfortunately, Semevsky referred to schemes never carried out and indeed kept in great secrecy. The one important reform on the list, the emancipation of the serfs in the Baltic provinces, proved to be a dubious blessing. Because serfs were emancipated without land in Estonia in 1816, in Courland in 1817, and in Livonia in 1819, their general position was only made worse by the reform. Even Alexander I's decision not to give state peasants with state lands into private ownership and serfdom, much praised in traditional historiography, was proved by N. M. Druzhinin and some other Soviet historians to have been more a matter of style than substance: such grants of populated estates continued, but they came to be designated as hereditary leases rather than outright gifts. And yet the issue of serfdom and its abolition were apparently in the emperor's mind throughout his reign. The last burst of government activity in that connection, secret or semisecret to be sure, occurred in 1820 and the years immediately following, at the same time that Alexander I was approving, in principle, Novosiltsev's constitutional project. It appeared that both constitutionalism and the abolition of serfdom remained possible alternatives for Russia as long as "the enigmatic tsar" presided over its destinies.

Why did Alexander I fail to abolish autocracy and serfdom and reform Russia?

To begin with, there was the subjective side. Alexander I was twenty-three years old when he ascended the Russian throne. His personality and manner of dealing with people had thus already been formed, and it is the psychology of the emperor that has fascinated those who became acquainted with him, both his contemporaries and later scholars. Moreover, there seems to be little agreement about Alexander I, beyond the assertion that he was the most complex and elusive figure among the emperors of Russia. This unusual sovereign has been called "the enigmatic tsar," a sphinx, and "crowned Hamlet." Striking contradictions, or alleged contradictions, appear in the autocrat's character and activities. Thus Alexander I was hailed as a liberal by many men and women, Thomas Jefferson among them, and denounced as a reactionary by numerous others, including Byron. He was glorified as a pacifist, the originator of the Holy Alliance, and in general a man who did his utmost to establish peace and a Christian brotherhood on earth. Yet this "angel"—an epithet frequently applied to Alexander I, especially within the imperial family and in court circles—was also a drill sergeant and a parade-ground enthusiast, given to uncontrollable rages over military trifles. Some students of Alexander I's foreign policy have concluded that the tsar was a magnificent and extremely shrewd diplomat, who consistently bested Napoleon. Napoleon himself, it might be added, called him a "cunning Byzantine." But other scholars, again on good evidence, have emphasized the Russian ruler's mysticism, his growing detachment from reality, even hinting at madness.

Various elements in the emperor's background have been cited to help account for his baffling character. There was, first, Alexander's difficult childhood and boyhood, in particular his ambiguous relations with his father, Paul, and his grandmother, Catherine the Great, who hated each other. Alexander spent more time with Catherine than with his parents, and he learned early the arts of flattery, dissimulation, and hypocrisy, or at least so his boyhood letters indicate. He also developed a penchant for secrecy. The empress took a great liking to Alexander from the very beginning and apparently wanted to make him her successor, bypassing Paul. Quite possibly only the suddenness of her death upset that plan. Catherine took a personal interest in Alexander's education and saw to it that with the help of LaHarpe, and indeed the entire orientation and atmosphere of her court, Alexander grew up as a devoted disciple of the Age of Reason. But, versed in Enlightenment ideology, he had little knowledge of Russian reality. The contrast between theory and practice characteristic of Alexander I's reign has been attributed by some scholars to this one-sided education. The tragic circumstances of Alexander I's accession to the throne have also been analyzed for their effect on his character and rule. Alexander found himself in a precarious position during Paul's reign, especially because Paul thought of divorcing his wife and disinheriting Alexander and his other sons by her. The young grand duke almost certainly knew of the conspiracy against his father, but the murder of Emperor Paul came to him apparently as a surprise and a shock. Some critics see in that event the basis for the new emperor's strong feeling of guilt and his later mysticism and lack of balance.

Behind Alexander I's reactions to particular incidents and situations of his life there was, of course, his basic character. Alexander I remains a mystery, in the sense that human personality and behavior have not been and perhaps cannot be fully explained. Yet his psychological type is not uncommon, as psychiatrists, psychologists, and observant laypersons attest. The emperor belonged with those exceedingly sensitive, charming, and restless men and women whose lives display constant irritation, search, and disappointment. They lack balance, consistency, and firmness of purpose. They are contradictory. Alexander I's inability to come to terms with himself and pursue a steady course explains his actions much better, on the whole, than do allegations of cynicism or Machiavellianism. As is characteristic of the type, personal problems grew with the passage of time: the emperor became more and more irritable, tired, and suspicious of people, more dissatisfied with life, more frantically in search of a religious or mystical answer; he even lost some of his proverbial charm. More and more willful, as well as suspicious of others, he was not going to share his power in practice, much as that might have looked good in theory. (And he proved to be a poor constitutional ruler of the Kingdom of Poland.) The autocrat died in 1825, only forty-eight years old. A few specialists even insist that Alexander I did not die then but escaped from the throne to live in Siberia as the saintly hermit Fedor Kuzmich, although the evidence for that possibility seems insufficient. Suicide might offer another explanation for a certain strangeness and confusion associated with the sovereign's death.

Of course, there were "objective" as well as subjective factors affecting Alexander I's policies and the destiny of Russia, and the two sets of factors often combined in a complex manner. Many commentators believed that the Russian emperor did best in 1812, when the great French invasion made basic issues desperately clear, and when he chose to fight Napoleon until the eventual total triumph over him. But "crowned Hamlet" had constantly to make important decisions that most rulers, whatever their characters or preferences, would have found difficult. As a student of the foreign ministers of the Russian sovereign concluded: "They all were caught in the unreconciled dilemma between Alexander's enlightened aims, with which they had to sympathize to succeed, and his fundamental quest for peace and social stability—in whose interest he might pursue the most despotic conduct—to which they had to be willing to submit."[21] Yet even when the emperor could be blamed for a lack of resolve, procrastination, or a self-defeating effort to please all sides concerned, the issues, dilemmas, and attendant difficulties involved were basically not of his making. Even the financial stringency given by Alexander I to Viazemsky as the reason for postponing the introduction of a constitution was real enough. Still more threatening was the fact that constitutional rule and abolition of serfdom were, or at least were considered to be by the emperor and some of his closest assistants, at cross-purposes. Political participation would add power to the gentry, probably especially the upper gentry, the social class most opposed to the abolition of serfdom. Although enthusiastic on the subject of constitutions, Alexander I was apprehensive from the start of the possible emergence of an oligarchy, which he associated with "the Senate party" and the very narrow view of representation held by that clique. Later he was deeply suspicious of the orientation of such gentry groups as the one around the *Spirit of Journals* (*Dukh Zhurnalov*), published from 1815 to 1820. On the horns of that dilemma, it seemed incumbent to decide which goal, constitutionalism or the emancipation of the serfs, was the more important one to pursue. In the end, the emperor did not sufficiently pursue either.

How feasible were these two great liberal aims in early nineteenth-century Russia? Alexander I and his friends of the Unofficial Committee were stunned by the backwardness of Russia and by the manifold difficulties of reforming it, once they turned to that task. And these were eager, intelligent, and well-meaning, if somewhat naive and doctrinaire, young men. Most of their educated contemporaries, as well as subsequent commentators, concurred. With half of the population enserfed and almost all of it illiterate, the ideas of the Enlightenment seemed to belong, and indeed did belong, to a different world. To be sure, the serfs wanted freedom, and in that they agreed with the *philosophes*. However, the implication of their emancipation for social stability, reason, and progress could well be another matter. Alexander I himself was born only a few years after the great Pugachev rebellion, and he knew of the continuous explosive peasant hostility to the landlords, for instance in 1812, when the peasants fought the French even on their own but also sometimes used the French invasion to throw off the authority of their masters. Emancipation would presumably diminish the danger of a massive peasant rebellion, especially over a period of time, but some were afraid that the act itself would immediately ignite the worst explosion of all. The landlords, for their part, were not willing to give up the very valuable property on which much of their sustenance and way of life was based. As to constitutionalism, especially liberal constitutionalism, as distinct from a narrow oligarchical rule, it had few supporters and no obvious and effective social base. There are excellent reasons for arguing that both a fundamental social and a fundamental political reform were doomed in Russia at the time, for causes much more basic than the character or predilections of a particular monarch.

Yet doubt lingers. It is extremely likely that most Russian landlords were opposed to the emancipation of the serfs not only in the reign of Alexander I but also in 1861, when the emancipation took place. Once abolished, serfdom as such could not return. Constitutions, even bad constitutions, once enacted, sometimes acquire lives of their own; the most important step could be to begin.

In any case, Alexander I, coming to the throne after a century of Enlightened rule in Russia, still failed "to catch up with the West" and transform his country according to the dictates of the Age of Reason. His brother and successor, Emperor Nicholas I, would try a different approach.

However, before Nicholas I established himself firmly on the throne, the Age of Reason made, so to speak, one last bid to transform Russia. This time its agents were not sovereigns, such as Catherine the Great or Alexander I, nor statesmen, like Novosiltsev and Speransky, but young officers of the guard, who came to be known after their unsuccessful uprising in December 1825 as the Decembrists. The military uprising to seize power was a prerequisite for the transformation. Most of the Decembrists were army officers, often from aristocratic families and elite regiments, who had received a good education, learned French and sometimes other foreign languages, and obtained a firsthand knowledge of the West during and immediately after the campaigns against Napoleon. Essentially, the Decembrists were liberals in the tradition of the Enlightenment and the French Revolution; they wanted to establish constitutionalism and basic freedoms in Russia, and to abolish serfdom. More specifically, the Decembrist plans ranged from those of Nikita Muraviev, who advocated a rather conservative constitutional monarchy and supported the idea of a constituent assembly to decide the future structure of Russia, to those of the authoritarian Colonel Paul Pestel, the author of *Russian Justice*, who favored a strongly centralized republic along Jacobin lines, as well as a peculiar land reform program that would divide land into a public and a private sector and guarantee every citizen his allotment within the public sector. *Russian Justice* was meticulous, precise, and comprehensive, although it remained incomplete; Pestel, like Speransky, was a brilliant devotee of the *ésprit de système* of his age.

At first the liberals who later became Decembrists were eager to cooperate with the government on the road of progress, and their early societies—the Union of Salvation, founded in 1816, and the subsequent Union of Welfare—were concerned with such issues as the development of philanthropy, education, and the civic spirit in Russia rather than with military rebellion. Only gradually, as reaction grew and hopes for a liberal transformation from above faded away, did the more stubborn liberals begin to think seriously of change by force and to talk of revolution and regicide. The movement acquired two centers, St. Petersburg in the north and Tulchin, the headquarters of the Second Army, in southern Russia. The northern group lacked leadership and accomplished little. In the south, by contrast, Pestel acted with intelligence and determination. The Southern Society grew in numbers, developed its organization, discovered and incorporated the Society of the United Slavs, and established contacts with a Polish revolutionary group. The United Slavs, who pursued aims vaguely similar to those of the Decembrists and had the additional goal of a democratic federation of all Slavic peoples, and who accepted the Decembrist leadership, consisted in particular of poor army officers, more democratic and closer to the soldiers than were the aristocrats from the guard. Yet when the hour of rebellion suddenly arrived, the Southern Society, handicapped by Pestel's arrest, proved to be little better prepared than the Northern.

Alexander I's unexpected death in southern Russia in December 1825 led to a dynastic crisis, which the Decembrists utilized to make their bid for power. The deceased emperor had no son or grandson; therefore, Grand Duke Constantine, his oldest brother, was his logical successor. But the heir presumptive had married a Polish aristocrat not of royal blood in 1820 and, in connection with the marriage, had renounced his rights to the throne. Nicholas, the third brother, was thus to become the next ruler of Russia, the entire matter having been stated clearly in 1822 in a special manifesto confirmed by Alexander I's signature. The manifesto, however, had remained unpublished, and very few people had received exact information about it; even the two grand dukes were ignorant of its precise content. Following Alexander I's death, Constantine and the Polish kingdom where he was commander-in-chief swore allegiance to Nicholas, but Nicholas, the Russian capital, and the Russian army swore allegiance to Constantine. Constantine acted with perfect consistency. Nicholas, however, even after reading Alexander I's manifesto, also felt impelled to behave as he did: Alexander I's decision could be challenged as contrary to Paul's law of succession and also for remaining unpublished during the emperor's own reign, and Nicholas was under pressure to step aside in favor of his elder brother, who was generally expected to follow Alexander I on the throne. Only after Constantine's uncompromising reaffirmation of his position, and a resulting lapse of time, did Nicholas decide to publish Alexander's manifesto and become emperor of Russia.

On December 26, 1825 (December 14, Old Style), when the guard regiments in St. Petersburg were to swear allegiance for the second time within a short while, this time to Nicholas, the Northern Society of the Decembrists staged its rebellion. Realizing that they had a unique chance to act, the conspiring officers used their influence with the soldiers to start a mutiny in several units by entreating them to defend the rightful interests of Constantine against his usurping brother. Altogether about three thousand misled rebels came in military formation to the Senate Square in the heart of the capital. Although the government was caught unprepared, the mutineers were soon faced by troops several times their number and strength. The two forces stood opposite each other for several hours. The Decembrists failed to act because of their general confusion and lack of leadership; the new emperor hesitated to start his reign with a massacre of his subjects, hoping that they could be talked into submission. But, as verbal inducements failed and dusk began to fall, artillery was brought into action. Several canister shots dispersed the rebels, killing sixty or seventy of them. Large-scale arrests followed. In the south, too, an uprising was easily suppressed. Eventually, five Decembrist leaders, including Pestel and the firebrand of the Northern Society, the poet Conrad Ryleev, were executed, while almost three hundred other participants suffered lesser punishment.

As already emphasized, the Decembrists belonged wholly to general European culture and were carried by main currents of European thought. Appropriately, some of the Decembrist material has come down to us in French, while parts of their Russian Nachlass read like translated French. More precisely, their immediate ambiance, like that of Alexander I and his Unofficial Committee, was that of the late Enlightenment and of the years of the French Revolution and Napoleon. At least a dozen major thinkers of the Age of Reason exercised important influence on Pestel, while on the whole he can perhaps be best described as a Jacobin. Nikita Muraviev's constitution reflected, among other Western sources, the French Constitution of 1791, the Spanish Constitution of 1812, and the United States Constitution. While more recent studies have stressed newer elements in Decembrist thought, such as its historical sense, patriotism, nationalism, and even a certain xenophobia,[22] these trends, although indeed present among the Decembrists and indicative of changing times, did not seriously affect the thoroughly Age of Reason allegiance and ideology of the Decembrist movement. They belonged to the future, Decembrism—to the past.

The problem of the relationship of the Decembrists to the government continues to fascinate scholars. Aristocrats and officers of elite regiments, the members of the movement belonged to the top of Russian society. As already emphasized, they resembled friends and advisers of Alexander I in their social background, French culture, general education, and ideology of the Age of Reason. Progressive reforms and constitution-making preoccupied both groups. The early Decembrist societies naturally wanted to further the good intentions of the government. Even later, when philanthropic associations were becoming conspiracies, Alexander I made his famous comment on an informer's report to the effect that it was not for him to punish these men and these ideas. In fact, the Decembrist movement, or rather many of its members, remained psychologically so close to the government and so permeated by the concept of enlightened despotism that their position was ambivalent to the end. This psychological ambiguity helps to explain the critical collapse of the Decembrist leadership, especially in the North, at the time of the uprisings. Colonel Prince Sergei Trubetskoi, who had been elected "dictator" for the occasion, and his ranking assistants, Colonel Alexander Bulatov and Captain Alexander Iakubovich, all deserted the rebel cause. The Decembrists who did lead their troops in rebellion on December 14 showed a crucial lack of initiative during the hours of confrontation. It is generally agreed that their one hope of success lay in quick and decisive action; but nothing was done. And these were some of the bravest and most daring officers of Russia. The psychological ambiguity must also account in large part for the collapse of the Decembrists during the interrogation and the trial, when many of them confessed and repented and also tried desperately to enlighten the monarch about the true condition of Russia so he would reform it. Nicholas I, it should be added, made full and detailed use of this major psychological weakness of the conspirators.

But the Decembrists' clinging to the monarch and the government could be a result not only of an intellectual tradition going back to Peter the Great, or of emotion, but also of a sense of reality. Once the Decembrists made the break, they were horribly isolated. In addition to their own small numbers—and even some of their own, as I have just shown, proved unreliable at the critical moment—they could expect understanding and backing only from some other young members of the cultural elite, including such literary luminaries as Alexander Pushkin and Alexander Griboedov, as well as a broader personal sympathy in the high society to which they belonged, especially after they were cruelly punished. All this amounted to very little in terms of overthrowing the imperial regime and reforming Russia. The Decembrists could not expect support from their own social stratum, because that stratum was already ruling the country—quite literally ruling as governors huge parts of it, as in the case of Pestel's father or of Dmitri Zavalishin's. The Decembrist rebellion was, among other things, a remarkable generational revolt. Only ten Decembrists were over forty years old, only one over forty-six. Even more striking, in this thoroughly military uprising, a mere lieutenant had to command troops in the Senate Square. A possible Decembrist appeal to the gentry as a whole was bound to suffer from the limited education of the gentry, as well as from the emphasis of the Decembrists on the abolition of serfdom and their other attacks on gentry rights. Although Pestel, Nikita Muraviev, and their friends wanted to promote the middle classes in Russia, they had no connection with these classes, and their very hopes for them referred only to the future. Similarly, the Decembrists had no connection with the peasants and indeed were afraid of peasant rebellions and determined to keep the people quiet while transforming Russia—although the huge crowds in and around the Senate Square were certainly on the Decembrist side. Even soldiers were to follow their Decembrist officers because of discipline and personal loyalty, not out of ideological conviction. The military historian of the uprising, G. S. Gabaev, pointed out that the revolt of December 14 was staged by units whose honorary head was Grand Duke Constantine, as opposed to those whose patron was Grand Duke Nicholas.[23] An untrustworthy but appropriate story claimed that for soldiers in the Senate Square, shouts for Constantine and constitution meant Grand Duke Constantine and his wife. In the south, efforts to propagandize the soldiers for the Decembrist cause were few and late, although occasionally strikingly antimonarchist. All in all, the balance of forces would seem to indicate that ultimately the Decembrists had very slight chances of success, even if they were to gain some initial advantage by decisive action in the capital.

Contrary to what the government claimed, the Decembrists were not immature criminals but remarkably well educated, gifted, and precocious representatives of their generation, a true elite. Even in terms of careers, they were faring excellently until the catastrophe of December 14. Moreover, the Decembrists did their best to adapt the principles of the Age of Reason to Russia, mounting a frontal attack on serfdom and proposing many other eminently relevant and practical reforms in the army and elsewhere. On the whole, they represented the best and the most far-reaching response made, within the framework of the Enlightenment, by the Russian educated public to the needs of Russia. What was missing in the Decembrist plans to transform their native country—as well as in the original intentions of Alexander I's Unofficial Committee and the later constitutions prepared for the emperor, all of which, so to speak, remained hanging in the air—was not intelligence or ideas but context and support. The special tragedy of the Decembrist effort was that at the end of it five prominent Decembrists were hanging from the gallows. (Pushkin kept doodling gallows in one of his manuscripts.)

The Reign of Nicholas I, 1825–1855, and the New Intellectual Climate

*Here [in the army] there is order, there is a strict unconditional
legality, no impertinent claims to know all the answers, no
contradiction, all things flow logically one from the other; no one
commands before he has himself learned to obey; no one steps in front
of anybody else without lawful reason; everything is subordinated to
one definite goal, everything has its purpose. That is why I feel so well
among these people, and why I shall always hold in honor the calling
of a soldier. I consider the entire human life to be merely service,
because everybody serves.*

—Nicholas I

*Our common obligation consists in this that the education of the
people be conducted, according to the Supreme intention of our
August Monarch, in the joint spirit of Orthodoxy, autocracy, and
nationality.*

—S. S. Uvarov

*Every age, every nation contains in itself the possibility of original
art, provided it believes in something, provided it loves something,
provided it has some religion, some ideal.*

—A. S. Khomiakov

The reign of Nicholas I can be treated in terms of continuity as well as of change. Indeed, it resembled in many important and less important ways that of his older brother and predecessor.[1] Neither sovereign challenged the fundamental Russian realities of autocracy and serfdom. Both, however, enacted certain more modest and limited reforms. Nicholas I's reorganization of state peasants can be considered a rather substantial contribution to the kind of partial improvement in peasant life inaugurated by such measures of Alexander I as the law concerning the free agriculturists. Similarly, Speransky's codification of Russian law represented a logical continuation of improvements to the structure and functioning of the Russian government and polity in the earlier reign. In foreign policy, the younger brother was only too conscious of continuity with the older, of the legacy of the Congress of Vienna and the alliance system. In terms of principles, Nicholas I maintained the Russian tradition as both the head and the first servant of the state, and he admired Peter I fervently. Even as to character, it is worth remembering that Alexander I too was a perfectionist and a drill sergeant, suspicious, given to rages, and determined to keep all authority to himself in matters great and small. Both militarism and obscurantism existed in Russia before 1825 as well as after.

But the difference was also important. It was as if Nicholas I's rule reproduced and developed comprehensively and consistently many basic aspects of his brother's rule. Alexander's reign, however, like the emperor's baffling and contradictory character, had another side, which Nicholas's regime and Nicholas conspicuously lacked. Alexander I was an autocrat, but an autocrat in love with constitutions. He was a despot, but a despot who believed in Enlightenment. Even his foreign policy could not be simply summarized as legitimism and a defense of the status quo. Whereas Alexander I talked to Prince Peter Viazemsky and others about his determination to introduce Novosiltsev's constitution in Russia, a project that was to him "sacred," Nicholas I, after the recapture of Warsaw, wrote as follows to Prince Ivan Paskevich, the Russian commander, concerning that same constitution, which the Poles had found and published.

> Chertkov brought me a copy of the constitutional project for Russia found in Novosiltsev's papers. The publication of this paper is most annoying. Out of a hundred of our young officers ninety will read it, will fail to understand it or will scorn it, but ten will retain it in their memory, will discuss it—and, the most important point, *will not forget it.* This worries me above everything else. This is why I wish so much that the guards be kept in Warsaw as briefly as possible. Order Count Witt to try to obtain as many copies of this booklet as he can and to destroy them, also to find the manuscript and send it to me.[2]

Novosiltsev, to be sure, remained as a senior statesman of the empire. Indeed, the efforts and aspirations of such figures as Novosiltsev, Kochubei, and Speransky himself, under Alexander I and under Nicholas I, illustrate admirably the continuity, but also the change, between the two reigns.

Nicholas I was well suited to follow a simple and straight line of behavior. By contrast with his predecessor's psychological paradoxes, ambivalence, and vacillation, the new sovereign displayed determination, singleness of purpose, and an iron will. He also possessed an overwhelming sense of duty and a great capacity for work. In character, and even in his striking and powerful appearance, Nicholas I seemed to be the perfect despot. Appropriately, he always remained an army man, a junior officer at heart, devoted to his troops, to military exercises, to the parade ground—in fact, as emperor, he ordered alterations of the uniforms, even changing the number of buttons. And in the same spirit, the autocrat insisted on arranging and ordering minutely and precisely everything around him. Engineering, especially the construction of defenses, was Nicholas's other enduring passion. Even as a child, "whenever he built a summer house, for his nurse or his governess, out of chairs, earth, or toys, he never forgot *to fortify* it with guns—*for protection.*"[3] Later, specializing in fortresses, he became head of the army corps of engineers and thus the chief military engineer in his country, perhaps his most important assignment during the reign of his brother; still later, as emperor, he staked all on making the entire land an impregnable fortress.

Nicholas's views fitted his personality to perfection. Born in 1796 and nineteen years younger than Alexander, the new ruler was brought up not in the atmosphere of the late Enlightenment like his brother but in that of wars against Napoleon and of reaction. Moreover, Nicholas married a Prussian princess and established particularly close ties with his wife's family, including his father-in-law, King Frederick William III, and his brother-in-law, King Frederick William IV, who ruled Prussia in succession. Devotion to the defense of the established order against subversion and revolution implied pessimism. In contrast to the organic optimism of the Enlightenment and its expanding vistas, the new intellectual and emotional climate stressed duty, endurance, holding the line, performing one's task to the end. And Nicholas I bore his immense burden faithfully for thirty years, into the catastrophe of the Crimean War. When his diplomatic system collapsed, the weary monarch commented: "Nothing remains to me but my duty as long as it pleases God to leave me at the head of Russia."[4] "I shall carry my cross until all my strength is gone."[5] "Thy will be done."[6] Rarely does one find such congruity between a historical period and a man's character and convictions.

The government ideology, which came to be known as Official Nationality, was proclaimed on April 2, 1833, by the new minister of Education, Sergei Uvarov, in his first circular to the officials in charge of the educational districts of the Russian empire. Uvarov (1786–1855), that "fortunate and flexible nature,"[7] a precocious product of the Enlightenment and even something of a freethinker, as well as a scholar, a writer, and from 1818 the president of the Academy of Sciences, belonged to those liberal European aristocrats, who, in changed political circumstances, discovered religion, authority, and tradition.[8] It was Uvarov who, in the circular quoted in the epigraph to this chapter, declared that all education in Russia must be conducted in the joint spirit of Orthodoxy, autocracy, and nationality.

The minister proceeded to propound and promote his three cardinal principles throughout the sixteen years during which he remained in charge of public instruction in Russia. In reports to the emperor, as well as in orders to subordinates, he presented these principles invariably as the true treasure of the Russian people and the

Russian state. For instance, Uvarov discussed the matter as follows in the survey of his first decade in office, submitted for imperial approval.

In the midst of the rapid collapse in Europe of religious and civil institutions, at the time of a general spread of destructive ideas, at the sight of grievous phenomena surrounding us on all sides, it was necessary to establish our fatherland on firm foundations upon which is based the well-being, strength, and life of a people; it was necessary to find the principles which form the distinctive character of Russia, and which belong only to Russia; it was necessary to gather into one whole the sacred remnants of Russian nationality and to fasten to them the anchor of our salvation. Fortunately, Russia had retained a warm faith in the sacred principles without which she cannot prosper, gain in strength, live. Sincerely and deeply attached to the church of his fathers, the Russian has of old considered it the guarantee of social and family happiness. Without a love for the faith of its ancestors a people, as well as an individual, must perish. A Russian, devoted to his fatherland, will agree as little to the loss of a single dogma of our *Orthodoxy* as to the theft of a single pearl from the tsar's crown. *Autocracy* constitutes the main condition of the political existence of Russia. The Russian giant stands on it as on the cornerstone of his greatness. An innumerable majority of the subjects of *Your Majesty* feel this truth; they feel it in full measure although they are placed on different rungs of civil life and although they vary in education and in their relations to the government. The saving conviction that Russia lives and is protected by the spirit of a strong, humane, and enlightened autocracy must permeate popular education and must develop with it. Together with these two national principles there is a third, no less powerful: *nationality*.[9]

It was for his long service to the three sacred principles that Uvarov was made a count. Still more appropriately, Nicholas I granted him the words "Orthodoxy, autocracy, nationality" as his family motto.

The doctrine of Official Nationality constituted the Russian version of the general European ideology of restoration and reaction that accompanied the fall of Napoleon and a substantial restoration of the old order on the Continent. "Orthodoxy" referred to the official Church and its important role in Russia, but also to the ultimate source of ethics and ideals that gave meaning to Russian life and society. "Autocracy" meant the affirmation and maintenance of the absolute power of the sovereign, which was considered to be the magnificent and indispensable foundation of the Russian state. "Nationality"—*narodnost* in Russian—referred to the particular nature of the Russian people, which, so the official doctrine asserted, made this people a mighty and dedicated supporter of its Church, dynasty, and government. However, with some proponents of Official Nationality, especially professors and writers such as Michael Pogodin and Stephen Shevyrev, "nationality" acquired far-reaching Romantic connotations. In particular, the concept for them embraced a longing for a great future for Russia and Slavdom. The dynastic and the Romantic emphases continued to be present in the doctrine of Official Nationality, in mutual support but also in opposition and strife, throughout the effective existence of that doctrine, that is, not only until the death of Nicholas I in 1855 but until 1917, although in the government, at least, the dynastic approach prevailed.[10]

Many poets, writers, professors, and journalists proved eager to echo Uvarov's battle cry, sometimes with a respectful bow in his direction; Stephen Shevyrev, to give one example, followed the minister in 1841 in his analysis of Russia and the West for the first issue of the journal the *Muscovite*. He asserted, in his usual ponderous and involved manner:

> But even if we did pick up certain unavoidable blemishes from our contacts with the West, we have on the other hand preserved in ourselves, in their purity, three fundamental feelings which contain the seed and the guarantee of our future development. We have retained our ancient religious feeling. The Christian cross had left its sign on our entire religious education, on the entire Russian life. . . . The second feeling which makes Russia strong and which secures its future well-being is the feeling of our state unity, again derived by us from our entire history. There is certainly no country in Europe which can boast of such a harmonious political existence as our fatherland. Almost everywhere in the West dissension as to principles has been recognized as a law of life, and the entire existence of peoples transpires in heavy struggle. Only in our land the tsar and the people compose one unbreakable whole, not tolerating any obstacle between them: this connection is founded on the mutual feeling of love and faith and on the boundless devotion of the people to its tsar. . . . Our third fundamental feeling is our consciousness of our nationality and our conviction that any enlightenment can be firmly rooted in our land only when it is assimilated by our national feeling and expressed by our national thought and national word. . . . Because of the three fundamental feelings our Russia is firm, and her future is secure. A statesman of the Council of the Tsar, to whom are entrusted those generations which are being educated, already long ago expressed them in a profound thought, and they have formed the foundation of the upbringing of the people.[11]

In addition to the *Muscovite*, a score or more other periodicals proclaimed "Orthodoxy, autocracy, and nationality" as their articles of faith. They ranged from the fantastically reactionary, obscurantist, and nationalist *Lighthouse* to formal and pedantic government publications, such as Uvarov's own *Journal of the Ministry of Education*. A newspaper with a very wide circulation, the *Northern Bee*, published by the grammarian Nicholas Grech and the most notorious journalist of the period, Thaddeus, or Faddei, Bulgarin, was of particular assistance in disseminating the minister's views throughout the length and breadth of Russia. So was a similarly popular magazine, the *Reader's Library*, produced by another notorious and fantastic Pole who was a gifted orientalist: Joseph, or Osip, Senkovsky. In fact, until the end of the reign of Nicholas I, Uvarov's brief formula dominated most of the Russian press. The three sacred principles appeared in many different works, in and out of context, but they became especially common in textbooks and popularizations with a wide circulation.

Indeed, before long "Orthodoxy, autocracy, nationality" came to represent much more than Uvarov's attempt at philosophizing, more even than the guiding principles of the Ministry of Education. The formula expanded in application and significance to stand for the Russia of Nicholas I. Military cadets were enjoined to become "Christians," "loyal subjects," and "Russians," in that order. [12] The entire nation was to rally for "faith, tsar, and fatherland," the phrase used, for instance, in the famous, and to many contemporaries and later scholars baffling, 1848 manifesto defying the revolutionary West.[13] The emperor himself dedicated his life to the service of Orthodoxy, autocracy, and Russia, and everyone else in the government was expected to follow the monarch. At the same time, a considerable part of the educated Russian public, led by prominent professors, writers, and journalists, hoisted the three words as their banner. These adherents ranged from some figures of surpassing genius, such as Gogol, Tiutchev, and, to some extent, Pushkin, to humdrum scribblers and poetasters, from true believers to careerists and adventurers. "Orthodoxy, autocracy, nationality" were interpreted to mean the past, the present, and the future of Russia, Russian tradition as well as Russian mission, Russian culture as much as Russian politics.

To be sure, the proponents of Official Nationality did not do full justice to the first article of their creed, Orthodoxy. While emphasizing devoted membership in the Orthodox Church and proclaiming Orthodox Christianity as the ultimate measure and goal of human existence, they were generally suspicious of all philosophy, even of theology—practiced, for example, by some of their Slavophile contemporaries. Nor, whatever their goodwill and intent, were they successful in implementing their Christian ideals in life. Instead, the Russian school system and the literature of Official Nationality teemed with moral lessons intended to edify and instruct the Russian people. Crude at best, these lectures became extremely cheap and vulgar when dispensed by such shady and facile journalists as Bulgarin, with his innumerable moral tales. But, avoiding Bulgarin, one might cite a true literary giant, Gogol, whose *Selected Passages from Correspondence with Friends*, published in 1847, gave an equally authentic, even exaggerated, expression to official ideology and produced a scandal in Russian intellectual circles. For example, Gogol advised a landlord:

> Take up the task of landlord as it should be taken up in the true and lawful sense. First of all, gather the peasants and explain to them what you are and

what they are: that you are the landlord over them not because you want to rule and be a landlord, but because you are already a landlord, because you were born a landlord, because God will punish you if you were to exchange this condition for any other, because everyone must serve God in his own place, not someone else's, just as they, having been born under authority, must submit to the same authority under which they were born, for there is no authority which is not from God. And right then show it to them in the Gospel so that they all, down to the last one, will see it. After that tell them that you force them to labor and work not at all because you need the money for your pleasures, and, as a proof, burn right there in front of them some bills, and make it so that they actually see that money means nothing to you. Tell them that you force them to work because God decreed that man earn his bread in labor and sweat, and right there read it to them in Holy Writ so that they will see it. Tell them the whole truth: that God will make you answer for the last scoundrel in the village, and that, therefore, you will all the more see to it that they work honestly not only for you, but also for themselves; for you know, and they know it too, that, once he has become lazy, a peasant is capable of anything—he will turn into a thief and a drunkard, he will ruin his soul, and also make you answerable to God. And everything that you tell them confirm on the spot with words from Holy Writ; point with your finger to the very letters with which it is written, make each one first cross himself, bow to the ground, and kiss the book itself in which it is written. In one word, make them see clearly that in everything that concerns them you are acting in accordance with the will of God and not in accordance with some European or other fancies of your own. [14]

A different instance of the religious mentality of the proponents of Official Nationality is the following statement by Count Alexander Benckendorff, the chief of gendarmes and one of the closest associates of the emperor: "Kiev was selected as the place for the new university, this city being, on the one hand, the ancient cradle of Orthodoxy, and, on the other, the headquarters of the First Army, which offered all the necessary facilities for the surveillance of a large gathering of young people." [15] No wonder that the appeal to "Orthodoxy" in the doctrine of Official Nationality has frequently been considered a gigantic fraud or, at least, a thorough misuse of religion. Religion was utilized to preach obedience to the emperor, the officer, and the landlord. The government, which taught meekness and charity, distinguished itself by despotism and brutality. Even the Church itself was controlled by the state and generally did its bidding. Unfortunately, it fell to those living in the twentieth century to witness the work of governments totally unencumbered by religious and moral principles.

The second article of the creed of Official Nationality, "autocracy," usually included at least two items: the absolute nature of imperial power, and the link between the emperor and God. The law of the land declared: "The Tsar of all the Russias is an autocratic and absolute monarch. God Himself commands us to obey the Tsar's supreme authority, not from fear alone, but as a point of conscience." [16] For, in the last analysis, God provided the foundation for the authority of the tsar; and most proponents of Official Nationality were well aware of the connection. Such statements as "the heart of the tsar is in the hand of the Lord," Pogodin's favorite, indicated this awareness. It also found expression in the constant joining of the images of the monarch and of God, one of the most common motifs in the poetry and the prose of Official Nationality. Typically, in such composite pictures the tsar was represented as the absolute ruler of his great realm yet begging guidance and support from the ultimate ruler of the world, God.

The belief in autocracy was also based on the conviction of the inherent weakness and even wickedness of human beings, and of the resulting need for a strong, authoritarian rule over them. As is true of most conservative or reactionary teachings, Official Nationality was a profoundly pessimistic doctrine. Its low estimate of humanity fitted neatly into the Christian framework, if at the cost of neglecting certain basic aspects of Christianity. One of Uvarov's favorite arguments, in his classical research as well as in his other writings, dealt with the fall of man from his initial state of grace, the fact "which alone contains the key to all history."[17] Similarly, Pogodin found everywhere "proofs of the fall of man (which continued in us), of our impaired nature."[18] Grech's *Memoirs* refer to mankind as a "despicable and ungrateful tribe" and note, in connection with Alexander I's sponsorship of the Bible Society, that "human viciousness turns even a medicinal drink into poison, and by its machinations extracts damage and poison from the Word of God."[19] Even Senkovsky's allegiance to Official Nationality has been credited to his skeptical view of the Russian people.[20] The same pessimism and disillusionment constituted fundamental traits in the personality of Nicholas I himself.

Because men were feeble and perverse, they had to be driven by a benevolent supreme authority in order to achieve desirable social ends. Pogodin combined loud praise of the Russian people, in line with new Romantic philosophy, with some reservations on the subject. As early as 1826 he observed: "The Russian people is marvellous, but marvellous so far only in potentiality. In actuality it is low, horrid, and beastly." And he went on to assert that Russian peasants "will not become human beings until they are forced into it."[21] Grech proclaimed dogmatically: "Men are not angels; there are many devils among them. Therefore, police, and a severe police, is a necessity both for the state and for all private individuals."[22] He commented as follows on the reign of Nicholas I as contrasted to that of his predecessor:

> Pepper too is required in a salad! Alexander was too meek replacing during the first years firmness of character with kindness and compassion. This is too good for the vile human species. Now there, I love our Nicholas! When he is gracious, he is really gracious, but when he hits, then willy-nilly they

sing: "God, save the Tsar!" Truthfulness, directness, sincerity compose, in my opinion, the greatness of any person, especially of a tsar. Why be crafty, when one can issue orders and use the whip? [23]

While social betterment depended on government initiative, the state had a still more immediate and fundamental task to perform: to preserve law and order. Bulgarin wrote with unusual conviction:

> It is better to unchain a hungry tiger or a hyena than to take off the people the bridle of obedience to authorities and laws. There is no beast fiercer than a raging mob! All the efforts of the educated class must be directed toward enlightening the people concerning its obligations to God, to lawful authorities and laws, toward the establishment of the love of man in the heart, toward the eradication of the beastly egoism inborn in man, and not toward exciting passions, not toward generating unrealizable hopes. Whoever acts differently is a criminal according to the law of humanity. One who has seen a popular rebellion knows what it means.[24]

The government knew. Nicholas I and his officials proceeded to emphasize above all the perfect maintenance of discipline and order, punishing relentlessly all opposition and disaffection. In theory, too, Tiutchev and other ideologists stressed the role of the Russian emperor as the mainstay of law, morality, and civilization against individual license, subversion, and revolution.

Not only did an autocrat embody the ideal form of supreme rule, but at lower levels of government, too, everything depended on men. Echoing Karamzin's earlier opinions, and in particular his emphasis on fifty good governors as the true need of Russia, Pogodin explained the matter as follows.

> There is no institution or law which cannot be abused, something that is being done promptly everywhere; therefore, institutions and laws are not as important as the people on whom depends their functioning. [25]
>
> One educated, zealous, active superior—and the entire department entrusted to him is, under the system of publicity, aiding other departments by its example, organization and training officials. One governor with such qualities—and one-fiftieth part of Russia is prosperous, a second, a third—and all the people cannot recognize themselves, they will be the same and yet not the same in this general uplift. [26]

Force had to be at the ready, and sometimes it had to be applied, but the political and social ideal of Official Nationality remained not state terrorism but a paternal or patriarchal relationship. Pogodin, the historian, wrote:

> There it is, I shall add here, the secret of Russian history, the secret which not a single Western sage is able to comprehend. Russian history always depicts Russia as a single family in which the ruler is the father and the subjects the

children. The father retains complete authority over the children while he allows them to have full freedom. Between the father and the children there can be no suspicion, no treason; their fate, their happiness and their peace they share in common. This is true in relation to the state as a whole, but one notices a reflection of the same law also in parts; the military commander must be the father of his soldiers, the landlord must be the father of his peasants, and even servants in the house of every master were called children of the house in the expressive old language. As long as this union is sacred and undamaged, so long there is peace and happiness—as soon as it begins to waver, no matter where, there appear disorder, confusion, and alarm. [27]

Gogol made the same general point: "Do not forget that in the Russian language ... a superior is called father."[28]

As Pogodin's discussion of "the secret of Russian history" indicated, autocracy found justification not only in religion and in the nature of man, but also in history. Sharing in new currents of thought, the proponents of Official Nationality showed a remarkable awareness of history and the historical approach. Nicholas I read avidly everything dealing with the Russian past, both original documents and secondary works. It was in his reign that chairs of Russian history, as distinct from world history, were established in the universities of the empire, and large sums of money were devoted to the gathering and publication of source materials. Historians and historians of literature, such as Pogodin and Shevyrev at the University of Moscow and Nicholas Ustrialov at the University of St. Petersburg, made important contributions to the development and dissemination of the ideology of the state. Academic writing was supplemented by journalism and fiction. The age of Romanticism proved to be especially favorable in Russia, as elsewhere, to historical drama, novel, and story. Their qualities ranged from such rare masterpieces as Pushkin's *Boris Godunov* to Michael Zagoskin's trite novels, Nestor Kukolnik's feeble plays, and even Bulgarin's insipid tales about the early Slavs. Most of these works were very poor history, but they helped to provide sustenance and form to the interest in the past. History, in one way or another, became the center of attention and controversy. "The historian represented"—in the words of Pogodin—"the crowning achievement of a people, for through him the people came to an understanding of itself."[29]

The work that presented best the salutary impact of autocracy on Russia was Karamzin's brilliant twelve-volume *History of the Russian State*, interrupted at the Time of Troubles by its author's death in 1826.[30] Karamzin held the position of official historian, and he also won immense favor with the reading public. Repetitions of his theme and variations on it became extremely common in the reign of Nicholas I. Autocracy received incessant praise for binding the Russians together and leading, or driving, them to new prosperity, power, and glory. Highly representative of this approach was Ustrialov's *Russian History*, which Uvarov adopted as a textbook in the schools of the empire and which he commended enthusiastically in a report to the monarch. [31]

The entire history of Russia foreshadowed and justified Nicholas I's regime, but its direct line of descent stemmed from Peter the Great. The proponents of Official Nationality, from the monarch himself downward, admired, almost worshiped, the titanic emperor. The historians among them, Pogodin, Shevyrev, and Ustrialov, paid special attention to his personality and reign. Pogodin, to take the most interesting example, fell in his youth, if not earlier, under the fascination of the great reformer, this "Russian to the highest degree," the "human god." [32] Later, although specializing in an earlier period of Russian history, he taught a course on Peter the Great's reign, collected documents related to it, and wrote on the subject both as historian and publicist. The reforming emperor even inspired Pogodin to compose a tragedy in verse, "Peter I," which dealt with a particularly painful episode of Peter's life, his condemnation of his own son Alexis to death, and which was written as an apotheosis of his sense of duty and of his services to Russia. [33]

Pogodin's preoccupation with Peter the Great was dull, blunt, crude, and obsessive; Pushkin's treatment of him was brilliant, graceful, and sensitive but also obsessive. The difference emphasized the chasm between awkward prose and magnificent verse, and, beyond that, between mediocrity and supreme genius. Yet both writers were under the spell of the great emperor, and the themes they kept repeating in their works showed profound similarities. Pushkin dealt with him in such accomplished pieces as "Poltava" and "The Bronze Horseman," as well as in notes, letters, and conversation. He was working on a history of Peter the Great when he was killed in a duel. Pushkin's Peter, as well as Pogodin's, was above all the glorious hero of Poltava, the almost superhuman leader of his country, who gave Russia new life and a new history, symbolized by St. Petersburg, Pushkin's beloved city. He stood for reform, light, progress, for the present strength of the nation, and for its future destiny. Still, Pushkin was concerned for the common man writhing in the clutches of the leviathan emperor and state. In his extensive study of the time of Peter the Great, the poet became increasingly impressed by the ruthlessness and cruelty of the overwhelming monarch and his measures. Pushkin's own life seemed to repeat the same tale: he found himself controlled, restricted, directed, and generally hounded at every turn by Peter the Great's state and by Peter's successor, another powerful and autocratic emperor, Nicholas I.

These elements and, no doubt, many others went into the making of Pushkin's masterpiece "The Bronze Horseman." In this story of a poor, ordinary man, Eugene, who lost his beloved in a St. Petersburg flood, went mad, dared challenge the bronze statue of the builder of the city, and then ran in mortal terror, pursued by it, the poet presented both the might and the harshness of Peter the Great and of Russian autocracy. While extending sympathy to the unfortunate Eugene, Pushkin depicted the Bronze Horseman as an infinitely majestic, almost divine figure, the greatness and permanence of whose work the poet affirmed powerfully in the introduction.

The astounding lines devoted to the emperor, not those describing Eugene, became a treasure of Russian verse. Pushkin's tale is a tragedy, but its composite parts are not evenly balanced: above all rises the autocratic state sweeping on to its grand destiny, undeterred by the obstacles of nature, such as swamps and floods, and impervious to the pain, the sorrow, and even the opposition of the individual, exemplified by Eugene's miserable plight and his pathetic rebellion. Pushkin's "Bronze Horseman," as well as his treatment of Peter the Great in general, represented his closest approach to the doctrine of Official Nationality. It was, so to speak, the poet's compromise with Russian historical reality: one course open to those who were fortunate to survive 1825 unharmed.[34]

The third article of the government creed, *narodnost,* or nationality, was at the time and has since remained the most obscure, puzzling, and controversial element of the official trinity. While "Orthodoxy" and "autocracy" were relatively precise referring to an established faith and a distinct form of government, "nationality" possessed no single, generally accepted meaning. It has been most often interpreted as merely an appendage to "autocracy," an affirmation that the Russian people were happy, docile, and obedient subjects of their tsar and their landlords. According to that view, it served mainly as a propaganda device and possessed no significance of its own. Indeed, it has been equated by some simply with the defense of serfdom.

This assessment of "nationality" is largely valid, but it is incomplete. For, and to repeat, the term also had, in addition to its reactionary, dynastic, and defensive connotations, a Romantic frame of reference. And on the Romantic plane, "Russia" and "the Russian people" acquired a supreme metaphysical, even mystical, importance, leading to belief in the great mission of Russia, to such doctrines as Panslavism and such practices as Russification. Theories attempting to buttress the antique Russian regime met German Idealistic philosophy with its dizzying new vistas: Restoration met Romanticism. As mentioned earlier, the dynastic and the nationalistic elements in Official Nationality not only complemented but also contradicted each other. Their contrast and antagonism found expression in the strife between different groups of government ideologists. It was reflected more subtly in the change of position by certain proponents of the state views, while in still other instances, the contradictions remained concealed and implicit. In general, the concept of nationality accounted for the tensions and conflicts within the government doctrine—all the way to 1917.

The dynastic view was represented by Nicholas I himself, as well as by most members of his government and his court. It also found expression in such a loyal newspaper as the *Northern Bee* with its well-known editors, Grech and Bulgarin. The nationalist wing was led by the Moscow professors, Shevyrev and especially Pogodin, and it included the poet and publicist Tiutchev, as well as numerous participants in the *Muscovite.* The members of the latter group stood close to the Slavophiles—who will be discussed later—although they remained separated from them, primarily by the issue of the nature and role of the Russian state.[35] Moreover, judging by Barsukov's meticulous listing of Pogodin's contacts, nationalist student reactions, gendarmerie reports, and other evidence, they enjoyed considerable support among the Russian public. Indeed, the nationalists possessed, together with their much humbler background, a much wider appeal than the proponents of a dynastic orientation. But Romantic, nationalist ideas penetrated even the Russian government, increasingly affecting some of the ministers and other high officials, although they never grew strong enough to replace the essentially dynastic and *ancien régime* outlook of the emperor and of most of his aides. The proponents of the dynastic view centered in St. Petersburg, the capital; the nationalists in Moscow.

Uvarov, in his key position of minister of education, reflected these opposing influences in a striking manner. An aristocrat by origin, an outspoken defender of serfdom, and a man fully identified with the existing Russian regime, he nevertheless patronized nationalistic professors, dabbled in quasi-Romantic ideology in composing the famous triple formula, and wanted to play the role of a forward-thinking intellectual. The revolutions of 1848 made him recoil from nationalism and toe the line of extreme Russian reaction. Yet his support of official policy was found to be insufficiently complete and single-minded, and in 1849 Uvarov was forced to resign his ministry.

Official Nationality was part and parcel of European reaction, and all of its intellectual proponents were intimately connected with the West and Western culture. In fact, with the single important exception of Karamzin, no Russian writer influenced them as much or as significantly as did dozens of Western ones. A certain crudeness and lack of talent of the school served only to emphasize the derivative nature of its thought. [36] Even Shevyrev's extravagant account of the decline of the West was borrowed, in part, from a French publicist, Philarète Chasles. [37] When, after the revolutions of 1848, the government decided to isolate Russia completely from the intellectual development of the rest of Europe and proceeded to institute a ban on philosophy, Alexander Nikitenko noted in his diary: "Again a persecution of philosophy. It has been proposed to limit its teaching in the universities to logic and psychology, entrusting both to the clergy. The Scottish school is to serve as the foundation."[38]

The impact of the West varied, of course, in each individual case, being decisively affected by such factors as Uvarov's thoroughly cosmopolitan education and interests, Pogodin's and Shevyrev's voracious academic learning and eager travels abroad, Tiutchev's residence abroad, including some twenty years in Munich, where he came to know Schelling well personally, Grech's German background and Lutheran faith, Zhukovsky's immersion in Romantic literature and his marvelous ability to translate and adapt Western originals from many lands, or the aristocratic upbringing in the tradition of legitimism and Restoration of Nicholas I himself. Particular differences and nuances were very many. Yet at least one more general point needs to be made. The nationalists had an extremely high opinion of German Idealistic philosophy, above all of Schelling, and they were profoundly affected by that philosophy. Nicholas I and most of his dynastically oriented followers, on the other hand, paid no attention to Schelling and were suspicious and critical of the entire German school. It was at this intersection of opinion most especially that old reaction met new Romanticism.

Second rate at best intellectually, Official Nationality proved historically important for one reason: for thirty years it governed Russia. In particular, Nicholas I's reign reflected in a striking manner both the character and the principles of the ruler, that "most consistent of autocrats."[39] Nicholas's regime became preeminently one of militarism and bureaucracy. The emperor surrounded himself with military men, to the extent that in the later part of his reign, there were almost no civilians among his immediate assistants. He relied heavily on special emissaries, most of them generals of his suite, who were sent all over Russia on particular assignments to execute immediately the will of the sovereign. Operating outside the regular administrative system, they represented an extension, so to speak, of the monarch's own person. In fact, the entire machinery of government came to be permeated by the military spirit of direct orders, absolute obedience, and precision, at least as far as official reports and appearances were concerned. Corruption and confusion, however, lay immediately behind this facade of discipline and smooth functioning.

In his conduct of state affairs Nicholas I often bypassed regular channels, and he generally resented formal deliberation, consultation, or other procedural delay. The importance of the Committee of Ministers, the State Council, and the Senate decreased in the course of his reign. Instead of making full use of them, the emperor depended more and more on special devices meant to carry out his intentions promptly while remaining under his immediate and complete control. As one favorite method, he made extensive use of ad hoc committees standing outside the ordinary state machinery. The committees were usually composed of a handful of the most trusted assistants of the emperor, and because these were very few, the same men in different combinations kept forming committees throughout the reign. As a rule, the committees were secret, thus adding to the confusion.

The first, and in many ways the most significant, of Nicholas I's committees was that established on December 6, 1826, and lasting until 1832. Count Victor Kochubei served as its chairman, and the committee contained five other leading statesmen of the period. In contrast to the restricted assignments of later committees, the Committee of the Sixth of December had to examine the state papers and projects left by Alexander I, to reconsider all major aspects of government and social organization in Russia, and to propose improvements. The painstaking work of this select group of officials led to negligible results: entirely conservative in outlook, the committee directed its effort toward hair-splitting distinctions and minor, at times merely verbal, modifications; and it drastically qualified virtually every suggested change. Even its innocuous "law concerning the estates," which received imperial approval, was shelved after criticism by Grand Duke Constantine. This laborious futility became the characteristic pattern of most of the subsequent committees during the reign of

Nicholas I, in spite of the fact that the emperor himself often took an active part in their proceedings. The failure of one committee to perform its task merely led to the formation of another. For example, some nine committees in the reign of Nicholas I tried to deal with the issue of serfdom.

His Majesty's Own Chancery proved to be more effective than the special committees. Organized originally as a bureau to deal with matters that demanded the sovereign's personal participation and to supervise the execution of the emperor's orders, the Chancery grew rapidly in the reign of Nicholas I. As early as 1826, two new departments were added to it: the Second Department was concerned with the codification of law, and the Third with the administration of the newly created corps of gendarmes. In 1828 the Fourth Department was formed for the purpose of managing the charitable and educational institutions under the jurisdiction of the Dowager Empress Mary. Eight years later, the Fifth Department was created and charged with reforming the condition of the state peasants; after two years of activity, it was replaced by the new Ministry of State Domains. Finally, in 1843, the Sixth Department of His Majesty's Own Chancery came into being, a temporary agency assigned the task of drawing up an administrative plan for Transcaucasia. The departments of the Chancery served Nicholas I as a major means of conducting a personal policy that bypassed the regular state channels.

The Third Department of His Majesty's Own Chancery, the political police—which came to symbolize to many Russians the reign of Nicholas I—acted as the autocrat's main weapon against subversion and revolution and as his principal agency for controlling the behavior of his subjects and for distributing punishments and rewards among them. Its assigned fields of activity ranged from "all orders and reports in every case belonging to the higher police" to "reports about all occurrences without exception"![40] The new guardians of the state, dressed in sky-blue uniforms, were incessantly active:

> In their effort to embrace the entire life of the people, they intervened actually in every matter in which it was possible to intervene. Family life, commercial transactions, personal quarrels, projects of inventions, escapes of novices from monasteries—everything interested the secret police. At the same time the Third Department received a tremendous number of petitions, complaints, denunciations, and each one resulted in an investigation, each one became a separate case.[41]

The Third Department also prepared detailed, interesting, and remarkably candid reports for the emperor, supervised literature—an activity ranging from minute control over Pushkin to ordering various "inspired" articles in defense of Russia and the existing system—and fought every trace of revolutionary infection. The two successive heads of the Third Department, Count Alexander Benckendorff and Prince Alexis Orlov, probably spent more time with Nicholas I than any of his other assistants; they accompanied him, for instance, on his repeated trips of inspection throughout Russia. Yet most of the feverish activity of the gendarmes seemed to be to no purpose. Endless investigations of subversion, stimulated by the monarch's own suspiciousness, revealed very little. Even the most important radical group uncovered during the reign, the Petrashevtsy, fell victim not to the gendarmerie but to its great rival, the ordinary police, which continued to be part of the Ministry of the Interior.

The desire to control in detail the lives and thoughts of the people and above all to prevent subversion also guided the policies of the Ministry of Education, and in fact served as an inspiration for the entire reign. As in the building of fortresses, the emphasis was defensive: to hold fast against the enemy and to prevent his penetration. The sovereign himself worked indefatigably at shoring up the defenses. He paid the most painstaking attention to the huge and difficult business of government, did his own inspecting of the country, rushed to meet all kinds of emergencies, from cholera epidemics and riots to rebellions in military settlements, and bestowed special care on the army. Beyond all that, and beyond even the needs of defense, he wanted to follow the sacred principle of autocracy, to be a true father of his people, concerned with their daily lives, hopes, and fears.

Education continued to attract the attention of the emperor and his assistants. During the thirty years of Official Nationality, with Uvarov himself serving as minister of education from 1833 to 1849, the government tried to centralize and standardize education; to limit the individual's schooling according to his social background, so that each person would remain in his assigned place in life; to foster the official ideology exclusively; and, especially, to eliminate every trace or possibility of intellectual opposition or subversion.

As to centralization and standardization, Nicholas I and his associates did everything in their power to introduce absolute order and regularity into the educational system of Russia. The state extended its minute control to private schools and even to education in the home. By a series of laws and rules issued in 1833–1835, private institutions, which were not to increase in number in the future, except where public schooling was not available, received regulations and instructions from central authorities, while inspectors were appointed to assure their compliance. "They had to submit to the law of unity which formed the foundation of the reign." [42] Home education came under state influence through rigid government control of teachers: Russian private tutors began to be considered state employees, subject to appropriate examinations and enjoying the same pensions and awards as other comparable officials; at the same time, the government strictly prohibited the hiring of foreign instructors who did not possess the requisite certificates testifying to academic competence and exemplary moral character. Nicholas I himself led the way in supervising and inspecting schools in Russia, and the emperor's assistants followed his example.

The restrictive policies of the Ministry of Education resulted logically from its social views and aims. In order to ensure that each class of Russians obtained only "that part which it needs from the general treasury of enlightenment," the government resorted to increased tuition rates and to such requirements as the special certificate of leave that each pupil belonging to lower layers of society had to obtain from his village or town before he could attend secondary school. Members of the upper class, by contrast, received inducements to continue their education, with many boarding schools for the gentry being created for that purpose. Ideally, in the government scheme of things—and reality failed to live up to the ideal—children of peasants and of the lower classes in general were to attend only parish schools or other schools of similar educational level; students of middle-class origin were to study in the district schools; secondary schools and universities catered primarily, although not exclusively, to the gentry. Special efforts were made throughout the reign to restrict the education of the serfs to elementary and "useful" subjects. Schools for girls, which were under the patronage of Dowager Empress Mary and the jurisdiction of the Fourth Department of His Majesty's Own Chancery, served the same ideology as those for boys. Educational opportunities for women were limited, not only by their social origin but also by their sex. As in other countries, women had no access to higher education.

The inculcation of the true doctrine, that of Official Nationality, and a relentless struggle against all pernicious ideas constituted, of course, essential activities of the Ministry of Education. Only officially approved views received endorsement, and they had to be accepted without question rather than discussed. Teachers and students, lectures and books were generally suspect. In 1834, full-time inspectors were introduced into universities to keep vigil over the behavior of students outside the classroom. Education and knowledge, in the estimation of the emperor and his associates, could easily become subversion. With the revolutionary year of 1848, unrelieved repression set in. "Neither blame, nor praise is compatible with the dignity of the government or with the order which fortunately exists among us; one must obey and keep one's thoughts to oneself." [43]

Still, the government of Nicholas I made some significant contributions to the development of education in Russia. The Ministry of Education spent large sums to provide new buildings, laboratories, and libraries, and other aids to scholarship, such as the excellent Pulkovo observatory; teachers' salaries were substantially increased—extraordinarily increased in the case of professors, according to the University Statute of 1835; and in general, the government of Nicholas I showed a commendable interest in the buildings and equipment necessary for education and in the material well-being of those engaged in instruction. Nor was quality neglected. Uvarov, in particular, did much to raise educational and scholarly standards in Russia in the sixteen years during which he headed the ministry. Especially important proved to be the establishment of many new chairs, the corresponding opening up of numerous new fields of learning in the universities of the empire, and the practice of sending promising young Russian scholars abroad for extended training. The Russian educational system, with all its fundamental flaws, came to emphasize academic thoroughness and high standards. Indeed, the government utilized the standards to make education more exclusive at all levels of schooling. Following the Polish rebellion, the Polish University of Vilna was closed; in 1834, a Russian university was opened in Kiev instead. The government of Nicholas I created no other new universities, but it did establish a number of technical and "practical" institutions of higher learning, such as a technological institute, a school of jurisprudence, and a school of architecture, as well as schools of arts and crafts, agriculture, and veterinary medicine.

But Nicholas I, demanding and decisive in little things, could not even approach major reform. The emperor personally disapproved of serfdom. He saw that it produced misery in the army and in the country at large, and he remained constantly apprehensive of the danger of insurrection. Besides, he had no sympathy for aristocratic privilege when it clashed with the interests of the state. Yet, as he explained the matter in 1842 in the State Council: "There is no doubt that serfdom, as it exists at present in our land, is an evil, palpable and obvious to all. But to touch it *now* would be a still more disastrous evil. . . . The Pugachev rebellion proved how far popular rage can go."[44] In fact, throughout his reign the emperor simultaneously feared two different revolutions. There was the danger that the gentry might bid to obtain a constitution if the government decided to deprive the landlords of their serfs. On the other hand, an elemental popular uprising might also be unleashed by such a major shock to the established order as the coveted emancipation.

Determined to preserve autocracy, afraid to abolish serfdom, and suspicious of all independent initiative and popular participation, the emperor and his government could not introduce fundamental reforms. Important developments did nevertheless take place in certain areas, where change would not threaten the fundamental political, social, and economic structure of the Russian empire. Especially significant proved to be the codification of law and the reform in the condition of the state peasants. In spite of its defects, the new code, produced in the late 1820s and the early 1830s by the immense labor of Speransky and his associates, marked a tremendous achievement and a milestone in Russian jurisprudence. In January 1835 it replaced the ancient Ulozhenie of Tsar Alexis, dating from 1649, and it was in effect until 1917. The reorganization of the state peasants followed several years later, after Count Paul Kiselev became head of the new Ministry of State Domains in 1837. Kiselev's reform, which included the shift of taxation from persons to land, additional allotments for poor peasants, some peasant self-government, and the development of financial assistance, schools, and medical care in the villages, received almost universal praise from prerevolutionary historians. However, the leading Soviet specialist on the subject, N. M. Druzhinin, claimed, on the basis of impressive evidence, that the positive aspects of Kiselev's reform had a narrow scope and application, while fundamentally it placed an extremely heavy burden on the state peasants, made all the more difficult to bear by the exactions and malpractices of local administration. [45] Finance Minister Kankrin's policy and, in particular, his measures to stabilize the currency—often cited among the progressive developments in Nicholas I's reign—proved to be less effective and important in the long run than Speransky's and Kiselev's work.

But even limited reform became impossible after 1848. Frightened by European revolutions, Nicholas I became completely reactionary. Russians were forbidden to travel abroad, an order that hit teachers and students especially hard. The number of students without government scholarships was limited to three hundred per university, except for the school of medicine. Uvarov had to resign as minister of education in favor of an entirely reactionary and subservient functionary, Prince Plato Shirinsky-Shikhmatov, who on one occasion told his assistant: "You should know that I have neither a mind nor a will of my own—I am merely a tool of the emperor's will."[46] New restrictions further curtailed university autonomy and academic freedom. Constitutional law and philosophy were eliminated from the curricula; logic and psychology were retained, but were to be taught by professors of theology. In fact, in the opinion of some historians, the universities themselves came close to being eliminated, and only the timely intervention of certain high officials prevented this disaster. Censorship reached ridiculous proportions, with new agencies appearing, including the dreaded "censorship over the censors," the so-called Buturlin committee. The censors, to cite only a few instances of their activities, deleted "forces of nature" from a textbook in physics, probed the hidden meaning of an ellipsis in an arithmetic book, changed "were killed" to "perished" in an account of Roman emperors, demanded that the author of a fortunetelling manual explain why in his opinion stars influenced the fate of men, and worried about the possible concealment of secret codes in musical notations.[47] Literature and thought were stifled. Even such a staunch supporter of Nicholas I and of Official Nationality as Pogodin was impelled in the very last years of the reign to accuse the government of imposing upon Russia "the quiet of a graveyard, rotting and stinking, both physically and morally."[48] It was in this atmosphere of suffocation that Russia experienced its shattering defeat in the Crimean War.

Official Nationality not only dominated Russia for thirty years but also found application in foreign policy. Indeed, it had emerged as part of the reaction of established European regimes against the French Revolution and Napoleon and thus had been international from the beginning. Nicholas I was determined to maintain and defend the existing order in Europe, just as he considered it his sacred duty to preserve the archaic system in his own country. He saw the two as closely related, as the whole and its part, and he thought both to be threatened by the same enemy: the many-headed hydra of revolution, which had suffered a major blow with the final defeat of Napoleon but refused to die. In fact, it rose again and again, in 1830, in 1848, and on other occasions, attempting to undo and reverse the settlement of 1815. True to his principles, the resolute tsar set out to engage the enemy. In the course of the struggle, the crowned policeman of Russia became also the "gendarme of Europe."

Although not to the exclusion of other considerations, this determined championing of legitimism—that international equivalent of autocracy—and established order explains much in Nicholas I's foreign policy in regard to such crucial developments as the Münchengrätz and Berlin agreements with Prussia and Austria, Russian policy toward the revolutions of 1830 and 1848, including the large-scale military intervention in Hungary in 1849, and the Russian emperor's persistent hostility to such products of revolutions as Louis-Philippe's monarchy in France and the new state of Belgium. The great Polish uprising of 1830–1831 only helped to emphasize to the monarch the direct connection between European revolution and revolt in his own domains, and, long after the military victory, the suppression of the Polish danger remained his constant concern. From Don Carlos in Spain to Ernest Augustus in Hanover, Nicholas I was ready to support, or at least sympathize with, all manifestations of European reaction.

Yet even for Nicholas I not every issue could be entirely clear. Unusually complex and difficult in his reign was the so-called Eastern Question, which led to a war between Russia and Persia in 1826–1828, to the naval battle of Navarino in 1827 and a war between Russia and Turkey in 1828–1829 in connection with the Greek struggle for independence, and to such striking diplomatic developments as the Treaty of Unkiar Skelessi of 1833, the Treaty of London of 1840, and the Straits Convention of 1841—and which finally exploded in the Crimean War. Still, although opinions differ on most particular points, it would seem rash to dissociate Nicholas I's policy in the Near East from his general orientation. The Persian dynasty survived its defeat, the Russian emperor refusing to support its revolutionary opponents. The Treaty of Adrianople of 1829 represented a moderate settlement that might have saved the Ottoman empire from destruction. The Treaty of Unkiar Skelessi, whatever its exact nature and implications, resulted from Nicholas I's quick response to the sultan in his hour of need against Mohammed Ali of Egypt, another revolutionary rebel in the eyes of the tsar. Even Nicholas's eventual interest in partitioning the Turkish empire can be construed as a product of the conviction that Turkey could not survive in the modern world, and that therefore the leading European states had to arrange for a proper redistribution of possessions and power in the Balkans and the Near East, in order to avoid popular self-determination, anarchy, revolution, and war. In other words, Nicholas I's approaches to Great Britain can be considered sincere, and the ensuing misunderstandings all the more tragic.

However, one other factor must also be weighed in an appreciation of Nicholas I's Near Eastern policy: Orthodoxy. The Crimean War was provoked partly by religious conflicts. Moreover, the tsar himself retained throughout his reign a certain ambivalence toward the sultan. He repeatedly granted the legitimacy of the sultan's rule in the Ottoman Empire but remained, nevertheless, uneasy about the sprawling Muslim state, which believed in the Koran and oppressed its numerous Orthodox subjects. To resolve the difficulty, on one occasion Nicholas I actually proposed to the Turkish representative that the sultan become Orthodox![49] Once the hostilities began, the Russian emperor readily proclaimed himself the champion of the Cross against the infidels. [50]

Yet there was intellectual change as well as political torpor in Russia in the second quarter of the nineteenth century, and the intellectual situation in the country at the end of Nicholas I's reign was different from that at the beginning. Significantly, the single sovereign Enlightenment image of Peter the Great, which had presided over Russia for more than a century, was replaced by three competing images. More exactly, the great Enlightenment image of the emperor split in two. One of the two, that is, Official Nationality, as already discussed, emphasized such elements as power, a leading role in Europe, and a modern and effective organization of the state with a paternalistic care for all its inhabitants. The other of the two, which came to be associated in particular with the Westernizers, stressed progress, the West, and a further modernization of Russia. But before turning to the Westernizers, it is appropriate to recognize the third and new image of Peter the Great and his work: a comprehensive negative image provided by the Slavophiles.

Whereas Official Nationality continued the eighteenth-century ideology of the beneficent ruler, put on the defensive, so to speak, by the French Revolution, it also acquired, as already indicated, a Romantic wing, with its wild dreams and sweeping vistas. As to Slavophilism, it was all Romantic. In fact, it represented the fullest, most cohesive, and most authentic expression of Romantic thought in Russia.

As was usual after Peter the Great, Russia was borrowing from the West, where in the early decades of the nineteenth century, Romanticism and German Idealistic philosophers—I treat the two very broadly speaking together—replaced the Enlightenment and French *philosophes* as guides for much current thought. The new intellectual *Zeitgeist* affirmed deep, comprehensive knowledge, often with mystical or religious elements, in opposition to mere rationalism, an organic view of the world as against a mechanistic view, and a historical approach to society in contrast to a utilitarian attitude with its vision limited to the present. It also emphasized such diverse doctrines as struggle and the essential separateness of the component parts of the universe, in place of the Enlightenment ideals of harmony, unity, and cosmopolitanism. And it stressed the supreme value of art and culture. In the new world of Romanticism, such strange problems as the true nature of nations and the character of their missions in history came to the fore.

Romanticism and Idealistic philosophy penetrated Russia in a variety of ways. For example, a number of professors, typified by Michael Pavlov, who taught physics, mineralogy, and agronomy at the University of Moscow, presented novel German ideas in their lectures in the first decades of the nineteenth century. Educated Russians continued to read voraciously and were strongly influenced by Schiller or Scott and other brilliant, as well as not-so-brilliant, Western writers. They knew French and sometimes other foreign languages and they traveled and on occasion studied abroad, especially in German universities. These Russians kept learning and had much to learn. Yet at best their response was supremely creative, as in the case of Lermontov's, or Tiutchev's, poetry. And they cannot be logically kept apart, whether on the grounds of uniqueness or backwardness, from other educated Europeans of the age.

In particular, two German philosophers, Schelling first and then Hegel, exercised strong influence on the Russians. Schelling affected certain professors and a number of poets—the best Russian expression of some Schellingian views can be found in Tiutchev's unsurpassed poetry of nature—and also groups of intellectuals and even schools of thought, such as the Slavophile. It was largely an interest in Schelling that led to the establishment of the first philosophic "circle" and the first philosophic review in Russia. In 1823 several young men who had been discussing Schelling in a literary group formed a separate society, with the study of German Idealistic philosophy as its main object. The circle chose the name "The Lovers of Wisdom" and came to contain a dozen members and associates, many of whom were to achieve prominence in Russian intellectual life. It published four issues of a journal, *Mnemosyne*. The leading Lovers of Wisdom included a gifted poet, Dmitri Venevitinov, who died in 1827 at the age of twenty-two, and Prince Vladimir Odoevsky (1803–1869), who developed interesting views concerning the decline of the West and the great future of Russia to issue from the combination and fruition of both the pre-Petrine and the Petrine heritages. The Lovers of Wisdom reflected the Romantic temper of their generation in a certain kind of poetic spiritualism that pervaded their entire outlook, in their worship of art, in their pantheistic adoration of nature, and in their disregard of the "crude" aspects of life, including politics. The group disbanded after the Decembrist rebellion in order not to attract police attention.

A decade later, the question of the nature and destiny of Russia was powerfully and shockingly presented by Peter Chaadaev. In his *Philosophical Letter*, published in the *Telescope* in 1836, Chaadaev argued, in effect, that Russia had no past, no present, and no future. It had never really belonged to either the West or the East, and it had contributed nothing to culture. In particular, Russia lacked the dynamic social principle of Catholicism, which constituted the basis of the entire Western civilization. Indeed, Russia remained "a gap in the intellectual order of things." Chaadaev, who was officially proclaimed deranged by the incensed authorities after the publication of the letter, later modified his thesis in his *Apology of a Madman*. Russia, he came to believe, did enter history through the work of Peter the Great and could obtain a glorious future by throwing all its fresh strength into the construction of the common culture of Christendom.

Chaadaev's postulates were truly seminal, although their separate impact should not be overemphasized, because much of the general European and even already some Russian thought was going in the same direction. The affirmation of Peter the Great and his work in *Apology of a Madman*, Peter the Great who wrote on a blank sheet of paper "Europe" and "the West" and thus gave meaning to his country and determined its future, had an absolute metaphysical character, much beyond the Enlightenment calculations of reasonableness and utility. It could well serve as the slogan or the mantra of Westernizers for generations to come. But Chaadaev's central argument of religion activating culture and history was to be developed by the Slavophiles, not the Westernizers, although, of course, they were to stress the positive impact of Eastern Orthodoxy, not of Roman Catholicism. From a different angle, the entire teaching of the Slavophiles has been sometimes considered as their answer to Chaadaev's shattering declaration in the *Philosophical Letter* that Russia had no past, no present, and no future.

The Slavophiles were a group of Romantic intellectuals who formulated a comprehensive and remarkable ideology centered on their belief in the superior nature and supreme historical mission of Orthodoxy and of Russia. The leading members of the group, all of them landlords and gentlemen-scholars of broad culture and many intellectual interests, included Alexis Khomiakov, who applied himself to everything from theology and world history to medicine and technical inventions; Ivan Kireevsky who has been called the philosopher of the movement; his brother Peter, who collected folk songs and left very little behind him in writing; Constantine Aksakov, a specialist in Russian history and language; Constantine's brother Ivan, later prominent as a publicist and a Panslav; and George Samarin, who was to have a significant part in the emancipation of the serfs and who wrote especially on certain religious and philosophical topics, on the problem of the borderlands of the empire, and on the issue of reform in Russia. This informal group, gathering in the salons and homes of Moscow, flourished in the 1840s and 1850s, until the death of the Kireevsky brothers in 1856 and of Khomiakov and Constantine Aksakov in 1860.

Slavophilism expressed a fundamental vision of integration, peace, and harmony among human beings. On the religious plane, it produced Khomiakov's concept of *sobornost,* an association in love, freedom, and truth of believers, which Khomiakov considered the essence of Orthodoxy. [51] Historically, so the Slavophiles asserted, a similar harmonious integration of individuals could be found in the social life of the Slavs, notably in the peasant commune, and in such other ancient Russian institutions as the *zemskii sobor.* Again, the family represented the principle of integration in love, and the same spirit could pervade other associations of human beings. Constantine Aksakov wrote as follows on the peasant commune, the most beloved social institution of the Slavophiles, which was to leave a remarkable record in Russian intellectual, as well as general, history:

> A commune is a union of the people who have renounced their egoism, their individuality, and who express their common accord; this is an act of love, a noble Christian act, which expresses itself more or less clearly in its various other manifestations. A commune thus represents a moral choir, and just as in a choir a voice is not lost, but follows the general pattern and is heard in the harmony of all voices: so in the commune the individual is not lost, but renounces his exclusiveness in favor of the general accord—and there arises the noble phenomenon of a harmonious, joint existence of rational beings

(consciousnesses); there arises a brotherhood, a commune—a triumph of the human spirit.[52]

As Nicholas Berdiaev commented: "The Slavophiles were under the influence of their *narodnik* illusions. To them the commune was not a fact of history, but something imposing which stands outside the realm of history; it is the 'other world' so to speak within this world." [53]

As against love, freedom, and cooperation, stood the world of rationalism, necessity, and compulsion. It, too, existed on many planes, from the religious and metaphysical to that of everyday life. Thus it manifested itself in the Roman Catholic Church—which had chosen rationalism and authority in preference to love and harmony and had seceded from Orthodox Christendom—and, through the Catholic Church, in Protestantism and in the entire civilization of the West. Moreover, Peter the Great introduced the principles of rationalism, legalism, and compulsion into Russia, where they proceeded to destroy or stunt the harmonious native development and to seduce the educated public. The Russian future lay clearly in a return to native principles, in overcoming the Western disease. After being cured, Russia would take its message of harmony and salvation to the discordant and dying West. It is important to realize that the all-embracing Slavophile dichotomy represented—as pointed out by Fedor Stepun and others—the basic Romantic contrast between the Romantic ideal and the Age of Reason.[54] In particular, as well as in general, Slavophilism fits into the framework of European Romanticism, although the Slavophiles showed considerable originality in adapting Romantic doctrines to their own situation and needs and also experienced the influence of Orthodox religious thought and tradition.

The problem for Russia was to move from the second stage, that of Petrine rationalism and alienation, to the third stage of Orthodox unity and harmony. It must be emphasized that the Romantic ideological structure was typically threefold. Furthermore, the third stage consisted of a return to the first. Often the pattern has been described as union, separation, and reunion. Yet the third stage, reunion, usually did not mean the exact replay of the initial union but, rather, a union made somehow richer through the experience and the overcoming of the period or stage of separation. In philosophical and historical terms, the Romanticists frequently defined the third stage as a conscious union, in contrast to the original unconscious one, as a fully understood and articulated and therefore stronger condition. It is remarkable to what extent that pattern prevailed throughout Romanticism.

Ivan Aksakov applied the Slavophile dialectic to St. Petersburg—that concentrated essence of Petrine Russia—as follows.

> St. Petersburg as the embodiment of a negative moment of history can not create anything *positive* in the Russian sense. According to a well-known dialectical law, it is possible to return to *the positive* only through *a negation of the negation itself*, in other words through a negation of the St. Petersburg

period, through a negation of St. Petersburg as a political *principle* that guided Russian life for almost two centuries. The result will be a Russian nation freed from exclusiveness and called into the arena of world history. Is that clear?[55]

The direction and the destination were clear. But the timing remained unknown. Like Romanticists in general, the Slavophiles situated themselves at the very end of the second stage and the impending coming of the third. They cited their own group on the one hand and what they considered the collapse of Europe and the failure of the Petrine course in Russia on the other as evidence for forthcoming change. That stance, with its clash of the two stages, provided much of the urgency and the dynamic of the Slavophile ideology. It also made Slavophilism unlikely to last, for the millennium would not arrive. Ivan Aksakov, for one, might have become a Panslav in the hope that a cataclysmic battle between the Slav and the Teuton would shake Russia to its very essence and thus bring about the third Slavophile stage.

In its application to the Russia of Nicholas I, the Slavophile teaching often produced paradoxical results, antagonized the government, and baffled Slavophile friends and foes alike. In a sense, the Slavophiles were religious anarchists, for they condemned all legalism and compulsion in the name of their religious ideal. Yet, given the sinful condition of man, they granted the necessity of government and even expressed a preference for autocracy: in addition to its historical roots in ancient Russia, autocracy possessed the virtue of placing the entire weight of authority and compulsion on a single individual, thus liberating society from that heavy burden; besides, the Slavophiles remained unalterably opposed to Western constitutional and other legalistic and formalistic devices. Yet this justification of autocracy remained historical and functional, therefore relative, never religious and absolute. Furthermore, the Slavophiles desired the emancipation of the serfs and other reforms, and above all, they insisted on the "freedom of the life of the spirit," that is, freedom of conscience, speech, and publication. As Constantine Aksakov tried to explain to the government: "Man was created by God as an intelligent and a talking being." [56] In addition, Khomiakov and his friends opposed such aspects of the established order as the death penalty, government intrusion into private life, and bureaucracy in general. No wonder Slavophile publications never escaped censorship and prohibition for long.

At the beginning of Alexander II's reign, Constantine Aksakov presented to the emperor a memorandum expounding the nature and the proper roles of the Russian people and the Russian government. He asserted that "the first relationship between the government and the people is the relationship of mutual non-interference," [57] and concluded as follows.

> May the ancient union of the government and the people, of the state and the land be reestablished on the firm foundation of true, fundamental Russian

principles. To the government the unlimited freedom of *rule*, which is its exclusive possession, to the people the full freedom of both external and internal *life*, which the government safeguards. *To the government the right of action*, and consequently of law; *to the people the right of opinion*, and consequently of speech.[58]

On other occasions, too, the Slavophiles kept emphasizing this division of spheres and the need for the government to remain strictly in its own area. "*Defense* in general, that is the meaning and the duty of the state. Its guardianship consists in providing greater comforts of life, and not at all in managing it. The state is in no way a preceptor."[59] "Its entire virtue must consist of its *negative* character, so that the less it exists as a state, the better it accomplishes its aim, as is the case in England." [60] And to eliminate all possible doubt: "The fewer points of contact the government has with the people, and the people with the government, the better." [61] A repudiation of enlightened despotism could hardly be more complete.

The fullest Russian expression of Romanticism and German Idealistic philosophy, Slavophilism disappeared as its few proponents died, and the intellectual climate changed. These "early Slavophiles" ("rannie slavianofily") were actually the only Slavophiles who ever existed, for none of their supposed successors shared with them the complex intellectual structure essential to Slavophilism. Yet, in a broader sense, the teaching had a major impact. It offered educated Russians a new identity, different from, indeed opposed to, the Enlightenment image of Russia that had been dominant for well over a century, opposed to the government, and also opposed to the emerging liberal, eventually radical, Westernizers' reading of the Petrine inheritance. While there were no true disciples, elements and aspects of the Slavophile synthesis apparently had their impact all the way from Herzen's and very many other radicals' emphasis on the peasant commune to some brilliant twentieth-century theology by Russian émigrés in Paris. Not always, to be sure, a matter of simple direct causation, the impact seems to be widespread and impressive enough to establish Slavophilism, broadly speaking, as a continuous part of Russian intellectual life and search for identity.

I shall mention only two or three examples, of necessity brief and fragmentary. Reference has already been made to Panslavism, which profited greatly not only from the tireless activities of Ivan Aksakov, both a Slavophile and a Panslav, but also from the writings and personal interests of Khomiakov, as well as from the general high standing of Slavdom in the Slavophile doctrine, where it occupied, nonetheless, a tertiary or secondary position at best. Or consider the following passage of Khomiakov and think of Dostoevsky, Vladimir Soloviev, and still other later Russian ideologists:

> Look at Germany. More than any other people of Europe she denied her nationality, was even partly ashamed of herself, and what happened? . . . Was this temporary renunciation really fruitless? No: Germany was rewarded by

the fact that when she returned to self-consciousness and self-respect, she brought with her from the period of her humiliation the ability to understand other peoples much better than a Frenchman, an Englishman or an Italian understands them. She practically discovered Shakespeare. We also renounced ourselves and humiliated ourselves more, a hundred times more than Germany. I hope, I am certain that when we return home (and we shall return home—and soon), we shall bring with ourselves a clear understanding of the entire world, such as the Germans did not even dream of. [62]

Or, as a still different example of the Slavophile connections with the future, assess the elements in Alexander Solzhenitsyn's ardent and continuous preaching against the West.

But to return to the reign of Nicholas I, Slavophilism had been formulated in the main by 1839 or 1840, and the following five or seven years witnessed the celebrated debate between the Slavophiles and another group of young intellectual enthusiasts, who came to be known as the Westernizers. The two circles read the same books, attended the same lectures, visited the same salons, even wrote in the same periodicals. Monday evenings were usually spent at Chaadaev's, Friday at the Sverbeevs', Sunday at the Elagins', Thursday at the Pavlovs'.

> The whole large literary society of the capital (Moscow) assembled there on Thursdays; there enthusiastic arguments continued late into the night: Redkin with Shevyrev, Kavelin with Aksakov, Herzen and Kriukov with Khomiakov. There the Kireevskiis used to appear, also Iurii Samarin, then still a young man. Chaadaev was a constant guest there, with his head as bald as his hand, his unexceptionable society manners, his civilized and original mind, and his eternal posing. This was the most brilliant literary time of Moscow. All questions, philosophical, historical, and political, everything that interested the most advanced contemporary minds, were discussed at these assemblies, to which the competitors came fully armed, with opposed views, but with a store of knowledge and the charm of eloquence. At that time Khomiakov led a fierce struggle against Hegel's Logic. . . . Similarly vehement disputations concerned the key problem of Russian history, the reforms of Peter the Great. Circles of listeners formed around the debaters; this was a constant tournament in the course of which knowledge, intelligence, and resourcefulness were all displayed. [63]

Intellectual closeness was even more important than physical proximity or community of interests. Both the Slavophiles and the Westernizers argued within the German Idealistic and generally Romantic intellectual framework, employed a kind of dialectic, and utilized the same or similar concepts, such as "old Russia" or "the contemporary West," as key elements of their theoretical constructions. Only usually, notably so in the case of Peter the Great, the values of these concepts were reversed: negative for one group, positive for the other, and vice versa. Thus, whereas the Slavophiles condemned the reformer as the evil genius who destroyed Orthodox and harmonious Old Russia and set the country on the vicious and disastrous Western course, the Westernizers staked the future of Russia and their own future on the success of the first emperor and his work. As Herzen, already a radical and in exile, wrote, remembering the Slavophiles and his differences with them: "The times of Peter, the great tsar, are gone; Peter, the great man, is no longer in the Winter Palace; *he is in us.*"[64] Ideological tension and certain other circumstances finally drove the Slavophiles and the Westernizers apart, and their close intellectual and personal association ended by about 1846, never to be forgotten by the participants, or in Russian intellectual history.[65]

The Westernizers were much more diverse than the Slavophiles, and their views did not form a single, integrated whole. Besides, they shifted their positions rather rapidly. Even socially the Westernizers consisted of different elements, ranging from Michael Bakunin, who came from a cultured gentry home like those of the Slavophiles, to Vissarion Belinsky, whose father was an impoverished doctor and grandfather a priest, and Basil Botkin, who belonged to a family of merchants. Yet certain generally held opinions and doctrines gave a measure of unity to the group. The Slavophiles and the Westernizers started from similar assumptions of German Idealistic philosophy, but they came to different conclusions. While Khomiakov and his associates affirmed the uniqueness of Russia and the superiority of true Russian principles over those of the West, the other party argued that the Western historical path was the model that Russia had to follow. Russia could accomplish its mission only in the context of Western civilization, not in opposition to it. Naturally, therefore, the Westernizers took a positive view of Western political development and criticized the Russian system. Contrary to the Slavophiles, they praised the work of Peter the Great, but they wanted further Westernization. In addition, whereas the Slavophiles anchored their entire ideology in their interpretation and appraisal of Orthodoxy, the Westernizers assigned relatively little importance to religion, while some of them gradually turned to agnosticism and, in the case of Bakunin, even to violent atheism. To be more exact, the moderate Westernizers retained religious faith and an essentially idealistic cast of mind, while their political and social program did not go beyond mild liberalism, with emphasis on gradualism and popular enlightenment. These moderates were typified by Nicholas Stankevich, who brought together a famous early Westernizer circle but died in 1840 at the age of twenty-seven, before the movement really developed, and by Timothy Granovsky, who lived from 1813 to 1855 and taught European history at the University of Moscow. The radical Westernizers, however, largely through Hegelianism and Left Hegelianism, came to challenge religion, society, and the entire Russian and European system, and even on occasion to call for a revolution. Although few in number, they included such major figures as Vissarion Belinsky (1811–1848), Alexander Herzen (1812–1870), and Michael Bakunin (1814–1876).

Belinsky, the most famous Russian literary critic and editor, exercised a major influence on Russian intellectual life in general. He had the rare good fortune to welcome the works of Pushkin, Lermontov, and Gogol and the debuts of Dostoevsky, Turgenev, and Nekrasov. Belinsky's commentary on the Russian writers became famous for its passion, invective, and eulogy, as well as for its determination to treat works of literature in the broader context of society, history, and thought, and to instruct and guide the authors and the reading public. Belinsky's own views underwent important changes and had not achieved cohesiveness and stability at the time of his death. His impact on Russian literature, however, proved remarkably durable and stable: it consisted above all in the establishment of political and social criteria as gauges for evaluating artistic works. As Nekrasov put it later, one did not have to be a poet, but one was under obligation to be a citizen.

Belinsky began his intellectual odyssey in the Stankevich circle, where he had much to learn from the better educated members, notably Stankevich and Bakunin. His devotion to Hegel and German Idealism reached its height when in 1839 and 1840, together with and probably following Bakunin, he interpreted Hegel's statement that the rational was the real as an affirmation of all reality, Russian reality in particular, and most especially Russian autocracy. Not surprisingly, the infatuation did not last long, and Belinsky wrote what became the most famous denunciation of Hegel and German Idealistic philosophy in Russian intellectual history. Always in search of faith, he turned instead to a belief in the individual and to the principle of what he called "sociality," perhaps best described as a humanitarian concern for fellow human beings. [66] In the name of the individual and of "sociality," Belinsky reaffirmed his support of the great French Revolution and of the entire progressive development in the West. As to Russia, that country needed "another Peter the Great," another mighty effort to advance along the common road of civilized humanity. Belinsky died in 1848, of consumption, thus probably escaping an imminent arrest.

Both Michael Bakunin and Alexander Herzen were to live much longer than Belinsky and to follow their striking debuts as Westernizers and as "men of the 'forties" with explosive, seminal, and inimitable prominence in the radical movements in their country and, in the case of Bakunin especially, also all over Europe. Bakunin's infatuation with Russian autocracy and Nicholas I lasted no longer than Belinsky's. After leaving Russia and arriving in Berlin in 1840, he joined actively and enthusiastically in German intellectual life, and he moved rapidly to the Left. Bakunin's arrival and establishment in the Prussian capital corresponded with Arnold Ruge's publicistic activities, the appearance in 1841 of Ludwig Feuerbach's *Essence of Christianity*, and in general the emergence of the so-called Young Hegelians. The sustained effort of the Hegelian Left to interpret Hegel's teaching as a theoretical justification of radical action suited Bakunin to perfection: it left many of his Hegelian, metaphysical, and even mystical premises intact, yet it offered him what he longed for most, rebellion. Fully converted in the winter of 1841–1842 and never one to keep in the background, Bakunin published in October 1842, in Ruge's

Deutsche Jahrbücher, a remarkable article entitled "Reaction in Germany: From the Notebooks of a Frenchman," signed "Jules Elysard." Typically, he argued especially against the compromisers, the people in the middle. There could be no compromise. The issue of the day was the struggle between democracy and reaction. The victory of democracy would produce a new heaven and a new earth. In the meantime, however, only the struggle, only negation mattered. The article concluded:

> All peoples and all men are full of presentiments. Everyone whose living organs are not paralyzed sees with trembling expectation the approach of the future which will utter the decisive word. Even in Russia, in that limitless and snow-covered empire, of which we know so little and which has before it perhaps a great future, even in Russia the dark storm clouds are gathering! The air is sultry, it is heavy with storms!
>
> And therefore we call to our blinded brothers: Repent! Repent! The Kingdom of God is coming nigh.
>
> Let us put our trust in the eternal spirit which destroys and annihilates only because it is the unsearchable and eternally creative source of life. The passion for destruction is also a creative passion. [67]

Michael Bakunin was well on his way to becoming "founder of nihilism and apostle of anarchy."

Alexander Herzen also followed the road from idealistic Westernism to radicalism. A brilliant writer, publicist, and polemicist, the author of perhaps the most remarkable depiction of that entire period in his autobiographical *My Past and Thoughts*, and eventually an inspiration to the entire Russian intelligentsia to which he had contributed so much, Herzen was born in the memorable year of 1812, an illegitimate but pampered son of a cultured and misanthropic landlord. His childhood and boyhood combined social and perhaps emotional isolation with fluency in three languages, including his mother's German, voracious reading, and the usual aristocratic education of private tutors. He studied at the University of Moscow and at the same time organized a circle of young intellectuals parallel to that of Stankevich. In 1834, however, Herzen was arrested when the government reacted very sharply to a few signs of disaffection among students. Although nothing could be demonstrated against Herzen beyond his interest in the writings of Saint-Simon, he had to spend ten months in prison and five more years in exile in provincial towns, distant Viatka from 1835 to the end of 1837, and then Vladimir until 1840. Prison and government service in the provinces both separated Herzen from his intellectual and social world and offered him a new look at Russia. When he was finally pardoned in May 1840, Herzen returned to his intellectual pursuits with his friends and proceeded, for several years, together with Granovsky, to carry the main burden of the Westernizer side of the celebrated debate with the Slavophiles.

Herzen liked to emphasize that he displayed early a more social, political, "French" orientation than those of his Romantic associates, and his claim is justified to an extent. Yet he was also a splendid representative of the age of Romanticism and German Idealistic philosophy. As a leading specialist has put it: "Young Herzen's main interest in Saint-Simon's doctrine was the philosophy of history, the revelation of a new religion and the announcement of a new 'organic age.' In Herzen's *Weltanschauung*, the influences of Saint-Simon and Pierre Leroux coexisted happily with the equally strong influences of Schelling and German Romantic philosophy."[68] Indeed, Schelling and certainly Schiller, Hegel, and some other German writers were at the foundation of Herzen's thought. And it was Herzen who immortalized in his autobiography the fantastic obsession of contemporary Russian intellectuals of his and related circles with Hegel and other German Idealistic philosophers. Herzen and his bosom friend, the poet and a kind of Schellingian Nicholas Ogarev, lived their Romantic convictions. Their celebrated friendship, to which they seemed to attach a supreme, even at times a metaphysical or quasi-religious importance, was itself a remarkable product of the age. Their loves were equally notable. In particular, Herzen's courtship of and marriage to Natalie Zakharina, during his exile, had almost cosmic overtones for the future great radical: Natalie became his reconciliation and his salvation, almost his religion and his philosophy, in a manner no Voltairian could comprehend.

While it is impossible to exclude Herzen from the history of Idealism and Romanticism in Russia, he refused to be permanently confined to that *Weltanschauung* either. A study of Hegel led to the Left Hegelians. It was Herzen who referred to Hegelianism as "the algebra of revolution." "The world is complete only in action . . . the living unity of theory and practice."[69] Finally, in 1847, Herzen left Russia forever, to publish eventually the *Bell* and become one of the most important and celebrated émigrés in Russian history. Yet abroad, too, Herzen could find no new satisfactory intellectual framework, let alone ideological security. He quickly discovered disasters in the West to match those in Russia. The optimistic Westernizer belief in Peter the Great and progress had to be abandoned, for the last time, after Herzen's total disappointment with the emancipation of the serfs and other "great reforms" as they were enacted by the Russian government. Bakunin's running after revolutions appeared to be childish and completely ineffective. If Herzen was maturing as man and thinker, he was maturing essentially toward skepticism and despair. Isaiah Berlin concluded on Herzen:

> The heart of his thought is the notion that the basic problems are perhaps not soluble at all, that all one can do is to try to solve them, but that there is no guarantee, either in socialist nostrums or in any other human construction, no guarantee that happiness or a rational life can be attained, in private or in public life.[70]

In 1834 Herzen had been accused of reading Saint-Simon; in the spring of 1849, the police in St. Petersburg arrested a whole group or society of young men gathering on Fridays at the home of Michael Butashevich-Petrashevsky and studying the works of another strange French utopian socialist, Francois-Marie-Charles Fourier (1772–1837), and other radical literature. The meetings had, in fact, been taking place from 1845. Fourier preached a peaceful transformation of the world into small, marvelously integrated and self-supporting communes, which would also provide for the release and harmony of human passions, according to a fantastic scheme of Fourier's own invention. The all-important point was to establish these initial phalanxes, or even a single phalanx, for after that, the obvious blessedness of the phalanx life and eager imitation by the outsiders will accomplish the rest. The world would become paradise. The Petrashevtsy, as these Russian enthusiasts of Fourier came to be known, were, to be sure, an informal group, with a considerable variety of opinion on many issues (for instance, on religion, especially because Fourier also advocated totally fantastic religious views of his own) and, for some of them, an unfortunate proclivity to combine Fourierism with attacks on the situation in Russia and even on Nicholas I himself. And the year 1849, after the revolutions of 1848, was a very bad one for the unfortunate culprits. Nicholas I would not found a phalanx. Instead, twenty-one men were sentenced to death, although the sentence was changed at the place of execution to less drastic punishment. It was as a member of the Petrashevtsy that Dostoevsky faced imminent execution and later went to Siberia. The Petrashevtsy, it might be added, came generally from lower—but educated—social strata than the Lovers of Wisdom, the Slavophiles, and the Westernizers, and included mostly minor officials, junior officers, and students.

The reign of Nicholas I has been described as a period of political despotism, social stagnation, military defeat in the Crimea, and economic backwardness and crisis, but also as part of the Golden Age of Russian literature, and as a creative and seminal segment of time for Russian intellectual development. Herzen referred to an amazing period of outward political slavery and inward intellectual emancipation. A lesser participant and observer, Paul Annenkov, focusing principally on the 1840s, called those years "a marvelous decade" (*zamechatelnoe desiatiletie*). [71] What these two and many other Russians glorified was the new richness of Russian thought and literary culture, no longer led and controlled by the government.

And the government knew it. Although finding widespread support in Official Nationality, the authorities generally considered ideologists and ideas highly suspect. Nicholas I never distinguished sharply between the two, and perhaps with reason. The Lovers of Wisdom disbanded their society in time and caused no trouble. Chaadaev, however, insisted on making his statement and had to be proclaimed insane. The government was offended by the Slavophiles in more ways than one. In addition to expressing nonsensical but clearly critical and oppositionist views, they usually failed to serve the state either in the army or the bureaucracy. Scions of good landholding families, they seemed to be engaged in some kind of gentry *fronde*. As a reprisal and a security measure, the authorities interfered drastically with Slavophile publishing, while no member of the immediate group obtained a position in the imperial educational establishment. The Westernizers ranged from suspicious liberal professors who had to be watched constantly to outright rebels, such as Bakunin and Herzen. The Petrashevtsy were worse, if anything. Lacking organization and professing a peaceful ideology, they seemed nevertheless to threaten the government with their bitter hostility. Moreover, their appearance marked, in a sense, a new stage in the alienation of progressive intellectuals from the state. Whereas Chaadaev, like some of the Decembrists, stood at one time close to Alexander I, and whereas Nicholas I could still admonish the Slavophile Samarin in person and even be impressed by Bakunin's stunning written confession to the autocrat,[72] no such ties existed between the young men who gathered at Petrashevsky's on Fridays and the rulers or Russia. In fact—although at the time this, of course, could be at best sensed rather than known—the Petrashevtsy, and possibly even more so the members of a related circle organized by the poet Sergei Durov, were in composition and attitude quite similar to the later revolutionary groups of the 1860s and 1870s. While the Petrashevtsy were holding their meetings in St. Petersburg, authorities uncovered yet another subversive society, the Brotherhood of Cyril and Methodius, in Kiev, arresting its members in March 1847. These few members, who included the historian Nicholas Kostomarov and the great Ukrainian poet of serf origin Taras Shevchenko, believed in the Messianic role of the Ukrainians and in a free democratic federation of Slavic peoples centered on Kiev.

How can one account for all these developments? What were the reasons that terminated, or at least so greatly impaired, the more than century-old intimate alliance between the government and the educated public in Russia, transforming the apparently monolithic image of the eighteenth century, and, still, of the 1830s, with the government virtually in complete control, into a picture of alienation and opposition? Most prerevolutionary Russian scholars and many Western specialists blamed directly the government itself, and more specifically Nicholas I. With a characteristically liberal, and occasionally radical, bias, they saw the educated public, in particular its intellectual leaders, as bearers of light and the conscience of Russia. These leaders naturally supported progressive Petrine reforms, and they offered their strong backing to the activities of Catherine the Great and the projects of Alexander I. But with Nicholas I, cooperation ceased. The new emperor refused to solve the pressing problems of the country, and he established a regime of unbearable reaction, oppression, and militarism. The last harrowing years of his rule, which followed the revolutions of 1848, raised oppression to an insane pitch and made a fundamental break between the state and all aware and self-respecting Russians inevitable. One is reminded of Alexander Nikitenko's bitter comment that the main failing of the reign of Nicholas I consisted in the fact that it was all a mistake.[73] And yet, at least in its simple form, the liberal view fails to carry conviction. For one thing, the last years of Nicholas I's rule were probably more painful than decisive in the relationship between the government and the educated public in Russia, because the split between the two had preceded their onset. More important,

Nicholas I was not called the most consistent of autocrats for nothing. The emperor's beliefs, aims, and policies remained essentially the same in the 1820s, 1830s, 1840s, and 1850s. It was the educated public that changed.

The educated Russian public was affected by many factors of diverse kinds and potency. Among the most persistent and important was the course of Russian foreign relations and the role that Russia played on the world stage in an increasingly nationalistic age. Peter Christoff spent much effort in his valuable books on the Slavophiles demonstrating that the hearts of his protagonists belonged to Russia. Soviet specialists kept insisting, again needlessly, on the patriotism of their radical heroes. In fact, every educated Russian—and many an uneducated one, for not quite the same reasons—was a patriot in that bright and naive dawn of Romantic nationalism in Russia, over which there shone the luminous light of 1812. That was true, in his own desperate way, even of the Chaadaev of the first "Philosophical Letter" (and not only of the Chaadaev of *Apology of a Madman* or the Chaadaev who fought at Borodino). Observers and later scholars noted, for instance, in what a united manner the Russian educated public reacted against the Poles when they staged their rebellion in 1830–1831. Throughout his reign, Nicholas I was concerned not by any lack of patriotism but by the nationalist wing within his own Official Nationality and by other nationalists outside government circles. Benckendorff kept citing in his annual gendarme reports "Russian patriots" or "Muscovite patriots" as the greatest source of critical discussion and discontent in the country, at least outside Poland, and, conversely, he continually reiterated his belief that nothing gained the sovereign so much approbation and support as measures meant to enhance the Russian national spirit. A dedicated patriot himself, Nicholas I was also a convinced conservative or reactionary, as well as the man actually responsible for state policies and their results. By temperament, conviction, and also certainly because of his position, he could not endorse the irresponsible nationalistic enthusiasms of many of his subjects. Tension and hostility, therefore, developed and are reflected in the writings of the Slavophiles and of many other educated Russians, including representatives of the nationalist wing of Official Nationality. The Crimean fiasco at the end of the reign constituted a terrible disaster for Russians in general, but especially for the nationalists among them. The government looked so strikingly isolated in 1855 precisely because it had lost all nationalist support.

In another respect, too, in regard to the West, the decades of Nicholas I's rule proved to be on the whole disastrous as well as, once again, highly significant for Russian public opinion. Throughout the eighteenth century and the reign of Alexander I, Russia enjoyed good press, everything considered, in other European countries. Many disparate phenomena, ranging from Catherine the Great's skill in dealing with the *philosophes* to a virtual European idolatry of Alexander I following his victory over Napoleon, contributed to this favorable image. Most important, the cosmopolitan European Enlightenment welcomed Russia as a promising, as well as enthusiastic, disciple. By 1813 or 1815, the land of the tsars was, to all appearances, already repaying its debt, leading other countries in the overthrow of Napoleonic tyranny and in the establishment of a new age of peace, stability, and happiness.

In subsequent years, and especially in the reign of Nicholas I, the image of Russia changed. The change was primarily determined by the increasing polarization of European politics and by the logical alliance of the Russian empire with the Right. Nicholas I's personal devotion to the conservative cause and his directness and rudeness accelerated and sharpened the process. In any event, whereas Alexander I had been hailed as the liberator of Europe, Nicholas I came to be known as its gendarme. Whereas Catherine the Great had been eulogized by Voltaire, Diderot, and d'Alembert, and whereas Alexander I had received praise from Jefferson, all liberals and radicals denounced Nicholas I, his system, and his country. Nor was the condemnation limited to the Left, no matter how broadly defined. The most famous literary attack on the Russia of Nicholas I, *La Russie en 1839*, was mounted by Astolphe Marquis de Custine, a conservative French aristocrat.[74] After Russian troops in the summer of 1849 suppressed the Hungarian revolt against the Habsbug crown, hatred of Nicholas I and of Russia became in a sense part of the Hungarian national creed. While the Hungarians reacted to a single decisive intervention, the Poles remained a constant enemy and source of trouble for the Russian ruler and state. Following the defeat of their rebellion in 1830–1831, many Poles migrated to the West, especially to Paris but also to London and other cities, where they formed effective centers of Polish nationalism and anti-Russian propaganda. Mickiewicz's great voice was only one of many calling attention to the tragedy of Poland and the brutality of its Russian oppressor. Violent denigration of Nicholas I reached remarkable extremes. Even the emperor's closest foreign associates, the rulers and governments of Prussia and Austria, were dissatisfied: the Prussians resented the fact that Nicholas I had taken the side of Austria during the momentous developments of 1848–1850; the Austrians felt that their interests were in conflict with those of Russia in the Balkans; both chafed under Nicholas's overbearing solicitude. The British, in addition to their general disapproval of Russian autocracy, developed an exaggerated dread of Russian designs in the East, fearing even for British India. As to France, Nicholas I hated both the July Monarchy, which was brought to the throne by a revolution, and Louis-Napoleon, after he declared himself Emperor Napoleon III. In the Crimean War, Russian isolation in European public opinion paralleled the diplomatic isolation of the country.

The situation at home was also alarming. Most specialists refer to a midcentury crisis of gentry agriculture, and almost all emphasize that serfdom had outlived its usefulness. Yet, although serfdom clearly represented both a major economic and a major moral problem, the government of Nicholas I failed, as we know, to do anything substantive about it. A student of the period notices that economic worries were prominent in the correspondence of such generally successful landowners as the Slavophiles; that scions of leading families, such as Prince Peter Viazemsky, had to enter state service to make ends meet; that Boris Chicherin's aforementioned celebrated account of social life in Moscow in the 1840s becomes, unexpectedly, a series of gentry bankruptcies. Less impressionistic is the enormous indebtedness of the landlords to the state on the eve of the emancipation. State service, too, created discontent, because of its perceived obsequiousness, stupidity, and stultification.[75] All the while the Russian educated public was becoming larger and more articulate, with a better, more varied, and more extensive periodical press, a greater number and more effective distribution of books, and higher standards in schools and universities. Even the very reactionary policies of the last years of the reign failed to stop that general advancement. The origins of the Russian intelligentsia, the establishment of writing in the country as an independent, as well as a brilliant, profession, the full participation of Russia in European university culture, and much else of similar importance are often dated from the reign of Nicholas I.

The issue of Russian identity and of the definition of Russia—referring always to the educated public—underwent striking, even explosive, changes in the second quarter of the nineteenth century. Russia experienced then two intellectual transformations: the change from the ideology of the Age of Reason, dominant for over a century, to Romanticism and Idealism, and the disintegration of the new worldview, or rather worldviews. The first change could well be considered by the government a blessing. Surely metaphysics, religion, art, or poetry were less of a threat in the eyes of the determined autocrat and of the Third Department than an active interest of society in politics would have been. Even better, historical, traditionalist, religious, and authoritarian arguments of the Romantic age were used to define and uphold the doctrine of Official Nationality. It was no mere coincidence that the Russian educated public did not mount a single violent attempt against the state throughout the entire age of Romanticism and Idealism, from the late Enlightenment of 1825 until the 1860s, when a neo-Enlightenment had become an active force.

Yet, as it turned out, the Russian government obtained its peace and the Russian educated public its more or less successful reconciliation with reality at an exorbitant price. The philosophy of the Enlightenment was probably the last truly unifying ideology of the Western world. In Russia, as elsewhere, it was followed by division and fragmentation, the common language of the rulers and the educated public by a babel of tongues. The poignancy and the special tragedy of the Radishchev episode had been due precisely to the fact that the critic and Catherine the Great belonged to the same intellectual camp. Even the Decembrists had found it difficult to separate their intentions and actions from those of the government of Alexander I, and their emotional attitude to their rulers had remained ambivalent to the end. But there was no way for Benckendorff to understand the Slavophiles, or for Nicholas I the Petrashevtsy. At the same time the thought of Russian intellectuals, and to a certain extent of the government, too, was becoming increasingly unreal. While scholars still argue whether an implementation of Speransky's main proposal would have fundamentally changed the course of Russian history, or dispute the practical merits and demerits of Novosiltsev's, Nikita Muraviev's, and even

Pestel's constitutions, no such debate swirls around the Slavophile program, Buta-shevich-Petrashevsky's phalanx, or Bakunin's anarchism.

To be sure, Russian intellectuals in the Romantic age made a valiant effort to for-mulate an effective new *Weltanschauung*, and they displayed in the process a greater originality of thought than had their predecessors in the Age of Reason. The Rus-sians were offered a choice from three national identities instead of a single one, not to mention Petrashevtsy's Fourierism, which bid to eliminate the very concept of national identity. But Official Nationality, eclectic and even contradictory to begin with, suffered greatly from the performance of the government for which it stood. Slavophilism, the most stable, complete, and impressive Russian Romantic ideology, led nowhere and remained in glaring contrast to reality. The Westernizers did try to come closer to that reality. It was the Westernizers who moved by thesis and antithe-sis, or at least through contradiction and argument, from Schelling to Hegel, the Left Hegelians, and beyond. It was thus they who exhibited best the disintegration of Romanticism and Idealism. The total picture was that of confusion, collapse, and defeat, with only some central concepts, such as "people" (*narod*) or "peasant com-mune" (*obshchina, mir*) as seminal legacies, in changing contexts, for a new and vastly different period of Russian intellectual history.

Russia from the Death of Nicholas I to the Abdication of Nicholas II, 1855–1917

*The Russian Empire fell apart in 1917 along fault-lines which were
inherent in its situation as an empire with extensive vulnerable borders
straddling Europe and Asia. For more than three centuries its structures
had been those of a multi-ethnic service state, not those of an emerging
nation. Social hierarchy and status were shaped by the need to provide the
sinews of that empire, through taxation, recruitment, administration and
military command. The economy was deflected from productive purposes
to sustain the army and the administrative apparatus. A nobility was
maintained in expensive non-productivity, absorbing an alien culture to
guarantee Russia's status as European great power.*

    *Most damaging of all, perhaps, Russia's church was compelled to
renounce its function as guarantor of the national myth to become the
marginalized prop of an activist secular state. A messianic national myth
which had demonstrated its viability in the crises of the sixteenth and
seventeenth centuries was spurned in favour of a cosmopolitan
Enlightenment project which required all the refinements of the "well-
ordered police state."*

                  —G. Hosking, *Russia: People and Empire, 1552–1917*

*Whole masses of the peasantry were dragging along so near to the
margin of subsistence that a crop-failure meant starvation—and so
came the great famine of 1891 and the lesser famines of earlier and
later date. Whether the general well-being of the peasantry had shown
improvement or decline— whether there had been within the peasant
mass a tendency to draw together or to draw apart—still, as the day of
revolt approached, there was no doubt of the existence in the
countryside of a morass of penury sufficiently large, an antithesis
between poverty and plenty sufficiently sharp, to give rise to whatever
results might legitimately be bred and born of economic misery and
economic contrast.*

                  —G. T. Robinson, *Rural Russia under the Old Regime:
A History of the Landlord-Peasant World and
a Prologue to the Peasant Revolution of 1917*

The main outlines of Russian history during the last several decades of tsarism are reasonably clear.[1] The conservative or reactionary policies of Nicholas I, centered above all on "holding the line," died with the emperor. Indeed, there is a strong but undocumented court and academic tradition that Nicholas I on his deathbed told his son and heir, Alexander II, to liberate the serfs. And it was high time to do so. With the growth of a money economy and competition for markets, the deficiencies of low-grade serf labor became ever more obvious. Many landlords, especially those with small holdings, could barely feed their serfs, and the gentry accumulated an enormous debt. Free labor, whether really free or merely the contractual labor of someone else's serfs, became more common throughout the Russian economy during the first half of the nineteenth century. Moreover, the serfs perhaps declined in absolute numbers in the course of that period, while their numerical weight in relation to other classes certainly declined: from 58 percent of the total population of Russia in 1811 to 44.5 percent on the eve of the "great reforms," to cite Blum's figures. Recent interpretations of the Russian economic crisis in mid–nineteenth century range all the way from Kovalchenko's emphatic restatement, with the use of quantitative methods, of the thesis of the extreme and unbearable exploitation of the serfs to Ryndziunsky's stress on the general loosening of the social fabric. But from either point of view, as well as most views in between, serfdom was becoming increasingly anachronistic. Moreover, the serfs kept rising against their masters. While no nineteenth-century peasant insurrection could at all rival the Pugachev rebellion, the uprisings became more frequent and on the whole more serious. Semevsky, using official records, had counted 550 peasant uprisings in the nineteenth century prior to the emancipation. A Soviet historian, Ignatovich, raised the number to 1,467 and gave the following breakdown: 281 peasant rebellions, that is, 19 percent of the total, in the period from 1801 to 1825; 712 rebellions, 49 percent, from 1826 to 1854; and 474 uprisings, or 32 percent, in the six years and two months of Alexander II's reign before the abolition of serfdom. Ignatovich emphasized that the uprisings also increased in length, in bitterness, in the human and material losses involved, and in the military effort necessary to restore order. Ignatovich's long list has been further expanded by other scholars. Besides rising in rebellion, serfs ran away from their masters, sometimes by the hundreds and even by the thousands. On occasion, large military detachments had to be sent to intercept them. Pathetic mass flights of peasants, for example, would follow rumors that freedom could be obtained somewhere in the Caucasus, while crowds of serfs tried to join the army during the Crimean War, mistakenly believing that they could thereby gain their liberty.[2]

Moral sentiments combined with practical reasons. The Decembrists, the Slavophiles, the Westernizers, the Petrashevtsy, and some supporters of Official Nationality, together with other thinking Russians, all wanted the abolition of serfdom. As education developed in Russia, and especially as Russian literature came into its own, humane feelings and attitudes became more widespread. Such leading writers as Pushkin and particularly Turgenev, who in 1852 published in book form his magnificent collection of stories, *Sportsman's Sketches,* in which serfs were depicted as full-blown, and indeed unforgettable, human beings, no doubt exercised an influence. In fact, on the eve of the abolition of serfdom in Russia, virtually no one defended that institution as such; the arguments of its proponents were usually limited to pointing out the dangers implicit in such a radical change as emancipation. The Crimean War might well have been the last straw, for it not only resulted in a shattering defeat, but also demonstrated the damage serfdom did to the Russian armed forces, including the fact that the government relied on a standing army without reserve, because it was afraid to allow discharged soldiers to return to villages.[3]

The formulation, passage through appropriate government instances, and eventual proclamation and enactment of emancipation legislation proved to be difficult, because landlords and conservatives in and out of government were reluctant to lose their huge possessions and, in fact, largely their way of life. Repeated imperial prodding proved necessary. The final result, the emancipation proclamation of the nineteenth of February 1861, with attendant enactments, has been called the greatest legislative act in world history. It directly affected the status of some fifty-two million peasants, over twenty million of them serfs of private landowners, and others mostly state peasants—compared, for example, with the almost simultaneous liberation of four million black slaves in the United States, obtained as a result of a huge Civil War, not by means of a peaceful legal process. In addition, the main Soviet criticism of the emancipation as a clever conspiracy of the government and the landlords at the expense of the peasants lacks substance: it is disproved both by the process of emancipation itself and by a sharp decline of the fortunes of the landlord class in its wake. Yet the emancipation was in fact a compromise, and criticism, even fundamental criticism, together with the praise, may also be in order—not a surprising situation, given the scope and the import of the measure.

The land allotted to the former serfs turned out to be insufficient. While in theory they were to retain the acreage that they had been tilling for themselves prior to 1861, in fact they received 18 percent less land, with heavy losses in the fertile southern provinces. In addition, in the course of the partitioning, former serfs often failed to obtain forested areas or access to a river, with the result that they had to assume additional obligations toward their onetime landlords to satisfy their needs. One expert estimated that 13 percent of the former serfs received liberal allotments of land; 45 percent, allotments sufficient to maintain their families and economies; whereas 42 percent had to manage with insufficient allotments. Another wrote: "The owners, numbering 30,000 noblemen, retained ownership over some 95 million dessyatins of the better land immediately after the Reform, compared with 116 million dessyatins of suitable land left to the 20 million 'emancipated' peasants."[4] Other scholars have stressed the overpopulation and underemployment among former serfs, who, at least after a period of transition, were no longer obliged to work for the landlord and at the same time had less land to cultivate for themselves. State peasants, although by no means prosperous, received, on the whole, better terms than did the serfs of private owners.

The financial arrangement proved unrealistic and impossible to execute. By the time the redemption payments were finally abolished in 1905, former serfs had paid, counting the interest, one and one-half billion rubles for the land initially valued at less than a billion. While the serfs were officially to redeem only the land, not their persons, the payments actually included a concealed recompense for the loss of their labor. Thus, more had to be paid for the first unit of land than for the following units. As a whole the landlords of southern Russia received 340 million rubles for land valued at 280 million; those of northern Russia, where *obrok* prevailed, 340 million rubles for land worth 180 million rubles.

The transfer of land in most areas to peasant communes rather than to individual peasants probably represented another major error. Arguments in favor of the commune ranged from the Slavophile admiration of the moral aspects of that institution to the desire on the part of the government to have taxes and recruits guaranteed by means of communal responsibility and to the assertion that newly liberated peasants would not be able to maintain themselves but could find protection in the commune. But the disadvantages of the commune outweighed its advantages. Of primary importance was the fact that the commune tended to perpetuate backwardness, stagnation, and overpopulation in the countryside, precisely when Russian agriculture drastically needed improvement and modernization.

The emancipation of the serfs made other fundamental changes that followed it much more feasible. These included the establishment of the so-called *zemstvo* system of local self-government, and municipal, judicial, and military reforms. The law enacted in January 1864 constituted a strong modernization and democratization of local government, as well as a far-reaching effort on the part of the state to meet the many pressing needs of rural Russia, largely by stimulating local initiative and activity. Institutions of self-government, *zemstvo* assemblies and boards, were created at both the district and provincial levels—the word *zemstvo* itself connotes land, country, or people, as distinct from the central government. The electorate of the district *zemstvo* assemblies consisted of three categories: the towns, the peasant communes, and all individual landowners, including those not from the gentry. Representation was proportionate to landownership, with some allowance for the possession of real estate in towns. The elections were indirect. Members of district assemblies, in turn, elected from their own midst, regardless of class, delegates to their provincial assembly. Whereas the district and provincial *zemstvo* assemblies, in which the *zemstvo* authority resided, met only once a year to deal with such items as the annual budget and basic policies, they elected *zemstvo* boards to serve continuously as the executive agencies of the system and to employ professional staffs. A variety of local needs fell under the purview of *zemstvo* institutions: education, medicine, veterinary service, insurance, roads, the establishment of food reserves for emergency, and many others. The municipal reform of 1870 applied many practices and principles of the *zemstvo* system to towns. The *zemstvo* system has been criticized for encompassing for a long time only the ethnically Russian central provinces, not the borderlands; for being heavily weighted in favor of landlords and property; for having an insufficient power of taxation and being in general a junior partner at best to respective governors and the entire central administration; for the fact that the smallest *zemstvo* unit, the district, proved too large for effective and prompt response to many popular needs, and on other grounds besides. Yet the system accomplished much for Russia, from its establishment in 1864 until its demise in 1917; criticisms refer more to the insufficient extent of the reform than to its substance. The year 1864 witnessed the enactment of another "great reform," that of the legal system. The Russian judiciary needed improvement probably even more than the local government. Archaic, bureaucratic, cumbersome, corrupt, based on the class privilege rather than on the principle of equality before the law, and relying entirely on a written and secret procedure, the old system was thoroughly hated by informed and thinking Russians. The legislation of 1864 marked a decisive break with that part of the Russian past. The most significant single aspect of the reform was the separation of the courts from the administration. Instead of constituting merely a part of the bureaucracy, the judiciary became an independent branch of government. Judges were not to be dismissed or transferred, except by court action. Judicial procedure acquired a largely public and oral character, instead of the former bureaucratic secrecy. The contending parties were to present their cases in court and have adequate legal support. In fact, the reform largely created the class of lawyers in Russia, who began rapidly to acquire great public prominence. Two legal procedures, the general and the abbreviated one, replaced the chaos of twenty-one alternate ways to conduct a case. Trial by jury was introduced for serious criminal offences, while justices of the peace were established to deal with minor civil and criminal cases. The courts were organized into a single unified system with the Senate at the apex. All Russians were to be equal before the law and receive the same treatment. Apart from the general system stood the military and ecclesiastical courts, as well as special courts for peasants who lived mostly by customary law. Later, the government sometimes tried to influence judges for political reasons, and, more important, in its struggle against revolution it withdrew whole categories of legal cases from the normal procedure, but the basic judicial reform of 1864 could not be undone in imperial Russia.

Even the military transformation of 1874 has been appropriately listed with the "great reforms." The obligation to serve was extended from the lower classes alone to all Russians, with recruits to be called up by lot, while at the same time the length of the active service was drastically reduced, and a military reserve was organized. New arrangements stressed military education and specialization but also, perhaps the most important point, introduced elementary education for all draftees. Minister of War Dmitri Miliutin's measures for the army were extended to the navy by Grand Duke Constantine.

The "great reforms" went a long way toward transforming Russia. To be sure, the empire of the tsars remained an autocracy, but it changed in many other respects. Vastly important in themselves, the government reforms also helped to bring about sweeping economic and social changes in the years and decades following. The growth of capitalism in Russia, the evolution of the peasantry, the decline of the gentry, the rise of the middle class, particularly the professional group, centered both in the *zemstvo* and the new legal institutions, and of the industrial proletariat—all were affected by Alexander II's legislation. Russia began to take long strides on the road to becoming a modern nation. Nor could the changes be reversed.

But the road was not an easy one. Alexander II acted as he did because after thirty years of Nicholas I's rule, there was no other way out. In contrast to Peter the Great (or Lenin later), he was a conservative, not a radical reformer, with no hatred for the old or passion for the new, and he was effectively aided only by some liberal or at least utterly loyal bureaucrats. The repeated failures and the ultimate defeat in the Crimean War had already cost the government much support throughout the spectrum of public opinion, from right to left. The reforms, particularly the emancipation of the serfs, did receive considerable, especially liberal, endorsement, but they brought new problems. Before long, the authorities abandoned their liberal course. From then until 1905, and after that in a sense again from 1907 until 1917, the liberals remained on the margin of Russian politics. Moreover, the most prominent opponents of the established system were no longer Westernizing university professors or quixotic Slavophiles but dedicated radicals and revolutionaries. The intellectual climate had changed drastically and very rapidly—a fact that is still insufficiently recognized by the students of the period. Such prominent participants in the scene as Fedor Dostoevsky, Constantine Pobedonostsev, and Michael Katkov responded much more quickly as they veered sharply to the right in reacting against what they saw on the left.

The new intellectual climate, like all the preceding ones from the time of Peter the Great, came to Russia from the West. It was an uneasy but dogmatic and inspiring combination of utilitarianism, positivism, materialism, scientism, and realism, more especially critical realism. Sometimes the entire process has been described as a transition from Romanticism to realism. Only material, scientific reality deserved recognition. Science at the time, it has been pointed out, was conquering ever-new fields and, indeed, linking its fields together toward a total scientific view of the universe. Moreover, it was claimed that a high school education should be sufficient to acquire that complete true knowledge. Many specialists have argued that while sharing in the general realistic and materialistic character of the age in Europe, Russians tended to be more extreme, because of such special circumstances as a reaction to the stifling of intellectual life under Nicholas I, the autocratic and oppressive nature of the regime, the weak development of the middle class or other elements of moderation and compromise, as well as a rather sharp democratization of the educated public. But whether especially extreme or not, educated Russians were part of the Western world. In science proper, to cite the most telling example, it was Dmitri Mendeleev's periodic table of elements (1869) that organized modern chemistry and beyond that made a major contribution to the above-mentioned total scientific view of the world. And in literature it was the great Russian novelist Ivan Turgenev (1818–1883), who in his celebrated novel *Fathers and Sons* (1862; more exactly *Fathers and Children*) and other works presented the most memorable account of the clash of the two generations, and ages, and established the term "nihilist" forever after.

Whereas the "fathers," the men of the 1840s, grew up on German Idealistic philosophy and Romanticism in general, with its emphasis on the metaphysical, religious, aesthetic, and historical approaches to reality, the "sons," the men of the 1860s, hoisted the banners of materialism, positivism, utilitarianism, and especially "realism." "Nihilism"—and, in large part, "realism," particularly "critical realism"—meant above all a fundamental rebellion against accepted values and standards: against abstract thought and family control, against polite manners and art for art's sake, against lyric poetry and school discipline, against religion and rhetoric. The earnest young men and women of the 1860s wanted to cut through every polite veneer, to get rid of all conventional sham, to get to the bottom of things. What they usually considered real and worthwhile included the natural and physical sciences, simple and sincere human relations, and a society based on knowledge and reason rather than on ignorance, prejudice, exploitation, and oppression. The casting down of idols—and there surely were many idols in mid-nineteenth-century Russia, as elsewhere—emancipation, and freedom constituted the moral strength of nihilism. Yet few in our age would fail to see the narrowness of its vision, or neglect the fact that it erected cruel idols of its own. Interestingly, critics debate to this day whether Turgenev presented Bazarov, the nihilist, as a positive or a negative character.

Bazarov's most striking counterpart in life was a young literary critic at the *Russian Word*, Dmitri Pisarev (1840–1868). A long arrest and, after that, death by drowning at an early age made him in a sense a transitional figure, open to speculation as to his possible later course of development. But he did express strikingly the new nihilist negation and apparently had readers all over Russia. As the critic stated his creed: "what can be broken, that should be broken; what survives the blow, that can be of use; what breaks into bits, that is garbage; in any case, strike right and left. This will do no harm, and can do no harm." Or, a little differently: "Words and illusions perish; facts remain." And to underline the directness and simplicity of the new faith: "True science leads to tangible knowledge; and what is tangible, what can be seen by one's eyes and felt by one's hands, that will be understood by a ten-year-old boy, as well as by a simple peasant, by an educated person or by a learned specialist."[5] Natural sciences and technical and professional skills should replace useless philosophy and esthetics. Pisarev is perhaps best remembered for his denigration of Pushkin and his assertion that a pair of boots is of a greater value than Shakespeare.

Nihilism concentrated on the individual, whom it promised to liberate from all the prejudices and all the false gods hemming human existence, although presumably more and better critical realists would eventually improve society. But the social program, as such, had to be found elsewhere. Pisarev himself admired much in the work of Chernyshevsky, who was probably the most influential writer in Russia in the second half of the nineteenth century, certainly so among the radicals. Nicholas Chernyshevsky (1828–1889) was an erudite, a scholar, a literary critic, a publicist, and an intellectual of many parts. An outstanding economist, he also concerned himself with esthetics, developing further Belinsky's ideas on the primacy of life over art; and with nineteenth-century French history, where he aimed to demonstrate the failure of liberalism, as well as with Darwinism, which he regarded as an enormous advance in science but criticized for its Malthusian bias;[6] not to mention a variety of Russian problems. The most important writer and editor of a leading periodical, the *Contemporary,* from 1855 to 1862, Chernyshevsky was arrested in the latter year for connections with radical figures and underground literature. Although no criminal complicity was ever established in his case, he was eventually condemned to fourteen years' hard labor and banishment for life to Siberia. Chernyshevsky was allowed to return to European Russia, specifically Astrakhan, only in 1883. Perhaps more so than in regard to any other figure in Russian intellectual history, there was an astounding contrast between Chernyshevsky's few years and limited possibilities of activity and his colossal impact on his countrymen and women. The reader must keep firmly in mind the spirit of the time and thank such guides as Irina Paperno.[7]

Much more a scholar than Pisarev, Chernyshevsky tried to analyze in some detail the Russian economy and to prescribe its future course. In the process, he became a major contributor to the emerging general doctrine of populism, because he endorsed the peasant commune and a noncapitalist way of development for his country. Yet it is also important to realize the nature of qualifications that Chernyshevsky included in his endorsement, as well as to see how that endorsement fit into Chernyshevsky's general outlook as a progressive intellectual and "enlightener." To follow Andrzej Walicki:

> Of particular interest in this respect in his article "A Critique of Philosophical Prejudices against the Communal Ownership of the Land." Although he declared that there were no features typical of society that could not be deduced from characteristics of individuals, Chernyshevsky nevertheless posited the existence of a universal evolutionary law, which he summed up as follows: "As far as form is concerned, the highest stage of development everywhere represents a return to the first stage which—at the intermediate stage—was replaced by its opposite." Since individuals can "skip" the intermediate stage, he argued, why should not societies—which are only aggregates of individuals—be able to do so as well? If individuals can evolve at a

faster pace symbolized in the progression 1, 4, 64, . . . , then social development can follow the formula 1A, 4A, 64A, . . .

This argument was used by Chernyshevsky to prove that Russia could
bypass the capitalist stage and that the communal ownership of the land
could serve as a basis for the socialist development of agriculture. . . . The
evolution of forms of ownership progressed from the communal property of
the tribe through private ownership (which reached its culmination under
capitalism) to modern communal ownership by associations; Chernyshevsky had no doubt that this last stage would soon replace capitalist property relations in the developed countries. Communal landholdings in Russia,
Chernyshevsky thought, were a form of ownership corresponding to the first
phase of the universal development of mankind; since a direct transition to
the third phase—that of postcapitalist collectivism—seemed likely, there was
no point in abolishing the village commune and thus destroying the collec-
tivist traditions alive among the Russian people. On the contrary, attempts
should be made to modernize the commune and to transform it along
rational lines into an association similar to the workers' associations existing
in Western Europe.[8]

The whole was a remarkable combination of the Enlightenment, even of Romanticism with its triple beat, and of the newer currents of the age, all in the burgeoning
spirit of radical and revolutionary optimism.

But Chernyshevsky's greatest coup proved to be his novel *What Is to Be Done?*
written after his arrest in 1862 and published in the main in the *Contemporary*
through the government's mistaken permissiveness. Still strange, controversial, and
puzzling in places—perhaps largely because its peculiar provenance prevented a
certain kind of direct talk—and, without literary merit, Chernyshevsky's work
became the bible of young radicals and revolutionaries throughout Russia, all the
way to Lenin's brother, executed in 1887 for conspiring to assassinate Alexander III
and indeed to young Lenin himself. Its heroes and heroines, Vera Pavlovna,
Lopukhov, Kirsanov, and especially Rakhmetov, represented the new generation
with its critical realism and superior morality, while Vera Pavlovna's dress atelier
marked a new type of cooperative social organization. Rakhmetov, at least, a dedicated ascetic revolutionary (as a type of revolutionary saint, Chernyshevsky came
from a priest's family), looked beyond personal problems and adjustments to the
great day.

Chernyshevsky's closest collaborator and friend at the *Contemporary* was a talented young literary critic, Nicholas Dobroliubov (1836–1861). Less learned than his
mentor and without Chernyshevsky's philosophical background and great variety of
interests, Dobroliubov embodied the new orientation in its pristine form. He
believed in facts and in social progress, and he judged writers by their faithfulness in
presenting the former and contributing to the latter. Even more than Chernyshevsky,

he clashed with the members of the preceding generation, in particular the famed Westernizers, as well as with many of his contemporaries. All these were "superfluous men," whether embodied in Lermontov's Pechorin or in Goncharov's Oblomov. The cleavage, or rather the chasm, between the radicals and the liberals in Russia had never been so strikingly presented. Herzen was stunned and enraged by the nature and the ferocity of the attack. Dobroliubov's literary criticism was, of course, highly subjective, frequently substituting the critic's ideas for those of the author, little concerned with the aesthetic qualities of what he analyzed, and otherwise deficient. Yet it gave a fine, impassioned expression to some of the main currents and attitudes of the age. It is in that sense that such articles as "What Is Oblomovism?" remain classics. Dobroliubov died at the age of twenty-five of consumption.

Chernyshevsky, as already mentioned, gave strong support to the peasant commune, reinforced by the great prestige he had acquired in radical circles and beyond. Yet he was far from idolizing that Russian agrarian institution: communal, it merely represented the first stage in the three-stage evolution of human society, and it deserved preservation and had a socialist future only because the forthcoming triumph of socialism in the West would make it possible for Russia to bypass capitalism and join the new socialist world. Yet Russia also contained some unconditional, almost idolatrous, admirers of the peasant commune. Most prominent were Constantine Aksakov and the Slavophiles in general, with their glorification of "a moral choir," "a triumph of human spirit." It is very likely that Herzen, who had argued indefatigably the Westernizer cause against the Slavophiles, turned around, once he had migrated to the West, and borrowed the Slavophile arguments to defend Russia to Michelet and other disparaging critics. In any case, Herzen's defense of the Russian peasant commune was much more emotional and spiritual than Chernyshevsky's, and, again, it was, apparently, influential. Bakunin too, already a full-fledged anarchist, put his confidence in the peasant masses, with special faith in their revolutionary nature, which needed only an initial spark to explode. At the time, Russia was still 90 percent peasant, and that fact was bound to be reflected in the ideologies, literature, and general culture of the country. It also accounted for some peculiarities of the Russian radical and revolutionary movement and for certain differences between it and its counterparts to the west. However, the connection between the two sides, Russian and Western, still could be observed, especially if the issue is considered in broad terms. As Martin Malia wrote recently in the polemical manner:

> The point here is that the Russian revolutionary intelligentsia, from its inception in Left Hegelianism in the 1840s to the 1880s, was in constant symbiosis with German and French radicalism. In fact, in Russia no less than in Germany or France, the Socialism of the intellectuals was a variant of modern Europe's common quest for a perfect, egalitarian democracy founded on the people. Russian Populism was not a radical species apart, as is usually

assumed; it was an adaptation to backward Russian conditions of a common European aspiration.[9]

As the 1860s turned into the 1870s and the Russian radical and revolutionary movement continued its wayward course, some new populist writers became important and influential. The two most frequently mentioned as amplifying and deepening the doctrine of populism were Peter Lavrov (1823–1900) and Nicholas Mikhailovsky (1842–1904). Lavrov, a colonel and a professor of mathematics at the Artillery Academy, was also a philosopher, a historian of science, and a notable publicist. Linked to the radical movement in Russia, he was forced—and fortunate—to leave the country in 1869 and to continue his activities abroad, where he published the periodical *Forward,* first in Zurich, then in London, and, later edited the journal of the revolutionary society Will of the People from Geneva. Lavrov's works included, among others, *A Survey of the Issues in Practical Philosophy* (1860), *A Survey of the Physical and Mathematical Sciences* (1866), *A Survey of the History of Thought* (1874), and *Problems in Understanding History* (1898), as well as a study of the Paris Commune, in which he had taken part. Lavrov became instantly famous and a leading figure on the Left with the appearance in 1868–1869 in the periodical the *Week* of his series of essays known under the general title *Historical Letters.*

A positivist, broadly speaking, Lavrov proposed to base his own view and activity, and by extension those of populism, on the so-called subjective sociology, a heroic, if not always consistent, effort to uphold the identity, importance, and efficacy of the individual in an age of science, materialism, and determinism:

The basic assumption of "subjective sociology" (an unfortunate and not particularly accurate label) can be summed up under three headings. First, it was a defense of ethical standards, and implied that men had the right to judge everything from their own point of view and to protest even against the "objective laws of history"—that indeed they were obliged to protest against human suffering even where the situation seemed hopeless. Second, it was an epistemological and methodological standpoint that disputed the possibility of "objective" knowledge in the social sciences; "subjectivism" in this sense implied that historical and sociological knowledge could never be really objective because they were colored by the scholar's social position, his unconscious emotions, or consciously chosen ideals. Third, it was a philosophy of history that claimed that the "subjective factor"—human will and consciousness (expressed in the activity of a revolutionary party or in deliberate state intervention)—could effectively oppose the spontaneous-development trend and influence the course of history. For the Populist revolutionaries this last point was, of course, the most important; on it Lavrov based his "practical philosophy," which proclaimed that by forming a party and establishing a common program "critically thinking individuals" could become a significant force capable of changing reality and realizing their "subjective" aims.[10]

Critically thinking individuals were thus the true bearers of progress, and Lavrov was certain that they would perform their historical obligation. Indeed: *"The development of personality in its physical, mental, and moral aspects, the incarnation of truth and justice in social forms*—here is the brief formula, which encompasses, so it seems to me, all that can be considered progress."* Or: "progress is the process of development in humanity of a consciousness and incarnation of truth and justice, by means of the work of the critical thought of individuals on the material of their contemporary culture." And: "Any human being who thinks critically and decides to embody his thought in his life can be an agent of progress." Although it was the critically thinking individuals who advanced society, a disjunction between their interests and the interests of the masses was illusory:

> The interests of an individual clearly understood demand that the individual attempt a realization of common interests; common aims can be obtained only in individuals. Therefore the true social theory demands neither a *subordination* of the social element to the individual, nor an *absorption* of the individual by society, but a *merging* of the social and the individual interests. The individual must develop an understanding of social interests which are also those of the individual.[11]

Science, philosophy, art, literature, all the advantages of critically thinking individuals were obtained at the price of heavy labor, ignorance, even savagery, of the masses. "History demanded victims." And: "A better historical future had to be won." Every critically thinking individual, therefore, had the choice of joining the struggle for progress, whatever the cost, or supinely watching the evil around him or her and, so to speak, sanctioning it. The figure of a repentant nobleman—Lavrov himself came from a landowning family—or, more broadly, of the debt of the intelligentsia to the people, so often associated with populism, received a rich and striking expression in Lavrov's writing. In fact, even in his "anthropological" studies, Lavrov emphasized three phases in the development of the animal and human world: the original Hobbesian dog-eat-dog principle; the instinctive "unconscious solidarity" of certain species in the struggle for survival; and the human conscious solidarity.[12] The peasant commune was thus to mark the Russian future and to swallow private property, although, characteristically, Lavrov also stressed the need to work with and to educate the people, because they were to carry out the transformation.

Nicholas Mikhailovsky has frequently been cited as an even more quintessential populist theoretician and intellectual than Lavrov. A leading literary critic and publicist, as well as a notable sociologist, Mikhailovsky provided a broad sociological doctrine for populism and at the same time wrote striking essays on more specific topics. Rather constant in his views and determined in his defense of the peasant commune and populism in a Russia that was becoming increasingly capitalist and increasingly the subject to Marxist and certain other approaches, the critic dotted his "i's" and in the process provided much evidence for the interpretation of populism as a backward peasant utopia.

Like Lavrov, Mikhailovsky was deeply concerned with the relationship between the individual and the masses, and, again like Lavrov, he favored the subjective method in sociology, based on one's moral judgment. "As unconditioned justice is impossible for a human being, as pure art without tendentiousness is impossible, so is impossible an exclusively objective method in sociology. . . . The objective method avoids in a most coarse and crude way the evaluation of the inner meaning of phenomena and glides on their surface." In fact, however, "the human individuality, its fate, its interests that is what . . . must be placed as the cornerstone of our theoretical thought in the area of social issues and of our practical activity." Mikhailovsky too believed that there was no contradiction between the interests of the individual and of the people, stressing the consideration that the basic identification of the individual is the individual's work, whereas the people constituted the working classes of society. The search for truth-verity (*pravda-istina*, objective truth) and truth-justice (*pravda-spravedlivost*, subjective truth, based on the social ideal) and their synthesis represented one of the fundamental problems of sociology, which Mikhailovsky was trying to resolve.

In turning from the individual to society, social history, and social evolution, Mikhailovsky relied heavily on his own rather peculiar sociological framework. He conceded that, as the Russian (or Baltic German) embryologist Karl Ernst von Baer and other scholars had established, in the organic world progress proceeded by means of an increasing complexity and differentiation. The human organism itself demonstrated this principle. But, Mikhailovsky insisted, not human society, because society is not an organism but a totality of indivisible organisms. "In an organism it is not parts, but the whole that suffers or rejoices, in society the opposite is true."

> They keep repeating their line: society progresses when, like an organism it is subject to a differentiation and divides into several parts. Well and good, let *society progress*, but do understand that in that case the *individual regresses*. If one is to consider only this aspect of the matter, then society is the first, the nearest and the most vicious enemy of the human being against which the human being must be constantly on guard.

Thus, a peasant in a village does everything himself: he is a carpenter, a cabinet-maker, a house-painter, a weaver, and so forth. Once he moves to town and to a factory, he specializes in one productive activity, or a part of such activity, and he forgets all the rest. Society gains from the shift, but the individual loses, for he sacrifices a harmonious, many-sided development of his integral personality. Mikhailovsky came to distinguish between the type and the level of development. In the given example, the peasant belonged to a higher type of human being, although a skilled worker in a modern factory may well have reached a much higher level within his type. The critic postulated the following definition of progress:

> Progress is the gradual approach towards the wholeness of individuals, towards the fullest and the most many-sided possible division of labor among human organs and the least possible division of labor among human beings. Immoral, unjust, irrational is everything that delays that development. Moral, just, wise, and useful is only that which diminishes the heterogeneity of society, thus strengthening the heterogeneity of its individual components.

Russia, and in particular the Russian peasant commune, embodied a higher type of social development than anything the West had to offer, superior though the latter was in boosting to higher and higher levels the social institutions it did possess. Therefore, Russia could have its own historical evolution, avoiding the bourgeois system of Europe and relying instead on its native communal arrangements. In 1872 Mikhailovsky wrote:

> In Europe the labor question is a revolutionary question, because there it demands *a transfer* of the means of production into the hands of the laborer, expropriating the present owners. The labor question in Russia is a conservative question, for here it demands only the *preservation* of the means of production in the hands of the laborer, a guarantee of what they own to the present owners. Here, right next to Petersburg, that is, in one of the most Anglicized localities, a locality sprinkled with factories, industrial plants, parks, summer houses, there are villages, the inhabitants of which live on *their own* land, burn *their own* wood, eat *their own* bread, dress in kaftans and coats of *their own* work, made from the wool of *their own* sheep. Give them a firm guarantee of that kind of *their own*, and the Russian labor question is solved. [13]

Yet it is a measure of Mikhailovsky's worry at the time and uncertainty for the future that, in spite of his radical credentials, he wanted the autocratic Russian government to guarantee the peasant commune and peasant property.

A reference to the spirit of the age and Russian radicalism helps us to understand the peculiar course of Russian history in the 1860s and 1870s. As the government proceeded with its necessary but, in a sense, unwelcome reforms, trouble quickly came to occupy center stage. In the early 1860s there were numerous peasant uprisings, student disturbances, even the still unexplained fires of 1862. Poland, which had received a liberal treatment from Alexander II, rose in 1863 in a mighty rebellion. And on April 4, 1866, Dmitri Karakozov, an unbalanced student and a revolutionary, attempted and barely failed to assassinate the emperor. To be sure, the Polish rebellion was defeated, and the rights of the Poles were further greatly reduced, with the government even receiving strong support, somewhat to its surprise, from Russian nationalists, led by Katkov. But, especially after Karakozov's shot, there seemed to be a continuous danger on the Left and a continuous struggle of the imperial government against the revolution, all the way to 1917.

Whereas in the 1860s revolutionary acts were usually individual and revolutionary circles embryonic, there were many more radicals in the 1870s, and they were better indoctrinated and organized. Populism by that time had become the dominant radical ideology in Russia. And while relatively few men and women appeared to be ready to take it to a murderous and revolutionary extreme, they seemed to have little difficulty in replenishing their ranks and even profiting from a certain tolerance, if not approval, of broader layers of society.

The climax came in 1873, 1874, and the years immediately following. When in 1873 the imperial government ordered Russian students to abandon their studies in Switzerland—where Russians, especially women, could often pursue higher education more easily than in their fatherland—and return home, a considerable number of them, together with numerous other young men and women who had stayed in Russia, prepared to "go to the people." And in the summer of 1874 they went to the villages, some two and a half thousand of them, to become rural teachers, scribes, doctors, veterinarians, nurses, or storekeepers. Some meant simply to help the people as best they could. Others nurtured vast radical and revolutionary plans. In particular, the followers of Bakunin put their faith in a spontaneous, elemental, colossal revolution of the people, which they had merely to help start, while the disciples of Lavrov believed in the necessity of gradualism—more exactly, in the need for education and propaganda among the masses before they could overturn the old order and establish the new. The populist crusade failed. On the whole, the masses did not respond. The only significant uprising that the populists produced resulted from an impressive but forged manifesto in which the tsar ordered his loyal peasants to attack his enemies, the landlords. Indeed, the muzhiks on occasion handed over the strange newcomers from the cities to the police. The police, in turn, were frantically active, arresting all the crusaders they could find. Mass trials, of the 193 and of the 50 in 1877–1878, marked the sad conclusion of the "going to the people" stage of populism. The peasants, to repeat, would not revolt, nor could satisfactory conditions be established to train them for later revolutionary action.

Yet one more possibility of struggle remained: the one advocated by another populist theoretician, Peter Tkachev (1844–1886) and by an amoral and dedicated revolutionist, Sergei Nechaev (1847–1882). It was given the name "Jacobin," in memory of the Jacobins who seized power to transform France during the great French Revolution. If the peasants would not act—and, according to Tkachev, they would never act on their own—it remained up to the revolutionaries themselves to fight and defeat the government. Tkachev believed in conspiracy, centralization, and discipline, as well as, it might be added, in contrast to the mainstream of populism, in a leveling of human beings rather than in a many-sided development of personalities. Several years of revolutionary conspiracy, terrorism, and assassination ensued. The first instances of violence occurred more or less spontaneously, sometimes as counter-measures against brutal police officials. Thus, early in 1878, Vera Zasulich shot and wounded the military governor of St. Petersburg, General Fedor Trepov, who had ordered a political prisoner to be flogged; but, although there was no doubt concerning her action, a jury failed to convict her, with the result that political cases were withdrawn from regular judicial procedure. Ironically, Zasulich herself rejected terrorism as revolutionary strategy. But before long an organization emerged that consciously put terrorism at the center of its activity. The conspiratorial revolutionary society "Land and Freedom," founded in 1876, split in 1879 into two groups: the "Black Partition," or "Total Land Repartition," which emphasized preparation and propaganda, and the "Will of the People," which mounted an all-out terroristic offensive against the government. Members of the Will of the People believed that, because of the highly centralized nature of the Russian state, a few assassinations could do tremendous damage to the regime, as well as provide the requisite political instruction for the educated society and the masses. They selected the emperor, Alexander II, as their chief target and condemned him to death. What followed has been described as an "emperor hunt," and in certain ways it defies imagination. The Executive Committee of the Will of the People included only about thirty men and women, led by such persons as Andrew Zheliabov, who was born a serf, and Sophia Perovskaia who came from Russia's highest administrative class, but it fought the entire Russian Empire. Although the police made every effort to destroy the revolutionaries and although many terrorists perished, the Will of the People made one attempt after another to assassinate the emperor. Time and again Alexander II escaped through sheer luck. Many people were killed when the very dining room of the Winter Palace was blown up, while at one time the emperor's security officials refused to let him leave his suburban residence, except by water! (The government was isolated further, and in a major way, by the extremely negative reaction in the country to the decisions of the Congress of Berlin, which, in the summer of 1878, changed the provisions of the Treaty of San Stefano, a Russian diplomatic defeat for which the public held the government responsible.)

After the explosion in the Winter Palace and after being faced by industrial strikes, student disturbances, and a remarkable lack of sympathy on the part of the educated public, as well as by the dauntless terrorism of the Will of the People, the emperor finally decided on a more moderate policy that could lead to a rapprochement with the public. He appointed General Count Michael Loris-Melikov first as head of a special administrative commission and several months later as minister of the interior. Loris-Melikov was to suppress terrorism but also to propose reforms. Several moderate or liberal ministers replaced a number of reactionaries. Loris-Melikov's plan called for the participation of representatives of the public, both elected and appointed, in considering administrative and financial reforms—not unlike the pattern followed in the abolition of serfdom. On March 13, 1881, Alexander II indicated his willingness to consider Loris-Melikov's proposal. On the same day, he was finally killed by the remaining members of the Will of the People.

Although it took Alexander III a number of months to change top personnel and to make reactionary policy explicit, that policy was to continue to the end of his reign, as well as in the reign of Nicholas II until the Revolution of 1905. The promoters of reaction included Constantine Pobedonostsev, formerly a noted jurist at the University of Moscow, who had served as tutor to Alexander and had become in 1880 the ober-procurator of the Holy Synod; Dmitri Tolstoy, who returned to the government in 1882 to head the Ministry of the Interior; and Ivan Delianov, who took charge of the Ministry of Education in the same year. Pobedonostsev, the chief theoretician as well as the leading practitioner of reaction in the last decades of the nineteenth century, characteristically emphasized the weakness and viciousness of man and the fallibility and dangers of human reason, hated the Industrial Revolution and the growth of cities, and even wanted "to keep people from inventing things." The state, he believed, had as its high purpose the maintenance of law, order, stability, and unity. In Russia, that aim could be accomplished only by means of autocracy and the Orthodox Church.

"Temporary Regulations" to protect state security and public order, issued late in the summer of 1881, gave officials in designated areas broad authority in dealing with the press and with people who could threaten public order. Summary search, arrest, imprisonment, exile, and prompt trials by courts-martial became common occurrences in Russia.[14] The Temporary Regulations were aimed primarily at the Will of the People, which lasted long enough to offer the new ruler peace, on conditions of political amnesty and the convocation of a constituent assembly! Although the Will of the People had been largely destroyed, even before the assassination of the emperor, and although most of its remaining members soon fell into the hands of the police, the Temporary Regulations were not rescinded but instead applied, as their vague wording permitted, to virtually anyone whom officials suspected or simply disliked. For many years after the demise of the Will of the People, terrorism died down in Russia, although occasional individual outbreaks occurred. Yet the Temporary Regulations, introduced originally for three years, were renewed. Indeed, the tsarist government relied on them during the rest of its existence, with the result that Russians lived under something like a partial state of martial law.

Alexander III's government also enacted "counterreforms" meant to curb the sweeping changes introduced by Alexander II and to buttress the centralized, bureaucratic, and class nature of the Russian system. New press regulations made the existence of radical journals impossible and the life of a mildly liberal press precarious. The University Statute of 1884, which replaced the more liberal statute of 1863, virtually abolished university autonomy and also emphasized that students were to be considered as "individual visitors," who had no right to form organizations or to claim corporate representation. In fact most policies of the Ministry of Education, whether they concerned the emphasis on classical languages in secondary schools, the drastic curtailment of higher education for women, or the expansion of the role of the Church in elementary teaching, consciously promoted the reactionary aims of the regime.

The tsar and his associates used every opportunity to help the gentry and to stress their leading position in Russia, as, for example, by the creation in 1885 of the State Gentry Land Bank. At the same time, they imposed further restrictions on the peasants, whom they considered to be essentially wards of the state rather than mature citizens. The policies of bureaucratic control of the peasants and of emphasizing the role of the gentry in the countryside found expression in the most outstanding "counterreform" of the reign, the establishment in 1889 of the office of *zemskii nachalnik*—*zemstvo* chief, or land captain. That official—who had nothing to do with the *zemstvo* self-government—was appointed and dismissed by the minister of the interior, following the recommendation of the governor of the land captain's province. His assigned task consisted in exercising direct bureaucratic supervision over the peasants and, in effect, managing them. Thus the land captain confirmed elected peasant officials, as well as decisions of peasant meetings, and he could prevent the officials from exercising their office, and even fine, arrest, or imprison them, although the fines imposed by the land captain could not exceed several rubles and the prison sentences, several days. Moreover, land captains received vast judicial powers, thus, contrary to the legislation of 1864, again combining administration and justice. In fact, these appointed officials replaced for the peasants—that is, for the vast majority of the people—elected and independent justices of the peace. The law of 1889 stipulated that land captains had to be appointed from members of the local gentry who met a certain property qualification. Each district received several land captains; each land captain administered several *volosts*, that is, townships or cantons. Russia obtained in this manner a new administrative network, one of land captaincies.

The following year, 1890, the government made certain significant changes in the *zemstvo* system. The previous classification of landholders, that of 1864, had been based only on the form of property, so that members of the gentry and other Russians who happened to hold land in individual ownership were not distinguished. But in 1890 the members of the gentry became a distinct group—and their representation was markedly increased. Peasants, on the other hand, could thenceforth elect only candidates for *zemstvo* seats, the governor making appointments to district *zemstvo* assemblies from these candidates, as recommended by land captains. In addition, the minister of the interior received the right to confirm chairmen of *zemstvo* boards in their office, while members of the boards and their employees were to be confirmed by their respective governors. In 1892, the town government underwent a similar "counterreform," which, among other provisions, sharply raised the property requirement for the right to vote. After its enactment, the electorate in St. Petersburg decreased from twenty-one thousand to eight thousand, and that in Moscow from twenty thousand to as little as seven thousand.

The reign of Alexander III also witnessed increased pressure on non-Orthodox denominations and a growth of the policy of Russification. Even Roman Catholics and Lutherans, who formed majorities in certain western areas of the empire and had unimpeachable international connections and recognition, faced discrimination: for instance, children of mixed marriages with the Orthodox automatically became Orthodox, and all but the dominant Church were forbidden to engage in proselytizing. Old Believers and Russian sectarians suffered greater hardships. The government also began to oppose sharply non-Christian faiths, such as Islam and Buddhism, which had devoted adherents among the many peoples of the empire.

Russification went hand in hand with militant Orthodoxy, although the two were by no means identical, for peoples who were not Great Russians, such as the Ukrainians and the Georgians, belonged to the Orthodox Church. Although Russification had been practiced earlier against the Poles—especially in the western provinces following the rebellions of 1830–1831 and 1863 and to somewhat lesser extent in Poland proper—and was also apparent in the attempts to suppress the budding Ukrainian nationalism, it became a general policy of the Russian government only late in the nineteenth century. It represented in part a reaction against the growing national sentiments of different peoples of the empire with their implicit threats to the unity of the state and in part a response to the rising nationalism of the Great Russians themselves. Alexander III has often been considered the first nationalist on the Russian throne. Certainly, in his reign, measures of Russification began to be extended not only to the rebellious Poles but also, for example, to the Georgians and Armenians in Transcaucasia and even gradually to the loyal Finns.

The Jews, who were very numerous in western Russia as a result of the invitation of late medieval Polish kings, were bound to suffer in the new atmosphere of aggressive Orthodoxy and Russification. And indeed, old limitations came to be applied to them with a new force, while new legislation was enacted to establish additional curbs on them and their activities. In contrast to the former lax enforcement of rules, Jews came to be rigorously restricted to residence in the "Pale of Jewish Settlement," that is, the area in western Russia where they had been living for a long time, with the added proviso that even within the Pale they could reside only in towns and smaller settlements inhabited by merchants and craftsmen, but not in the countryside. Educated or otherwise prominent Jews could usually surmount these restrictions, but the great bulk of the poor Jewish population was tied to its location. In 1887, the government established quotas for Jewish students in institutions of higher learning: 10 percent of the total enrollment within the Pale of Jewish Settlement, 5 percent in other provinces, and 3 percent in Moscow and St. Petersburg. In 1881, pogroms—the sad word entered the English language from the Russian—that is, violent popular outbreaks against the Jews, occurred in southwestern Russian towns and settlements, destroying Jewish property and sometimes taking Jewish lives. Pogroms were to recur sporadically until the end of imperial Russia. Local authorities often did little to prevent pogroms and on occasion, it is rather clear, even encouraged them. As

Pobedonostsev allegedly remarked, the Jewish problem in Russia was to be solved by the conversion to Orthodoxy of one-third of the Russian Jews, the emigration of one-third, and the death of the remaining third. It should be added that the Russian government defined Jews according to their religion; Jews who converted to Christianity escaped the disabilities imposed on the others.

Nicholas II, Alexander III's eldest son, born in 1868, became the autocratic ruler of Russia after his father's death in 1894. The last tsar possessed certain attractive qualities, such as simplicity, modesty, and devotion to his family. Indeed the extent of his patience and resignation to the will of God have become fully apparent only with the publication of new documents after the fall of the Soviet regime.[15] But these positive personal traits, and even Christian virtues, mattered little in a situation that demanded strength, determination, adaptability, and vision. It might well be argued that another Peter the Great could have saved the Romanovs and imperial Russia. There can be no doubt that Nicholas II did not. In fact, he proved to be both narrow-minded and weak, unable to remove reactionary blinders even when circumstances forced him into entirely new situations with great potentialities, and at the same time unable to manage even reaction effectively. The unfortunate emperor struck many observers as peculiarly automatic in his attitudes and actions, without the power of spontaneous decision, and—as his strangely colorless and undifferentiating diary so clearly indicated—also quite deficient in perspective. Various, often unworthy, ministers made crucial decisions that the sovereign had failed to evaluate. Later in the reign the empress, the reactionary, hysterical, and willful German princess Alexandra, became the power behind the throne, and with her even such an incredible person as Rasputin was able to rise to the position of greatest influence in the state. A good man, but a miserable ruler lost in the moment of crisis—no wonder Nicholas II has often been compared to Louis XVI. As Trotsky and other determinists have insisted, the archaic, rotten Russian system, which was about to collapse, could not logically produce a leader much different from that ineffective relic of the past. Or, as an old saying has it, the gods blind those whom they want to destroy.

Reaction continued unimpeded. The new emperor, who had been a pupil of Pobedonostsev, relied on the ober-procurator of the Holy Synod and on other reactionaries, such as his ministers of the interior, Dmitri Sipiagin and Viacheslav Plehve. The government continued to apply and extend the Temporary Regulations, to supervise the press with utmost severity, and, as best it could, to control and restrict education. The *zemstvo* and municipal governments experienced further curtailments of their jurisdictions. For example, in 1900 the limits of *zemstvo* taxation were strictly fixed, and the stockpiling of food for emergency was taken away from *zemstvo* jurisdiction and transferred to that of the bureaucracy. Moreover, the authorities often refused to confirm elections of *zemstvo* board members or appointments of *zemstvo* employees, trying to ensure that only people of unimpeachable loyalty to the regime would hold public positions of any kind.

Religious persecution grew. Russian sectarians suffered the most, in particular those groups that refused to recognize the state and perform such state obligations as military service. Many of them were exiled from central European Russia to the Caucasus and other distant areas. It was as a result of the policies of the Russian government that the *dukhobory* and certain other sects—helped, incidentally, by Leo Tolstoy—began to emigrate in large numbers to Canada and the United States. The state also confiscated the estates and charity funds of the Armenian Church and harassed other denominations in numerous ways. The position of the Jews, too, underwent further deterioration. Additional restrictions on them included a prohibition from acquiring real estate anywhere in the empire, except in the cities and settlements of the Jewish Pale, while new pogroms erupted in southwest Russia, including the horrible one in Kishinev in 1903.

But the case of Finland represented, in many respects, the most telling instance of the folly of Russification. As an autonomous grand duchy since the time it was won from Sweden in 1809, Finland received more rights from the Russian emperor, who became the Grand Duke of Finland, than it had had under Swedish rule, and remained a perfectly loyal, as well as a relatively prosperous and happy, part of the state until the very end of the nineteenth century and the introduction of the policy of Russification. Finnish soldiers helped suppress the Poles, and in general the Finns participated actively and fruitfully in almost every aspect of the life of the empire. Yet the new nationalism demanded that they too be Russified. While some preliminary measures in that direction had been enacted as early as in the reign of Alexander III, real Russification began with the appointment of General Nicholas Bobrikov as governor-general of Finland and of Plehve as state secretary for Finnish affairs in 1898. Russian authorities argued that Finland could remain different from Russia only as far as local matters were concerned, while it had to accept the general system in what pertained to the entire state. With that end in view, a manifesto concerning laws common to Finland and Russia and a new statute dealing with the military service of the Finns were published in 1899. Almost overnight, Finland became bitterly hostile to Russia, and a strong though passive resistance developed: new laws were ignored, draftees failed to show up, and so on. In 1901, freedom of assembly was abrogated in Finland. In 1902, Governor-General Bobrikov received the right to dismiss Finnish officials and judges and to replace them with Russians. In 1903, he was vested with extraordinary powers to protect state security and public order, which represented a definitive extension of the Temporary Regulations of 1881 to Finland. In 1904, Bobrikov was assassinated. The following year, the opposition in Finland became part of the revolution that spread throughout the empire.

Revolution came to Russia in 1905 for a number of reasons. As already indicated, from as early as the 1860s, the Russian government found it difficult to control the country or operate in a normal manner. Foreign affairs added to the tensions, whether in the case of the war against Turkey in 1877–1878, which Russia won but from which it had to limit its gains under pressure of other powers, or in the case of adventurous competition and eventually war and defeat administered by Japan, which led directly to the revolution of 1905. After the unification of Germany in January 1871, the new state became the greatest power on the European continent, leading to numerous diplomatic alignments and realignments that resulted eventually in a world war. Most important, the Russian government kept clinging for dear life to the old system at home, while the country was changing rapidly.

The gentry class declined after the "great reforms," a fact all the more significant because, as I have shown, the government did all it could to support and promote that class. Members of the gentry owned 73.1 million *desiatinas* of land, according to the census of 1877; 65.3 million, according to the census of 1887; 53.2 in 1905, according to a statistical compilation of that year; and only 43.2 million in 1911, according to one expert.[16] At the same time, to quote Robinson: "The average size of their holdings also diminished, from 538.2 *desiatinas* in 1887 to 488 in 1905; and their total possession of work horses from 546,000 in 1888–1891 to 499,000 in 1904–1906—that is, by 8.5 percent."[17] Although the emancipation settlement was on the whole generous to the gentry, it should be kept in mind that a very large part of the wealth of that class had been mortgaged to the state before 1861, so that much of the compensation that the landlords received as part of the reform went to pay debts, leaving rather little for development and modernization of the gentry economy. Moreover, most landlords failed to make effective use of what resources and opportunities they had. Deprived of serf labor and forced to adjust to more intense competition and other harsh realities of the changing world, members of the gentry had little in their education, outlook, or character to make them successful capitalist farmers. The important fact, much emphasized by Soviet scholars, that a small segment of the gentry did succeed in making the adjustment and proceeded to accumulate great wealth in a few hands does not fundamentally change the picture of the decline of a dominant class.

If the "great reforms" helped push the gentry down a steep incline, they also led to the rise of a Russian middle class, and in particular industrialists, businessmen, technicians, and other professional people—and neither result was intentional. Indeed, while the populist intelligentsia kept promoting Russia as the land of the peasants, and the Ministry of the Interior and many other government agencies increased their efforts to preserve the old agrarian and hierarchical system, the world around them was undergoing change. Russian industry continued to grow, and in the 1890s it expanded at an amazing rate, estimated by Gerschenkron at 8 percent a year on the average. Russian industrialists could finally rely on a better system of transportation, with the railroad network increasing in length by some 40 percent between 1881 and 1894 and doubling again between 1895 and 1905. In addition to Russian financial resources, foreign capital began to participate on a large scale in the industrial development of the country: foreign investment in Russian industry has been estimated at 100 million rubles in 1880, 200 million in 1890, and over 900 million in 1900. Most important, the Ministry of Finance—that great and much more modern rival of the Ministry of the Interior, especially when under the able and energetic leadership of Sergei Witte—not only built railroads and attracted foreign capital but also did everything possible to develop heavy industry in Russia. To subsidize that industry, Witte, himself a railroader and a businessman, increased Russian exports, drastically curtailed imports, relied on the tax on alcohol, balanced the budget, introduced the gold standard, and used heavy indirect taxation on items of everyday consumption to squeeze the necessary funds out of the peasants. Thus, in Russian conditions, the state played the leading role in bringing large-scale capitalist enterprise into existence.

The new Russian industry displayed certain striking characteristics. Because Russia industrialized late and rapidly, the Russians borrowed advanced Western technology wholesale, with the result that Russian factories were often more modern than their Western counterparts. Yet this progress in certain segments of the economy went along with appalling backwardness in others. Indeed, the industrial process frequently juxtaposed complicated machinery with primitive manual work performed by a cheap, if unskilled, labor force. For technological reasons, but also because of government policy, Russia acquired huge plants and large-scale industries almost overnight. Before long, the capitalists began to organize: a metallurgical syndicate was formed in 1902, a coal syndicate in 1904, and several others in later years. Russian entrepreneurs and employers came from different classes—from gentry to former serfs—with a considerable admixture of foreigners. Their leaders included a number of old merchant and industrialist families who were Old Believers, such as the celebrated Morozovs. As to markets, since the poor Russian people could absorb only a part of the products of Russian factories, the industrialists relied on huge government orders and also began to sell more abroad. In particular, because Russian manufacturers were generally unable to compete successfully in the West, export began on a large scale to the adjacent Asiatic countries of Turkey, Persia, Afghanistan, Mongolia, and China. Again, Witte and the government helped all they could by such means as the establishment of the Russo-Persian Bank and the building of the East China Railway, not to mention the Trans-Siberian. As already suggested, Russian economic activity in the Far East was part of the background of the Russo-Japanese War.

And the country acquired a considerable working class. While Russians began to work in factories and mines in the Urals and elsewhere far back in history, a sizeable industrial proletariat grew in Russia only late in the nineteenth century. Russian industrial workers numbered over 2 million in 1900 and perhaps 3 million out of a population of about 170 million in 1914. Not impressive in quantity in proportion to total population, the proletariat was more densely massed in Russia than in other countries. Because of the heavy concentration of Russian industry, over half the industrial enterprises in Russia employed more than five hundred workers each, with many employing more than a thousand each. The workers thus formed large and closely knit groups in industrial centers, which included St. Petersburg and

Moscow. These workers, to be sure, came usually from the village, and were often slow to break their village ties. Thus they frequently left their families behind, returned to their village for the harvest, and sought to retire to the village to end their days in peace. And even after their ties to the village had been severed, Russian workers could not immediately abandon their peasant mentality and outlook. Nevertheless, the Marxists were right in their argument with the populists in emphasizing the continuing growth of capitalism and the proletariat in Russia. With all due qualifications, an industrial working class had come to constitute a significant component of Russian population, an essential part of Russian economy, and a factor in Russian politics.

Significant labor legislation began in the 1880s, when Minister of Finance Nicholas Bunge tried to eliminate certain abuses of the factory system and also introduced factory inspectors. Although Bunge was forced to resign in 1887 under pressure from conservative interests, labor legislation resumed its course, largely as a response to the St. Petersburg strikes of 1896 and January 1897. A law in 1897, applicable to industrial establishments employing more than twenty workers, limited day work of adults to eleven and one-half hours and night work to ten hours. A pioneer labor insurance law, holding the employers responsible for accidents in connection with factory work, came out in 1903. However, in spite of labor legislation, and also in spite of the fact that wages probably increased in the years preceding World War I—a point, incidentally, strongly denied by Soviet scholars—Russian workers remained in general in miserable condition. Poorly paid, desperately overcrowded, and with very little education or other advantages, the proletariat of imperial Russia represented, in effect, an excellent example of a destitute and exploited labor force, characteristic of the early stages of capitalist development and described so powerfully by Engels and Marx.

Not surprisingly, the workers began to organize to better their lot. Indeed, they exercised at times sufficient pressure to further labor legislation, notably in the case of the law of 1897, and they could not be deterred by the fact that unions remained illegal until after the Revolution of 1905 and were still hampered by the government thereafter. The first significant strikes occurred in St. Petersburg in 1870, 1878, and 1879, in Kreenholm in 1872, and at a Morozov textile factory near Moscow in 1885. The short-lived but important Northern Workers' Union, led by a worker and populist, Stephen Khalturin, helped to organize the early labor movement in the capital. Major strikes took place in the 1890s, not only in St. Petersburg but also in Riga, in industrial areas of Russian Poland, in central Russia, especially in 1895, and in new plants in Ukraine. In addition, railwaymen struck in several places. The strike movement again gathered momentum in the first years of the twentieth century, culminating in the Revolution of 1905.

And at the bottom of Russian society there remained the enormous peasant world, still at least three-quarters of the total population of the country, according to the census of 1897. Their absolute numbers increasing rapidly, it was not clear whether Russian peasants were generally better off or worse off in the aftermath of the "great reforms." That they were badly off there was no doubt, and they experienced a major famine as late as 1891. The peasants too were ready for a revolution.

Education was of special importance in the evolution of the country. The death of Nicholas I and the coming of the "great reforms" meant liberalization in education as in other fields. The university statute of 1863 reaffirmed the principle of university autonomy, while Nicholas I's special restrictions on universities were among the first regulations to disappear in the new reign. The *zemstvo* reform of 1864 opened vast opportunities to establish schools in the countryside. In towns or rural areas, the increasing thirst for knowledge on the part of the Russians augured well for education in a liberal age. However, as already mentioned, official liberalism did not last long, and reaction logically, if unfortunately, showed a particular anxiety about education. As a result, the growth of education in Russia, while it could not be stopped, found itself hampered and to an extent deformed by government action.

After Dmitri Tolstoy replaced Alexander Golovnin in 1866 as minister of education, the ministry did its best to control education and to direct it into desirable channels. High standards were used in universities and secondary schools to keep the number of students down, hindering especially the academic advancement of students of low social background. In secondary education, the emphasis fell on the so-called *gimnaziia*, which became the only road to universities proper, as distinct from more specialized institutions of higher learning. These *gimnazii* concentrated on teaching the classical Latin and Greek languages, to the extent of some 40 percent of the total class time. Largely because of the rigorous demands, less than one-third of those who had entered the *gimnazii* were graduated. In addition to the natural obstacles that such a system presented to "socially undesirable" elements, ministers of education made direct appeals in their circulars to subordinates to keep "cook's sons" out of the *gimnazii*, as did one of Dmitri Tolstoy's successors, Ivan Delianov, in 1887. In general, the government tried to divide education into airtight compartments that students as a rule could not cross. Under Alexander III and Pobedonostsev, Church schools received special attention. Following the statute of 1884 concerning Church-parish schools, an effort was made to entrust elementary education as much as possible to the Church, the number of Church-parish schools increasing from forty-five hundred in 1882 to thirty-two thousand in 1894. While inferior in quality, these educational institutions were considered "safe."

Yet, in spite of all the vicissitudes, education continued to grow in Russia. The impact of the *zemstvos* proved especially beneficial. Thus, according to Charnolusky's figures, the sixty provinces of European Russia in 1880 possessed 22,770 elementary schools with 1,140,915 students,[18] 68.5 percent of the schools having been established after the *zemstvo* reform of 1864. In addition to the exclusive classical *gimnaziia*, the Realschule, which taught modern languages and science in place of Greek and Latin, provided a secondary education that could lead to admission to technical institutions of higher learning. Other kinds of school also developed. In addition to the activities of the ministries of education, war, and the navy and of the Holy Synod, Witte promoted commercial schools under the jurisdiction of the Ministry of Finance, establishing some 150 of them between 1896 and 1902, and well over 200 altogether. In 1905 these schools were transferred to the new Ministry of Trade and Industry.

It was also in the second half of the nineteenth century and going into the twentieth that Russian scientists made significant contributions in almost every area of knowledge. Such scholars as Pafnuty Chebyshev in mathematics, the already-mentioned Dmitri Mendeleev in chemistry, Peter Lebedev in physics, Alexander Kovalevsky in zoology and embryology, his brother Vladimir Kovalevsky in paleontology, Elijah Mechnikov in bacteriology, Ivan Sechenov in physiology, and Ivan Pavlov in physiology and psychology, among many other Russians in different fields, all advanced their specialties. To be sure, Ivan Pavlov, for example, belonged also to later periods, but his epoch-making studies of the reactions of dogs to food and his resulting postulation of conditioned reflexes began in the 1880s. Russian inventors included such notable pioneers as Paul Iablochkov, who worked before Edison in developing electric light, and Alexander Popov, who invented the radio around 1895, shortly before Marconi. But Russian inventors, even more than Russian scholars in general, frequently received less than their due recognition in the world, both because of the prevalent ignorance abroad of the Russian language and Russia and because of the backwardness of Russian technology, which often failed to utilize their inventions.

It was Russian literature that received at that time recognition in the world. That was primarily an achievement of three supreme novelists, Ivan Turgenev (1818–1883), Fedor Dostoevsky (1821–1881), and Leo Tolstoy (1828–1910), and a creator of the modern short story and brilliant playwright Anton Chekhov (1860–1904). There were, of course, numerous other authors then on the Russian intellectual and cultural scene, popular and important at home, if not abroad, such as the novelist Ivan Goncharov, the creator of *Oblomov;* the writer with an inimitable style and much knowledge of provincial clergy, old-fashioned merchants, and other rarely presented social strata, Nicholas Leskov; the populist and pessimist Gleb Uspensky; the satirist Michael Saltykov (best known under the pseudonym of N. Shchedrin); or the indefatigable and highly talented Alexander Ostrovsky, who from about 1850 until his death in 1886 contributed much of the basic repertoire of the Russian theater. It has been frequently pointed out that in Russia literature came to mean much more than entertainment, or even than esthetic expression—perhaps in part as compensation for the paucity of opportunities in the political and social fields—and that, for example, the three Russian giants of the novel were also major figures in Russian intellectual history.

In that respect, Turgenev was the least original of the three. A lifelong Westernizer and liberal, he became famous around 1850 with the gradual appearance of his *Sportsman's Sketches,* which depicted peasants in an unforgettable manner and, in the opinion of many, contributed to the emancipation. It might be added that, in spite of his greatness as a novelist, some specialists consider him to have been even better as a story writer. Turgenev proceeded to describe in six novels, the first of which appeared in 1855 and the last in 1877, the evolution of Russian educated society and of Russia itself, as he witnessed it. The novels were, in order of publication, *Rudin, A Gentry Nest, On the Eve*, the celebrated *Fathers and Sons, Smoke*, and *Virgin Soil*. Turgenev depicted Russia from the time of the iron regime of Nicholas I, through the "great reforms," to the return of reaction in the late 1860s and the 1870s. He concerned himself especially with the idealists of the 1840s and the later liberals, nihilists, and populists. I have already described how Turgenev's presentation of the clash of generations, of protagonists such as Bazarov, and of concepts such as "nihilism" came to be indissolubly connected with the epoch the author described.

Fedor Dostoevsky also became well known before the "great reforms." He was the author of a novel, *Poor Folk*, which was acclaimed by Belinsky when it was published in 1845, and of other writings, when he became involved, as already mentioned, with the Petrashevtsy and was sentenced to death, the sentence being commuted to Siberian exile only at the place of execution. Next, the writer spent four years at hard labor and two more as a soldier in Siberia before returning to European Russia in 1856, following a general amnesty proclaimed by the new emperor. Dostoevsky recorded his Siberian experience in a remarkable book, *Notes from the House of the Dead*, which came out in 1861. Upon his return to literary life, the onetime member of the Petrashevtsy became an aggressive and prolific right-wing journalist, contributing to a certain Slavophile revival, Panslavism, and even outright chauvinism. His targets included the Jews, the Poles, the Germans, Catholicism, socialism, liberalism, and the entire West. While Dostoevsky's journalism added to the sound and fury of the period, his immortal fame rests on his late novels, four of which belong among the greatest ever written. These were *Crime and Punishment, The Idiot, The Possessed*, and *The Brothers Karamazov*, published in 1866, 1868, 1870–1872, and 1879–1880, respectively. In fact, Dostoevsky seemed to go from strength to strength and was apparently at the height of his creative powers in working on a sequel to *The Brothers Karamazov* when he died.

Dostoevsky has often been described as the most Russian of writers and evaluated in terms of Russian messiahship and the mysteries of the Russian soul—an approach to which he himself richly contributed. The emphasis, going straight back to the Slavophiles and beyond, was on the Christian and panhuman nature of the Russian people, who properly responded to and represented all of humanity and its future, whereas other peoples were limited by their specific individual essences—the subject of Doestoevsky's celebrated Pushkin oration and certain other pieces. Yet a closer consideration quickly reveals the fragility and even the entirely imaginary quality of Dostoevsky's "Russianness." To the contrary, Dostoevsky could be called the most international or, better, the most human of writers, because of his enormous concern with and penetration into the nature of man. The strange Russian author was a master of depth psychology before depth psychology became known. Moreover, he viewed human nature in the dynamic terms of explosive conflict between freedom and necessity, faith and despair, indeed good and evil. Of Dostoevsky's several priceless gifts, the greatest was to fuse into one his protagonists and the ideas they expressed—or rather, the state of their soul and entire being—as no other writer has ever done. Therefore, where others are prolix, tedious, didactic, or confusing in mixing different levels of discourse, Dostoevsky is gripping, in places almost unbearably so. As Gleb Uspensky reportedly once remarked, into a small hole in the wall, where the generality of human beings could put perhaps a pair of shoes, Dostoevsky could put the entire world. One of the greatest antirationalists of the second half of the nineteenth century, together with Nietzsche and Kirkegaard, Dostoevsky became with them an acknowledged prophet for the twentieth, inspiring existential philosophy, theological revivals, and scholarly attempts to understand the catastrophes of our time—as well as, of course, modern psychological fiction.

Although Dostoevsky has been singled out frequently and, on the whole, correctly as the greatest opponent of the Russian radical and revolutionary movement—to the extent that in the Soviet period, one edition of his complete collected works appeared without *The Possessed*—he too contributed to the broad and dominant ideology of populism. His gift to it consisted, in the first place, in his fervent belief in the God-bearing quality of the Russian people, of the peasant masses, a belief that could be more powerful and persuasive than sociological demonstrations or economic explanations of their importance. In fact, although increasingly embattled, populism, with its faith in the peasant, in one way or another continued to permeate the Russian scene, at least all the way to the constituent assembly of January, 1918, where the Socialist Revolutionaries, the political party version of populism, had a majority. The assembly was disbanded by Lenin.

Not surprisingly, therefore, the third and last giant of the novel to be mentioned, Tolstoy, also paid his dues to populism. Very different from Dostoevsky, not at all an antirationalist but a desperate rationalist, the sage of Iasnaia Poliana found the reason and reasonable life he had been looking for, *mirabile dictu*, among the peasants, with their simplicity, closeness to nature, hard physical work, and the rejection, or rather absence, of the monumental falsehood of the contemporary society and culture. Tolstoy actually tried to become a peasant in his own person, appearance, work, and life, and that in spite of the fact that he could write devastatingly of the ignorance, superstition, and misery of the masses in such a play as *The Power of Darkness*.

Count Leo Tolstoy lived a long, full, and famous life. Born in 1828 and brought up in a manner characteristic of his aristocratic milieu—magnificently described in *Childhood, Boyhood, and Youth*—he received a cosmopolitan, if dilettante, education; engaged in merry social life; served in the army, first in the Caucasus and later in the siege of Sevastopol; and became a happy husband, the father of a large family, and a progressive landowner much concerned with the welfare of his peasants.

In addition to these ordinary activities, however, Tolstoy also developed into one of the greatest writers in world literature and later into an angry teacher of human-kind, who condemned civilization, including his own part in it, and called for the abandonment of violence and for a simple, moral life. In fact, he died in 1910 at the age of eighty-two as he fled from his family and estate in yet another attempt to sever his ties with all evil and falsehood and find truth. It is indeed difficult to deter-mine whether Tolstoy acquired more fame and influence in his own country and all over the world as a writer or as a teacher of nonresistance and unmasker of modern civilization, and whether *Anna Karenina* or *A Confession*—an account of the crisis that split his life in two—carries the greater impact. In Russia, at least, Tolstoy's position as the voice of criticism that the government dared not silence, as moral conscience, appeared at times even more extraordinary and precious than his liter-ary creations.

But, whatever can be said against Tolstoy as thinker—and much has been justly said about his extraordinary naïveté, his stubborn and at the same time poorly thought-out rationalism, and his absolute insistence on such items as vegetarianism and painless death as parts of his program of salvation—Tolstoy as writer needs no apologies. While a prolific author, the creator of many superb stories and some wonderful plays, Tolstoy, like Dostoevsky, is remembered best for his novels, espe-cially *War and Peace*, published in 1869, and *Anna Karenina*, published in 1876. In these novels, as in much else written by Tolstoy, there exists a boundless vitality, a driving, overpowering sense of life and people. And life finds expression on a sweep-ing scale. *War and Peace* contains sixty protagonists and some two hundred distinct characters, not to mention the unforgettable battle and mob scenes and the general background. The war of 1812 is depicted at almost every level: from Alexander I and Napoleon, through commanders and officers, to simple soldiers, and among civil-ians from court circles to the common people. *Anna Karenina*, while more restricted in scope, has been praised no less for its construction and its supreme art.

As to Tolstoy's teaching, *tolstovstvo*, it represented a moral and intellectual chal-lenge to some and a virtual religious cult to others, throughout the world but espe-cially among certain Russian sectarians, who often combined it with their original unorthodox views. After condemning his own life as well as the society around him, Tolstoy turned first to the Orthodoxy of his childhood and youth. But before long he was developing a religion of his own, based on an absolute opposition to force and coercion and on a view of Christ not as God, but as a supreme preacher of morality founded entirely on reason and thus incontrovertible and accessible to all who had ears to hear and eyes to see. The excommunication of Tolstoy by the Holy Synod thus was, whatever its other aspects, technically correct. The content of Tolstoy's "rational Christianity" could be described, as already suggested, as a quixotic form of pop-ulism. It was, of course, many other things besides. Notably, it represented a far-reaching form of anarchism, although certainly of the nonviolent kind. If Tolstoy's heroic attempt to become a peasant demonstrated one extreme of populism in

Russia, the great writer's total rejection of coercion and his refusal to condone the legalization of compulsion of any sort illustrated the depth of the break between the government and some of the educated public, which had been for a long time its chief support.[19]Anarchism in Russia, it is worth remembering, had already had a brilliant and militant representative in Michael Bakunin, who had moved in his own person in the 1840s from a frenetic "Hegelian" admiration of Nicholas I, the emperor's family, and the emperor's Russia to preach pan-destruction. Many Russian men and women were to follow Bakunin or other similar leaders in the second half of the nineteenth century and on into the twentieth, with the black flag of anarchism often accompanying the red one of radical revolution. At least one of the younger group, Prince Peter Kropotkin (1842–1921), deserves a note of his own. Indeed, Russian anarchism was destroyed as a radical and revolutionary movement, as was so much else, only by the Soviet regime.

While Bakunin has been often deemed the most destructive of the famous Russian anarchists, and Tolstoy the most quixotic, Kropotkin concentrated on the constructive ideals of anarchism. Like Tolstoy a member of the Russian aristocracy, as well as a distinguished scientist, Peter Kropotkin received an elite military education and served of his own choice from 1862 to 1867 in a cossack regiment in Siberia, in the distant Amur district, where he studied ethnography, geology, and geography. He went on to continue successfully his scientific work at the University of St. Petersburg, but he also became deeply involved in anarchism, populism, and the revolutionary movement. Imprisoned in 1874 in the dreaded Peter and Paul fortress, he escaped some two years later, and then again escaped abroad. There Kropotkin became a leading and well-known European anarchist, by means of the journal *Le Révolté*, which he founded in 1879 in Switzerland, and numerous books and articles, which he wrote in French, Russian, and English. Kropotkin's most popular book, *Memoirs of a Revolutionist,* was written in English in 1898–1899 for the *Atlantic Monthly*, although he was imprisoned in France, as well as earlier in Russia, and suffered some other vicissitudes in his career of an anarchist. Kropotkin lived long enough to return to Russia in 1917 and write blistering letters to Lenin concerning the great ethical failings of the Russian revolution and the new regime, before dying in 1921.

Prince Peter Kropotkin is a striking example of an extremely intelligent scientist who nevertheless was a true believer in the simplistic scientistic ideas, which, as already indicated, formed an essential component of the new intellectual climate in Russia in the 1860s. Nor, penetrating observers noted, would he change his views even as advanced scientific thought itself became more sophisticated and perhaps more ambivalent. Religious, metaphysical, and other nonscientific approaches to the world did not matter at all, or they had a negative value, when they interfered with the true perception of reality. Biology was simply an extension of chemistry, and sociology of biology. Newton and Darwin provided a magnificent scientific framework for human knowledge. Unfortunately, as Kropotkin argued in *Mutual*

Aid, a Factor in Evolution, and other works, Darwin and Thomas Huxley, while they gave full play to competition and the struggle for survival in the evolution of the species, did not pay equal attention to cooperation and mutual aid in that same evolution. And yet the latter could be as important as the former, whether one was considering ants, beavers, or human beings. By contrast, Kropotkin's anarchist world of the future was to be a triumph of cooperation and mutual aid. Kropotkin called his ideal "anarchistic communism" or "pure communism," and he disdained property, wages, and salaries, not to mention Marxist "state socialism." Perfectly free communes, such as the Russian peasant *obshchiny,* would produce everything their members needed or wanted, and with the continuous advance of science and technology, production would be quick and easy. It would be an egalitarian world, with minimal differentiation in occupation or status. But Kropotkin was willing to provide even for those who had other intentions, such as a craving for special luxuries—they might perhaps form a different kind of commune.

The Left did not monopolize the Russian intellectual scene. In fact, some commentators on the second half of the nineteenth century in Russia emphasize especially the emergence of a "modern" Right. To be sure, there remained always the old Right of Official Nationality, represented most prominently in the late nineteenth century by Constantine Pobedonostsev (1827–1907), together with numerous other supporters in and out of government. It can even be said that once the "great reforms" were over, the members of that grouping ruled Russia. Yet their position was not an enviable one. Once again, they were guarding the ramparts, although the enemy had already penetrated their defenses and the threatening trends both inside and outside Russia were accelerating their pace. They themselves did not believe in any kind of victory. No wonder that Pobedonostsev not only hated Western political institutions but, more generally, wanted to prevent people from inventing. There were also a few more original pessimists, the most outstanding among them being the brilliant writer and interesting thinker Constantine Leontiev (1831–1891), who, however, saw nothing but doom as Russia was losing her Byzantine foundations.

The modern Right was something else. It has been argued that it was in the second half of the nineteenth century and, more precisely, from the Polish rebellion in 1863 to the culmination of Balkan uprisings and war in 1878 that popular nationalism emerged as a force in Russia.[20] The government was surprised both by the broad support it received against the Poles and against the European powers that spoke for them, and by the great public interest in the complicated events in the Balkans. Modern Russian nationalism closely resembled other nationalisms. Its recognized leader was the former Westernizer, professor of philosophy, and supporter of the "great reforms" Michael Katkov (1818–1887), who, however, became obsessed with the danger to the Russian state of separatism. Hence his all-out campaign against Poland. But once the Poles were defeated, Katkov turned his attention to what he considered similar threats in the Baltic provinces, Finland, Transcaucasia, and elsewhere. The answer had to be, in each case, strong government and Russification, an approach that betrayed at least some of Katkov's originally liberal heritage. Katkov's main means was the press, which he used ably and energetically to gain support, to the point of being frequently listed in historical literature simply as a journalist or a publicist. In Russia, as elsewhere, intellectuals were in the vanguard of modern nationalism.

Although Russian nationalism obviously had enough to be preoccupied with at home, such ideologies usually look outside, as well as inside, in search of still broader possibilities. In the Russian case, the search led to Panslavism. Nationalism and Panslavism could often be mutually reinforcing or complementary, but their association also produced certain dangers. Most important, which was to claim supreme loyalty, Russia or Slavdom? (In a parallel situation, Germany or the "Aryan race"?)

Modern Panslavism was produced in Europe in the first part of the nineteenth century by two related intellectual and cultural phenomena: the new Romantic ideology, centered on organicism and, increasingly, historicism, and the establishment of modern philology. The first provided the fundamental *Weltanschauung* for at least the early stages of Panslavism; the second pinpointed the object of allegiance and devotion, the organism to which one belonged, namely Slavdom, as attested by the use of a Slavic language. Some pioneers of new thought, notably Herder, had not only provided the necessary framework for Panslavism, but also themselves dealt in an important and favorable manner with the Slavs. Ironically, that new thought, although many-sided, rich, and eventually as extensive as Western civilization itself, could also be regarded as most especially German. Slavophiles, such as Khomiakov and Constantine Aksakov, and even adherents to the Romantic wing of Official Nationality, notably Pogodin, also made their contributions to Panslavism, although neither Slavophilism nor Official Nationality were primarily concerned with Slavdom. One Slavophile, Ivan Aksakov, 1823–1886, later became a leader of the Panslavs.

The Russian Panslav movement proper of the second half of the nineteenth century is usually traced to the Moscow Slavic Benevolent Committee founded in January 1858 and to its later sections or more autonomous organizations in such cities as St. Petersburg, Kiev, and Odessa. The committees devoted themselves to cultural and philanthropic enterprises, such as scholarships for Balkan students in Russia and some financial aid to schools and churches in the Orthodox parts of the Ottoman and Hapsburg empires. They also served as a fulcrum for Panslav thought, with special emphasis on the Russian language as the obvious common language for the Panslav world. A Panslav congress was held in Moscow in 1867, with eighty-one Slavic guests from abroad, but it produced no tangible results, the question of Poland remaining the most intractable divisive issue. Russian Panslavism experienced a great revival during the Balkan wars of the late 1870s, as thousands of Russian volunteers flocked to fight for the Bulgarians and the Serbs against the Turks before Russia itself joined the fray. But if the Treaty of San Stefano of 1878 could be considered the high point for Russian Slavic sentiments and Panslavism, its remaking that same year at the Congress of Berlin came as a sharp disappointment. In the decades following, further strife in the Balkans fueled Panslav expectations, until in the summer of 1914 Russia actually came to the aid of Serbia against Austria-Hungary to start World War I. The results of the war, however, were not what the Russian Panslavs had hoped for.

Together with world politics, the intellectual climate also changed, on the Right as well as on the Left. Whereas Panslavism stemmed from Romanticism and developed for decades within the Romantic framework, in the second half of the nineteenth century it came to be influenced and even dominated by new trends of thought: "realistic" (as in *Realpolitik*), pragmatic, and at the same time scientistic, that is, applying, or rather misapplying, scientific categories to human society and history. Nicholas Danilevsky's *Russia and Europe*, serialized in the periodical press from 1869, published as a book first in 1871, and frequently referred to as the "Bible of Panslavism," may be considered the epitome of the new approach.[21] An able natural scientist, Danilevsky (1822–1885) concluded that universal history and culture were delusions and that the only reality consisted in the existence and evolution of entirely separate linguistic-ethnographic entities. He discovered about a dozen such entities, as well as some peoples who did not properly belong to history, because they offered either nothing or only destruction. Five laws were basic to the historical process: (1) language identified race or family of peoples; (2) for its particular civilization to develop, that entity had to have political independence; (3) the basic principles of each entity were unique and could not be transmitted to another cultural-historical type; (4) to obtain the full richness of development, each entity should be a federation of states and not absorbed by one of them; (5) as in the case of perennial monocarpic plants, the period of growth of these cultural-historical types was indefinite, but the florescence and fruition of each occurred briefly and only once. The next step in history was to be the replacement of the Romano-Germanic, or European, by the Slavic type, led, of course, by Russia—as, in the expectations of late Ivan Aksakov and other Panslavs, a titanic war loomed on the horizon. Once victorious, the Slavs might well institute the first society harmoniously synthesizing all four main aspects of human activity: the religious, the cultural, the political, and the social-economic (it was especially in the last respect that the earlier cultural-historical types had proved so far deficient). In the meantime, only the Slavic success mattered, not chimeras of universal civilization, universal standards, or humanity itself. It should be emphasized that the Panslavs never controlled the Russian government, which generally considered them troublesome quacks, but they certainly added to the furies and counterfuries of the age.

One more new claimant to establishing the nature and realizing the destiny of Russia must be mentioned: Marxism. George (Georgy Valentinovich) Plekhanov (1857–1920) earned his frequent designation as the father of Russian Marxism. Brilliant, well-educated, very scholarly, and eventually recognized as a specialist in many fields, from philosophy, economics, and history to literary criticism, Plekhanov became prominent in his youth as a revolutionary populist but turned to Marxism after he left Russia for the West in 1881. He proceeded to preach Marxism and publish such works as *Socialism and the Political Struggle* (1883), *Our Disagreements* (1885), *Concerning the Development of a Monistic View of History* (1895), and *A Survey of the History of Materialism* (1896), which became basic texts for Russian Marxists, as well as weapons of special importance in the ongoing struggle between the Marxists and the populists. Plekhanov's disciples included, for a number of years, Lenin, together with uncounted other young men and women in the Russian radical and revolutionary movement. Plekhanov had an advantage over the populists, because industrial capitalism was indeed penetrating Russia and the Marxist diagnosis and prognosis appeared to be more correct than those of their rivals. Yet he also deserved personal credit for the effective way in which he presented his powerful teaching: Marxism, and Marxism as taught by Plekhanov, had precisely the comprehensiveness, clarity, and finality that populism so sadly lacked. Not that everything was beyond dispute. An orthodox Marxist who had incorporated violence and revolution into his thought, Plekhanov nevertheless emphasized Marxist determinism and considered Russia entirely unprepared for a quick revolutionary transition to socialism. In the words of Walicki:

> For Plekhanov the most important thinkers were Hegel and Spinoza. . . . What he admired in the system of Spinoza and Hegel was their monism and strict determinism—determinism conceived as an ontological necessity inherent in the rational structure of the universe. Plekhanov's necessity, therefore, was essentially the rational necessity of Spinoza made dynamic and historical by Hegel and reinterpreted scientifically by Marx. The principle of determinism (causality), widely accepted in the natural sciences, was extended by Plekhanov to the social sciences and raised to the rank of a "rational" necessity—of greater significance, therefore, than an ordinary empirical necessity or regular pattern that could be empirically deduced.[22]

Not surprisingly, therefore, Plekhanov considered Lenin's revolution of 1917 not a triumph but a voluntaristic transgression of the proper course of history and thus potentially a disaster, which, however, he did not live to see for very long. Not surprisingly, too, Russia got Marxism according to Lenin, not according to Plekhanov.

Near the turn of the century, the opposition began to organize. The frightful famine of 1891–1892 marked the end of a certain lull in Russia and the resumption of social and political activity, with a very emphatic criticism of the regime. The liberals, who could boast of many prominent names in their ranks and who represented at that time the elite of the opposition, eventually formed in 1903 the Union of Liberation, with its organ, *Liberation*, published abroad by the noted political economist Peter Struve. In 1905, they organized the Constitutional Democratic Party—or "Cadet," a word based on two initial letters in the Russian name (the formal designation of the party, however, was Party of the People's Freedom)—led by the historian Paul Miliukov and encompassing liberals of different kinds, both constitutional monarchists and republicans.

At roughly the same time, the radicals formed two important parties. The Socialist Revolutionaries represented the great populist tradition of Russia, and they emerged as a political party in 1901, with Victor Chernov as their most prominent leader.

But the other radical party, the Social Democrats, were Marxists and, as already mentioned, rather new on the Russian political scene. Marxist association with the Russian labor movement dated from 1883, when Plekhanov organized the Emancipation of Labor Group, but a Marxist political party, as such, appeared only in 1898 or, better, 1903. The founding congress of 1898, held in Minsk, proved abortive, with most of its few participants being arrested in short order. The Social Democratic party became a reality only after the second congress, held in Brussels and London in 1903. At that time, the party also split into the Bolsheviks, led by Vladimir Ulianov, better known as Lenin, who wanted a tightly knit organization of professional revolutionaries, and the Mensheviks, who preferred a somewhat broader and looser association. In time, the ramifications of that relatively slight initial difference acquired great importance.

As the twentieth century opened, Russia was in turmoil. Strikes spread throughout the country. Student protests and disturbances became more frequent, constituting an almost continuous series from 1898 on. Sporadic peasant disturbances kept the tension high in rural areas and offered increased opportunities to the Socialist Revolutionaries, just as the growth of the labor movement encouraged the Social Democrats. In 1902, 1903, and early 1904, committees dealing with the national economy, conferences of teachers and doctors, and other public bodies all demanded reforms. Moreover, the Socialist Revolutionaries resumed the terrorist tactics of their predecessors, such as the Will of the People. Their "Battle Organization" assassinated a number of important officials, including two reactionary ministers of the interior, Dmitri Sipiagin in 1902 and Viacheslav Plehve in 1904 and, early in 1905, Grand Duke Sergei, commanding officer of the Moscow military region and Nicholas II's second cousin and brother-in-law. The war against Japan and the resulting series of defeats added fuel to the fire. In November 1904, a *zemstvo* congress, meeting in St. Petersburg, demanded a representative assembly and civil liberties. The same demands were made with increasing frequency by numerous other public bodies. In particular, professional organizations, such as unions of doctors and teachers, and other associations spread rapidly throughout Russia and made their voices heard. Several months after the *zemstvo* congress, fourteen professional unions united to form a huge Union of Unions, led by the Cadets. The government tried both repression and some conciliation, appealing for confidence, but its generally ineffectual efforts only helped to swell the tide of opposition.

January 22, 1905, came to be known in Russian history as "Bloody Sunday." On that day, the police of the capital fired at a huge demonstration of workers led by an adventurer and priest named George Gapon, killing, according to the official estimate, 130 persons and wounding several hundred. Ironically, Gapon's union of Russian factory workers had been essentially a "police union," part of police official Sergei Zubatov's plan to infiltrate the labor movement and direct it into officially desirable loyalist channels. Ironically, too, the workers were converging on the Winter Palace—unaware that Nicholas II was not there—with icons and the tsar's portraits, as faithful subjects, nay, children of their sovereign, begging him for redress and help. The entire ghastly episode thus testified to official incompetence in more ways than one. The massacre led to a great outburst of indignation in the country and gave another boost, an unexpected one, to the revolutionary movement. In particular, as many authorities assert, it meant a decisive break between the tsar and those lower classes of society who had until that "Bloody Sunday" remained loyal to him.[23]

Under ever-increasing pressure, Nicholas II declared early in March his intention to convoke a "consultative" assembly; in further efforts toward pacification, he proclaimed religious tolerance and repealed some legislation against ethnic minorities. Nevertheless, the revolutionary tide kept rising. The summer of 1905 witnessed new strikes, mass peasant uprisings in many provinces, active opposition and revolutionary movements among national minorities, and even occasional rebellions in the armed forces, notably in the celebrated instance of the battleship *Potemkin* on the Black Sea. On August 19, an imperial manifesto created an elective *duma* with consultative powers, but that too failed to satisfy the educated public or the masses. The revolutionary movement culminated in a mammoth general strike that lasted from October 20 to October 30, a strike that has been described as the greatest, most thoroughly carried out, and most successful in history. Russians seemed to act with a single will, as they made perfectly plain their unshakable determination to end autocracy. It was in the course of the strike, and in order to direct it, that workers in St. Petersburg organized a *sovet*, or council. Paralyzed in their essential activities and forced at last to recognize the immensity of the opposition, Nicholas II and his government finally capitulated. On October 30, the emperor, as advised by Witte, issued the October Manifesto. That brief document guaranteed civil liberties to the Russians, announced a legislature (or *duma*) with the true legislative function of passing or rejecting all proposed laws, and promised a further expansion of the new order in Russia. In short, the October Manifesto made the empire of the Romanovs a constitutional monarchy.

It also split the opposition. Most liberals and moderates of all sorts felt fundamentally satisfied. The radicals, such as the Social Democrats, on the contrary, considered the tsar's concession entirely inadequate and wanted in any case a constituent assembly, not handouts from above. Thus divided, the opposition lost a great deal of its former power. In the middle of December, the government arrested the members of the St. Petersburg Soviet. The Soviet's appeal for revolution found effective responses only in Moscow, where workers and some other radicals fought bitterly against the police and the soldiers, including a guards' regiment, from December 22 until January 1.

The year 1905 thus ended in bloody fighting. However, the revolution had spent itself with that last effort. In the course of the winter, punitive expeditions and summary courts-martial restored order in many troubled areas. The extreme Right joined the army and the police; Rightist squads, known as the "Black Hundreds," beat and even killed Jews, liberals, and other intellectuals. Protofascist in nature, this newly awakened Right represented an extreme wing of the rising Russian nationalism, throve on ethnic and religious hatreds, and appealed especially to wealthy peasants and to members of the urban lower middle classes. Still more important, the great bulk of the people was tired of revolution and longed for peace. It might be added that Witte further strengthened the hand of the government by obtaining a large loan from France.

On May 6, 1906, virtually on the eve of the meeting of the First Duma, the government promulgated the Fundamental Laws. These laws provided the framework of the new Russian political system; the October Manifesto had merely indicated some of its guiding lines. According to the Fundamental Laws, the emperor retained huge powers. He continued in complete control of the executive, the armed forces, foreign policy—specifically making war and peace—succession to the throne, the imperial court, imperial domains, and so forth. He maintained unchanged his unique dominating position in relation to the Russian Church. And he even retained the title of autocrat. He was to call together the annual sessions of the *duma* and to disband the *duma*, in which case, however, he had to indicate the time of the election and of the meeting of the new *duma*. He had the power of veto over legislation. Moreover, in case of emergency when the *duma* was not in session, he could issue *ukazes* with the authority of laws, although they had to be submitted for approval to the next session of the *duma* no later than two months after its opening.

The *duma*, to be sure, received important legislative and budgetary rights and functions by the Fundamental Laws, but these rights were greatly circumscribed. Notably, almost 40 percent of the state budget, encompassing such items as the army, the navy, the imperial court, and state loans, stayed outside of the purview of the *duma*, while the remainder, if not passed by the *duma*, was reenacted in the amounts of the preceding year. Ministers and the entire executive branch remained responsible only to the emperor, although the Laws did contain complicated provisions for interpellation, that is, questioning of ministers by the *duma*. Furthermore, the State Council, which had functioned since its creation by Alexander I as an advisory body of dignitaries, became, rather unexpectedly, the upper legislative chamber, equal in rights and prerogatives to the *duma* and meant obviously as a counterweight to it. "No more than half" of the membership of the upper house was to be appointed by the emperor—appointed not even for life but by means of annual lists—and the other half elected as follows: fifty-six with very high property standing by the provincial *zemstva*, eighteen by the gentry, twelve by commerce and industry, six by the clergy, six by the Academy of Sciences and the universities, and two by the Finnish Diet.

The results of the revolution of 1905 represented a compromise: Russia became a constitutional state with an elected legislature and numerous concessions to liberalism, but the emperor still largely ruled the state, and its many problems remained unresolved. Not surprisingly the First Duma (1906) and the Second Duma (1907) failed to agree with the government on such issues as combating terrorism and the redistribution of land. Only illegal and far-reaching changes in the electoral law in 1907 produced a sufficiently cooperative legislature. The Third Duma thus lasted its full term of five years, 1907–1912, and the Fourth had almost done so when another revolution struck in 1917. As to further reforms, the only major government effort was Peter Stolypin's controversial attempt to break up, by the laws of 1906, 1910, and 1911, the peasant commune and rely on, as the future of Russia, individual peasant farmers. That project, like so much else, was cut short by World War I.

But the last years of imperial Russia were by no means a period of stagnation. Once the revolution of 1905 was contained, economic and social development resumed its course, even at a quickened pace. Russia experienced another industrial spurt in the constitutional period, with output increasing at, perhaps, 6 percent a year. The working class was growing in numbers, and after the Lena gold field massacre of 1912, it was also again becoming more militant. Education spread as never before, and at all levels. Russia even produced early in the twentieth century a remarkable cultural outburst known as the Silver Age.

Foreshadowed by certain literary critics and poets in the 1890s, the new period has often been dated from the appearance in 1898 of a seminal periodical, the *World of Art*, put out by Sergei Diaghilev and Alexander Benois. What followed was a cultural explosion. Almost overnight, there sprung up in Russia a rich variety of literary and artistic creeds, circles, and movements. As Mirsky and other specialists have noted, these different and sometimes hostile groups had little or nothing in common, except their denial of "civic art" and their high standards of culture and craftsmanship. While much of the creative work of the Silver Age tended toward pretentiousness, obscurity, or artificiality, its best products were very good indeed. And even when short of the best, the works of the Silver Age indicated a new refinement, richness, and maturity in Russian culture.

In literature, the new trends resulted in a great revival of poetry and literary criticism, although some remarkable prose was also produced, for example, by Boris Bugaev, known as Andrei Bely. Among the poets, the symbolist Alexander Blok, who lived from 1880 to 1921 and wrote verses of stunning magic and melody to the mysterious Unknown Lady and on other topics, has been justly considered the greatest of the age and one of the greatest in all Russian literature. But Russia suddenly acquired many brilliant poets; other symbolists, for example, Innokenty Annensky, Bely, Valery Briusov, and Constantine Balmont; "acmeists," such as Nikolai Gumilev and Osip Mandelstam; futurists, such as Velemir Khlebnikov and Vladimir Maiakovsky;

or peasant poets, such as Sergei Esenin. The poet and novelist Boris Pasternak, who died in 1960, and the poet Anna Akhmatova, who lived until 1966, as probably the last Russian poet of the first rank, also belong fully to the Silver Age. In literary criticism, too, the new trends continued to enrich Russian culture after 1917, producing notably an interesting school of formalist critics, until these trends were destroyed by Soviet regimentation and "socialist realism."

The Silver Age brought a renaissance in fine arts as well as in literature. In music, where Alexander Scriabin initiated the change, it marked the appearance of the genius of Igor Stravinsky and of other brilliant young composers. In a sense, the new ballet masterpieces, for example, Stravinsky's ballets *The Firebird, Petrushka*— which also belongs to Benois—and *Le Sacre du printemps*, combining as they did superb music, choreography, dancing, and sets and staging, expressed best the cultural refinement, craftsmanship, and many-sidedness of the Silver Age. The Russian ballet received overwhelming acclaim when Diaghilev brought it to Paris in 1909, starring such choreographers as Michael Fokine and such dancers as Anna Pavlova and Waslaw Nijinsky. From that time on, Russian ballet has exercised a fundamental influence on ballet in other countries. On the eve of 1917, Russia could also boast of leading artists in other musical fields, for instance, the bass Fedor Chaliapin, the conductor Sergei Koussevitzky, and the pianist, conductor, and composer Sergei Rachmaninov, to mention three of the best-known names.

Diaghilev's ballets made such a stunning impression in the West in part because of the superb sets and staging. Benois, Constantine Korovin, Leonid Bakst, and other gifted artists of the Silver Age created a school of stage painting that gave Russia world leadership in that field and added immeasurably to operatic and theatrical productions, as well as to the ballet. Other Russian artists, notably Marc Chagall and Vasily Kandinsky, broke much more radically with the established standards and became leaders of modernism in painting. Still another remarkable development in the Silver Age was the rediscovery of icon painting: both a physical rediscovery, because ancient icons had become dark, had been overlaid with metal, or even had been painted over, and began to be restored to their original condition only around 1900; and an artistic rediscovery, because these icons were newly appreciated, adding to the culture and the creative influences of the period.

Theater, like the ballet a combination of arts, also developed splendidly in the Silver Age. In addition to the fine imperial theaters, private ones came into prominence. The Moscow Art Theater, directed by Constantine Stanislavsky, who emphasized psychological realism, achieved the greatest and most sustained fame and exercised the strongest influence on acting in Russia and abroad. But it is important to realize that it represented only one current in the theatrical life of a period that was remarkable for its variety, vitality, and experimentation. Russian art, as well as Russian literature, in the Silver Age formed an inseparable part of the art and literature of the West, profiting hugely, for example, from literary trends in France and from German thought, and in turn contributing to virtually every form of literary and artistic argument and creative expression. In a sense, Russian culture was never more "Western" than on the eve of 1917.

The Silver Age affected Russian thought as well as Russian literature and art. Notably, it marked a return to metaphysics, and often to religion eventually, on the part of a significant sector of Russian intellectuals. Other educated Russians, especially the writers and the artists, tended to become apolitical and asocial, often looking to esthetics for their highest values. The utilitarianism, positivism, and materialism dominant from the time of the 1860s finally had to face a serious challenge.

Philosophy in Russia experienced a revival in the work of Vladimir Soloviev and his followers. Soloviev, a son of the historian Sergei Soloviev, a poet and an encyclopedic scholar—in fact, the philosophy editor of the most important Russian encyclopedia—lived from 1853 until 1900 and wrote on a variety of difficult philosophical and theological subjects, such as the theory of knowledge, and the need for an effective union of the Roman Catholic and the Orthodox Churches and for a world theocracy. A study in ethics, *A Justification of the Good*, is generally considered his masterpiece. A trenchant critic of the radical creed of the age, as well as of chauvinism and reaction, Soloviev remained a rather isolated individual during his lifetime but came to exercise a profound influence on the intellectual elite of the Silver Age. In effect, almost everything he had stood for, from imaginative and daring theology to a sweeping critique of the radical intelligentsia, suddenly came into prominence in the early twentieth century. Only Dostoevsky's influence could rival that of Soloviev in the Silver Age. And indeed, in retrospect, some commentators saw Vladimir Soloviev's life and achievement, with its many-sided brilliance and great promise, as well as a certain incompleteness and an early ending, as a faithful premonition of the entire Russian culture of the Silver Age.

The new critique of the intelligentsia found its most striking expression in a slim volume entitled *Signposts* (*Vekhi*) that appeared in 1909. *Signposts* contained essays by seven authors, including such prominent converts from Marxism as Peter Struve, Nicholas Berdiaev, and Sergei Bulgakov, and constituted an all-out attack on the radical intelligentsia: Russian radicals were accused of an utter disregard for objective truth, religion, and law, and of an extreme application of the maxim that the end justifies the means, with destruction as their only effective passion. Although *Signposts* represented a minority of Russian intellectuals and attracted strong rebuttals, a new cleavage among educated Russians became apparent—a cleavage all the more revealing because the critics of the intelligentsia could by no means be equated with the Right. Eventually Struve (1870–1944) became a leading thinker and political figure of the moderate conservatives; Berdiaev (1874–1948) acquired world fame as a personalist philosopher and champion of "creative freedom"; and Bulgakov (1871–1944) entered the priesthood and developed into the most controversial Orthodox theologian of the twentieth century. Other prominent intellectuals of the Silver Age included the "biological mystic" Vasily Rozanov, who was especially concerned with the problem of sex, and the brilliant antirationalist Leo Shestov (a pseudonym of Leo Schwartzmann), as well as the metaphysicians Semen Frank (another contributor to *Signposts*) and Nicholas Lossky. By comparison with the 1860s, or even the 1890s, the Russian intellectual scene had indeed changed on the eve of World War I.

The Silver Age, like other cultural outbursts, defies easy or complete explanation; and it is also difficult to integrate it with the general course of Russian history. The issue was complicated by what many observers considered the premature and violent end of that age in Soviet Russia, although many important developments would continue among the Russian émigrés. Some critics found connections between the nervous, tense, at times even apocalyptic aspects of much of the new mentality and the cataclysmic revolution that followed these premonitions so promptly. Others emphasized the frequently made promise of the coming of the new world and new humanity, which was to find its unexpected embodiment in the Five-Year plans. To be sure, the Silver Age was an abstraction, and any study of its impact must deal with numerous and very different individuals. Thus it was Blok who in January 1918 composed "The Twelve," perhaps the greatest poem ever devoted to revolution, though, appropriately, also a most controversial poem. And it was the futurist Maiakovsky who became in effect the bard of the new Soviet regime during its early years—much to the chagrin of Lenin, whose own tastes in literature were more conservative. Still, the dissonances between the Silver Age and the Soviet ideology and world were much greater than the consonances. The first had to be repressed in the name of the second. Indeed, it has been argued that the Silver Age demonstrated that the Russian educated public was finally moving away from the simple materialistic, utilitarian, and activist beliefs professed by Lenin and his devoted followers. Therefore, the latter had to succeed quickly, if at all. In the event, they just made it.

General estimates of the constitutional period of Russian imperial history are many, but most of them can be readily classified as either optimistic or pessimistic. Optimistic students of the development of Russia from the Revolution of 1905 to World War I and the revolutions of 1917 have emphasized that the country had finally left autocracy behind and was evolving toward liberalism and political freedom. The change in 1907 in the electoral law, reactionary though it was, indicated that the *duma* could no longer be abolished. Moreover, the reformed Russian legislature proceeded to play an important part in the affairs of the state and to gain ever-increasing prestige and acceptance at home, among both government officials and the people, as well as abroad. As an Englishman observed, "the atmosphere and instincts of parliamentary life" grew in the empire of the Romanovs. Besides, continue the optimists, Russian society at the time was much more progressive and democratic than the constitutional framework alone would indicate, and it was becoming increasingly so every year. Modern education spread rapidly at different levels and was remarkably humanitarian and liberal—as were Russian teachers as a group—and not at all likely to serve as a buttress for antiquated ideas or obsolete institutions. Russian universities enjoyed virtually full freedom and a rich creative life. Elsewhere, too, an energetic discussion went on. Even the periodical press, in spite of various restrictions, gave some representation to every point of view, including the Bolshevik. Government prohibitions and penalties could frequently be neutralized by such simple means as a change in the name of a publication or, if necessary, by sending the nominal editor to jail, while important political writers continued their work. To be sure, as many optimists acknowledge, grave problems remained, in particular economic backwardness and the poverty of the masses. But, through rapid industrialization on the one hand and Stolypin's land reform on the other, they were on the way to being solved. Above all, Russia needed time and peace.

Pessimistic critics have drawn a different picture of the period. Many of them refused even to call it "constitutional," preferring such terms as Max Weber's *Scheinkonstitutionalismus*, that is, sham constitutionalism, because, both according to the Fundamental Laws and in fact, the executive branch of the government and the ministers in particular were not responsible to the *duma*. In any case, the critics asserted, whatever the precise character of the original arrangements, they were destroyed by the arbitrary electoral change of 1907. On the whole, the government refused to honor even its own niggardly concessions to the public. Nonentities, like the twice—prime minister Ivan Goremykin and the minister of war Vladimir Sukhomlinov, and the fantastic Grigory Rasputin himself, were logical end products of the bankruptcy of the regime. Other aspects of the life of the country, ranging from political terrorism, both of the Left and of the Right, to Russification and interminable "special regulations" to safeguard order, emphasized further the distance that Russia had to travel before it could be considered progressive, liberal, and law-abiding. Social and economic problems were still more threatening, according to the pessimists. Fundamental inequality and widespread destitution could not be remedied by a few large-scale "hothouse" industries and by a redivision of the peasants' inadequate land, always safeguarding that of the landlords. Workers in particular, including those concentrated in St. Petersburg and in Moscow, were becoming more radical and apparently more responsive to Bolshevik slogans. Moreover, the argument continues, the government never wanted real reform, because it was devoted to the interests, first, of the landlords and, second, of the great industrial capitalists. Russia was headed for catastrophe.

The optimists, thus, believe that a basically sound imperial Russia was ruined by World War I. The pessimists maintain that the war merely provided the last mighty push to bring the whole rotten structure tumbling down. Certainly it added an enormous burden to the load borne by the Russian people. Human losses were staggering. To cite Golovin's figures, in the course of the war, the Russian army mobilized 15,500,000 men and suffered greater casualties than did the armed forces of any other country involved in the titanic struggle: 1,650,000 killed, 3,850,000 wounded, and 2,410,000 taken prisoner. The destruction of property and other civilian losses and displacement escaped count. The Russian army tried to evacuate the population as it retreated, adding to the confusion and suffering. It became obvious during the frightful ordeal that the imperial government had again failed in its tasks, as in the Crimean War and the Russo-Japanese War, but on a much larger scale. The Russian minister of war and many other high officials and generals proved to be incompetent in the test of war. Russian weapons turned out to be inferior to the enemies', Russian ammunition in short supply. Transportation was generally bogged down, and on numerous occasions it broke down completely. Together with the army, the urban population suffered as a result of this, because it experienced difficulties obtaining food and fuel. Inflation ran rampant. Worst of all, the government refused to learn any lessons: instead of liberalizing state policies and relying more on the public, which was eager to help, Nicholas II, in an anachronistic gesture, handed over supreme power to the reactionary empress, and through her to Rasputin, when the tsar assumed command at the front.

Uncounted Russian soldiers were dying in the hecatombs of World War I fighting "for God, tsar, and fatherland," just as their ancestors had died in the heroic defense of Sevastopol in the Crimean War sixty years earlier. Yet the situation was not quite the same. In the intervening period, educated Russians, and their numbers were always increasing, participated more than ever before in the beliefs and obsessions of the West, modifying them, as everywhere else, to the conditions of their own country. Thus Russian radicalism was predominantly peasantist, from Herzen until the victory of Lenin's creed. Dostoevsky found his ideal in the soul of the Russian peasant; Tolstoy in his way of life. The Panslavs were cousins, as well as natural enemies, of the Pangermans. Russia, as well as Great Britain or France, claimed to bring enlightenment to the non-European world. Potentially most significant, however, was the change in the Russian masses. The Muscovite uncompromising adoration of the tsar was coming to its end. Basic to Muscovite history and still very much in evidence in the eighteenth and even nineteenth centuries, it apparently faded out by the end of the latter. While the events of "Bloody Sunday" certainly cannot account for the fadeout, they may serve as a symbol of the separation of the tsar and his people. Devotion to the tsar was not prominent in 1917 or in the years of civil war that followed, and the dedicated fighters on the White side were officers of the army and navy, not masses rallying for the true tsar. This erosion of a quasi-religious support of the ruler by the masses went for a long time almost unnoticed in historiography, until the appearance of some interesting recent works. Thus, Geoffrey Hosking in his fine book *Russia: People and Empire, 1552–1917* not only focused on that loss of support but even asserted: "The imperial state's humiliation of the church which underpinned its legitimizing ideology was perhaps its gravest mistake and certainly a fundamental cause of the revolution of 1917."[24] But Hosking did not explain how the old reverence for the tsar could be retained in the modern secularized world, and he wrote almost as if he did not realize how thoroughly Orthodox Nicholas II and most of the imperial Russian rulers had been.

If not the Orthodox tsar, then what? The obvious candidate, as in so many other countries, was modern nationalism. And indeed, it was rising in Russia. A good case can be made for the emergence of modern Russian nationalism in the period from 1863 to 1878, as well as in the years following, with its own professors, journalists, writers, students, books, periodicals, and newspapers. An aggressive and even violent nationalist Right, though not to be confused with more moderate main currents, was its appropriate component. Such basic developments leading to modern nationalism in France and other countries as popular education, improved communications, and compulsory statewide military service were present in Russia. The empire of the Romanovs lagged behind in many of these important matters, but its retardation could be readily cured with the passage of time.

Yet obstacles in the path of Russian nationalism were many. The Russian educated public was, on the whole, more opposed to the government than intellectuals elsewhere, and it devoted its interest and support more willingly to radical and revolutionary movements. The ruling stratum, even in 1917, was in many ways still that of an *ancien régime* rather than a modern national state. Statesmen like Dmitri Miliutin, Witte, and Stolypin were rare, while the last emperors and most of their ministers tried simply to hold the line, to defend what they could from internal or external attack. The religious bond, so important in Russian history, was itself on the decline, and the government, it is generally believed, made matters worse by treating the Church and different religious issues in its usual authoritarian and bureaucratic manner. Moreover, the Russian empire was a multiethnic state, out of place in the age of nationalism. Finland, for example, was indeed ruled more appropriately by its own grand duke, with its own constitution and rights, than by the same personage as the autocratic Russian emperor. The fundamental difference between *rossiiskii,* the adjective for the Russian empire, and *russkii,* meaning Russian ethnically, has been recognized by most critics. More novel are some suggestions that it was the second that was sacrificed to the first. Finally, it seems precipitous to find the best solution for imperial Russia in becoming a modern national state. Germany did just that, quickly and brilliantly, with the process eventuating in Hitler.

Soviet Russia, 1917–1991

Quiet, quiet. Beyond the polar circle
There sleep without separating their arms
Next to a faithful friend, an inseparable friend,
A dead friend a dead friend.

         —Ivanov

The issues of belief and identity had some very striking characteristics in the Soviet Union.[1] No other state in history was so explicitly and thoroughly based on an ideology, teaching it in schools and inculcating it by all other means possible, spreading it to almost every detail of human existence and maintaining that stupendous effort for almost three-quarters of a century. Even Nazi Germany, often compared to the U.S.S.R. as its twin totalitarian state, could not claim such a performance, because its ideology was much more mushy, confusing, and incomplete, and the practical realization of that ideology—most dreadful and tragic, to be sure—lasted twelve rather than seventy-four years.

A great deal has been written about communist ideology, including ideology in the Soviet Union. And yet that ideology needs more rather than less emphasis. Failures to appreciate it fully range from suspicions of intellectual history as basic causation to the omnipresence of the official dogma and doctrine to the point that it appears as something obvious and natural rather than imposed. A very large number of misconceptions stems from the substitution of a struggle of leaders for power—their vanity, suspiciousness, pride, vengeance, conspiracies, and so on and on—for Marxism-Leninism. Usually the error is simply mixing the levels of discourse. It is not that Soviet protagonists were free from the above-mentioned vices and rivalries in all their forms. It is rather that their vices and rivalries took place within the basic framework of their ideology, by no means eliminating that ideology. A comprehensive ideology is of a fundamental importance in the first place, because that is how those who believe in it, whether they are aggressive or passive, honest or dishonest, vain or modest, see the world. And that is how the world was seen from the Kremlin from 1917 to 1991.

In fact, the Soviet leadership, from Lenin, to Stalin, to Khrushchev, to Brezhnev, to Andropov, to Chernenko, to Gorbachev, as well as their numerous associates and assistants, demonstrated a remarkable ideological consistency. Lenin, whose contributions extended Marxism to Marxism-Leninism, has often been accused of fanaticism, but not of unbelief. Stalin, whose almost entire intellectual, particularly theoretical, baggage was limited to Marxism, considered that, after Lenin, he became its true seer and leader. On a more naive and less murderous plane, Khrushchev put his heart into the competition of his socialist fatherland with the capitalist world, especially the United States, and was still counting Soviet gains in the production of milk, meat, and eggs as he was dismissed from office. Brezhnev's long rule came to be known as a period of stagnation precisely because no fundamental changes took place, and the U.S.S.R. continued on its established dogmatic course. Many observers noted a decline in enthusiasm for old beliefs and goals, but there was nothing to replace them. Nor did the leadership of Andropov, and after him Chernenko, transform the scene; besides, both died very shortly after attaining the highest position.

Even the last occupier of that position, the reformer who finally arrived, Gorbachev, was in his own way as much a Marxist-Leninist as Khrushchev. In addition to impeccable communist service prior to his elevation, he praised the Soviet system—for example, for having successfully solved the problem of nationalities, just before that problem exploded—and spoke of the wonderful potentialities of the Party, to general amazement, even after being rescued from the putsch of the hardliners. Gorbachev's authentic vision was that of a dynamic Leninism, restored to its full glory. Fate willed otherwise.

Since the collapse of the U.S.S.R. and the new availability of primary sources, scholars have found only further confirmation of the enormous role of ideology in Soviet Russia. In particular, at the highest Party and government level, there seems to be no instance, no matter how private or secret, of a cynical use of Marxism to trick the unwary or mislead the masses. One confronts certainly a community of believers, although it is fair to speculate that with the passage of time that community contained fewer fanatics.

Intellectual history is not the only important aspect of history, which is a record of a complex, many-sided development of a society over centuries. Marxism, which ruled Russia for seventy-four years, was at best of tertiary significance in the evolution of the United States, while Hitler and many other heralds of Nazism would have probably remained isolated cranks if located in Soho. More to the point, of course, even the dominant and official Soviet Marxism had its major limitations.

First, Marxism simply did not cover some important areas of state activity. Classical Marxism offered no manual on foreign policy after the revolution, for the good reason that there was to be no such policy, but instead of division, diplomacy, and war, a united proletarian world. Lenin and his associates looked for that world in the Russian revolution itself and especially in revolutionary outbreaks in central and eastern Europe, as well as in the invasion of Poland by the Red Army. But when the revolution failed to spread, they had to improvise, and improvise they did, from the Treaty of Brest-Litovsk, signed on March 3, 1918, to the collapse of the Soviet Union in 1991. Bereft of comprehensive guidance, the Soviet leaders used their Marxism in specific instances, including the creation and the entire activity of the Comintern and later the Cominform. It is also only with reference to Marxism that one can understand the Soviet expectation of a war between the United States and Great Britain (the new capitalism challenging the old capitalism) or the light treatment of the rise of Nazi power in Germany, which represented to the Soviets the last gasp of dying imperialism, to be followed by a major struggle against the social democrats for the allegiance of the German people. (Western observers and even governments came to equally incorrect conclusions from different assumptions, such as the expectations that once in power the Nazis would acquire conservatism, moderation, and even good manners.)

Second, theory had to be translated into practice, and that almost inevitably means adaptation and change. A textbook example was provided by the First Five-Year Plan, with its remarkable ups and downs, but essentially with its relentless drive to produce (or collectivize) as much as possible and even beyond the possible. The drive would stop only at the edge of the precipice and even beyond that edge, with millions of peasants perishing during collectivization. But there were other and more subtle forms of adaptation. The end product, whether in economics, social policy, or culture, would be connected to the plan, of course, but also greatly changed by Soviet reality. Third, the dominant position of Soviet Marxism did not exclude some roles for certain subordinate, even contradictory, teachings, such as nationalism and anti-Semitism—in the 1930s but especially in connection with World War II and its aftermath in the Soviet Union and abroad.

In the fourth place, but perhaps most important, was the issue of spread and per-meation, of the extent to which Marxism-Leninism became the inspiration and the guiding light of the masses. Witness the colossal effort of the Party and the govern-ment to create a new socialist, eventually communist, country, inhabited by the new Soviet men and women. But the results of the effort proved to be extremely complex and controversial; and in any case, the beliefs and aspirations of the masses should not be simply assimilated with official Soviet history or with the often lengthy pro-nouncements of the leaders. They deserve a separate consideration, to be given at the end of this chapter.

Lenin believed ardently in the teaching of Marx and Engels and even made some valuable contributions to it. While not at the same level as the creation of the found-ing fathers who established the entire basic framework, Lenin's addenda helped to point Marxists in the direction of the colonial countries of the world and even to an extent toward peasants. Originally strictly industrial, urban, and European, Marx-ism and Marxists, Lenin argued, once capitalism reached the stage of imperialism, found their natural allies in the exploited colonial peoples. As to peasants—a fact of great significance for a peasant country such as Russia—even they could be of help to revolution: while rich peasants were its natural enemies, the poor peasants and the agricultural laborers were its logical supporters, and even middle peasants could be an asset, if properly managed. Lenin was also the main figure in the creation and the evolution of the Bolshevik (later Communist) party in Russia, with its emphasis on exclusiveness, intolerance of other opinions, and discipline. Whether or not these qualities were naturally ingrained in Marxism and the Marxist vision of the world, they were certainly part of Lenin's character. The much-disputed larger question of whether Leninism was true creative Marxism or a heresy, with legitimate succession perhaps to be found in some other teaching, such as a more peaceful and evolutionary social democracy, defies a simple answer. Marx and Engels wrote and argued very much, over a long period of time, and not always consistently. It may be best to consider Leninism as one appropriate teaching to come out of Marxism without denying the authenticity of some other.

Lenin's crucial decision and role in the October revolution was based on his Marxist beliefs, but also on his own extreme interpretation of the situational advantages for revolution in Russia at that moment, a judgment initially not shared even by other Bolsheviks, let alone other socialists, who considered the country entirely too backward for immediate socialism. It was thus both a "scientific" Marxist evaluation and a gamble, with Lenin feeling repeatedly in 1917 that everything was lost. Even more eagerly than his associates, he was looking for any sign of the spread of the revolution in Europe, which was to validate and support the Russian overturn. But that Marxist expectation failed.

The years following brought instead a tremendous civil war at home, an unbearable strain and even collapse of the national economy, and hostility and isolation in foreign affairs. The fighting itself, with its attendant executions and massacres, and (even more) starvation, typhus, and other diseases, took uncounted millions of lives, exceeding by far in numbers or in the percentage of population the casualties of other revolutions in modern European history. The country also lost a million or two people by emigration, quite in line with Soviet social policies, although those who departed were by no means all "exploiters." The period from 1918 to 1921 came to be known as that of "War Communism," and many of its horrors were indeed linked directly to the civil war. However, War Communism also marked the height of revolutionary utopianism, of the effort by Lenin and his lieutenants to achieve socialism immediately or within a few months. Walicki's summary of the draft of the Party Program, written in March 1918, said:

> As we can see, at this early stage Lenin's program envisioned not only a countrywide socialist organization of production, coupled with the forced allocation of labor, but also a complete and final replacement of trade by "planned, organized distribution" to be followed by the gradual abolition of all forms of monetary exchange; it demanded strict collective control over individual consumption of all well-to-do people and postulated that individual households should be replaced by communal catering for large groups. In other words, it was a program for a drastic collectivization of all spheres of life, including private consumption. It did not, as yet, demand the expropriation

of the bourgeoisie but made up for this by abolishing the market, introducing universal control, and compulsorily organizing the whole population into consumer and producer communes.[2]

A number of studies have traced the utopian aspects of War Communism in considerable detail,[3] while others have slighted it, usually by concentrating almost entirely on mobilization for war.

The Red Army won, but War Communism lost. Reference has already been made to the utter devastation of the land and ruin of the economy by 1921. The New Economic Policy (N.E.P.) of 1921–1927 was thus a forced temporary retreat from the original communist vision to a mixed economy, and it was so argued by Lenin. The Party, of course, retained full political control. In economics, the state kept its exclusive hold on the "commanding heights," that is, on finance, large and medium industry, modern transportation, foreign trade, and all wholesale commerce. Private enterprise, however, was allowed in small industry and in retail trade. Perhaps still more important, requisitioning produce from the peasants, characteristic of War Communism, was replaced by a tax in kind, particularly in grain, and later by a money tax. The peasants could keep and sell on the free market what remained after the payment to the state, an obvious incentive to produce more.

By most counts, the N.E.P. was a great success. Economy revived, and according to many economic indicators, Russia had returned from the abyss and registered scores comparable to those in the last years of tsarist rule, and even slightly better. But the problems were numerous, and the frequently expressed opinion that the Soviet authorities should have left the N.E.P. to run its natural course probably lacked realism. The state and the private sectors of the economy did not work well together. While it proved possible in general to restore prewar industry, its further development required capital investment and determined leadership, which were sadly lacking. Peasants, for their part, were not eager to exert themselves on the land when they could get so little in exchange for their produce. Moreover, whatever their potential in economic theory, the embodiment and beneficiaries of the new course, the Nepmen—that is, small traders and manufacturers, as well as rich peasants—became increasingly irritating, and indeed threatening, to the Marxist-Leninist rulers of the country and their communist supporters. After all, what had the revolution and the civil war been fought for, and to whom did the Soviet Union belong? Again the ideology was playing a major role.

It was thus, so to speak, ideological logic, as well as economic, social, and other reasons, that turned the Soviet leadership against the N.E.P., which had in any case been accepted only as a temporary expedient in dire circumstances. Socialist and, after that, communist ideals were to be achieved through industrialization, collectivization of land, and the spread of Communism throughout society and down to each individual, including every detail of his or her private life. *Totalitarianism* is not a bad word for it, although economists may prefer to speak of a command economy. Writ large, it became the story of the Five-Year plans, of *kolkhozy* and *sovkhozy*, of the police control of society, forced labor, purges, and concentration camps.

To be sure, there is nothing in classical Marxism about the Five-Year plans. It may well be considered ironic that instead of happening in the most advanced industrial society, the socialist revolution occurred in a huge, backward borderland, which, after that, made a desperate, even partly successful, effort to industrialize. The doctrine of the weakest link of capitalism and much else has been adduced to explain the October Revolution in Marxist terms.[4] And every student of the Soviet Union knows how prominent the concepts of "proletarians," "proletariat," and "proletarian" as an adjective were in Soviet history, especially in its first decades, when they were virtually omnipresent. They represented, of course, a clear legacy of Marxism-Leninism.

Again, Marx and Engels did not write about *kolkhozy* and *sovkhozy*, but collectivization of agriculture was the greatest Soviet move into socialism, announcing the destruction of the old world and the creation of the new. And, in fact, because it affected most Russians in a fundamental way, the year 1929 marked the most important turning point in all Russian history, with the probable exception of the year 988. Those who liken the *kolkhoz* to the peasant commune, well known to the Russian peasants, are wrong. Members of a commune possessed their land in common, but they farmed their assigned lots separately, undisturbed, and in their own traditional way. Organization and regimentation of labor became the very essence of the *kolkhoz*.

It is remarkable to what extent the Soviet leaders resented the remnants of private farming within the collectives, namely the small private plots allotted to *kolkhoz* peasants. These plots were diminished in size and even forbidden, only to be reinstated because peasants wanted them, and certainly made a very much better use of them than of socialized fields. Over the years, the *kolkhozy* were increasing in size but declining in number. Another continuous trend in Soviet agriculture was the growth of the *sovkhozy*, in effect state agricultural factories, at the expense of the *kolkhozy*, and thus a further socialization of production. As usual in the U.S.S.R., the direction came from the highest level. One of Stalin's greatest ambitions was the socialization of Soviet agriculture. It was apparently especially in that connection that he came to consider himself the architect of the second Communist revolution in Russia, which would surpass in its results even that of Lenin. Khrushchev, in turn, concentrated on agriculture as his special domain. His unrealized projects included even that of *agrogoroda*, entire agricultural towns that would replace scattered collective farms and thus eliminate the very concepts of peasants and countryside. The abandoned buildings, fields, and materiel, hostile critics calculated, would surpass all the destruction in the Soviet Union during World War II. Soviet leaders were still socializing and improving agriculture when the U.S.S.R. collapsed.

Of the major Soviet policies, that of conducting purges, especially the great purges of the 1930s, is most difficult to explain. A setting for extreme, arbitrary violence, it is true, had already been provided by Lenin and Marxist ideology. In the words of Walicki:

> Lenin's conception of dictatorship as authority "absolutely unrestricted by any rules whatever" was an extreme case of "teleocratic" thinking, of a resolute and contemptuous opposition to all sorts of "nomocracy." It is therefore not enough to treat Lenin as "probably the most extreme utilitarian" in history: utilitarianism as such does not necessarily involve contempt for all rules. The existence of some rules, on the contrary, may be justified on purely utilitarian grounds. Neither does it suffice to define Lenin as a "legal nihilist"; typical legal nihilists, especially in the Russian tradition, condemned law in the name of morality, whereas in Lenin's case contempt for all rules extended to morality as well. In his view proletarian morality had to be strictly teleocratic, that is, consistently subordinated to the struggle for communism, as defined by the vanguard party."[5]

Practice illustrated theory. The Cheka, the political police, was established as early as December 20, 1917. The frightful cruelty of the civil war, displayed on the Red as well as on the White side and in numerous peasant rebellions, seemed impossible to trump. Lenin's personal cruelty has been richly confirmed by new archival evidence, and the same was true of other Soviet leaders, such as Trotsky, or, for that matter, Tukhachevsky. After the relatively quiet several years of the N.E.P. came the unbelievably brutal collectivization, with its victims—men, women, and children— counted in the millions. Solzhenitsyn had good reasons to rage that it was not necessary to wait for the execution of a Zinoviev or a Bukharin to find cruelty in the Soviet Union. What, then, could the great purges of the 1930s add to the Soviet experience, and why should they not be considered simply another characteristic manifestation of the Soviet system?

The purges were unique for several reasons. For one thing, these purges meant a tremendous—"fantastic" would not be too strong a word—annihilation of the ruling elite in Soviet Russia, in the Party, in the government, in the armed forces. Any analysis of what transpired makes this point stunningly clear. It was almost as if the Whites had won the civil war and proceeded to exterminate the Communists. The method of purging, with much public display, except in the case of the military, and confessions to most unlikely and even impossible crimes, turning the builders of Soviet Russia into its deadliest enemies, defied all imagination. Confessions can now be firmly explained by the mass use of torture, as well as by threats and action against family members and false promises of pardon. However, the need to obtain most extravagant confessions in each case and the entire surrealistic performance make little or no sense. Collectivization, too, had taken millions of lives, but its aim, lethal as it turned out, was clear: to destroy the kulaks and all other assumed enemies of collectivized agriculture and establish socialism in the countryside. The purges of the 1930s, as they spread in all directions and to every kind of people, defied explanation. Many explanations, of course, have been proposed, from advancing new cadres to strengthening the army for the forthcoming war (by virtually destroying its command). Some scholars have emphasized the significance of local conditions, rivalries, and struggles and their impact on the cleansing. Yet all these interpretations of what happened seem at best accounting only for a small part of an enormous and fantastic centrally directed enterprise. And the director, most scholars have concluded, could only be Stalin.

As a fine example of the Stalin approach, one might turn to Robert C. Tucker's book *Stalin in Power: The Revolution from Above, 1928–1941* (1990). Tucker writes:

> From late 1932 Soviet Russia was the scene of a conspiracy to seize total power by terrorist action. This was the gist of the secret letter circulated by Stalin's office to party committees in July 1936. In a way the charge was true. There *was* a conspiracy. It had its inception in 1932, and took final shape in 1934. It was carefully organized, and sought total power through terrorist action against much of the party-state's leadership.
>
> Beyond that point, fact leaves off and fiction begins. Those accused of being leaders of the conspiracy—Zinoviev, Kamenev, Trotsky and others—were among its intended victims; and the one named in the letter as the chief intended victim—Stalin—was the archconspirator. The secret letter was projective. Through a glass darkly it revealed what happened: from the time Stalin came to see himself as the target of a plot by a multitude of masked enemies, he began conspiring against them. Their conspiracy was fictional; his was real.[6]

Tucker proceeds to describe in an impressive, even stunning, manner the fantastic and fascinating great purge, as organized in general, and often in particular, by Stalin to destroy his enemies and suspected enemies, in order to establish himself as the only and absolute successor to Lenin. His ego and his self-doubt could never rest, and he had to keep killing. A reader readily shares the author's hatred of the supreme criminal, and ardently wishes with him that Mikhail Tomsky or Sergo Ordzhenikidze had killed the monster to whom they had a ready access rather than merely denouncing him to his face and committing suicide. Clear and powerful, Tucker's explanation of the purges has its weaknesses. By its very nature, it minimizes factors other than Stalin, such as the nature of Marxism and the aforementioned characteristics of the Soviet system. And its psychological argument can be challenged. Stalin is presented as a cold-blooded and calculating mass murderer. Yet he needs confessions from the victims, and that is Tucker's explanation for the confessions: that Stalin needed to be able to keep convincing himself that it was they and not he who committed crimes. After arranging the assassination of Kirov (and Tucker is absolutely certain that Stalin arranged it, although some other specialists are not), did Stalin need Zinoviev's confession to convince himself that Zinoviev was really the guilty party? And if that double-entendre was an exception, what were the other exceptions? Was Stalin insane?[7] The systematic and situational reasons combine poorly with abnormal psychology, and it is best to keep both approaches firmly in mind when dealing with Stalin and the purges.

Moving from the lethal Georgian party secretary to the Soviet supreme leadership in general, as established by Lenin and Stalin and continued until 1991, one must note that personal dictatorship, occasionally modified by a narrow oligarchy of a few, became the standard form. Whether that was based on the Marxist-Leninist belief in one correct answer to everything and one correct policy or should be ascribed to more adventitious circumstances is a matter for debate. Once, in 1964, the established dictator, Khrushchev, was overthrown by his elite associates. Some scholars make a special category of the period of "high Stalinism," when the Politburo did not meet for a very long time and Stalin appeared to be entirely on his own. Yet then, as in earlier years, he prosecuted his policies relying only on a few trusted assistants (usually, as it happened, members of the Politburo). More difficult to explain from the Marxist point of view is the cult of personality of the leader, already strong under Lenin, achieving fantastic proportions under Stalin and continuing under Khrushchev (the quip was that the country acquired a cult, but no personality, at least none to compare to that of Khrushchev's predecessor) and beyond. In fact, in some ways most remarkable was the cult of Brezhnev, which reached its heights in his last years, when the barely surviving invalid was presented as a dashing hero, while uncounted editions of his works were published, to be promptly ground for pulp. Brezhnev's successors, Iury Andropov, Constantine Chernenko, and Mikhail Gorbachev, could also claim supreme power and regard until the first two died quickly in office and the third brought the entire system down.

But, in any case, the ideology was never absent from the purges, although it often looked like Marxism-Leninism edited by Alice and her acquaintants in Wonderland, as the devil Trotsky waged his war against the Party and Stalin, while most associates of Lenin turned out to be traitors plotting for years the destruction of their own work. On a slightly different level, it is worth noting that in 1937 Stalin declared that as the country progressed toward socialism, social antagonisms and struggle would become sharper. That view was condemned in 1956.

The issue of Russian nationalism as part of Soviet ideology has produced much disagreement among specialists. At one extreme, scholars followed Timasheff's argument of the "great retreat"[8] and other conservative interpretations of Soviet reality to claim that the Communist revolution had spent itself and that Stalinization meant the restoration, or at least a partial restoration, of traditional values connected with family, school, history, and, perhaps indirectly, nationalism. Russian nationalism became more direct in the frightful years of World War II, when the government appealed to it to save the country. A very important ingredient of the new orientation was a greater permissiveness in regard to religion, especially Orthodoxy. The Orthodox Church obtained a patriarch, strengthened its organization, and in general made a certain recovery after what had been one of the most devastating religious persecutions in world history. Heroes from the Russian past, even some clerical heroes, competed with Communist stalwarts for public attention. Indeed, some observers believed that Stalin became a Russian nationalist, modeling himself on Ivan the Terrible or Peter the Great, rather than on Marxist theoreticians or his Georgian ancestors.

Yet the opposite view has the better argument. For the Marxist elite ruling the Soviet Union—and it is the ideology of that elite that I have been so far discussing— any serious resort to nationalism, tradition, non-Marxist history, or religion had a manipulative, but not a substantive, value. Dire circumstances forced retreats and allowances, but the basic direction and goal never changed. Thus religious persecution resumed its course, and the Church experienced its nadir probably at the time of Khrushchev. While history in schools became patriotic, its fundamental framework remained Marxist-Leninist with no exceptions and no other approach allowed at any level of schooling. As to the transformation of Stalin into a Russian nationalist, one should remember that the supreme leader never considered himself a Russian and referred to the Russians as "they," not "we." To the end of his days, he was more comfortable speaking Georgian than Russian. (His first published pieces were poems, in Georgian.) Much as he admired other powerful and decisive rulers, they were not allowed to transgress his basic Marxist intellectual framework. Once a foreign visitor asked Stalin how Peter the Great compared to Lenin; Stalin answered: like a drop of water to an ocean.[9]

Stalin's death on March 5, 1953, registered as a tremendous shock in the Soviet Union, but it did not change the country. If anything, there was a certain reassertion of a more dogmatic Marxism-Leninism, emphasizing the Party and not only its secretary, resuming regular meetings of the Politburo, and paying a new attention to the formal functioning of Soviet political and Party institutions. Much stress was put on collective leadership and proper Communist procedure. Khrushchev's secret speech about the crimes of Stalin's regime, delivered on February 25, 1956, following the Twentieth All-Union Communist Party Congress, and certain later efforts at de-Stalinization, notably at the Twenty-Second Congress in October, 1961, bore some fruit. The process of a rehabilitation of the victims of Stalin's purges began and gained momentum. Part of draconian antilabor legislation was repealed, notably the law of 1940 tying workers to their jobs and holding them criminally responsible for absenteeism and simply for being late. Perhaps most important, the concentration camp empire, the notorious gulag, largely disbanded, releasing millions of prisoners. Not surprisingly, however, de-Stalinization proved to be in a sense sporadic, fragmentary, and overall very difficult. Stalinism could not be separated from its crimes—after all, it was the history of the Soviet Union—and the guilt involved the entire governing elite, as well as many others, except for the very young. One could condemn particular repressions and "rehabilitate" specific victims, usually dead, but one could not—or was it that one did not dare?—go deeper and try to explain why criminal transgressions on such an enormous scale could occur in a Marxist country, in the land of socialism. And that was the question asked not only by critics of all sorts, but also by such allies and associates as the head of the Italian Communist Party, Palmiro Togliatti. There was no answer given, beyond references to the apparently magic evil powers of "the cult of personality." Possibly even more significant than the extremely sensitive and explosive personal aspect of de-Stalinization was the fact that the Communist government and elite saw no alternative to what they received in bequest from Lenin and Stalin. So they carried out more Five-Year plans, spread Marxist education to the point where they could claim to have the best-educated working force in the world, proclaimed their country to have reached the stage of developed socialism, and added Brezhnev's vacuous volumes to the reading list.

In foreign policy, the Soviet Union and its east European satellites continued to confront the United States and its allies. Indeed, not only Europe but most of the world came to be divided between the two camps. Although not predicted in Marxist classics, the confrontation was a most impressive and lasting demonstration of the mobilized might and hostility of the two sides. Very fortunately, the "Cold War" remained basically cold, although the crisis over Soviet missiles in Cuba and several other incidents came close to the precipice. From the point of view of Soviet ideology, a war between the two superpowers was both unnecessary and undesirable, except possibly in Stalin's mind during the weird last months of his life. Marxism does not intend to conquer by invasion but rather by historical logic, by the inevitable evolution of a given society. Moreover, international developments were going well from the Soviet point of view. From their insecure toehold in Russia in 1917, communists appeared to be already ruling half the world in the late twentieth century. Yet the danger of an atomic war was great. It could happen through a mistake or a misunderstanding. In addition, although the Communists had no need to storm capitalist fortresses, capitalism or, in its final stage, imperialism, at bay could launch a preventive war as its last chance of survival. Some military experts kept emphasizing the advantages of the first strike. It was perhaps to calm themselves and others that Soviet authorities in the late Brezhnev years stressed that the balance of power on our planet had already shifted in favor of socialism and that, therefore, the imperialists would not dare start a war. But how could they be certain?

The problem of nationalities in the U.S.S.R. and of their roles in Soviet ideology and politics has at least to be mentioned, although it is almost impossibly many-sided and complex. Again, we are faced with Marxist theory and its specific interpretations, needs, and opportunities of the moment, changes of the Party line, suspicion, sweeping purges, and so on and on. "Nation" or "nationality" is not a basic Marxist category, and the problem for Marxists is, therefore, to fit nations or nationalities into their own framework in theory, and sometimes also, as in the remarkable Soviet case, in practice. To simplify, the Soviet solution was based on a specific application of the dialectic, in itself a clear indication of its abstract intellectual origin. Communists believed in a transformed unitary society as their goal. However, they concluded that that aim could be reached best not by mixing different peoples in different stages of development but by having each nationality evolve to its own highest level, from which each could consciously and freely join others in a new higher synthesis. The dialectic thus postulated the greatest evolution and differentiation to achieve the most effective unity. Nor would socialism be at all jeopardized, because, according to the famous formula, each evolution will be national in form and socialist in content.

In practice, the Soviet Union came to be divided into, eventually, fifteen union republics and, within them, over a hundred smaller subdivisions, based again on the ethnic principle. Soviet authorities made a great effort to build up the culture of all ethnic units to the point of establishing full-fledged academies of sciences in the union republics. But the buildup was across the board. It has even been argued that the greatest gainers were the smallest nationalities, which had little cultural baggage to begin with and obtained much, including, when needed, alphabets.[10] Whole native intelligentsias were thus created in the 1920s and 1930s. Results, of course, varied from great ancient cultures of Armenia and Georgia to some primitive tribes of Siberia and the Far East, but the effort was always there. With Stalinization and its aftermath, suspicion and purges became the order of the day, sometimes wiping out the intelligentsia that had just been created. Ethnic emphasis suggested separatism and even independence. In the case of Ukraine, guerilla warfare lasted for months and even years after the successful conclusion of hostilities with Germany.

Moreover, after a controlled measure of Great Russian patriotism and nationalism became respectable in the Soviet Union, Stalin and the Politburo began to stress the Russian language and the historical role of the Great Russian people as binding cement of their multinational state. This trend continued during World War II and in the postwar years. Some peoples of the U.S.S.R. switched to the use of the Cyrillic in place of the Latin alphabet for their native tongues, while the Russian language received emphasis in all Soviet schools. Histories had to be rewritten again to demonstrate that the incorporation of minority nationalities into the Russian state was a positive good rather than merely the lesser evil as compared to other alternatives. The new interpretation was fitted into Marxist dress by such means as stress on the progressive nature of the Russian proletariat and the advanced character of the Russian revolutionary movement, which benefited all the peoples fortunate enough to be associated with Russians. But Stalin, and some other Soviet leaders as well, went further, giving violent expression to some of the worst kind of prejudices, notably the quite un-Marxist vice of anti-Semitism. Yiddish intellectuals were among the groups virtually wiped out by the purges of 1948–1952, and Stalin's and Zhdanov's notorious pursuit of "cosmopolitans" had Jews as a main focus. As to Russians proper, some might have enjoyed their assigned role of "elder brother" and the privileged position of their language and culture, but, to repeat, they generally shared the pain and tribulations of the other citizens of the Soviet Union and even were denied a separate Academy of Sciences or a distinct section of the Party. The Russian standard of living was lower than those in several other republics of the

U.S.S.R. Soviet authorities were very proud of their "solution" of the problem of nationalities, and their optimism was shared by many outside observers, including specialists. Granted some remnants of religious prejudices and certain other archaic traits in the older generations, younger people guaranteed a truly progressive and united multicultural Soviet socialist state. It was difficult to be more wrong.

But what did the Soviet people, in particular the Russian people, who form the subject of this book, really believe during some seventy-five years of Communist rule? So far, I have discussed only the huge governing layers, and it is time to turn in our ignorance to the masses. The official answer is simple: they all believed in Marxism-Leninism (and for a long time also Stalinism), only to a different depth and degree of comprehension, ranging from the gloriously enlightened leadership in Moscow to remarkably obdurate remaining class enemies and clods in backwaters. Education was the answer. And the Soviet Union may be considered a tremendous experiment in education, with some very impressive results. Education brought backward individuals and peoples into the modern world; in addition, so they would be correctly oriented, there were courses in Marxism-Leninism to be taken in almost every school and at almost every level of learning. By contrast, all dissenting or competing views were excluded to the greatest degree possible. Often only specialists were allowed to read crucial foreign works in their field, mainly to denounce them in print. Indeed, as some critics emphasize, it was only in the last part of the twentieth century, when technological and economic developments made this extraordinary intellectual isolation impossible, or at least extremely difficult, that the Soviet Union went down. As a recent study brought out forcefully, education, careers, appointments, and almost everything else in the Soviet Union came to be presented in the form of a generous gift from the leader and the Party that the recipient could never fully repay, although he or she was expected to try to do so throughout life.[11] The disparity between the two sides of the deal could hardly be made more striking.

Every effort was tried to convert and inspire the masses. The typical Soviet novel became the story of such Communist illumination of the hero or heroine.[12] All was to be in black and white, clear and simple for the mass reader to understand. Optimism was prescribed. The great poet Anna Akhmatova was denounced for her eroticism and her loneliness, while the composer Dmitri Shostakovich was told to simplify his music. Socialist realism became the dominant creative mode. Claiming association with the superb realistic tradition in prerevolutionary Russian literature, it became in fact simplistic Soviet propaganda. Indeed, it was explained that writers must depict human beings and society as they should and will be under socialism and Communism rather than look for blemishes around them. As one émigré critic put it, socialist realism was "a method of 'realistic' depiction of unrealistic phenomena, absent in reality."[13]

The colossal effort of Soviet education and propaganda to make the population of the country enthusiastically support Marxism, their leader, and the Party line had some foundation in facts. The October overturn and its immediate aftermath represented a social revolution, as well as a conspiratorial coup leading to the annihilation of whole classes of society. In the process, there were winners as well as losers. In spite of some remarkable proletarian detachments on the White side, workers in general fought for the Reds, and they were for many years afterward considered by the Communists as the most reliable social element, in particular if they had already been workers in tsarist time. Ironically, it was this dedicated, often fanatical element, composed of professional revolutionaries, workers, soldiers, sailors, and other sundry radicals, that was largely wiped out in the great purges of the 1930s. Peasants and peasants as soldiers battled on all sides, including their own peasant wars, but in the end they did obtain the landlords' land and kept their coveted prize until collectivization. Collectivization meant death to millions of people, and in fact the destruction of traditional Russian peasantry. Some other Stalinist and generally Soviet measures proved, however, more promising. Notably, there was the tremendous drive in education, which eventually transformed a more than half-illiterate country into one of the best educated in the world. Education went together with industrialization and urbanization, with all these processes affecting, in the framework of the Soviet Union, tens of millions of people. In its own way, the U.S.S.R. was a land of opportunity, for the government never had enough qualified personnel for its endless undertakings. Whatever the reasons for the purges, one of their results was a contribution to social mobility, as millions of jobs became open, sometimes more than once in rapid succession. In addition to the opportunities of a dynamic society, Soviet citizens enjoyed such special advantages as free medical help, very low rent, and rather effective general access to education. Authorities spent generously on the arts of almost every kind, although, of course, without forgetting the requirements of Marxism-Leninism and socialist realism. Soviet citizens could be justly proud of many scientists, musicians, athletes, and chess players.

On the whole, it is not surprising that, in addition to outspoken admirers of the Soviet Union, many of its critics also credited it with important achievements. The issue often became whether it had demonstrated enough success and stability to be a generally accepted and quasi-permanent member of the nations of the world. Some writers found that success and stability in modernization, in particular in industrialization and the development of education, or, later, in the Soviet achievements in space. Others saw the conclusive proof of the success and value of the Soviet system in its victory over Germany in World War II. Certain commentators emphasized the rise of the new middle class, with its interests and orientation quite different from those of old Communists. Most often the stress was on the present and future generations, not crippled by Stalin and the purges, who would revitalize the system and take it to new achievements. Now that Communism has collapsed in Russia, the inevitable additional question is: what went wrong? Or—to put it in terms of the Russian people, most germane to this study—did the Marxist government ever have the mass support of the people, and if so, when and why did it lose it? Earlier I considered the dogmatic ideological government and what it offered to the people. What was the popular response?

Although my answer is bound to be mere speculation, I would suggest—and I have no claim to originality—that the Communist Party and the Soviet government never had popular majority support. Most striking is the destruction of their own people by the rulers and the attempts of the people to escape the system whenever possible. The tragedy began with the October Revolution, the horrible civil war, and the virtual collapse of the country under War Communism. The New Economic Policy allowed for some recovery and even produced a certain kind of stability. But it was a temporary device, followed by Stalin's socialist offensive. The offensive meant a murderous collectivization and a frantic industrialization to the breaking point and often even beyond. At the same time, great purges swept the land, destroying both old and new cadres, and occasionally, it seemed, anyone of any prominence. When war came, the Red armed forces suffered catastrophic defeats, while many civilians, and not only in borderlands, welcomed the Germans. To be sure, the country staged a tremendous rally inspired by patriotism, nationalism, in part religion, and other un-Marxist sentiments, to which even the government itself at that point paid respect. Still, many thousands of Russian prisoners of war aligned themselves—as Vlasovites, that is, followers of General Andrei Vlasov—with the enemy, while many of them and many more other refugees did all they could, often including suicide, not to be returned eventually to their socialist fatherland. Although the Vlasovites, who changed sides mainly because of quite literal starvation in German camps and sometimes also because of their hatred of Communism, did not represent perfectly the total population of the U.S.S.R., few strangers who came to know them well could retain any illusions about the Soviet Union. Victory spelled a return where needed and a full reemphasis of the Soviet system. Indeed, the gulag archipelago received its greatest expansion, encompassing for the first time very many prisoners of war and some other citizens from abroad. As already mentioned, Stalin's death and efforts at de-Stalinization gradually emptied most of the camps but did not otherwise change the police nature of the state. Escape, permanent or even temporary, became a little easier, although still fraught with difficulties, as in the special case of the migration of Soviet Jews to Israel or of the numerous "cultural exchanges" between the Soviet Union and the outside world. Finally, after Gorbachev appeared on the scene, it was popular participation— through *glasnost*, elections, and other means—that brought about the precipitous crash of the Soviet empire and of the Soviet Union itself.

What went wrong with the Communist plan for the Union of Soviet Socialist Republics? To begin with, the enormous and impressive ideological indoctrination and education of the people had serious weaknesses. In retrospect, it seems that it was in general too crude and pitched at too low a level, especially as the population came to know its masters better and also as it acquired some awareness of life abroad. Surfeit of propaganda could even backfire. I remember a chauffeur of the

Academy of Sciences telling me that he knew that there was no race problem in the United States; when, taken somewhat aback, I asked him how he knew it, he answered: because the Soviet media talk about that alleged problem and its devastating impact day and night.[14]

Still, the main problem for the Communists was not that they delivered their message to the people in an ineffective manner but the message itself. Utopia in power was disjoined from reality and in many ways increasingly so with the passage of time, as its promises failed to be realized. Moreover, the drastic utopian demands were not superficial, but went to the heart of Marxism-Leninism. Most far-reaching was the need to abolish religion and, indeed, God. Frequently underplayed at present, it proceeded straight from the classics of Marxism to Lenin and the entire antireligious policy of the Soviet Union. To quote an entry from the chronological table at the end of M. Geller's and A. Nekrich's second volume: "1932, 15th of May. There is declared 'an anti-religious Five-Year Plan,' the aim of which is the liquidation by the first of May 1937 of all the houses of prayer in the U.S.S.R. and 'the expulsion [*izgnanie*] of the very concept of god.'"[15] That this policy was not a Russian aberration can be seen from similar efforts of other Marxist governments, two of which, the communist rulers of Albania and the Khmer Rouge in Cambodia, claimed eventually to have already achieved the liquidation of all religious buildings and activities in their countries. Communist China, in the meantime, continues its struggle against religion, often reminding one of the past efforts of the Soviet Union. But the Russian people remained, to a remarkable extent, religious. The official census of 1937, for example, found them more religious, percentage-wise, than the French. It was that finding that probably contributed to the suppression of the census, although the main reason might well have been the catastrophic figure for the total population of the country that was revealed by the census. Because religion would not go away, in spite of all the persecution, a certain compromise became necessary, especially during World War II and also after. Nevertheless, Khrushchev mounted another mighty liquidation of "the houses of worship" and some other aspects of religion, looking forward to its total elimination. In the end, however, religion survived, and Communism went down. Although there were many reasons for its collapse, the brutal and sustained antireligious policy represented probably the greatest cleavage between the rulers and the ruled in the U.S.S.R. Whereas religion meant, overwhelmingly, Orthodoxy for the Russians, that is, for the Great Russians, the Ukrainians, and the White Russians (Belarus) as well as for the Georgians and for some smaller ethnic groups, the Soviet state also persecuted Islam in the Muslim republics, Judaism, Buddhism, and other non-Christian and Christian creeds. The ultimate aim was always the same, although the particular circumstances varied greatly, including the pitting of the Orthodox Church against the Uniates and the Roman Catholics in western Ukraine and Belarus.

Class struggle and extermination also created cleavages. Martin Malia and some other specialists stressed the much more thorough social displacement following the October Revolution in Russia, compared to the social changes brought about by the great revolutions in England, France, or the United States.[16] In Soviet Russia, entire classes disappeared, either immediately, as in the case of the landlords, or at the end of the New Economic Policy, as was the fate of commercial and industrial small bourgeoisie. Indeed, the entire former upper and middle classes, broadly speaking, had no place in the new society. They consisted of "former people," defeated in the revolution and the civil war. As individuals, to be sure, many members of these classes could and did serve the new state as technical specialists and in many other capacities, or they could migrate, as up to two million of them did (although the emigrants included many cossacks and other people not usually classified as upper or middle class). Those who remained in the Soviet Union suffered from legal and social discrimination, and they formed particularly attractive material for forthcoming purges and punishments. Still, most of them survived and became part of the Soviet technical and general intelligentsia, which was being rapidly mass produced in schools and universities.

The case of the peasants was much more tragic. They constituted perhaps 85 percent of the population of the Russian empire at the time of the Revolution and thus could by no means be marginalized as fading remnants of the old order. The problem was to bring them into the new system. The method selected by Stalin to do so, namely rapid collectivization, was in a sense successful, because it destroyed forever the old Russian peasant world. But the cost was tremendous. Most economists believe that the reform was a failure and that Soviet agriculture became a disaster area from 1929 to the collapse of the U.S.S.R. in 1991. In human terms, the results were worse. The unbelievable brutality of collectivization, with cannibalism and millions starving to death, while the government pretended that everything was going well and prevented any import of food into the area, defies description. Was it five million human beings that perished or perhaps more? Even if we stress miscalculations, droughts, and disorganization rather than a deliberate decision to punish properly recalcitrant peasants, or, some argue, Ukrainians, it seems hardly possible to think of any approval of Communist plans or Communism in the countryside. And more than half of the Soviet citizens lived in the countryside, even for a number of years after World War II.

Great purges followed collectivization. Again, millions of people died, and other millions were sent to labor camps, from which many of them never returned. However, while collectivization had a clear goal of destroying the kulaks—which came to mean, in practice, all peasants objecting to collectivization—and establishing socialist agriculture, the new campaign, although as cruel as the preceding one, remained a mystery. Best known for its execution of Communist leaders and of a large part of the Communist elite, it quickly acquired a mass character.

People were arrested because of their social origin, because of their nationality, because of their religion, because of their contact with those who had already been condemned, because of their political past, because of their profession. The arrested were accused of most fantastic crimes and were forced by means of torture to denounce their relatives, friends, and colleagues. Those mentioned during the interrogations became new victims.[17]

The categories mentioned here by no means exhausted the victims of the purges or the accusations against them. In addition, while the costs of collectivization were kept secret as much as possible and were generally little known, the great purges became public and immediately presented a conundrum to the inhabitants of the Soviet Union and of the world.

The question most often asked is: how were the great purges at all possible? How could the authorities destroy millions of people of every kind, everywhere in the land, with no objective evidence for their action, and not be stopped in their tracks?[18] What was the popular reaction? To be sure, people were stunned, and most of them probably remained stunned throughout. Some must have believed the official explanation or rather explanations, difficult though it is for us to imagine that. Although suddenly threatened by the deadly enemy in their midst, they could at least find support in the vigilance of the state and feel relatively secure themselves, because they knew that they were not and had no association with Japanese spies or British saboteurs. Those less naive, apparently, often attributed the explosive new developments to some kind of internal Party struggle and tried to find their security in lying low and in not being involved in any intrigues themselves. Purges also contributed to some local scores being settled, and they even have been presented as a major Soviet way to advance in office—by denouncing one's superior or superiors. And indeed, many jobs became open. Still, it should be remembered that as the purges gathered momentum, denunciations were demanded almost from all and almost all the time. Therefore, producing a denunciation could have more to do with attempting to save one's own skin than with aiming for a higher position or better housing. Finally, whether Stalin had a comprehensive overall plan or not when he instituted the purges, locally they generally became separate and even disjointed events, subject also to local conditions. There was no center, not even a central personality, to rally the discontent.

If, as is my opinion, most Russians did not simply accept the Party and Communism as their hallowed guides in everything, what did they believe in? My first answer would be survival. I was time and again surprised to what extent the possibility of obtaining a room or the quality of potatoes mattered. Endurance rather than any kind of enthusiasm was the norm. Endurance may not be an Aristotelian political category, but it has its uses in politics and in life. It held the Germans at Stalingrad, as was beautifully described by Vasily Grossman in *Life and Fate*, and it also made it possible for the people to survive the other enormous trials and tribulations of the

Soviet period, mostly homemade. Russians readily accepted the advantages of the Soviet system, such as general education, but few—and, it seems, with the passage of time, always fewer—were inspired by the Marxist vision of universal proletarian blessedness. In that sense, too, Communism and the Soviet Union failed.

Were these recalcitrant Russians inspired by anything else? Or at least by something beyond mere survival? A full answer would require much knowledge we do not possess, all the more so because there was no freedom of speech in the Soviet Union, no alternative systems to communism were ever offered, and in a sense there was even no opposition. Still, the arguments were not only over the quality of the potato harvest. The most important rival of Communism was, of course, religion, which meant, in Russia, primarily the Orthodox Church. Lenin saw that well in his own time. While not a secular ideology like Marxism-Leninism, let alone a political party, Orthodox Christianity offered a totally different system of values and understanding of the world.

Other non-Marxist views—*ideologies* would be in most cases too strong and formal a term—widespread in the Soviet Union included many kinds of nationalism or patriotism. Russian nationalism was on the rise and, to repeat, in spite of very serious and numerous obstacles, Russia was in many ways in the process of becoming a modern nation-state when the October Revolution turned it in a different direction. Lenin hated especially Russian nationalism, and in the great civil war, the nationalist cause was associated, quite logically, with the Whites, not the Reds. Yet the Red victory did not settle the matter for good. Geller and Nekrich are probably correct in emphasizing the importance of *smenovekhovstvo*, an ideology created by the brilliant Nicholas Ustrialov and several other émigré intellectuals and publicists but prominent also in the 1920s in the U.S.S.R.[19] Even the Soviet authorities welcomed that heretical teaching to an extent, both because it split the émigrés and because it provided a rationale for people of different convictions to serve the Soviet government. As the name implies, the doctrine meant "a change of orientation," from hostility to the Communist state to cooperation with it. The argument was that the Soviet Union had proved itself to be the true and only representative of Russia and Russian interests at the given time in history, and thus deserved the support of every Russian. Bolshevism was a passing phase, whereas Russia will remain. Ustrialov returned to Russia and was shot in the purges; but many Russians must have continued serving their country with some degree of patriotism or nationalism, as well as hope for a better future—even if they never heard of Ustrialov.

World War II brought nationalism and patriotism to the fore. The authorities themselves engaged in direct appeals to these sentiments, and made important gestures in their direction. While their new attitude was, in my opinion, manipulative rather than an indication of a change in belief, it was nevertheless welcome to many people. The long "Cold War" provided further occasion for thinking and feeling in dichotomous quasi-national, as well as Marxist, terms. Patriotic nationalism certainly helped the Soviet government in war, and even in peace, but it always had to be controlled and was ultimately irreconcilable with Marxism-Leninism. In addition, the Soviet authorities had to be concerned not only with the Russians, but also with all their other nationalities.

The Soviet system did not allow for an opposition, and in that respect, in a sense, it succeeded. After other political parties and, following that, factions within the Party were proscribed, there remained no one to object legally to the Party line. The situation changed radically only with Gorbachev's *glasnost*. Individual dissenters and small groups of dissenters eventually emerged, and certain of their publications, *samizdat* when published clandestinely in the country and *tamizdat* when published abroad, obtained some circulation. But all this was little, and the police specialized in restricting and punishing the culprits. More successfully, during the later Brezhnev years, a number of critics could utilize international treaties signed by the Soviet Union and thus acquire a legal standing for their protests. In any case, future students of Soviet history will have to know the names of Solzhenitsyn and Sakharov as well as those of Dzerzhinsky and Beria.

Violence against authorities was a great crime, and it was apparently not very much in use, certainly not to be compared to the violence of the authorities against the people. This disproportion has been ascribed to many causes, ranging from the efficiency of a totalitarian system to the passivity of the Russian character. Still, previous to and even more so after the opening of the archives, there has been conclusive evidence of strikes, protests, attendant massacres, rebellions in forced labor camps (sometimes leading to ameliorations in the labor camp regime), and other forms of violence. Communist agitators were killed by peasants for years after the end of the civil war, and their graves were often desecrated. Even all that may be considered little, taking into account the magnitude of the subject.

But one should not mistake passivity or acquiescence for approval. Concentration camp memoirs form a devastating genre of twentieth-century literature. It is a multilingual, international species of writing, frequently set in Russia or in Germany. There are even outsiders, Poles and others, who went through labor camps in both systems and returned to tell the story. Typically, they identify the German camps with the German people, but not the Russian camps with the Russian people. Rather, they are prone to regard Russians, both convicts and those outside the camps, as living in an invaded territory, although the invaders are also Russians. Correspondingly, it was very difficult to escape from a German camp but easy to escape from a Russian one, mainly because the Russians, in contrast to the Germans, almost invariably helped fugitives, sometimes for months on end. Of course, most Germans were not Nazis. They enjoyed, however, an easy identification with their state and their authorities, which most of the Russians, or at least very many Russians, lacked—and that is precisely the point.

Conclusion

You are both scanty,
And you are bountiful,
You are both mighty,
And you are impotent,
Mother-Russia!

                                                        —Nekrasov

Once before I finished a book on Russian history by emphasizing that the ideologies and the expectations of the given period had failed and that the way was open for new opinions and new developments.[1] At issue was the end of the reign of Nicholas I, the death of the emperor, and the transition from the ideologies and the men of the 1840s to those of the 1860s.[2] Yet the earlier case can almost be considered a study in continuity, compared to the collapse of the Soviet Union. In the former instance, the government remained, as did essentially its doctrine of Official Nationality. Moreover, then the Russian population, overwhelmingly peasant, while properly Orthodox and monarchist, was generally left alone. By contrast, the enormous Communist indoctrination and penetration impacted everyday life for all Russians, and, after seventy-five years of complete sway and control, it suddenly disappeared.

The shock was enormous, mixed for very many Russians with great joy at the collapse of Communism. Most people, both at home and abroad, welcomed enthusiastically the arrival of a new age. But the nature of that new age never became clear. Gorbachev, who initiated the age, delayed and confused matters by clinging desperately to socialism and even Leninism, retreating only under pressure and step by step. Yeltsin demonstrated no such Leninist allegiance, for he saw better that the Soviet system or anything like it could not last. Perhaps for that very reason, he headed the search for a new sustaining and redemptive teaching. A large committee of specialists was appointed by the government to establish the true nature of Russia: their first task—admirably academic—was to gather everything that has been written and said on their subject. Even individual journals and newspapers offered prizes for the best definition of Russianness. As the saying goes, all that would be funny, if it were not so sad.

However, as already mentioned, certain beliefs remained. One institution that profited enormously from the fall of Communism has been the patriarchal Russian Orthodox Church. It survived because of the unexpectedly strong support of the faithful, and the ensuing compromise on the part of the authorities. With the fall of

Communism, the Church suddenly emerged from what has been described as the greatest religious persecution in human history to a central and privileged position. At present, the Church is favored by Vladimir Putin (apparently himself Orthodox) as it has been by Yeltsin and by almost all political parties and groupings, with even Gennady Zyuganov and his Communists proclaiming that they no longer oppose religion and even on occasion treasure it as Russian patrimony! Its expanding membership includes perhaps one-third of the Russian people, although many of them do not regularly attend services. What is more, repeated polls indicate that the population has a higher regard for and more confidence in the Church than in anything else in the country, be it the government, the armed forces, or the political parties. At its hierarchical council in the summer of the year 2000, the Church discussed and approved "The Foundations of the Social Concepts of the Russian Orthodox Church," a powerful as well as pioneering document, because the Russian Orthodox Church had never before dealt in a connected and comprehensive way with social and political matters. Still, one of the problems of the Church is its eagerness to play a greater role in education and in related matters in what is, after all, a secular state. In the autumn of 1997 the legislature passed and President Yeltsin signed what has been described as a religious protection bill, which declared Orthodoxy, Islam, Judaism, and Buddhism as the established religions of Russia; this made it more difficult for other religious groups to operate in the country, especially where they had not been previously entrenched over a period of time. Enjoying vast popular support as a proper measure against evangelical Christians, as well as Mormons, Hare Krishnas, and other religious groups that flooded Russia in search of converts after the fall of Communism, the bill was internationally denounced as an infraction of the freedom of religious expression. Other complex problems concerned ecclesiastical jurisdiction in newly independent states, such as Ukraine and the Baltic republics. In addition, the persecution and aggressive de-Christianization of the Soviet period left a difficult legacy. The Church is short of everything, and the large-scale construction and restoration of church buildings represents only a portion of the most visible part of its needs. At times, the Church seems to operate as a missionary establishment rather than one that recently celebrated a thousand years of its existence.

Russian nationalism and patriotism remained and profited greatly from the collapse of the Soviet Union. Indeed, it can be argued that it was especially the refusal of Yeltsin and the Russian republic to support the U.S.S.R. that spelled its doom. The remarkable present popularity of Putin, bolstered powerfully by the tragic Chechen wars, reflects the general view that he understands and represents Russian interests better than his disappointing predecessors. Nationalism combines readily with a broad spectrum of political opinions, from the extreme Right to the Left, although perhaps not the extreme Left. Although when it is moderate it is not necessarily antidemocratic or hostile to outsiders, it can survive political and economic defeats and failures, and even grow in response to challenges, especially in our nationalistic age. The Putin regime, formally democratic—and in many ways much more than merely formally, because there has been, since *glasnost,* an active public opinion and because there are elections, a parliament, a judiciary system, and so on—relies on the already-mentioned endurance of the Russian people and on their patriotism or nationalism. This compatibility between the leader and the people does not promise long-term political stability, nor does it eliminate justifiable worries about the dictatorial tendencies of the regime, about the future relationships between the center and the periphery, particularly between the central government and the eighty-nine regions into which Russia is divided, or about the impoverishment of the masses and other unresolved economic problems. It should be added that such prominent figures as Solzhenitsyn and the recently deceased Dmitri Likhachev preach, in spite of their impeccable nationalist credentials, moderation. Solzhenitsyn repeatedly insisted that Russians should not rule over non-Russian peoples. Likhachev carried as one of his banners in the ongoing ideological battle the assertion that there was no special Russian idea or historical mission.[3]

To be sure, the extreme Right has been very loud and determined to draw attention to itself. It has had the advantages of novelty and excitement, because its views could not be expressed, at least entirely and explicitly expressed, in the Soviet Union. It is only since *glasnost* that its members have fully entered the public domain, and they have been going strong ever since. A confusing and contradictory jumble, ranging from pseudohistory to occultism and from astrology to racism, these views have reflected in their own way the collapse of the established intellectual framework and the disarray, even chaos, of the time. Many observers see their rationale in the desperate effort to affirm the importance and power of the Russian people, severely battered in the real world, by emphasizing their identity with mythical Aryans or still other great races and civilizations. Greatness in the past promises greatness in the future. The largely historic stress on Orthodoxy has been sometimes supplemented or replaced by a fantastic neopaganism. Writers such as A. T. Fomenko have redrawn the entire course of human history along lines perhaps acceptable in science fiction but nowhere else. Some of these wild ideas have located themselves at the margins of the academic world and even occasionally entered that world.

Politically, the Far Right has so far failed. Its groupings have been characterized by small numbers and endless splitting. Time and again, its candidates lost miserably in popular elections. The one exception was the passing prominence of Vladimir Zhirinovsky and his so-called Liberal Democratic Party of Russia (LDPR). Zhirinovsky became politically significant rather suddenly in 1991, when he came in third in the first Russian presidential election won by Yeltsin. Even more striking, indeed stunning for many Russians and foreigners alike, were the results of the *duma* election of December 12, 1993, when Zhirinovsky's party took 23 percent of the total vote. Of course, much of Zhirinovsky's support was a protest vote for a man who challenged the government, the establishment, and even the world in a most extreme and vulgar manner, including physical assault on his opponents in the *duma*; who promised everything to all; and who never hesitated to lie or to deny well-known facts. Yet, beyond that amazing behavior, many observers seemed to detect a fundamental fanaticism, even as Zhirinovsky proposed such solutions for establishing peace in the world as another major war to destroy Turkey and the Turks and ensure the legitimate Russian expansion to the south. But the December 15, 1995, *duma* election reduced the vote for the LDPR from 23 to 11 percent, and even Zhirinovsky's own antics appeared gradually to lose, in spite of his inventiveness, much of their impact and news value.

"Eurasianism," absent in tsarist Russia and banned in the U.S.S.R., became a popular self-identification in certain Russian circles during the post-Soviet years. Eurasianism emerged quite formally and officially in 1921, when four young Russian émigré intellectuals published a collective volume, *Iskhod k Vostoku*, or *Exodus to the East*.[4] The four were Prince N. S. Trubetskoy, to be famous as a distinguished linguistic scholar, P. N. Savitsky, an economist-geographer and specialist in many subjects, P. P. Suvchinsky, a gifted music critic and many-sided intellectual, and G. V. Florovsky, a theologian, an intellectual historian, and also a person of numerous interests with a remarkable breadth of knowledge. The joint volume consisted of an introduction and ten essays. The introduction spoke of a world cataclysm—the year, to repeat, was 1921—of a catastrophic change of scenes, of a new age, of the dying of the West and the imminent rise of the East. It concluded: "Russians and those who belong to the peoples of 'the Russian world' are neither Europeans nor Asiatics. Merging with the native elements of culture and life which surround us, we are not ashamed to declare ourselves *Eurasians*."

Ten articles, and eventually many more articles and books, followed, supporting and developing the new claim of identity. The great originality of the Eurasians consisted in the fact that they were the first Russian ideologues to separate Russia completely from its European moorings and fundamental connections. (The Slavophiles, of course, protested against the West, but precisely because it failed to recognize and do justice to its Eastern brothers; Nicholas Danilevsky placed Russia squarely within Slavdom; and so on.) The issue, difficult for most Russians to understand, let alone accept, was not the extent of Asian influence on their country, but the much more basic assertion that their country was not Russia but Eurasia, quite distinct, for instance, from France or Japan, but a symbiotic organic unit bordering on the Pacific, the Himalayas, and central Europe. True, Savitsky's geopolitics, Trubetskoy's and Roman Jakobson's brilliant philological studies, George Vernadsky's voluminous historical works, and other Eurasian literature ultimately fail to convince the reader, although some of them represent useful contributions to their particular disciplines. Although there is no reason to doubt the sincerity of the devotion of the Eurasians to their newly discovered identity, that identity, namely Eurasia, would save the Russian empire (or the Soviet Union) in the age when other empires crumbled. And indeed, if the Russian empire were a symphonic unity of peoples—more than that, if there were no Russian empire at all but only one organic Eurasia—the issue of separatism would lose its meaning.

Fantastic already in émigré circles, Eurasianism abandoned all rhyme or reason when it was taken up by post-Soviet intellectuals in Russia:

> They have rediscovered the post-revolutionary, émigré theories of Eurasianism and its heretofore suppressed late Soviet-era exponents such as L. N. Gumilev. As purveyed by Gumilev and his epigones, classic Eurasianism has been leavened with messianism, racism (including anti-Semitism), anti-Americanism, conspiracy theories and cosmism. The resultant brew constitutes a veritable Russian New Age movement, noteworthy for its obscure and ideosyncratic ideology, which is not accessible to the general public. The ideology does have a following—a veritable cult has grown up around the posthumously published works of Gumilev—but has yet to become anything approaching a mass movement.[5]

But to return from the fringes to the main lines of development. In the second decade after the collapse of the Soviet Union and Communism, Russia is still in a state of transition and even confusion, contrary to the expectations of many observers, but perhaps not surprising, given the magnitude of the change. The ideological search and disarray illustrate the situation in the country well. With the dreadful exception of Chechnya, the transition in the Russian federation itself has been rather peaceful. Nor is Russia eager to fight other former Soviet republics or still other neighbors or nonneighbors. Democratic institutions have replaced the Party and the Soviet government, and they have claimed the allegiance of the authorities ever since Gorbachev, although they look much better on paper than in practice. And they may not be invulnerable to challenges from the Right or from the Left. Economic change has resulted in the impoverishment of a great many, as well as a fantastic enrichment of a few. Corruption has been immense. Crime is rampant. With popular support, and helped by such special circumstances as the high price of oil and natural gas on the world market, Putin seems to have obtained some kind of stability; but it is not clear for how long. Such Russian assets as great natural resources and an educated population, of course, remain. Since the demise of the U.S.S.R., Russia has confounded pessimists as well as optimists.

To repeat Nekrasov, "You are both mighty, and you are impotent, Mother-Russia!"

Notes

Introduction

1. The epigraph to this introduction is from F. I. Tiutchev, *Polnoe sobranie sochinenii* (St. Petersburg, 1913), p. 202.

2. Gellner, who died on November 5, 1995, was a gifted and productive scholar. For an introduction to his views on nationalism, see especially: Ernest Gellner, *Nations and Nationalism* (Ithaca, N.Y., 1983).

3. Benedict Anderson, *Imagined Communities: Reflections on the Origin and Spread of Nationalism,* rev. ed. (London, 1983).

4. Stanford, Calif., 1976.

5. See especially: Nicholas V. Riasanovsky, *A History of Russia,* 6th ed. (New York, 2000). In this book I limit myself mainly to identification in footnotes of certain direct references. Italics in quoted texts belong to the original. I am using a modified version of the so-called Library of Congress transliteration from the Russian (without noting the soft signs and with a preference for "y" rather than "ii" name endings in the text, as distinct from direct bibliographical references).

Chapter 1

1. The epigraph is a statement ascribed to the historian Dmitri Ivanovich Ilovaisky that has become a classic in Russian academic circles. I could not find it in print.

2. B. A. Rybakov, *Iazychestvo drevnikh slavian,* 2nd ed. (Moscow, 1994), pp. 217–284.

3. A student's comment that this strange circumstance was explainable by the common knowledge that the Yorkshiremen were speaking their own language, whereas the African Americans were brought from a different linguistic and social environment to an English-speaking country, missed the point: it is precisely that kind of "common knowledge" that we do not have for prehistory.

4. Marija Gimbutas, *The Slavs* (London, 1971), pp. 17–18.

5. Ibid., p. 14.

6. Ibid., p. 27.

7. Ibid., p. 98.

8. Johanna Nichols, "The Linguistic Geography of the Slavic Expansion," in *American Contributions to the Eleventh International Congress of Slavists,* edited by A. Timberlake (Columbus, Ohio, 1993), pp. 377–391, quotation from p. 378. The two striking opinions cited earlier serve as examples from a rich literature.

9. Tikhomirov's basic book was translated into English: M. Tikhomirov, *The Towns of Ancient Rus* (Moscow, 1959).

10. See such studies as: Georges Dumézil, *L'idéé tripartie des indo-européens* (Brussels, 1958), and *Les dieux des indo-européens* (Paris, 1952). A good introduction to Dumézil's work is provided in: C. Scott Littleton, *The New Comparative Mythology: An Anthropological Assessment of the Theories of Georges Dumézil,* rev. ed. (Los Angeles, 1973).

11. Soviet scholars in particular paid considerable and generally favorable attention to Slavic paganism. Rybakov's already-mentioned huge volume, meant to be only the first part of the total undertaking, is an outstanding example. While frequently disagreeing with the author, I find his contribution extremely interesting and eminently quotable. Of the earlier literature, see especially E. V. Anichkov, *Iazychestvo drevnikh slavian* (St. Petersburg, 1914).

12. Rybakov, *Iazychestvo drevnikh slavian,* p. 598.

13. The Russian is *Rod* and *rozhanitsy.* My translation is inadequate, but at least it helps to emphasize the essence of the cult, especially as presented by Rybakov.

14. Rybakov, *Iazychestvo drevnikh slavian,* p. 600.

15. Ibid., p. 600.

16. Ibid., p. 601–602.

17. Ibid., p. 602.

18. Ibid., p. 604.

19. Ibid.

20. The Russian word used here, "ograzhdenie," meaning also "defense" or "enclosure," refers in particular to the defensive line built against the steppe invader.

21. Rybakov, *Iazychestvo drevnikh slavian,* p. 605.

22. Ibid., p. 548.

23. Ibid., p. 552.

24. Ibid., p. 553.

Chapter 2

1. A fine introduction in English to Kievan Russia is provided in: George Vernadsky, *Kievan Russia* (New Haven, Conn., 1958). The emphasis on trade, based on the celebrated account of Constantine VI Porphyrogenitus, a Byzantine emperor and scholar, and other primary sources and evidence, can be found in most older histories of Russia, for instance in the first volume of V. O. Kliuchevsky's brilliant five-volume presentation, unfortunately poorly translated into English: V. Kliuchevskii, *Kur russkoi istorii,* chap. 1; I have at hand the 4th edition, published in Moscow in 1911. B. D. Grekov, whose views came to dominate Soviet historiography, did the most to shift the emphasis to peasants, agriculture, and the protofeudal, and even feudal, nature of the mighty and advanced Kievan state. B. D. Grekov, *Kievskaia Rus* (Moscow, 1944). See also: B. D. Grekov, *Krestiane na Rusi s dreneishikh vremen do XVII veka* (Moscow, 1946). Recent scholarship, both in Russia and elsewhere, treats, on the whole, Kievan state and society as more

primitive. See especially, I. Ia. Froianov, *Kievskaia Rus: Ocherki sotsialno-ekonomidieskoi istorii* (Leningrad, 1974); I. Ia. Froianov, *Kievskaia Rus: Ocherki sotsialno-politicheskoi istorii* (Leningrad, 1980); and an outstanding American study, Daniel H. Kaiser, *The Growth of the Law in Medieval Russia* (Princeton, N.J., 1980). See: David B. Miller, *The Kievan Principality in the Century before the Mongol Invasion: The Inquiry into Recent Research and Interpretation, Harvard Ukrainian Studies* 5, no. 112 (June 1986), pp. 214–240.

2. Vernadsky, *Kievan Russia*, p. 340; the chapter entitled "Russia and the Outside World in the Kievan Period," pp. 317–365, arranged by countries, contains several, sometimes lengthy, discussions of matrimonial alliances.

3. George P. Fedotov, *The Russian Religious Mind: Kievan Christianity*, (Cambridge, Mass., 1946), p. 412.

4. Michael T. Florinsky, *Russia: A History and an Interpretation*, 2 vols. (New York, 1953), vol. 1:142–144.

5. Father Georges Florovsky (Georgii Vasilevich Florovskii, 1893–1979), most of whose writings are now available in English, treated in a particularly incisive and masterful manner many of the topics mentioned in the preceding pages. In fact, Father Florovsky wrote with such power that the reader will do well to keep in mind that often his views represented only one of the possible positions on usually highly complex issues. See especially: G. V. Florovskii, *Puti russkogo bogosloviia* (Paris, 1937), translated under the title *Ways of Russian Theology*, vols. 5 and 6 of *The Collected Works of Georges Florovsky* (Belmont, Mass., 1979, 1987). Fourteen volumes of the *Works* were published.

6. Fedotov, *Russian Religious Mind*, p. 84.

7. Written frequently by monks and reflecting the position of the Church and certain other influences, the old Russian chronicles were essentially fine historical literature. They have been praised by specialists for their historical sense, realism, and richness of detail. They indicated clearly the major problems of Kievan Russia, such as the struggle against the peoples of the steppe and the issue of princely succession. Still more important, they have passed on to us the specific facts of the history of the period. The greatest value attaches to the *Primary Chronicle*—to which I have already made references—associated especially with two Kievan monks Nestor and Sylvester and dating from around 1111. The earliest extant copies of it are the fourteenth-century Laurentian and the fifteenth-century Hypatian. The *Primary Chronicle* forms the basis of all later general Russian chronicles. Regional chronicles, such as those of Novgorod or Vladimir, some of which survive, also flourished in Kievan Russia. See especially: D. S. Likhachev, *Russkie letopisi i ikh kulturno-istoricheskoe znachenie* (Moscow, 1947).

It was certain princes and some monasteries, urban in the Kievan period, that collected books, patronized scholars and schools, and generally supported education and culture. More recently, discoveries of the *beresta* or birchbark writing, centering very heavily on Novgorod, indicated a considerable spread of literacy, although of a limited and functional kind, among artisans and other broad layers of townspeople, touching slightly even peasants in the surrounding countryside.

8. For the latest discussion of *dvoeverie* see: V. Ia. Petrukhin, "Drevnerusskoe dvoeverie: Poniatie i fenomen," *Slavianovedenie*, no. 1 (1996), pp. 44–47.

9. D. S. Likhachev, "Kreshchenie Rusi i gosudarstvo Rus," *Novyi mir*, no. 6 (June 1988), pp. 243–268, quotation from p. 253. For an English translation of the article see: D. S. Likhachev, *Reflections on Russia* (Oxford, 1991), pp. 97–117.

10. Likhachev, "Kreshchenie Rusi i gosudarstvo Rus," p. 256.

11. The actual numbers of the invaders remain much in dispute. On the one hand, Russian sources, like the aforementioned one, produce the image of countless hordes; and they are supported by the fact that nomadic societies, the Mongols in particular, were so organized that they could mobilize almost every man for war. On the other hand, we must discount natural exaggeration, enhanced by the mobility of the nomadic cavalry and often the surprise and the coordination of the attack.

12. Indeed, I recollect how a colleague of mine, a member of a Russian émigré family that had been prominent in imperial Russia in diplomacy and war, was utterly horrified during the fighting in Vietnam by our American emphasis on body count as a measure of achievement. He told me of his grandfather, a commanding general, who after a campaign had to do strict penance before being admitted to Communion.

13. "Pouchenie Vladimira Monomakha," in *A Historical Russian Reader: A Selection of Texts from the Eleventh to the Sixteenth Centuries*, edited by John Fennell and Dimitri Obolensky (Oxford, 1969), pp. 52–62, quotation from p. 56.

14. Fedotov, *Russian Religious Mind*, p. 89.

Chapter 3

1. V. Kliuchevskii, *Kurs russkoi istorii*, pt. 2, 3rd ed. (Moscow, 1912), p. 19.

2. The autopsy suggests, but does not prove, murder by poison; arsenic was used at the time also as medicine and, in small doses, as an antidote to poisoning. A defective curvature of the spine indicated that Ivan IV must have been in constant pain.

3. Dimitri Obolensky, *Byzantium and Slavic Christianity: Influence or Dialogue?* (Berkeley, Calif., 1997), p. 34. "Lecture III: The *Hesychast* Tradition," pp. 29–44, presents an excellent brief up-to-date summary and interpretation of its subject.

4. The Old Believers have frequently been praised as more literate, better acquainted with religious texts, and in general much more able to maintain religious discourse and argument than mainline Orthodox. They were also usually more sober and more industrious; an Orthodox village or settlement often presented a sad contrast to its Old Believer neighbor. Yet, although this manifold praise is at least in part correct (there were all kinds of Old Believers and all kinds of Orthodox), it does not refer to theology. There Old Belief had virtually nothing to offer except a desperate defense of the established Russian religious practice, erroneous or correct, utterly minor or relatively more important. By contrast to the Reformation in the West, to which it has occasionally been compared, Old Belief never developed such issues as salvation by faith as against salvation by works, or even the relationship of the individual Christian to his or her Church. Perhaps the most striking explication of the deep essence of Old Belief is A. V. Kartashev's claim that within Orthodoxy, in constant search for the right way between the extremes of Nestorianism and Monophysitism, the Russian Church and the Old Belief that proceeded from it came to emphasize the sacredness on this earth of everything associated with the divine. See especially: A. V. Kartashev, "Russkoe khristianstvo," in *Transactions of the Association of Russian-American Scholars in the U.S.A.* (New York, 1989), 22:3–15; first published in *Put*, no. 51 (May—October 1936). See Kartashev's massive two-volume history of the Russian Church and other works. Kartashev was not an Old Believer but an outstanding Orthodox intellectual, public figure, and scholar of the so-called Silver Age. The latest major work on the subject, Georg Bernhard Michels, *At*

War with the Church: Religious Dissent in Seventeenth-Century Russia (Stanford, Calif., 1999), emphasizes the great extent and variety of that dissent, together with and usually apart from, the conventional narrower issues of the roles of Nikon, Avvakum, and the reform of the books.

5. As to the latest research on and interpretation of Muscovy, the seventeenth century in particular, I was unprepared for the degree of pessimism permeating the subject at the sessions devoted to it at a recent meeting of the American Association for the Advancement of Slavic Studies (the Twenty-Eighth National Convention of the American Association for the Advancement of Slavic Studies, November 14–17, 1996, Boston). Most notable in that respect was the session on "Violence in Late Muscovy," with papers presented by Richard Hellie ("Interpreting Violence in Late Muscovy from the Perspectives of Modern Neuroscience"), Georg Bernhard Michels ("Self-Immolation during the Russian Church Schism"), and Jennifer B. Spock ("Lay and Ecclesiastical Attitudes toward Violence in Muscovy: *Zhitie* and Miracle Tales as Exemplar"); David L. Ransel served as discussant and Marshall Poe as chairman. Hellie, one of the leading and most productive scholars on Muscovy, even argued for mass trauma, in the full clinical meaning of the term, in late Muscovite society, induced by the massacre of Russian troops by the Poles in mid-seventeenth-century fighting and by the general insecurity in the country.

For a more balanced presentation of the last part of the period under consideration in this chapter, see: Paul Bushkovitch, *Religion and Society in Russia: The Sixteenth and Seventeenth Centuries* (Oxford, 1992).

6. On military reforms see especially: Richard Hellie, *Enserfment and Military Change in Muscovy* (Chicago, 1971). I think, however, that Professor Hellie exaggerates the role of the government, as against long-term social processes, in the establishment of serfdom.

7. See my article "The Emergence of Eurasianism," *California Slavic Studies*, vol. 4 (Los Angeles, 1967), pp. 39–72. See: Otto Böss, *Die Lehre der Eurasier: Ein Beitrag zur russischen Ideengeschichte des 20. Jahrhunderts* (Wiesbaden, 1961).

8. George Vernadsky, *The Mongols and Russia* (New Haven, Conn., 1953), p. 335.

9. Ibid., p. 387.

10. N. P. Kondakov, *Izobrazheniia russkoi kniazheskoi semi v miniatiurakh XI v.* (St. Petersburg, 1906), pp. 54, 80.

11. This emphasis on the battle of Kulikovo marking a new stage in Russian consciousness and even Russian nationalism is common in Russian historical literature. See, e.g.: S. F. Platonov, *Lektsii po russkoi istorii* (St. Petersburg, 1904), pp. 128, 139.

12. The ancient Mongolian count by twenties was carried by some Mongolian peoples, such as the Buriats, into modern times. For particular references to this little-known subject, see my father's books: Professor V. A. Riasanovsky, *Customary Law of the Nomadic Tribes of Siberia* (Tientsin, 1938), pp. 42–43 (reprint, Bloomington, Ind., 1965), and *Customary Law of the Mongol Tribes (Mongols, Buriats, Kalmucks)*, pts. 1–3 (Harbin, 1929), p. 135 (reprint, Bloomington, Ind., 1965).

13. For an up-to-date and sober discussion of the Third Rome doctrine and its interpretations, see: Paul Bushkovitch, "The Formation of National Consciousness in Early Modern Russia," *Harvard Ukrainian Studies* 10, nos. 3–4 (December 1986), pp. 355–376, especially pp. 358–363.

On the position and power of rulers in old Russia and particularly on the limits of their power see especially: Vladimir Valdenberg, *Drevnerusskie ucherniia o predelakh tsarskoi vlasti* (Petrograd, 1916; reprint, Russian reprint series, The Hague, 1966). Valdenberg's precise, even punctilious, analysis leads notably to the conclusion that it is wrong to speak of any Byzantine tradition of rulership in Russia, both because of the inevitable difference between the two countries and because there was no single Byzantine tradition to borrow but a variety of even contradictory approaches (pp. 42–43, 58, 77–81, 451–452).

14. As an introduction to the fascinating subject of false rulers and popular rebellions in Russia, see especially: K. V. Chistov, *Russkie narodnye sotsialnopoliticheskie legendy XVIII—XIX vekov* (Moscow, 1967).

15. That religious severity of censorship led to such remarkable episodes as the banning of a poet's offer to give his soul and all else he had to his beloved on the ground that in that case there will be nothing left for God.

16. See such studies as: O. I. Podobedova, *Moskovskaia shkola zhivopisi pri Ivane IV: Raboty v Moskovskom Kremle 40–70kh godov XVI v.* (Moscow, 1972); and the brilliant: V. M. Zhivov and B. A. Uspenskii, *Tsar i Bog: Semioticheskie aspekty sakralizatsii monarkha v Rossii* (Moscow, 1987).

17. Daniel B. Rowland, "Moscow—The Third Rome or the New Israel," *The Russian Review* 55, no. 4 (October 1996), pp. 591–614. Rowland concluded: "We might finally note that there is nothing particularly exotic or Eastern about 'New Rome' theories, either. In the Middle Ages, at least six West European towns—Aix-la Chapelle, Tournai, Reims, Treves, Milan, and Pavia—were glorified by their chroniclers as 'Second Romes.' As Americans know (and as our coins would tell us if we forget), our founding fathers were preoccupied by the image of Rome. In 1803 the Irish poet Thomas Moore wrote mockingly of the pretensions of Washington, then a town barely and badly built, to be a 'second Rome':

> In fancy now, beneath the twilight gloom,
> Come, let me lead thee o'ver this 'second Rome'
> Where tribunes rule, where dusky Davy bows,
> And what was Goose-creek once is Tiber now." (p. 614)

Chapter 4

1. The epigraph to this chapter is from Count Egor Frantsevich Kankrin, minister of finance in the reign of Nicholas I, as quoted in: Faddei Bulgarin, *Vospominaniia*, 6 vols. (St. Petersburg, 1846–1849), vol. 1:200–201. This was not the only proposal to rename Russia "Petrovia."

2. For one introduction to this enormous subject, see my: *The Image of Peter the Great in Russian History and Thought* (Oxford, 1985).

3. The most striking and famous summary description of Peter the Great's associates is, as so often, Kliuchevsky's:

> Peter gathered the necessary men everywhere, without worrying about rank and
> origin, and they came to him from different directions and all possible
> conditions: one arrived as a cabin-boy on a Portuguese ship, as was the case of the
> chief of police of the new capital, de Vière; another had shepherded swine in
> Lithuania, as it was rumored about the first Procurator-General of the Senate,
> Iaguzhinskii; a third had worked as a clerk in a small store, as in the instance of

Vice-Chancellor Shafirov; a fourth had been a Russian house serf, as in the case of the Vice-Governor of Archangel, the inventor of stamped paper, Kurbatov; a fifth, i. e., Ostermann, was a son of a Westphalian pastor. And all these men, together with Prince Menshikov, who, the story went, had once sold pies in the streets of Moscow, met in Peter's society with the remnants of the Russian boyar nobility.

V. O. Kliuchevskii, "Petr Velikii sredi svoikh sotrudnikov," *Ocherki i rechi. Vtoroi sbornik statei* (Petrograd, 1918), pp. 454–495, quotation from p. 461. To qualify Kliuchevsky, it should be noted that the composition of the governing group was changing and becoming more "democratic" already in the decades preceding the rule of Peter the Great. For a rich and up-to-date treatment of both Peter the Great and his associates see especially the works of the leading present-day scholar in the field, N. I. Pavlenko, including: *Petr Pervyi;* "Petr I. (K izucheniiu sotsialnopoliticheskikh vzgliadov)," in *Rossiia v period reform Petra I,* edited by N. I. Pavlenko, L. A. Nikiforov, and M. Ia. Volkov (Moscow, 1973), pp. 40–102; *Poluderzhavnyi vlastelin* [Aleksandr Danilovich Menshikov]; *Ptentsy gnezda Petrova* [Boris Petrovich Sheremetev, Petr Andreevich Tolstoi, and Aleksei Vasilievich Makarov]. Most of Pavlenko's books, published in Moscow, have undergone several editions, with the later ones usually revised and enlarged.

The nature of Peter the Great's associates would make it difficult to generalize about their ideological stance on such concerns of this study as identity, self-definition, or Russia. Yet in fact they did fit well as a group, and usually as individuals, into the new Petrine Enlightenment.

4. W. F. Reddaway, ed., *Documents of Catherine the Great: The Correspondence with Voltaire and the "Instruction" of 1767 in the English Text of 1768* (Cambridge, 1931), p. 216.

5. The inscription on the monument, the celebrated Bronze Horseman, erected by Catherine the Great in St. Petersburg to Peter the Great.

6. Pavlenko, "Petr I," pp. 60–62.

7. B. H. Sumner, *Peter the Great and the Emergence of Russia* (London, 1950), pp. 59–60.

8. Quotation from Pavlenko, *Petr Pervyi,* p. 169.

9. Ibid., p. 315.

10. To his credit, Peter the Great realized the disparity between what he aimed to accomplish and what was actually happening in Russia, and he did not try to put a good face on disasters, inadequacies, or even his own mistakes. It was in the second half of the century that Catherine the Great, something of a genius in prevarication and public relations, asserted that her wars cost the country virtually nothing, that Russian peasants were already the happiest people in Europe, and that Russia was ahead of France in many respects in enlightenment.

11. See especially the huge and seminal work: P. Miliukov, *Gosudarstvennoe khoziastvo Rossii v pervoi chetverti XVIII stoletiia i reforma Petra Velikogo,* 2nd ed. (St. Petersburg, 1905).

12. See Pavlenko, *Petr Pervyi,* pp. 315–316, with some examples of these reasons.

13. *Iunosti chestnoe zertsalo ili pokazanie k zhiteiskomu obkhozhdeniiu. Sobrannoe ot raznykh Avtorov. Napechatasia poveleniem Tsarskago Velichestva, v Sanktpiterburkhe Leta Gospodnia 1717, Fevralia 4 dnia.* A facsimile edition of the *Mirror* was published in Moscow in 1976.

14. Peter the Great as translated in: Sumner, *Peter the Great and the Emergence of Russia,* pp. 59–60.

15. Feofan Prokopovich, *Kratkaia povest o smerti Petra Velikogo Imperatora Rossiiskogo* (St. Petersburg, 1819).

16. Personally, most Russian emperors and empresses were faithful, some of them ardent, Orthodox. The last in line, Nicholas II, was, indeed, recently canonized as a saint. Exceptions included Catherine the Great, probably a deist at heart but careful to observe proprieties as an Orthodox sovereign, and Alexander I, who, while a fully Orthodox monarch, tended repeatedly to go in his religious searches beyond strict Orthodoxy. Only the (in so many ways) unfortunate Peter III turned against Orthodoxy, but he was killed in a palace coup, and his reign was not long enough to affect seriously the Petrine religious arrangement. In fact, that arrangement, which combined a response to the secular climate of the modern age with the maintenance of the traditional faith of the people and which lasted until 1917, is a good example of the power of institutions.

17. Feofan Prokopovich, *Sochineniia* (Moscow, 1961), p. 144.

18. Ibid., p. 137.

19. K. V. Chistov, *Russkie narodnye sotsialnoutopicheskie legendy XVII–XIX vekov* (Moscow, 1967), especially pp. 96–109. The book is a fascinating, if highly controversial, examination of the Russian popular mind.

20. Ibid., pp. 99–100. For another stimulating treatment of the perception of Peter the Great as Antichrist, see B. A. Uspenskii, "Historia sub specie semioticae," in *Kulturnoe nasledie drevnei Rusi: Istoki, stanovlenie traditsii* (Moscow, 1976), pp. 286–292.

21. Peter I was, of course, Tsar Alexis's son, and the Old Believers were quick to note that he had been born in 1672, that is, six years after the decisive break between them and the established Church, and thus after divine grace and legitimacy had departed from the holders of the Russian throne. But there was even a version that Peter I was really the son of Patriarch Nikon, enemy number one of Old Belief. For the presence of that version as late as the second half of the twentieth century, see: Michael Cherniavsky, "The Old Believers and the New Religion," *Slavic Review* 25, no. 1 (March 1966), pp. 1–39, specifically p. 29, n. 122.

22. For perhaps the latest instance of such denunciation that attracted international attention see: Serge Schmemann, "Deep in Siberia, Three Centuries of Faith in God," *New York Times*, November 30, 1982, pp. 1, 7.

23. The standard work on the *Preobrazhenskii prikaz* and its activities is: N. B. Golikova, *Politicheskie protsessy pri Petre I. Po materialam Preobrazhenskogo prikaza* (Moscow, 1957).

24. Chistov, *Russkie narodnye sotsialnoutopicheskie legendy XVII–XIX vekov*, pp. 113–124.

25. Quotation from A. N. Pypin, "Petr Velikii v narodnom predanii," *Vestnik Evropy*, St. Petersburg, 32, no. 8 (August 1897), pp. 640–690, p. 665.

26. A. F. Nekrylova, "Predaniia i legendy, otrazivshie voennye sobytiia petrovskogo vremeni," in *Russkaia narodnaia proza. Russkii folklor* (Leningrad, 1972), vol. 13:103–110.

27. Nekrylova wrote:

> In its form of expression it still remains as if it were the story of a witness. It is
> remarkable that after more than a century and a half (the road was built in 1702
> whereas Mainov's writing the story down belongs to the 1880s) the narrative
> retained such details, as if the narrator himself witnessed this episode. Probably, a
> not insignificant role was played here by a solicitous attitude to the memory of
> Peter I, who was long considered in the North to be "one's own" tsar, who

understood the people, who did not disdain common labor, and who could accomplish anything. ("Predaniia i legendy," p. 104)

Chapter 5

1. The epigraph to this chapter is from: [Kheraskov, Mikhail Matveevich], "Stikhi ot izdatelia," in *Numa ili Protsvetaiushchii Rim* (Moscow, 1768), p. 180.

2. G. R. Derzhavin, "Petru Velikomu," *Sochineniia Derzhavina s obiasnitelnymi primechaniiami,* 4 vols. (St. Petersburg, 1895), vol. 1:10–12, p. 210 ns.

3. M. V. Lomonosov, "Slovo pokhvalnoe blashennyia pamiati Gosudariu Imperatoru Petru Velikomu, govorennoe aprelia 26 dnia 1755 goda," in *Polnoe sobranie sochinenii,* vol. 8, *Poeziia, oratorskaia proza, nadpisi, 1732–1764 gg.* (Moscow, 1959), pp. 584–612, editorial notes pp. 1044–1056, quotation from p. 611.

4. Aleksandr Petrovich Sumarokov, "Rossiiskii Vifleem," in *Polnoe sobranie vsekh sochinenii* (Moscow, 1787), vol. 6:302–303.

5. Aleksandr Petrovich Sumarokov, "Na pobedy Gosudaria Imperatora Petra Velikogo," in *Polnoe sobranie vsekh sochinenii,* 2:3–12, quotation from pp. 3–4. "Peter" is in capitals in the original.

6. Karen Rasmussen, "Catherine II and the Image of Peter I," *Slavic Review* 37, no. 1 (March 1978), pp. 51–69. The fullest treatment of the subject is to be found in Karen Malvey Rasmussen, "Catherine II and Peter I: The Idea of a Just Monarch," Ph.D. diss., University of California, Berkeley, 1973.

7. Rasmussen, "Catherine II and the Image of Peter I", p. 57.

8. *Polnoe sobranie zakonov* vol. 18, no. 12.597 (August 11, 1767), p. 222, col. 1. See, as two more instances of this assertion, Kheraskov's lines in the epigraph to this chapter and Sumarokov's poem:

> This bronze delineates the features of the face
> Of *Peter* the Great, Father of the Fatherland,
> He created this city, he organized the navy and the army;
> He raised Russia by means of Heroic deeds.
> As a sign of gratitude to him on the part of all of Russia
> *Catherine* erected this image.
> But if *Peter* were to rise from the dead in Russia now, again,
> He would erect a more beautiful monument to *Catherine.*
> *Peter* defeated internal and external enemies,
> He spread his sway on sea and on land,
> Having brought glory to the Russians he rewarded them with riches.
> *Peter* gave us existence, *Catherine* the soul.

Sumarokov, in *Polnoe sobranie vsekh sochinenii*, vol. 1:268. The names of the sovereigns were in capitals in the original.

9. "En attendant, madame, permettez-moi de baiser la statue de Pierre-le-Grand, et le bas de la robe de Catherine plus grande" (the letter of December 16, 1774), in *Documents of Catherine the Great: The Correspondence with Voltaire and the "Instruction of 1767 in the English Text of 1768,"* edited by W. F. Reddaway (Cambridge, 1931), p. 204.

10. Ibid., pp. 216–217. Numbers denote articles in the *Nakaz.* Italics in the original.

11. Ibid., pp. 216–217.

12. Ibid., p. xxvi.

13. Ibid., p. 219.

14. Ibid., p. 220.

15. Ibid., p. 293. Observe the competitiveness of the empress.

16. Ibid., p. 271.

17. Ibid., p. 30.

18. Ibid., p. 119.

19. Ibid., p. 67.

20. Ibid., p. 15.

21. The tombstone would declare: "Here lies an admirer of august Catherine, who had the honor of dying as he went to present his profound respect to her" (ibid., p. 34).

22. Ibid., p. 165.

23. Ibid., p. 37, and elsewhere.

24. Quotation from: G. Makogonenko, *Nikolai Novikov i russkoe prosveshchenie XVIII veka* (Moscow, 1951), p. 114.

25. The letter of December 16, 1774, in W. F. Reddaway, *Documents of Catherine the Great*, p. 13.

26. F. de Labriolle, "Le prosveščenie russe et les lumières en France (1760–1798)," *Revue des études slaves* 45 (1966), pp. 75–91; quotation from p. 75.

27. A. Lortholary, *Le Mirage russe en France au XVIIIe siècle* (Paris, n. d.).

28. The assertion belongs to S. E. Desnitsky, student of Adam Smith in Glasgow, professor of law at the University of Moscow, and one of the leading figures of the Russian Enlightenment. Quotation from: S. A. Pokrovskii, *Politicheskie i pravovye vzgliady S. E. Desnitskogo* (Moscow, 1955), p. 42.

29. To be fair to Derzhavin—and to provide something of a balance to that magnificent court poet's outrageous praise of Peter the Great, Catherine the Great, and some other mighty Russian contemporaries, as well as to return, perhaps, to the deepest roots of such praise—it is useful to remember Derzhavin's "last verses" (in *Sochineniia Derzhavina s obiasnitelnymi primechaniiami*, vol. 3:131):

> The river of time in its urgent course
> Carries away all the works of human beings
> And drowns in the abyss of oblivion
> Peoples, tsardoms, and tsars.
> And even if something remains
> Through the sounds of a lyre or a trumpet,
> It will be swallowed by the gullet of eternity
> And will not escape the common fate!

30. De Labriolle, "Le prosveščenie russe et les lumières en France (1760–1798)," p. 76. However, obtaining and mastering the latest literature is not the only definition of overcoming delay. Many scholars of the period, although agreeing that the Russian literati caught on fast, point to a certain thinness of the Russian Enlightenment, because Russia had not experienced earlier classical revivals, the Renaissance, the Reformation, and subsequent religious debates, etc., which formed part of the context of Western thought.

31. P. A. Viazemskii, *Zapisnye knizhki (1813–1848)* (Moscow, 1963), p. 221.

32. P. N. Berkov, *Istoriia russkoi zhurnalistiki XVIII veka* (Moscow, 1952), p. 377.

33. F. de Labriolle, "La Dramaturgie de Fonvizin," *Revue des études slaves* 46 (1967), quotations from pp. 65–66, 79.

34. G. V. Plekhanov, *Istoriia russkoi obshchestvennoi mysli* (Moscow, 1919), vol. 3:32.

35. For example, Sergei Uvarov's so-called Official Nationality formula of 1833 was and could only be "Orthodoxy, autocracy, nationality," not "Autocracy, Orthodoxy, nationality." (The latter would be my nominee for the most common mistake in Russian historiography, especially as practiced in the West.) Similarly, the best known military motto was "For God, tsar and fatherland," never "For tsar, God and fatherland."

Chapter 6

1. The epigraph for this chapter is from R. D. Charques, *A Short History of Russia* (New York, 1956), p. 151.

2. F. F. Vigel, *Zapiski*, pt. 1 (Moscow, 1891), pp. 177–178. The Easter Sunday theme is repeated in, e. g., Karamzin: R. Pipes, *Karamzin's Memoir on Ancient and Modern Russia: A Translation and Analysis* (New York, 1966), p. 136: "In houses and on the streets people cried with joy and embraced one another as on Easter Sunday."

3. A. V. Predtechenskii, *Ocherki obshchestvenno-politicheskoi istorii Rossii v pervoi chetverti XIX veka* (Moscow, 1957), pp. 64–65.

4. See especially the extremely informative study by Charles Corbet, *L'opinion française face à l'inconnue russe (1799–1894)* (Paris, 1967), particularly p. 95, for the specifics.

5. V. Orlov, *Russkie prosvetiteli 1790–1800kh godov*, 2nd ed. (Moscow, 1953), p. 227.

6. Ts. Ts., "O vernom sposobe imet v Rossii dovolno uchitelei," *Vestnik Evropy*, no. 8 (April 1803), p. 325.

7. "O novom obrazovanii narodnogo prosveshcheniia v Rossii," *Vestnik Evropy*, no. 5 (March 1803), quotations from pp. 49–56.

8. P. Alston, *Education and the State in Tsarist Russia* (Stanford, Calif., 1969), pp. 24–25.

9. From Born's speech quotation in: Orlov, *Russkie prosvetiteli 1790–1800kh godov*, p. 233.

10. N., "O knizhnoi torgovle i liubvi ko chteniiu v Rossii," *Vestnik Evropy*, no. 9 (May 1802), p. 62.

11. Ibid., p. 64.

12. Iu. M. Lotman, "Poeziia 1790–1810kh godov," in *Poety 1790–1810—kh godov* (Leningrad, 1971), p. 11.

13. On Speransky, see especially: M. Raeff, *Michael Speransky, Statesman of Imperial Russia, 1772–1839* (The Hague, 1957); and my review of that important work in *Journal of Modern History* 30 (September 1958), pp. 291–292.

14. B. Pares, *A History of Russia* (New York, 1953), p. 308.

15. It will be remembered that Catherine the Great, too, styled herself at times as a republican. Even Karamzin, already an ideologist of the Right, believed that the republican form of government was the best, but, because it depended on the virtue of the citizens, it was frequently impractical, certainly so in Russia. See especially: R. Pipes, "Karamzin's Conception of the Monarchy," *Harvard Slavic Studies* 4 (1957), pp. 35–58; and Pipes's discussion of Karamzin's political ideas in: R. Pipes, *Karamzin's Memoir on Ancient and Modern Russia: A Translation and Analysis* (New York, 1966), in particular

p. 90. For ideas, ideological groupings, government views, and public opinion of the period, see the informative book by Alexander M. Martin, *Romantics, Reformers, Reactionaries: Russian Conservative Thought and Politics in the Reign of Alexander I* (DeKalb, Ill., 1997).

16. "Plan gosudarstvennogo preobrazovaniia grafa M. M. Speranskogo," *Ulozhenie gosudarstvennykh zakonov 1809 g.* (St. Petersburg, 1905), pp. 1–120.

17. Literally, article 63 of Speransky's project defined and apportioned rights as follows: "1) General civil rights which belong to all subjects. 2) Particular civil rights which are to belong only to those who will be prepared for them by their manner of life and upbringing. 3) Political rights which belong to those who possess property." See: *M. M. Speranskii. Proekty i Zapiski* (Moscow, 1961), p. 186. Speransky's clever distinctions, notably his postulation of a particular civil right to own populated estates, represented his allowance for Russian reality, in the first place serfdom, which nevertheless remained incompatible at heart with his project.

18. "Gosudarstvennaia ustavnaia gramota Rossiiskoi Imperii" was published as an appendix to N. Shilder's (or Schilder's) standard court history of Alexander I: *Imperator Aleksandr I, ego zhizn i tsarstvovanie* (St. Petersburg, 1898), vol. 4:499–526. See also: G. Vernadsky, *La charte constitutionnelle de l'empire russe de l'an 1820* (Paris, 1933).

19. P. A. Viazemskii, *Zapisnye knizhki (1813–1848)* (Moscow, 1963), p. 148. Even as Alexander I was leaving in the autumn of 1825 on a journey south, a journey from which he was not to return alive, he kept talking, notably to Karamzin, about giving "fundamental laws" to Russia. The fullest account of Alexander I's last months, as well as of his life in general, is to be found in Shilder, *Imperator Aleksandr I*.

20. V. I. Semevskii, *Krestianskii vopros v Rossii v XVIII i pervoi polovine XIX veka* (St. Petersburg, 1888), vol. 1:482–483.

21. Patricia Kennedy Grimsted, *The Foreign Ministers of Alexander I: Political Attitudes and the Conduct of Russian Diplomacy, 1801–1825* (Los Angeles, 1969), p. 303.

22. See especially: S. S. Volk, *Istoricheskie vzgliady dekabristov* (Moscow-Leningrad, 1958); and H. Lemberg, *Die nationale Gedankenwelt der Dekabristen* (Cologne, 1963). In addition, very numerous Soviet writers emphasized the patriotism, and sometimes the "Russianness," of the Decembrists.

23. G. S. Gabaev, "Gvardiia v dekabrskie dni 1825 goda," appendix to A. E. Presniakov, *14 dekabria 1825 goda* (Moscow, 1926), p. 170.

Chapter 7

1. The epigraphs to this chapter are from the following sources. N. Shilder (or Schilder), *Imperator Nikolai Pervyi, ego zhizn i tsarstvovanie*, 2 vols. (St. Petersburg, 1903), quotation from vol. 1:147. S. S. Uvarov, "Tsirkuliarnoe predlozhenie G. Upravliaiushchego Ministerstvom Narodnogo Prosveshcheniia Nachalstvam Uchebnykh Okrugov 'o vstuplenii v upravlenie Ministerstvom,'" *Zhurnal Ministerstva Narodnogo Prosveshcheniia*, 1834, pt. 1, p. 1. A. S. Khomiakov, *Polnoe sobranie sochinenii*, 8 vols. (Moscow, 1900–1914), quotation from vol. 3:96.

2. Shilder, *Imperator Nikolai Pervyi*, quotation from vol. 2:390.

3. *Sbornik Imperatorskogo Russkogo Istoricheskogo Obshchestva*, 148 vols. (St. Petersburg, 1867–1917), quotation from vol. 98:36. Italics in the original.

4. From a letter to Frederick William IV of Prussia of August 26, 1854, in an appen-

dix to Professor Theodor Schiemann's standard four-volume history of the reign of Nicholas I, *Geschichte Russlands unter Kaiser Nikolaus I* (Berlin, 1904–1919), vol. 4:434–435.

5. In a letter to Prince Michael Gorchakov, the commander in the Crimea, quoted in: M. A. Polievktov, *Nikolai I. Biografiia i obzor tsarstvovaniia* (Moscow, 1918), p. 376.

6. Ibid.

7. I borrowed the phrase from the eulogistic introduction by L. Leduc to S. S. Uvarov, *Esquisses politiques et littèraires* (Paris, 1848), p. 11.

8. There is a remarkable consensus that Uvarov was an unprincipled, extremely vain, and egotistical, although brilliant, careerist. As one among many such judgments, see the discussion of the minister and his creed by the historian S. M. Soloviev, which reads in part: "Orthodoxy—while he was an atheist not believing in Christ even in the Protestant manner, autocracy—while he was a liberal, nationality—although he had not read a single Russian book in his life and wrote constantly in French or in German." S. M. Soloviev, *Moi zapiski dlia detei moikh, a, esli mozhno, i dlia drugikh* (Petrograd, n. d.), p. 59. Archival sources agree with the published materials. A notable example is an evaluation of Uvarov and his activity by the head of the gendarmerie, Count Alexander Benckendorff: "Otchet IIIgo Otdeleniia Sobstvennoi Ego Imperatorskogo Velichestva Kantseliarii i Korpusa Zhandarmov za 1839 god," Tsentralnyi gosudarstvennyi arkhiv Oktiabrskoi Revolutsii (now Gosudarstvennyi arkhiv Rossiskoi Federatsii), opis no. 85, edinitsa khraneniia no. 4. For a kinder view of the minister and ideologist, see: Cynthia Whittaker, *The Origins of Modern Russian Education: An Intellectual Biography of Count Sergei Uvarov, 1786–1855* (DeKalb, Ill., 1984).

9. S. S. Uvarov, *Desiatiletie ministerstva narodnogo prosveshcheniia, 1833–1843* (St. Petersburg, 1864), pp. 2–3.

10. For an extreme example of the dynastic emphasis see the assertion attributed to Nicholas I's minister of finance, Count E. Kankrin, that I used as the epigraph for chapter 4. More fully, the assertion reads:

> If we consider the matter thoroughly, then, in justice, we must be called not *Russians*, but *Petrovians*.... Everything: glory, power, prosperity and enlightenment, we owe to the Romanov family; and, out of gratitude, we should change our general tribal name of *Slavs* to the name of the creator of the empire and of its well-being. Russia should be called *Petrovia*, and we *Petrovians;* or the empire should be named *Romanovia*, and we *Romanovites.*

Faddei Bulgarin, *Vospominaniia*, 6 vols. (St. Petersburg, 1846–1849), vol. 1:200–201.

There is now a considerable historical literature on the doctrine of Official Nationality, but my study remains the only book-length treatment of the subject: Nicholas V. Riasanovsky, *Nicholas I and Official Nationality in Russia, 1825–1855* (Los Angeles, 1959). For the latest examination of the German sources of the doctrine, see: A. L. Zorin, "Ideologiia 'pravoslaviia—samoderzhaviia—narodnosti' i ee nemetskie istochniki," in *V razdumiakh o Rossii (XIX vek)*, edited by E. L. Rudnitskaia (Moscow, 1996), pp. 105–128.

11. S. P. Shevyrev, "Vzgliad russkogo na sovremennoe obrazovanie Evropy," *Moskvitianin*, pt. 1, pp. 292–295.

12. Quotation from: Polievktov, *Nikolai I*, p. 332.

13. About the manifesto see: N. Shilder, "Imperator Nikolai I v 1848 i 1849 godakh," first published in the *Istoricheskii Vestnik* for 1899 and later as an appendix to Shilder,

Imperator Nikolai Pervyi, vol. 2:619–639; the text of the manifesto is given on p. 269. Baron Modest Korff, who had helped the emperor draft the manifesto, remarked later that it contained a challenge to combat, referred to external threats that did not exist, and expressed hopes of victory while no hostilities were as yet in progress; p. 627.

14. N. V. Gogol, "Vybrannye mesta iz perepiski s druziami" ("Selected Passages from Correspondence with Friends"), in *Sochineniia*, vol. 8, edited by V. V. Kallash (St. Petersburg, n. d.), quotation from pp. 469–470.

15. Shilder, *Imperator Nikolai Pervyi*, vol. 2:680. Benckendorff's "Memoirs" for 1832–1837 form an appendix to the volume.

16. *Svod Zakonov Rossiiskoi Imperii* (St. Petersburg, 1832), article 1.

17. S. S. Uvarov, *Essai sur les mystères d'Eleusis* (Paris, 1816), p. 30.

18. M. P. Pogodin, *Prostaia rech o mudrenykh veshchakh* (Moscow, 1875), p. 91.

19. N. I. Grech, *Zapiski o moei zhizni* (Moscow, 1930), p. 209.

20. D. Korsakov, "Senkovskii, Osip Ivanovich," in *Russkii biograficheskii slovar*, vol. "Sabaneev" to "Smyslov" (St. Petersburg, 1904), p. 321.

21. N. P. Barsukov, *Zhizn i trudy M. P. Pogodina*, 22 vols. (St. Petersburg, 1888–1910), vol. 2:17.

22. Grech, *Zapiski o moei zhizni*, p. 104.

23. Ibid., p. 211.

24. Bulgarin, *Vospominaniia*, vol. 1:14–15.

25. Barsukov, *Zhizn i trudy M. P. Pogodina*, vol. 5:22.

26. M. P. Pogodin, *Istoriko-politicheskie pisma i zapiski v prodolzhenii Krymskoi Voiny, 1853–1856* (Moscow, 1874), p. 268. Except for "the system of publicity," which found no favor in the eyes of the emperor, Pogodin's statement represented faithfully the convictions of Nicholas I and of his associates.

27. M. P. Pogodin, *Rechi, proiznesennye v torzhestvennykh i prochikh sobraniiakh, 1830–1872* (Moscow, 1872), p. 90.

28. Gogol, "Vybrannye mesta iz perepiski s druziami," p. 163.

29. M. P. Pogodin, *Historische Aphorismen* (Leipzig, 1836), p. 8.

30. N. M. Karamzin, *Istoriia gosudarstva rossiiskogo*. Many editions.

31. Uvarov, *Desiatiletie ministerstva*, pp. 97–98. Ustrialov's discussion of the reign of Nicholas I was corrected by the emperor in person.

32. See especially: Barsukov, *Zhizn i trudy M. P. Pogodina*, vol. 1:56, 211; vol. 2:293. Shevyrev fell under the same spell as Pogodin. For instance, in 1829, at the age of twenty-three, he noted in his diary: "Each evening certainly, and sometimes in the mornings too, I assign to myself as an unfailing duty to read the life of Peter the Great and everything related to him." And he added the categorical imperative: "Be such a man as Christ, be such a Russian as Peter the Great." N. Ch., "Shevyrev, Stepan Petrovich," *Russkii biograficheskii slovar*, vol. "Shebanov" to "Shiutts" (St. Petersburg, 1911), p. 22.

33. But apotheosis was not enough. Nicholas I read the play and resolved: "*The person of Emperor Peter the Great must be for every Russian an object of admiration and of love; to bring it on to the stage would be almost sacrilege, and therefore entirely improper. Prohibit the publication.*" Barsukov, *Zhizn i trudy M. P. Pogodina*, vol. 4:13.

34. My interpretation of "The Bronze Horseman" is a common one. For a different view and rich material, see, for example: W. Lednicki, *Pushkin's Bronze Horseman. The Story of a Masterpiece* (Los Angeles, 1955).

35. See my: "Pogodin and Ševyrev in Russian Intellectual History," *Harvard Slavic Studies* vol. 4 (1957), pp. 149–167.

36. The issue here is of talent as ideologists; as literary figures, Gogol or Tiutchev were, of course, supreme.

37. S. P. Shevyrev, "Vzgliad russkogo na sovremennoe obrazovanie Evropy," *Moskvitianin*, no. 1 (1841), especially pp. 242–245. See: P. B. Struve, "S. P. Shevyrev i zapadnye vnusheniia i istochniki teorii-aforizma o 'gnilom' ili 'gniiushchem' Zapade," in *Zapiski Russkogo Nauchnogo Instituta v Belgrade* (Belgrade, 1940).

38. A. V. Nikitenko, *Moia povest o samom sebe i o tom "chemu svidetel v zhizni byl." Zapiski i dnevnik. (1804–1877 gg.)*, 2nd ed., 2 vols. (St. Petersburg, 1905), vol. 1:395.

39. Schiemann, *Geschichte Russlands unter Kaiser Nikolaus I*, vol. 2:xii.

40. I. M. Trotskii, *Trete otdelenie pri Nikolae I* (Moscow, 1930), pp. 34–35.

41. Ibid., p. 111.

42. S. P. Shevyrev, *Istoriia Imperatorskogo Moskovskogo Universiteta, napisannaia k stoletnemu ego iubileiu, 1755–1855* (Moscow, 1855), p. 483.

43. This imperial marginal comment is quoted from: Paul Milioukov (Miliukov), Ch. Seignobos, and L. Eisenmann, *Histoire de Russie*, 3 vols. (Paris, 1932–1933), vol. 2:785. For the context, see: Nikolai P. Barsukov, *Zhizn i trudy M.P. Pogodina*, 22 vols. (St. Petersburg, 1888–1910), vol. 10:525–538, especially p. 538.

44. *Sbornik Imperatorskogo Russkogo Istoricheskogo Obshchestva*, 148 vols. (St. Petersburg, 1867–1916), vol. 98:114–115.

45. N. M. Druzhinin, *Gosudarstvennye krestiane i reforma P. D. Kiseleva*, 2 vols. (Moscow, 1946–1958).

46. Nikitenko, *Moia povest o samom sebe i o tom "chemu svidetel v zhizni byl,"* vol. 1:441.

47. Nikitenko, *Moia povest o samom sebe i o tom "chemu svidetel v zhizni byl,"* 1:393–417, and M. O. Gershenzon, ed., *Epokha Nikolaia I* (Moscow, 1911), p. 105, on musical notations. Nikitenko himself served as a censor.

48. Pogodin, *Istoriko-politicheskie pisma i zapiski v prodolzhenii Krymskoi Voiny, 1853–1856*, p. 259.

49. Shilder, *Imperator Nikolai Pervyi*, vol. 2:271–272.

50. Historical literature on Russian foreign policy in the reign of Nicholas I, in particular on the Crimean War, is immense. As an introduction see: Brison D. Gooch, *A Century of Historiography on the Origins of the Crimean War* (Cambridge, Mass., 1957), which, obviously, does not cover the last fifty years of scholarship. My views are developed in the chapter "Official Nationality: Foreign Policy," in my aforementioned book on Nicholas I and Official Nationality in Russia, pp. 235–265. For an impressive recent work occupying the opposite position, see: John P. LeDonne, *The Russian Empire and the World: The Geopolitics of Expansion and Containment* (Oxford, 1997).

51. See my "Khomiakov on *Sobornost*," in *Continuity and Change in Russian and Soviet Thought*, edited with an introduction by Ernest J. Simmons (Cambridge, Mass., 1955), pp. 183–196, where I try to assess the intricate relationship between Romantic and traditional Christian elements in Khomiakov's crucial theological concept.

52. K. S. Aksakov, *Sochineniia istoricheskie* (Moscow, 1861), pp. 291–292.

53. N. A. Berdyaev (Berdiaev), *The Russian Idea* (London, 1947), p. 50.

54. F. Stepun, "Nemetskii romantizm i russkoe slavianofilstvo," *Russkaia Mysl*, March 1910, pp. 65–91, especially pp. 73–75.

55. I. S. Aksakov, *Sochineniia,* 7 vols. (Moscow, 1886–1891), vol. 5:632. Italics in the original.

56. N. L. Brodskii, *Rannie slavianofily* (Moscow, 1910), p. 95. This work contains, in addition to Brodskii's own contribution, Constantine Aksakov's celebrated memorandum "O vnutrennem sostoianii Rossii," and some of his editorials in *Molva.*

57. Constantine Aksakov, in Brodskii, *Rannie slavianofily,* p. 80.

58. Ibid., p. 96. Italics in the original.

59. K. S. Aksakov, *Sochineniia istoricheskie,* p. 552. Italics in the original.

60. I. V. Kireevskii, *Polnoe sobranie sochinenii,* 2 vols. (Moscow, 1911), vol. 2:272. Italics in the original.

61. K. S. Aksakov, "Zamechaniia na novoe administrativnoe ustroistvo krestian v Rossii," *Rus* (1883), nos. 3, 4, 5, p. 26.

62. Khomiakov, *Polnoe sobranie sochinenii,* vol. 3:210. See Constantine Aksakov's declaration:

> The Russian people is not a people; it is humanity; it is a people only because it is surrounded by peoples with exclusive national essences, and its humanity is therefore represented as nationality. The Russian people is free, it has no state element in itself, it contains nothing relative. . . . *Freedom* is the general essence of the Russian, true freedom and the absence of conditionality everywhere. (Aksakov, *Sochineniia istoricheskie,* p. 630)

63. B. N. Chicherin, *Vospominaniia, Moskva sorokovykh godov* (Moscow, 1929), pp. 5–6. The great Slavophile-Westernizer debate, which took the form of continuous swirling talk, went unrecorded. In trying to reconstruct it, scholars have to depend on their general knowledge of the views of the participants, on some relevant published pieces, and on the reminiscences of such figures as Herzen and Boris Chicherin (1828–1903) on the Westernizer side and Alexander Koshelev (1806–1883) on the Slavophile.

64. A. I. Gertsen, *Sobranie sochinenii v tridtsati tomakh,* 30 vols. (Moscow, 1954–1966), vol. 7:117. The commentary "Panslavisme moscovite et européisme russe" ("Muscovite Panslavism and Russian Europeanism"), pp. 101–118, was written in 1850 or 1851 and forms part of Herzen's *Du développement des idées révolutionnaires en Russie.*

65. The Westernizers and the Slavophiles retained mutual high regard for life. Ivan Aksakov used to measure degeneration in the camp of his enemies by comparing the latest Russian radicals to Granovsky. After Granovsky's death, Khomiakov had some kind words for "the good opponent." In his turn, Herzen, in *The Bell,* marked the deaths of Khomiakov and of Constantine Aksakov as follows:

> It is painful for those persons who loved them to know that these noble, tireless workers are no longer, that these *opponents,* who were closer to us than many of *ours,* no longer exist. The Kireevskiis, Khomiakov, and Aksakov *accomplished their task* . . . they stopped the stampeded public opinion and made all serious people think. With them begins *the turning point of Russian thought.* . . . Yes, we were their opponents, but very strange opponents: we had *one love,* but *not an identical one.* Both they and we conceived from early years one powerful, unaccountable, physiological, passionate feeling, which they took to be a recollection, and we—a prophecy, the feeling of boundless, all-encompassing love for the Russian people, Russian life, the Russian turn of mind. Like Janus, or like a two-headed eagle, we were looking in different directions while *a single heart was beating in us.*

A. I. Gertsen, *Polnoe sobranie sochinenii i pisem*, edited by M. K. Lemke, 22 vols. (Petrograd, 1915–1925), vol. 11:11. Italics in the original.

66. "By its very awkwardness this Anglicized equivalent of Belinski's term *sotsialnost* may serve to suggest the novelty of Belinski's own word, in its turn an awkward Russian equivalent of the French *socialité*." Herbert E. Bowman, *Vissarion Belinski, 1811–1848. A Study in the Origins of Social Criticism in Russia* (Cambridge, Mass., 1954), p. 143 n.

67. As translated in: E. H. Carr, *Michael Bakunin* (New York, 1961), pp. 115–116.

68. Andrzej Walicki, "Hegel, Feuerbach and the Russian 'philosophical left', 1836–1848," *Annali dell' Istituto Giangiacomo Feltrinelli*, Anno Sesto (1963), p. 108.

69. Quotation from: Martin Malia, *Alexander Herzen and the Birth of Russian Socialism, 1812–1855* (Cambridge, Mass., 1961), p. 247.

70. Isaiah Berlin, "A Marvellous Decade, 1838–1848," *Encounter*, May 1956, p. 29.

71. P. V. Annenkov, *Literaturnye vospominaniia* (Leningrad, 1928).

72. Chaadaev, a hero of Napoleonic wars, served as adjutant to Prince Hilarion Vasilchikov, commander of the Guard Corps; Samarin's family belonged to court circles; Bakunin came from a well-established gentry family and at least began his career as a gentleman and an officer (note also Bakunin's admiration for the emperor and the imperial family during his "reconciliation with reality").

73. Nikitenko, *Moia povest o samom sebe i o tom "chemu svidetel v zhizni byl,"* vol. 1:553.

74. A. Custine, *La Russie en 1839* (Brussels, 1843). Several editions appeared within a few years. In the words of a specialist: "Even more than Tocqueville in the case of the United States, it contributed to the formation of (French) opinion on Russia." Andre-Jean Tudesq, *Les Grands Notables en France (1840–1849). Etude historique d'une psychologie sociale* (Paris, 1964), vol. 2:799. On Custine, see: George F. Kennan, *The Marquis de Custine and His "Russia in 1839"* (Princeton, N.J., 1971).

75. To quote Viazemsky: "Well, all right, let the poor in spirit have the heavenly kingdom, but why are they also given kingdoms on earth?" P. A. Viazemskii, *Zapisnye knizhki (1813–1848)* (Moscow, 1963), p. 64.

Chapter 8

1. The epigraphs for this chapter are from Geoffrey Hosking, *Russia: People and Empire, 1552–1917* (Cambridge, Mass., 1997), p. 478; Gerold Tanquary Robinson, *Rural Russia under the Old Regime: A History of the Landlord-Peasant World and a Prologue to the Peasant Revolution of 1917* (Los Angeles, 1967), p. 116.

2. To cite from an immense literature only the most relevant works of the authors mentioned by name in my text: Jerome Blum, *Lord and Peasant in Russia from the Ninth to the Nineteenth Century* (Princeton, N.J., 1961); I. D. Kovalchenko, *Russkoe krepostnoe krestianstvo v pervoi polovine XIX v.* (Moscow, 1967); P. G. Ryndziunskii, *Gorodskoe grazhdanstvo doreformennoi Rossii* (Moscow, 1958); Vasilii I. Semevskii, *Krestianskii vopros v Rossii v XVIII i pervoi polovine XIX veka*, 2 vols. (St. Petersburg, 1888); Inna Ivanovna Ignatovich, *Borba krestian za osvobozhdenie* (Petrograd, 1924) *Pomeshchiki i krestiane nakanune osvobozhdeniia* (Moscow, 1910) "Krestianskie volneniia pervoi chetverti XIX veka; *Voprosy istorii*, no. 9 (1950), pp. 48–70.

3. See especially: A. J. Rieber, *The Politics of Autocracy: Letters of Alexander II to Prince A. I. Bariatinskii, 1857–1864* (Paris, 1966).

4. Peter I. Lyashchenko, *History of the National Economy of Russia to the 1917 Revolution* (New York, 1949), p. 393.

5. Quotation from: V. A. Riasanovsky, *Obzor russkoi kultury. Istoricheskii ocherk*, pt. 2, iss. 2 (New York, 1948), pp. 25–26.

6. See especially: Alexander Vucinich, *Darwin in Russian Thought* (London, 1988), pp. 146–149.

7. Irina Paperno, *Chernyshevsky and the Age of Realism* (Stanford, Calif., 1988).

8. Andrzej Walicki, *A History of Russian Thought from the Enlightenment to Marx* (Stanford, Calif., 1979), pp. 198–199.

9. Martin Malia, *Russia under Western Eyes: from the Bronze Horseman to the Lenin Mausoleum* (Cambridge, Mass., 1999), p. 171.

10. Walicki, *History of Russian Thought from the Enlightenment to Marx*, p. 233.

11. In this paragraph all quotations are from: Riasanovsky, *Obzor russkoi kultury. Istoricheskii ocherk*, pp. 15–16; italics in original.

12. Vucinich, *Darwin in Russian Thought*, pp. 342–343.

13. All Mikhailovsky quotations are from: Riasanovsky, *Obzor russkoi kultury. Istoricheskii ocherk*, pp. 17–21; Mikhailovsky's emphasis.

14. For those remarkable years both before and after the assassination, see especially: P. A. Zaionchkovskii, *Krizis samoderzhaviia na rubezhe 1870–1880 godov* ("The Russian autocracy in crisis at the turn of the 1870s to the 1880s") (Moscow, 1964).

15. See especially: Mark D. Steinberg and Vladimir M. Khrustalev, *Political Dreams and Personal Struggles in a Time of Revolution: Russian Documents Translated by Elizabeth Tucker* (London, 1995).

16. A *desiatina* equals 2.7 acres.

17. Robinson, *Rural Russia under the Old Regime*, p. 131.

18. V. I. Charnoluskii, "Nachalnoe obrazovanie vo vtoroi polovine XIX stoletiia," chap. 18, pp. 109–169, in *Istoriia Rossii v. XIX veke*, 9 vols. (St. Petersburg, n.d.), quotation from 7:165.

19. As I was walking in my city of Berkeley to the university campus and considering what I should write about Tolstoy within the confines of the present book, I saw a bumper sticker on a parked car that read: "Government is a crime against humanity." Tolstoy would have agreed.

20. See especially the writings of Professor Theodore R. Weeks.

21. I used: N. Ia. Danilevskii, *Rossiia i Evropa* (London, 1966).

22. Walicki, *History of Russian Thought from the Enlightenment to Marx*, p. 421.

23. See especially: Walter Sablinsky, *The Road to Bloody Sunday: Father Gapon and the St. Petersburg Massacre of 1905* (Princeton, N.J., 1976).

24. Geoffrey Hosking, *Russia: People and Empire, 1552–1917* (New York, 1996), p. 230.

Chapter 9

1. The epigraph for this chapter is from Georgii Ivanov, *Izbrannaia poeziia* (Paris, 1987), p. 86.

2. Andrzej Walicki, *Marxism and the Leap to the Kingdom of Freedom: The Rise and Fall of the Communist Utopia* (Stanford, Calif., 1995), pp. 361–362. Italics in the original.

3. For a more detailed presentation see, for instance: M. Geller and A. Nekrich,

Istoriia Rossii, 1917–1995. Utopiia u vlasti, 1917–1945 (Moscow, 1996), vol. 1:119–128, where the authors underline Lenin's own admissions of overoptimism and mistakes.

4. I even heard a Soviet speaker argue that in 1917 Russia was more economically advanced than Great Britain, because both must be considered in their totality, and Great Britain, with all of its empire, would be more backward, on the average.

5. Walicki, *Marxism and the Leap to the Kingdom of Freedom*, p. 303.

6. Robert C. Tucker, *Stalin in Power: The Revolution from Above* (New York, 1990), p. 271. For purges, see especially pp. 271–337.

7. The volume under discussion is Tucker's second sequential volume on Stalin. Much psychological analysis is to be found in the first, which I judged as impressive but not always convincing: Robert C. Tucker, *Stalin as Revolutionary, 1879–1929: A Study in History and Personality* (New York, 1973). See my review of it (together with Adam B. Ulam's *Stalin: The Man and His Era*): Nicholas V. Riasanovsky, "And Then There Was One," *Reviews in European History* 1, no. 2 (September 1974), pp. 247–251. An interesting recent contribution by the so-called revisionists on the subject of the purges was made at the Thirty-Second National Convention of the American Association for the Advancement of Slavic Studies, November 9–12, 2000, Denver, in a roundtable session entitled "Mass Terror Operations in the 1930's," held on November 10. The participants in the roundtable were professors Sheila Fitzpatrick, University of Chicago, J. Arch Getty, University of California, Los Angeles, Roberta Thompson Manning, Boston College, Steven E. Merritt, University of California, Riverside, David Randall Shearer, University of Delaware, and Lynn Viola, University of Toronto.

For Stalin's enigmatic and controversial last months and days, I would recommend the up-to-date and judicious article by A. A. Fursenko, "I. V. Stalin, Poslednie gody zhizni i smert," *Istoricheskie Zapiski* (Moscow) 3, no. 121 (2000), pp. 178–206.

8. Nicholas S. Timasheff, *The Great Retreat: The Growth and Decline of Communism in Russia* (New York, 1946).

9. Foreign Languages Publishing House, *Stalin on Lenin* (Moscow, 1946), p. 68.

10. On small peoples see especially: Yuri Slezkine, *Arctic Mirrors: Russia and the Small Peoples of the North* (London, 1994). For the general picture, at least up to World War II, consult the excellent study by Terry Martin, *The Affirmative Action Empire: Nations and Nationalism in the Soviet Union, 1923–1939* (London, 2001). Whereas I agree with most of the author's comprehensive and many-sided explanations of the evolving, and indeed changing, Soviet policy toward nationalities, such as the desire to keep national minorities satisfied within the boundaries of the U.S.S.R., or the extreme suspicion of those nationals who were strongly represented abroad, I would emphasize even more than the author does the belief in the original ideological paradox of full-scale national developments in a socialist state leading not to separatism, but to a more perfect union, without which belief the Soviet policy toward nationalities ultimately makes no sense.

11. Jeffrey Brooks, *Thank You, Comrade Stalin: Soviet Public Culture from Revolution to Cold War* (Princeton, N.J., 2000).

12. See especially: Katerina Clark, *The Soviet Novel: History as Ritual*, with a new afterword by the author, 2nd ed. (Chicago, 1985).

13. L. Rzhevsky cited in: Vera S. Dunham, *In Stalin's Time: Middleclass Values in Soviet Fiction* (Cambridge, 1976), p. 257.

14. For the most comprehensive and detailed account of the opinions of the Soviet citizens concerning the Soviet system, including many points of rapport between the two, see Alex Inkeles and Raymond A. Bauer, *The Soviet Citizen: Daily Life in a Totalitarian Society* (Cambridge, Mass., 1959). And for the more recent period: James R. Millar, ed., *Politics, Work and Daily Life in the U.S.S.R.: A Survey of Former Soviet Citizens* (Cambridge, 1987).

15. Geller and Nekrich, *Istoriia Rossii, 1917–1995*, vol. 2:96.

16. The unprecedented liquidation of entire classes as a result of the October Revolution is a leitmotif of: Martin Malia, *Comprendre la Revolution russe* (Paris, 1980). See also Malia, *The Soviet Tragedy: A History of Socialism in Russia* (New York, 1994).

17. *"Nam ostaetsia tolko imia . . .": Pamiatniki zhertvam politicheskikh repressii Petrograda-Leningrada* (St. Petersburg, 1999), p. 3.

18. Now that we are in the age of memorials to the victims of Soviet Communism, there is even a memorial in the political police museum in Moscow, still proud of its police past, to twenty thousand members of the service "unjustly repressed" (read shot) in the great purge.

19. Geller and Nekrich, *Istoriia Rossii, 1917–1995*, 1:150–159. On Russian patriotism and nationalism in the Soviet Union, broadly speaking, the most informative and interesting works include Mikhail Agursky's idiosyncratic *The Third Rome: National Bolshevism in the U.S.S.R.* (London, 1987), for the early part of Soviet history, and Yitzhak M. Brudny's *Reinventing Russia: Russian Nationalism and the Soviet State, 1953–1991* (London, 1998) for its last part. While both authors may be exaggerating the importance of their subject, and Agursky, in addition, expounds some strange views on the German role in Soviet history, the two specialists are generally good at tracing the difficult interplay between Marxism-Leninism and nationalism, without confusing the two ideologies. Brudny's book, in fact, can be summarized as a detailed exposition of the Communist leadership controlling, restricting, and at times utilizing recalcitrant nationalist currents.

Conclusion

1. The epigraph for this chapter is from N. A. Nekrasov, *Polnoe Sobranie stikhotvorenii v trekh tomakh* (New York, 1919), 3:254.

2. Nicholas V. Riasanovsky, *A Parting of Ways: Government and the Educated Public in Russia, 1801–1855* (Oxford, 1976).

3. For my view of Likhachev as nationalist see: Nicholas V. Riasanovsky, "Dmitrii S. Likachev and Russia: A Critical Appreciation," *Russian History/Histoire Russe* 23, nos. 1–4 (spring-summer-fall-winter 1996), pp. 141–154.

4. *Iskhod k Vostoku. Predchustviia i sversheniia. Utverzhdenie evraziitsev. Stati: Petra Savitskogo, P. Suvchinskogo, kn. N. S. Trubetskogo i Georgiia Florovskogo* (Sofia, 1921), translated, with a bibliographical essay, by Ilya Vinkovetsky under the title *Forebodings and Events. An Affirmation of the Eurasians. Articles: Petr Savitskii, P. Suvchinskii, Prince N. S. Trubetskoi, and Georgii Florovskii*, with additional translations by Catherine Boyle and Kenneth Brostrom, edited by Ilya Vinkovetsky and Charles Schlacks, Jr., and with an afterword by Nicholas V. Riasanovsky (Idyllwild, Calif.). See my article (also published in an abbreviated form in the preceding volume): "The Emergence of Eurasianism," *California Slavic Studies*, vol. 4 (Los Angeles, 1967), pp. 39–72.

5. John D. Klier, "The Dog That Didn't Bark: Anti-Semitism in Post-Communist Russia," in *Russian Nationalism Past and Present,* edited by Geoffrey Hosking and Robert Service (London, 1998), pp. 129–147, quotation from p. 141.

I found Professor Victor Shnirelman's studies especially useful for a wide-ranging sampling of the post-Soviet extreme Right: V. Shnirelman, "Evraziitsy i evrei," *Vestnik Evreiskogo Universiteta v Moskve,* no. 1 (11) (Moscow and Jerusalem, 1996), pp. 4–45; Victor Shnirelman and Galina Komarova, "Majority as a Minority: The Russian Ethno-Nationalism and Its Ideology in the 1970–1990s," in *Rethinking Nationalism and Ethnicity: The Struggle for Meaning and Order in Europe,* edited by Hans-Rudolf Wicker (Oxford, 1997), pp. 211–224; Victor A. Shnirelman, *Russian Neo-Pagan Myths and Anti-semitism* (Jerusalem, 1998); V. A. Shnirelman, "Vtoroe prishestvie ariiskogo mifa," *Vostok,* no. 1 (1998), pp. 89–107; V. A. Shnirelman, "The Idea of Eurasianism and the Theory of Culture," *Anthropology and Archeology of Eurasia* 36, no. 4 (spring 1998), pp. 8–31; V. A. Shnirelman, "Natsionalnye simvoly, etnoistoricheskie mify i etnopolitika," *Teoreticheskie problemy istoricheskih issledovanii* (Moscow), July 2, 1999, pp. 118–147; V. A. Shnirelman, "Passions about Arkaim: Russian Nationalism, the Arians, and the Politics of Archaeology," *Inner Asia* 1 (1999), pp. 267–282; Victor A. Shnirelman, "In Search of the Prestige Ancestors: Ethno-Nationalism and School Textbooks," *Information* 20, no. 1 (1999), pp. 45–52; Viktor Shnirelman, "Toska po Ariistvu. Mify russkogo neoiazychestva," *NG Religii* N 02 (73), January 31, 2001.

For Eurasianism in a different key, much more practical and political, and with a particular reference to Kazakhstan, see especially: N. A. Nazarbayev, *Evraziiskii soiuz: Idei, praktika, perspektivy 1994–1997* (Moscow, 1997).

Index

Abo, 114
Academy of Arts, 102
Adashev, Alexis, 38, 41
aeneolithic, 14
Afghanistan, 189
Age of Reason, 114, 128, 153, 166
  See also Enlightenment
agrogorod, agrogoroda, 216
Akhmatova, Anna, 205, 223
Aksakov, Constantine, 152, 154, 176, 198
Aksakov, Ivan, 153–155, 198–199
Alaska, 98
Albania, Albanians, 226
Alexander I, 111–129; 107–108, 110, 116, 124, 129, 137,
      143, 162, 165, 195, 203
  administrative and governmental reforms, 117,
    131
  as constitutional king of Poland, 120
  as creator of Council of State, 118
  death of, 123, 126
  educational and cultural reforms, 114–117
  first (liberal) period of reforms, 113–117
  personality of, 122
  popular reaction to accession to throne, 111–112
  reign as culmination of Russian Enlightenment
    of, 111, 113–114
  reign as viewed by other nations, 163–164
  second period of reforms, 114, 117–122
  stance towards autocracy and serfdom, 119–120
  versus Napoleon, 112, 122–123
Alexander II, 5, 154, 180
  assassination attempts of, 182–183
  legislative reforms, 172
  as liberator of serfs, 168
Alexander III, 175, 183, 185–187, 191
Alexander of Tyrnovo, 64

Alexandria, 56
Alexandrov, 41
Alexis, Metropolitan, 50–51
Ali, Mohammed, 149
Amur, 196
anarchism, 166, 195–196
anarchistic communism, 197
ancien régime, 110, 142, 210
Anderson, Benedict, 4
Andropov, Yuri Vladimirovich, 211–212, 219
Anhalt-Zerbst, 93
Anna Karenina (Tolstoy, Leo), 195
Anne, Empress, 88, 108
Annenkov, Paul, 161
Annensky, Innokenty, 204
anti-Americanism, 235
Antioch, 56
antirationalists, 194, 206
anti-Semitism, 213, 222, 235
Apollo, 13–14
Apology of a Madman (Chaadaev), 151, 163
appanage, 33–73
  definition and characteristics of Russian, 33–35,
    59, 61
  and Golden Horde, 66–71
  and Orthodox religion, 4–5, 59
  population movements during, 34
  princes of Russian, 33, 35–37, 63
  and reign of Ivan IV, the Terrible, 38–43
  and reigns of Ivan III and Basil III, 37–38, 66
  and rise of Moscow, 35–37, 65
  steppe frontier during, 59–61, 70
  and tsardom, 72
Arabic numerals, 80
Arakcheev, General Alexis, 120–121
archaeology, 7, 11

Archangel, 21, 40
Armenia, Armenians, 185, 187, 222
art
    Byzantine influence on Russian, 20–21, 25
    of Indo-European farmers, 9, 12
    influences of Nihilism and Critical Idealism on,
        173–174
    influences of Romanticism and Idealist
        philosophy on, 130, 150–151, 165
    from populist perspective, 178
    in Russian Enlightenment, 100–104
    Scythian animal style, 15–17
    in Silver Age, 204–206
Artemis, 13
Artillery Academy, 177
asceticism, 25, 59
Asia, Asians, Asiatics, 7, 69, 167, 189, 234
Astrakhan, 39–40, 42, 46, 60–61, 63, 67, 82, 174
astrology, 233
Augustus, Emperor, 66
Austria, Austrians, 112, 149, 164, 199
autocracy, autocrats, 61, 72, 93, 96–97, 99, 110, 123,
        145, 158, 162, 165, 202, 207
    as affected by "great reforms", 172
    as affecting Nicholas I's foreign policy, 149
    under critical attack in Russian Enlightenment,
        108
    15th century South Slav perspective, 64
    as fortified by Temporary Regulations, 183
    and monarchy, 6, 92, 96, 137
    as Muscovite rulers, 49, 65
    Nicholas I's personal views, 147
    and 1906 Fundamental Laws, 203
    and Official Nationality as defended by Nicholas
        I's Ministry of Education, 144
    in Petrovian society, 74, 77
    during reign of Alexander I, 117–122
    during reign of Nicholas I, 130–141
    Slavophilic perspective, 154–155
    as viewed by other countries, 164
    views of both educated public and uneducated
        masses in support, 92
Avars, 9–10
Avvakum, Archpriest, 56

Baal, 14
Baer, Karl Ernst von, 179
Bakst, Leonid, 205
Baku, 95
Bakunin, Michael, 157–160, 162, 166, 176, 181, 196
Balkans, 4, 8–10, 18, 26, 57, 60, 149, 164, 197–199
ballet. *See* Russian ballet
Balmont, Constantine, 204
Baltic Slavs. *See* Slavs

Baltics, 8–9, 13, 18–19, 40, 43, 103, 121, 179, 197, 232
baptizer of the Russians. *See* Vladimir, Prince
Barsukov, N. P., 142
Basil II, 36, 65, 70
Basil III, 35, 37, 38, 66, 71
Basque, 9
Bathory, Stephen, 42
Baumgarten, Nicholas P. S. von, 22
Bazhenov, Bazil, 102
Beccaria, Marchese De Cesare Bonesana Di, 97,
    104
Belarus, Belorussians, 4–5, 7, 20–21, 26, 34, 49, 58,
    226
Belgium, Belgians, 149, 201
Belinsky, Vissarion, 157–158, 174, 193
Bely, Andrei (Boris Bugaev), 204
Benckendorff, Count Alexander, 136, 144, 163, 165
Benois, Alexander, 204–205
Berdiaev, Nicholas, 153, 206
Beria, 230
Berlin, Sir Isaiah, 160
Beseduiushchii Grazhdanin. See Conversing Citizen
bespopovtsy, 57
Bestuzhev, Alexander, 116
Betsky, Ivan, 95
Bezborodko, Prince, 115
Biren (or Biron), Ernst-Johann, 88
Black Hundreds, 203
Black Partition. *See* Land and Freedom
Black Sea, 9, 18, 202
Blok, Alexander, 204, 207
Bloody Sunday, 201–202, 209
Blum, Jerome, 168
Bobrikov, General Nicholas, 187
Bohemia, 22
Bolotnikov, Ivan, 46–47, 49, 82
Bolsheviks, Bolshevism, Bolshevik revolution, 201,
    208, 213–214, 229
Boris Godunov (Pushkin), 139
Born, Ivan, 116
Borodino, battle of, 112, 163
Botkin, Basil, 157
boyars, 36, 38, 40–48
Brezhnev, Leonid Ilych, 211–212, 219, 221, 230
Brigadier, The (Fonvizin), 103, 106
British. *See* Great Britain, British
Briusov, Valery, 204
Bronze Age, 11, 13–14
Bronze Horseman, The, 93, 140–141
Brotherhood of Cyril and Methodius, 162
Brothers Karamazov, The (Dostoevsky), 193
Bruce, James, 104
Brussels, 201
Buddhism, 185, 226, 232

Bukharin, Nicholas, 217
Bulatov, Colonel Alexander, 127
Bulavin, Conrad, 82
Bulgakov, Sergei, 206
Bulgaria, Bulgarians, 7, 10, 26, 29, 60, 63–65, 70, 198
Bulgarin, Thaddeus (Faddei), 134–135, 138–139, 141
Bulgars, 8, 10, 20, 63
Bunge, Nicholas, 190
Butashevich-Petrashevsky, Michael, 160, 166
Buturlin committee, 148
Buzhinsky, Gabriel, 83
bylina, byliny, 21, 30
Byzantium, 22, 29–30, 37, 55, 62–67, 81, 107, 122, 197
    interactions with and impacts on Kievan Russia,
        18, 20–21
    Russian Church's break with, 51
    as source of Russian Christianity and culture, 20,
        23–27, 70–71

Cadet. *See* Constitutional Democratic Party
caesar, 63–64, 67
Cambodia, Cambodians, 226
Capetian, 36
capitalism, 4, 208, 213, 216, 221
    as affected by Alexander II's legislation, 172
    and early Russian capitalists' attempts at
        organization, 189
    as giving rise to labor legislation, 190, 200
    "great reforms'"s effects on, 188–189
    Russian hopes to bypass, 175–176
    and Russia's first significant strikes (1870, 1878,
        and 1879), 190
    and St. Petersburg strikes (1896 and January
        1897), 190
Carlos, Don, 149
Carpathians, 7, 9, 18
Cathedral of the Assumption of Our Lady, 27
Cathedral of Saint George, 27
Catherine II. *See* Catherine the Great
Catherine the Great, 75–77, 88–89, 104, 106–109, 111,
        113, 125, 162–165
    Age of Reason influences on, 94–98
    character traits, 93–94
    as educator of Alexander I, 122
    endorsement of absolute monarchy by, 96
    Peter the Great, 93–94
    influence of the *philosophes* on, 96–97, 99–100,
        103
    legal and legislative plans and reforms, 97
    personal background, 95–96
    as pioneer of women's education, 98
    posture towards effects of French Revolution on
        gentry and serfs, 98, 105, 110
    posture *vis-à-vis* Russia, 93
    reign's effect on literature, science, and art, 102

    rivalry with Peter the Great, 93–95
Catholicism, Catholics. *See* Roman Catholicism,
    Roman Catholics
censorship, 148, 154
census, 67–68, 84, 188, 190, 226
Chaadaev, Peter, 151–152, 156, 161–163
Chagall, Marc, 205
Chaliapin, Fedor, 205
Chancellor, Richard, 40
Charles XII, 99
Charnolusky, Vladimir, 191
Charques, 111
Chasles, Philarète, 142
Chebyshev, Pafnuty, 192
Chechnya, Chechens, 232
Cheka, 217
Chekhov, Anton, 192
Chernenko, Constantine, 211–212, 219
Chernigov, 21
Chernov, Victor, 201
Chernyshevsky, Nicholas, 174–176
chervonets, chervontsy, 121
Chicherin, Boris, 164
Childhood, Boyhood, and Youth (Tolstoy, Leo), 194
China, Chinese, 63, 69, 80, 189, 226
Chistov, K. V., 83–85
Choice of a Tutor, The (Fonvizin), 106
Chosen Council, 38, 41, 43
Christendom, 19–20, 23, 29, 53, 151, 153
Christianity, 6, 10, 14, 31, 51, 54, 63, 66, 70, 72, 84–85,
        92, 103, 113, 122, 152, 185–186, 193, 195, 226,
        229
    characteristics of Russian Orthodoxy, 59
    influence of baptism of the Rus, 5, 19
    influence of Byzantium on Kievan Russian,
        20–24, 27
    Kievan, 24
    Slavic form, 17
    as source of Russian identity, 24–30, 50, 132,
        134–135, 137
Christoff, Peter, 163
Christology, 24
Church, Russian, 19–22, 24, 33, 36–37, 39, 48–49, 59,
        61, 66, 69, 71–72, 79, 83–84, 86, 97, 100, 108,
        153, 183–184, 191, 210, 226, 229, 231
    acquisition of independent standing, 51
    as central Kievan institution, 25–28
    and cult of fertility, 12
    decline during Westernization process, 107
    as diocese of the Patriarchate of Constantinople,
        23, 25
    and heretics, 53
    ideological division between possessors and
        nonpossessors in, 54–55
    move from Kiev to Moscow by, 50

as part of Official Nationality, 133–136
persecution under Communist regime, 219–220
in Putin's regime, 232
and the *raskol*, 55–58
and the religious protection bill of Yeltsin, 232
reorganization under Peter the Great, 80–82
and Russification, 185–187
and schism of 1054, 20, 53
17th century apogee of, 51–52
stance regarding killing and wars, 30–31
struggles with paganism, 28–29
See also Orthodoxy, Eastern
Church of the Intercession of Our Lady, 27
Church Slavonic. *See* Old Church Slavonic
Cimmerians, 15–16
civil liberties, civil rights, 113–114, 119, 201–202
civil war, 18, 21, 25, 29, 43, 209, 214–215, 217, 225, 227,
    229–230
clergy, 41, 117, 192
    and the Fundamental Laws, 204
    and its appeal on behalf of Boris Godunov, 45
    and its deposing of Basil Shuisky, 48
    in Kievan period, 25, 30–31
    as only legitimate teachers, per Official
        Nationality, of logic and psychology, 142
    perception of the *raskol* reformers as being
        under influence of the Ukrainian, 58
    poor state of, as depicted by Kantemir, 104
    Tsar Alexis' attempts to improve the
        performance of, 56
collectivization, 213–217, 224–225, 227–228
Cominform, 213
Comintern, 212
Committee of Ministers, 143
Committee of the Sixth of December, 143
communes, communal, 57, 116, 152–153, 161, 175, 177,
    197, 215–216
    peasant, 152, 155, 166, 170, 174, 176, 178–180, 197,
        204, 216
Communism, communists, 214–215, 221, 223–229,
    231–232, 235
concentration camps, 216
*Concerning the Development of a Monistic View of
    History* (Plekhanov), 200
Condillac, Étienne Bonnot de, 99
Condorcet, Marquis de (Marie Jean Antoine
    Nicolas Caritat), 116
Confession, A (Tolstoy, Leo), 195
Congress of Berlin, 182, 199
Congress of Vienna, 131
conjurations, 11
conspiracy theories, 235
Constantine, Grand Duke, 126, 128, 143, 171
Constantinople, 19–21, 23, 25, 29, 51, 53–54, 56, 58,
    64, 66, 70–71, 99

See also Byzantium
Constitutional Charter of the Russian Empire, 120
Constitutional Democratic Party, 200
constitutionalism, 111, 201, 210
    and Alexander I's reign's failure to produce
        constitution, 117, 123–124
    and Alexander I's sponsorship of French Charter
        of 1814, 120
    and Alexander I's Unofficial Committee, 114, 119
    and constitutional monarchy, monarchists, 119,
        125, 201–202
    and constitutional period of Russian imperial
        history, 203–204, 207–208
    and the Decembrists, 125–129
    and Muraviev's constitution, 127
    and Novosiltsev's constitutional project, 120–122,
        131
    and October Manifesto, 202
    and oligarchic interlude of Empress Anne, 108
    and Pestel's constitution, 125
    and Polish constitution of 1815, 113–114, 120
    and reign of Nicholas I, 147–148
    following revolution of 1905, 5, 203–204
    Slavophilic opposition to, 154–155
    and state *duma* per Speransky, 119
Conversing Citizen, 104
cosmism, 235
cosmopolitanism, 76–77, 150
cossacks, 44, 46–48, 196, 227
Council of a Hundred Chapters, 39
Council of Florence, 51, 65, 71
Council of State, 118, 120
Council of the Tsar, 134
Courland, 40, 108, 121
Crete, 13
Crime and Punishment (Dostoevsky), 193
Crimea, 39–40, 60, 161
Crimean Tartars, 41–42, 49, 60
Crimean War, 132, 148–149, 164, 168–169, 172, 209
critical realism, 172–173, 175
Cuba, Cubans, 221
cult of personality, 219, 221
Custine, Astolphe Marquis de, 164
Cyrillic alphabet, 26, 222
Czartoryski, Prince Adam, 113
Czech, 7

d'Alembert, Jean Le Rond, 103
Danilevsky, Nicholas, 199, 234
Danube river, 8, 10
Darwinism, 174
Davlet-Geray, Khan, 42
Dazhbog, 14
Decembrists, 104, 116, 125–129, 162, 165, 168
Delianov, Ivan, 183, 191

Demidov Law School, 115
democratization, 170, 172
denga, dengi, 67
Denisov, Andrew and Simeon, 57
Denmark, 19
Derzhavin, Gabriel, 90–91, 102
despotism, despot, 22, 72, 123, 132, 136, 161
determinism, determinists, 74, 177, 186, 200
Deutsche Jahrbücher, 159
Diaghilev, Sergei, 204–205
Diderot, Denis, 99–100, 103, 164
dlia togo, 79
Dmitri Donskoi, Grand Prince, 50
Dmitri of Uglich, Prince, 45–47
Dnieper river, 8–9, 14, 16, 35
Dobroliubov, Nicholas, 175–176
Dobryi nastavnik. See Good Teacher, The
döcin, 69
dogma, dogmatic, 50, 56–57, 133,137, 172, 211–212,
    220, 225
Dolgoruky, Prince Iury, 35
Dolgorukiis, Princes, 89
Don river, 35, 84
Dorpat, 40, 114
Dostoevsky, Fedor, 155, 158, 161, 172, 192–195, 206,
    209
druzhina, 19
Druzhinin, N. M., 121, 147
Dukh Zhurnalov. See Spirit of Journals
dukhobory, 187
duma, 41, 47–48, 82, 119–120, 202–203, 207–208,
    233–234
Dumézil, Georges, 11
Durov, Sergei, 162
Dushan, Stephan, 63–64
Dvina river, 40
dvoeverie, 28–29
Dzerzhinsky, F. E., 230

East China Railway, 189
East Slavs. *See* Slavs
Eastern Europe, 9
Eastern Orthodoxy, 152
Eastern Question, 149
education, 52, 105, 120, 128, 159, 172, 188, 190, 194,
    196, 210
    of Alexander I by Catherine the Great, 122
    and Alexander I's Unofficial Committee, 119
    changes in, as one of the "great reforms" of
        Alexander II, 171
    changes in, during Alexander I's first reform
        period, 114–117
    and Church in Kievan period, 26
    contributions towards abolition of serfdom, 108

rise of humane feelings and attitude correlated
    to rise in, 168–169
and the Decembrists, 125, 127
and decline of its standards under Mongol
    presence, 62
in 18th century Russia, 76, 100, 103
Enlightenment as promoter of, 106–107
Fonvizin's treatment of, 106
and its effect on nationalism, 3–5
and Novikov, 109
and Official Nationality, 130, 142
and Peter the Great the Educator, 91
in Peter the Great's reign, 76, 79–80, 98
Popugaev's ideas regarding, 116
and populism, 181
in post-Stalin era, 221
under purview of *zemstvo* institutions, 170–171
rapid spread of, in Silver Age, 204, 207
under reign of Nicholas I by Minister of
    Education Uvarov, 132–135, 142, 145–148
under reign of Nicholas II by Minister of
    Education Dmitri Tolstoy, 186, 191
role played by present-day Church in, 232
Soviet Union as an experiment in, 223–225, 229
and university statute of 1863, 191–192
value of, in minds of citizens of Enlightenment,
    76
of women in Russia, 98, 146, 181, 184
Efimova, Alena, 85
1848,
    manifesto of Nicholas I, 135
    revolutions of, 142, 146, 148–149, 161–162
1812, War of, 4, 112, 123–124, 163, 195
Elizabeth, Empress, 88–90, 94, 98, 103, 109, 115
elk, 12, 16–17
Elysard, Jules. *See* Bakunin, Michael
Emancipation of Labor Group, 201
emigration, 223
    French, 114
    Jewish, 186
    Russian, 23, 155, 207, 214, 229, 234–235
Encyclopédie (Diderot and d'Alembert), 99, 103
England, 3, 22, 39, 40, 76, 104, 110, 117, 155, 227
    See also Great Britain
Engels, Fredrick, 190, 213–214, 216
enlightened despotism, 77, 84, 92, 94, 96, 98, 100,
    105–106, 108, 110, 112, 127, 131, 155
Enlightenment, 84, 87, 97, 99, 105, 107–108, 110, 112,
    118, 122, 124–125, 127, 129, 132, 155, 167, 175
    Alexander I as seen initially as representing best
        of Enlightenment, 113–114
    Catherine the Great as a child of, 95–96
    Catherine the Great's attempt to understand
        Peter the Great in terms of, 93–94

as cause of thoughts regarding improvement of
education, 116
and the Decembrists, 126
dominant themes in thought and literature of
Russian, 104
effects on governmental legislation, 98
as embodied in reign of Catherine the Great,
102–103,
as embodied in reign of Peter the Great, 76–78,
80, 82, 91
as facilitated by gentry, 89
as found wanting in Russia, 111
ideals of, 150–151
and image of Peter the Great the Enlightener in
literature of Russian, 91
influence of France on Russian, 103
influence of Germany on Russian, 103
influence of Great Britain on Russian, 104
influence on policies and legislative goals of
Peter the Great and Catherine the Great, 98
as an influence towards abolition of serfdom,
109, 119
and Novikov as Russian counterpart to French
philosophes, 106
reign of Alexander I as second, 111, 113–114, 131
Russia as bearer to non-European world of, 209
Russian version atypical of western nations'
versions of, 100–101
as a unifying ideology of western world, 165
and villages of, 116
as welcomer of Russia as promising and
enthusiastic disciple, 163
See also Age of Reason
epic, 11, 15, 18, 21, 23, 30
Esenin, Sergei, 205
Essence of Christianity (Feuerbach), 158
Estates General, 109
esthetics, 173–174, 206
Estonia, Estonians, 121
ethnicity, ethnic, 3, 5, 10, 15, 17, 21, 34, 167, 171,
202–203, 210, 222, 226
Eurasia, Eurasianism, Eurasians, 8, 62, 67, 69,
234–235
Europe, the West, Europeans, Westernization, 7, 13,
16, 19, 23–28, 30, 33, 35, 37–38, 43, 44, 49–50,
52, 55–60, 65, 67, 74, 81, 84, 89, 91, 95,
100–101, 104–106, 115–117, 125, 132–136, 138,
153–154, 162, 165, 167, 173–175, 177, 180,
187–189, 191, 193, 196, 198–200, 205–206, 209,
212–214, 221, 234
admiration of Alexander I, 112
battle at Poltava as initiator of closer ties to, and
as transformer of Russia into major power
in, 75–76, 82–83

Catherine the Great's perspective of Russia *vis-à-
vis* Europe, 75–76
emergence of Muscovy as major power, 99
and Enlightenment, 76–77
and French Revolution, 109–110
good press in 18th century from, 163–164
and Iaroslav the Wise, 22
Ivan IV's invitation to specialists from area to
serve tsar, 40
Kievan state understood as state of, 22
Nicholas I's reaction to post-French Revolution
disorder of, 133–134, 142, 148–149
Peter the Great's efforts to westernize, 60, 73, 71,
75–81
"proto"-Indo—Europeans' expansion from
Eurasia into Near East and, 8–9, 11
resumption of visits from, after Time of
Troubles, 73
Russian intellectual isolation from, following
revolutions of 1848, 142, 164
Russian isolation from, during appanage and
Muscovite periods, 20, 34, 40, 53, 62, 72–73
Russian participation in literary, scientific, and
artistic development of, 102–103
Russian suspicions of, traced to break between
Eastern and Western Churches, 20
and Russia's turn westward for social and
cultural models, 5, 76–77, 114, 118, 127
serfdom in, 108, 118
Slavic migrations and expansion of Slavic zone
in, 10–11
as a source of instruments of punishment and
torture, 69
as a source of new intellectual climate in
Alexander II's reign, 172
as standing closer to Russia than Mongol states,
70
and the Westernizers, 79–80, 88, 107, 150–152,
155–161, 166, 168, 176, 192, 197
Exodus to the East (Trubetskoy, Savitsky,
Suvchinsky, and Florovsky), 234

Fables, 104
fairy tales, 17
Falconet, Étienne-Maurice, 93
False Dmitri, 45–46, 52
False Dmitri the Second, 46–47
False Peter, 46, 72
famine, 45, 167, 191, 200
fanaticism, 211, 234
Far East, 189, 222
Far Right, 233
Fathers and Children. See *Fathers and Sons*
Fathers and Sons (Turgenev, Ivan), 173, 193

Fedor. *See* Theodore (Fedor), Tsar
Fedotov, George, 23, 27
Felon of Tushino. *See* False Dmitri the Second
feudalism, 31
Feuerbach, Ludwig, 158
Filaret, Patriarch, 52
Finland, Finns, Finnish, 4–5, 114, 120, 185, 187, 197, 204, 210
Finnic, 22, 46, 50, 84
Finnish Literary Society, 4
Finno-Ugric, 4
First Academic Expedition, 98
First Army, 136
First Five-Year Plan, 213
First Minor, The (Fonvizin), 106
First Turkish War, 94
Florinsky, Michael T., 23
Florovsky, G. V., 234
Fokine, Michael, 205
folk literature, folklore, folktales, folk songs, 9, 11, 13, 15, 20–21, 23, 87, 152
    See also myths and legends
Fomenko, A. T., 233
Fontenelle, Bernard de, 104
Fonvizin, Denis, 102–104, 106
forced labor, 216, 230
forest, 15–16, 50, 86–87
formalism, 55, 58–59
Forward, 177
Fourier, Francois-Marie-Charles, 161
Fourierism, 161, 166
France, French, 3–6, 22, 36, 39, 88–89, 96, 100, 104, 113, 116–117, 120, 123–125, 127, 142, 148–150, 158–159, 161, 174, 176, 181, 196, 205, 209–210, 226–227, 234
    Catherine the Great
        attempt to portray Russia as protector of freedoms and deplore their decline in, 97
        break of diplomatic relations with, 110
        view of, 103, 110
    expressions of gratitude towards Alexander I from, 112
    and French Academy of Sciences, 76
    Ivan IV's methods to unify and centralize were comparable to Louis XI's, 43
    Nicholas I's view of, 164
    as one source of Freemasonry, 109
    Paris Commune, 177
    Peter the Great's visit, 112
    wars with Napoleonic, 114
    Witte received large loan from, 203
Franciscans, 55
Frank, Semen, 207
Frederick the Great, 110

Free Economic Society, 105, 121
Freemasons, 109–110
French Academy of Sciences, 76
French National Assembly, 116
French Revolution, 3, 6, 109–110, 114, 125, 127, 148, 150, 158, 181
Fundamental Laws, 203, 208

Gabaev, G. S., 128
Galicia, 34
Gapon, George, 202
gathering of the Russian land, 35,—37, 40, 44, 51, 59, 65
Geller, M. and Nekrich, A., 226, 229
Gellner, Ernest, 3
gendarme of Europe, 148
    See also Nicholas I
gentry, Russian, 67, 70, 74, 115–117, 121, 124, 147, 157, 161, 170, 188–189, 203
    Alexander I's stance towards, 119
    attempts after Peter the Great's death to escape service and to increase advantage, 88
    Catherine the Great's Charter to and endorsement of, 98, 105
    and crisis of agriculture during reign of Nicholas I, 164–165
    debt accumulation during reigns of Nicholas I and Alexander II by, 168
    and the Decembrists, 128
    decline of, during reign of Alexander II and period of "great reforms," 172
    difficulties encountered during Time of Troubles by, 44
    educational advantages of, during reign of Nicholas I, 146
    emancipation of, 89, 98
    as facilitator of Russian Enlightenment, 89
    increase of political representation resulting from changes in *zemstvo* system for, 184
    interpretation of the *raskol* as protest against domination by, 57–58
    Ivan IV's general regulations for military service of, 39
    participation in Freemasonry by, 109
    after Peter the Great's death, 89
    request to King Sigismund III for Wladyslaw to become next Russian tsar by, 47–48
    service, 43–44, 48, 100
    stance of, during rebellion by Shakhovskoi and Bolotnikov, 46
    and the State Gentry Land Bank, 184
    uselessness and vices of, as depicted by Kantemir, 104
Gentry Nest, A (Turgenev, Ivan), 193

Georgia, Georgians, 185, 219–220, 222, 226

German Idealism, 158

Germany, Germans, 31, 75, 94, 104, 110, 117, 159, 173, 179, 186, 188, 193, 210–211, 213, 222, 224–225, 228, 230

acceptance of Ivan IV's invitation to serve tsar by specialists from, 40

Alexander I's revival of German university in Dorpat, 114

appanage Russian wars against German Knights, 34

Catherine the Great's admiration of Enlightenment of, 96

influence of Idealistic philosophy of, 3, 141–143, 150–151, 155–158, 160

influence on Russian Silver Age, 205–206

Kievan matrimonial alliances with, 22

as one source of Freemasonry, 109

and Panslavism, 198

as place of Catherine the Great's birth and childhood, 96

resemblance between Peter the Great's system of governmental reform and that of, 74

Russian revolutionary intelligentsia in symbiosis with radicalism from France and, 176

Russians studying in universities in, 150

as a source of Enlightenment in Russia, 103

as a source of instruments of punishment and torture, 69

Gimbutas, Marija, 9–10

gimnaziia, 191

Glagolithic alphabet, 26

glasnost, 225, 230, 233

Godunov, Boris, 43, 45, 51–52

Godunovs, 45–46

Gogol, Nikolai (Nicholas), 135, 139, 158

Golden Horde,

assistance to Muscovites in the gathering of Russian land by, 36

continued Russian warfare with successor states, 60

dissolution of, 37, 39

interpretation of lineage of Muscovite tsars as deriving from, 62–71

See also Mongols

Golitsyns, Prince, 89

Golovin, Nicholas, 208

Golovnin, Alexander, 191

Goncharov, Ivan, 176, 192

Good Teacher, The (Fonvizin), 106

Gorbachev, Mikhail, 211–212, 219, 225, 230–231, 235

Gordon, Patrick, 104

Goremykin, Ivan, 208

Goths, 10

gradualism, 157, 181

Granovsky, Timothy, 157, 159

Great Britain, British, 43, 104, 109, 118, 149, 164, 209, 213, 228

See also England

Great Lada, 13

Great Moravia, 10

Great Northern War, 60, 77–79

"great reforms," 5, 160, 168, 171–172, 188, 191, 193, 197

Great Russia, Great Russians, 5, 7, 17, 21–22, 26, 34–35, 49, 58, 61, 185, 222, 226

Grech, Nicholas, 134, 137, 141–142

Greece, Greeks, 10, 18, 21, 23–24, 26, 29, 51, 56, 63–64, 70, 99–100, 115

Greek Church. *See* Byzantium

Griboedov, Alexander, 128

Grimm, Friedrich Melchior, 96

Grossman, Vasily, 228

Groznyi, 38

gulag, 220, 225

Gumilev, Nikolai, 204, 235

Habakkuk. *See* Avvakum, Archpriest

Hadrian, Patriarch, 81, 84

Haltsonen, Sulo, 4

Hanseatic League, 40

Hapsburg empire, 4, 198

Hardrada, Harold, 22

Hare Krishnas, 232

hat of Monomakh, 66, 71

Hegel, Hegelianism, Hegelians, 151, 156–158, 160, 166, 176, 200

Young Hegelians, 158

Helsingfors. *See* Helsinki

Helsinki, 114

Henry IV, 22

Herder, Johann Gottfried von, 198

Hermogen, Patriarch, 51

Herodotus, 14, 17

Herzen, Alexander, 155–162, 176, 209

Hesychasm, 53–54

Hilarion, 24, 27, 32

Himalayas, 234

Historical Letters (Lavrov), 177

historicism, 198

History of the Russian State (Karamzin), 139

Hitler, Adolf, 210, 212

Holland, Dutch, 76, 79, 104

Holy Alliance, 113, 122

Holy Roman Emperor, 65

Holy Russia, 84

Holy Synod, 81, 183, 186, 192, 195

horin, 69

Hosking, Geoffrey, 167, 209

Hungary, Hungarians, 4, 19, 22, 42, 64, 149, 164, 199
Huns, 9
Huxley, Thomas, 197
Hyperboreans, 13

Iablochkov, Paul, 192
Iakubovich, Captain Alexander, 127
iarlyk, 67, 69
Iaroslav the Wise, 18, 22, 25, 29, 40, 50
Iaroslavl, 115
Iavorsky, Metropolitan Stephen, 81
icons, icon-painting, 20, 24, 49, 54, 59, 86, 202, 205
idealism. *See* German Idealism
identity, Russian, 45, 47, 177
    Christianity as part of, 20
    as defined by scholarship, 17
    difficulties in studying, 5
    extent of a group's traceable history, 7
    Imperial, 73, 82, 155, 165–166
    Kievan, 4–5, 27, 29–30
    Muscovite, 37, 49–50, 59–60, 63, 70
    post-Soviet, 62, 233–234
    Soviet, 6, 211
Idiot, The (Dostoevsky), 193
Ignatovich, Inna Ivanovna, 168
Illyria, 10
Ilovaisky, D. I., 7
Imagined Communities (Anderson), 4
Imperial Academy of Sciences, 79–80, 91, 98, 102, 132, 204, 222, 226
imperialism, 213, 221
Indo-European, 7–9, 11–14
industrialization, 188–190, 208, 215, 224–225
infidels, 60, 71, 150
Institut de France, 112
Instruction to the Legislative Commission (Catherine the Great), 75, 96
Iran, Iranians, 15, 63, 69, 149, 189
Isidore, Metropolitan, 51
Iskhod k Vostoku. See Exodus to the East
Islam, 19, 185, 226, 232
Israel, Israeli, 82, 225
Iuriev Polsky, 27
Ivan I (Kalita), 36
Ivan II (the Meek), 50
Ivan III (the Great), 35–37, 53, 55, 60–61, 65–66, 70, 73
Ivan IV (the Terrible), 35, 38–41, 43, 61, 63, 66–67, 70
Ivan V, 88, 108
Ivanov, George, 211

Jacobins, 181
Jakobson, Roman, 234
Japan, Japanese, 80, 188, 201, 228, 234

Jefferson, Thomas, 122, 164
Jenghiz Khan, 69, 72
Jesuits, 45, 114
Jew Zechariah, 53
John VIII Palaeologus, 65–66
Journal of the Ministry of Education (Uvarov), 134
Judaism, Jews, 19, 185–187, 193, 203, 222, 225–226, 232
Judaizers, 53

Kadinsky, Vasily (Basil), 205
Kaluga, 47
Kankrin, Egor, 74, 121, 147
Kantemir, Antioch, 102, 104
Karakorum, 68
Karakozov, Dmitri, 180–181
Karamzin, Nicholas, 109–110, 115–116, 138–139, 142
Kartashev, A. V., 72
Katkov, Michael, 172, 181, 197–198
Kavelin, Constantine, 156
Kazakov, Matthew, 102
Kazan, 38–41, 60–61, 63, 67, 114
kenoticism, 24
Kettler, Gotthard, 40
Khalturin, Stephen, 190
khans, 31, 36–37, 40, 62–63, 67–68, 71
Kharkov, 114–115
Khazars, 20, 30
Kheraskov, M. M., 88
Khlebnikov, Velemir, 204
Khlynov, 22
Khmer Rouge, 226
Khomiakov, Alexis, 130, 152, 154–157, 198
Khrushchev, Nikita, 211–212, 216, 219–220, 226
Khvorostinin, Ivan, 46
Kiev, Kievan Russia, 18–32; 4–5, 32, 36–38, 40, 44, 49–51, 53, 56, 58–62, 64–68, 70–71, 147, 162, 198
    city of, as belonging to tribe of Poliane, 10
    city of, as site of new university under reign of Nicholas I, 136
    culture and art, 22, 27–28
    description of "state", 18–19, 21–22, 28, 31
    economy, 19, 22, 31
    enthusiastic stance towards Christianity, 24
    as home of Russian Church, 33
    icon-painting in, 20–21
    importance of Byzantium's influence on, 20, 23, 27
    importance of saints in, 25
    and Kievan epic cycle, 11
    and Kievan Rus, 10–11, 18
    language, 26
    linguistic and ethnic differentiation of Kievan Russians into three peoples, 34
    monasteries in, 25

Mongol destruction of the city, 18
monks as source of most literature of, 27
occupation of city by Scandinavian princes, 18
popular appeal of warriors of, 30
populist and democratic element in system of, 19
readership in, 28
Russian Church in, 25–26
stone architecture in, 20, 28
and struggles with invading peoples of the
    Steppe, 29–30
ties with western European nations through
    numerous marriages, 22
towns and the middle class, 19
view of capital punishment, 30–31
view of participation in warfare, 30–31
as welcoming to newcomers, 23
Kievan Christianity, 23–25, 27
Kievan princes, 4, 22, 30–31, 61–62, 70–71
Kievan saints, 25
King Sigismund III, 47
Kireevsky, Ivan, 152
Kireevsky, Peter, 152
Kierkegaard, Søren, 194
Kirov, Serge, 218
Kiselev, Count Paul, 147–148
Kishinev, 187
Klin, 42
Klinger, Maximilian von, 116
Kliuchevsky, V. O., 36
Kochubei, Count Victor, 113–114, 131, 143
kolkhoz, kolkhozy, 87, 216
Kovalchenko, Ivan, 168
Koran, 149
Korovin, Constantine, 205
Kostomarov, Nicholas, 162
Kotoshikhin, Gregory, 63
Koussevitzky, Sergei, 205
Kovalevsky, Alexander, 192
Kovalevsky, Vladimir, 192
Kreenholm, 190
Kremlin, 27, 38, 42, 73, 83, 211
kritika, 104
Kropotkin, Prince Peter, 196–197
Krylov, Ivan, 104
Kublai Khan, 69
Kukolnik, Nestor, 139
kulak, kulaki, 217, 227
Kulikovo, 50, 60, 64
    battle of, 37
Kurbsky, Prince Andrew, 38, 41–42
Kuzmich, Fedor, 123

LaHarpe, Frederic-Cesar de, 113, 116, 122
Land and Freedom, 182

Latin, 20, 26, 79, 191, 222
Latinism, 20, 24, 56
Lato, 13
Latvia, Latvians, 4
Lavrov, Peter, 177–179, 181
Lay of the Host of Igor, 27
Lebedev, Peter, 192
Lefort, Francis, 83
Left, 157–158, 160, 164, 166, 176–177, 181, 197, 199, 208,
    232, 235
legends. *See* myths and legends
Legislative Commission, 95, 97
Leibniz, Gottfried Wilhelm, 78, 103
Lelia, 13
Lena gold field massacre, 204
Lenin (Vladimir Ulianov), 172, 175, 194, 196,
    200–201, 207, 209, 211–221, 226, 229
Leninism, 212, 214, 223, 231
Leontiev, Constantine, 197
Lermontov, Mikhail Yurievich, 151, 158, 176
Leroux, Pierre, 160
Leskov, Nicholas, 192
Leto, 13
Liberal Democratic Party of Russia, 233
liberalism, 98, 113, 120, 157, 174, 191, 193, 204, 207
Liberation, 200
Life and Fate (Grossman), 228
Lighthouse, 134
Ligne, Prince de, 94
Likhachev, Dmitri, 28, 233
linguistics, 4, 7
Lisle, Rouget de, 112
Lithuania, Lithuanians, 19, 34–35, 38, 40–42, 45, 47,
    51, 61, 63, 65, 66, 73
Livonia, Livonians, 42, 47, 121
Livonian Order, 40, 65
Logofet, Pakhomi, 65
Lomonosov, Michael, 91, 93, 98, 101–102
London, 164, 177, 201
Loris-Melikov, General Count Michael, 182–183
Los, 16
Lossky, Nicholas, 207
Louis XI, 43
Louis XIV, 118
Louis XVI, 109–110, 118, 186
Louis-Napoleon. *See* Napoleon III
Lovers of Wisdom, 151, 161
Lubeck, 40
Lutherans, 81, 142, 185

Mably, Gabriel Bonnot de, 99
Macarius, Metropolitan, 38–39
Maiakovsky, Vladimir, 204, 207
Makosh, 12

Malia, Martin, 176, 227
Mamai, 60
Mandelstam, Osip, 204
Marxism, Marxism-Leninism, 211, 214, 216, 218–219
  as claimant to establishing nature and realizing
    destiny of Russia, 199
  historical logic as means in, 221
  interpretation of paganism in Old Russia by, 29
  limitations of Soviet, 212–213
  Plekhanov as father of Russian, 199–200
  prominent converts from, 206–207
  qualities lacking in populism that were found in
    Plekhanov's teachings of, 200
  source of misconceptions about, 212
  Soviet people's stance *vis-à-vis*, 223–226
  after Stalin's death, 220–221
  views that survived Soviet era that were non-
    Marxist, 229–230
Marxist-Leninists, 212, 215, 219–220
Marxists, 74, 179, 190, 197, 200–201, 212–217,
  219–222, 224–226, 229
Mary, Empress, 144, 146
materialism, 172–173, 177, 206
Maximilian I, 65
Mechnikov, Elijah, 192
Mediterranean, 8, 99
Memoirs of a Revolutionist (Kropotkin), 196
Mendeleev, Dmitri, 173, 192
Mensheviks, 201
Menshikov, Prince Alexander, 89
merchants, 23, 43, 104, 119, 157, 185, 192
mesolithic, 11, 13
Messenger of Europe, The (Karamzin), 115–116
messianism, 235
metaphysics, 165, 206
metropolitan, 21–22, 24–25, 33, 37, 41, 50–52, 55,
  64
metropolitanate, 22, 51
Mickiewicz, Adam, 164
Mikhailovsky, Nicholas, 177–180
Miliukov, P. N., 58, 78, 201
Miliutin, Dmitri, 171, 210
Ministry of Commerce, 117
Ministry of Education, 114, 135, 145–146, 183
Ministry of Finance, 188, 192
Ministry of Police, 117
Ministry of State Domains, 144, 147
Ministry of the Interior, 145, 183, 188–189
Ministry of Trade and Industry, 192
Minsk, 201
Mirror of Youth, 79
Mirsky (Sviatopolk-Mirsky), Dmitrii P., 204
Mnemosyne, 151
Mniszech, Marina, 45, 47

monarchist, 231
monarchy, monarchs, 43, 70, 72, 76, 88, 90, 94, 96,
  99, 108, 115, 124, 135, 149, 164
  See also autocracy, autocrats; constitutionalism
monasteries, 20, 25, 28, 50–52, 54, 144
Monastery of the Caves, 25, 28, 37
monasticism, 25–26, 37, 50, 53–55, 59, 71
Mongolia, 70, 189
Mongols, 21–22, 30–31, 33, 36, 61, 73
  and battle of Kulikova, 37
  destruction of Kiev by, 18
  domination over Russia, 34, 62
  impact on Russia, 62–71
  invasion of Russia by, 59–60
  Ivan III as liberator of Russia from, 37, 60, 65
  Russia's repeated warfare with, 60
  the yoke of, 60
  See also Golden Horde
monks, 5, 23, 25, 27, 48, 50–52, 54, 56, 64, 90
Monomakh, Emperor Constantine, 66, 70–71
Monomakh, Iury, 66
Monomakh, Vladimir, 22–23, 27, 30–31, 36, 50,
  60–61, 63, 66, 71
Montesquieu, Baron de (Charles-Louis de
  Secondat), 94, 96, 104
moose, 12, 16
Moravia, Moravians, 10, 26
Mordva, 46
Mormons, 232
Morozovs, 189–190
Moscow Art Theater, 205
Moscow river, 35
Moscow Slavic Benevolent Committee, 198
Mount Athos, 25, 54, 56, 64
Mstislavsky, Theodore, 48
Münchengrätz and Berlin agreements, 149
Muraviev, Nikita, 125, 127–128, 165
Muscovy, Muscovites, Moscow, 33–73; 74–75, 77,
  80–83, 85, 88–89, 92–93, 95, 99, 102–103,
  105, 107–111, 114, 134, 141–142, 152, 156, 163,
  165, 184–185, 190, 198, 201–202, 205, 208–209,
  223
  as center for advocates of nationalist view of
    Russia during Nicholas I's regime, 142
  city of, as the new Constantinople, 64
  city of, as the Third Rome, 71
  competitors' inheritance customs as different
    from those of appanage, 36
  differences between Kievan Russia and, 37–38
  foreigners in service of, 73
  gathering of the Russian land in, 35–37, 59, 65
  Hesychasm in, 53–54
  history of the city, 35
  inadequacy of financial system, 78–79

intellectual and cultural contributions of other
  countries, 104
as isolated from Western Church, 53–54
Ivan I Kalita as counterpart to Kievan Vladimir
  Monomakh, 36
Khan Davlet-Geray burns city, 42
Kievan Russia linked to, 33
lack of development of middle class in, 100–101
metropolitan and metropolitanate move to city,
  22, 50
Mongol roots of the tsars of, 70
and the Mongols, 59–63, 65–71
Orthodoxy's leading characteristics in, 59
and Patriarch Nikon, 52–53, 55–56
and possessors versus nonpossessors, 54–55
and the *raskol*, 55–59
and reign of Ivan IV, the Terrible, 38–43
rise of, 35–37, 65
ritualism and formalism in culture of, 58
Russian Church in, 50–52
17th century as full flowering of, 48–49
succession after death of Tsar Theodore, 43–44
Time of Troubles in, 44–49
tsars in, as descendants of Kievan princes, 22
warfare as one source of self-identity in, 59–61
Mutual Aid, a Factor in Evolution (Kropotkin),
  196–197
muzhik, muzhiki, 100, 181
My Past and Thoughts (Herzen), 159
mysticism, 24, 122–123
myths and legends, 12, 15, 17, 86–87, 167
  See also folk literature, folklore, folktales, folk
    songs

NEP. *See* New Economic Policy
Nakaz, 96–97
Napoleon, 4, 99, 107, 112, 118, 122–123, 125, 127,
  132–133, 148, 163–164, 195
Napoleon III, 164
narod, 166
narodnik, 153
narodnost, 133, 141
Narva, 99
nationality, nationalism, 127, 164, 225, 228
  Alexander III as first nationalist on Russian
    throne, 185
  and the Black Hundreds, 203
  Christianity as a part of Russian, 20
  difficulties in studying Russian, 5–6
  emergence of popular, modern Russian, 197–198,
    209–210, 229, 232–233
  explanations of, 3–5
  and Official Nationality, 132–143, 145–146, 148,
    150, 161, 163, 165–166, 168, 197–198, 231

and Panslavism, 141, 155, 193, 198–199, 209
and Peter the Great, 82
Russian Romantic, 163
and Russification, 24, 141, 185, 187, 197, 208
Soviet Marxism's stance towards, 213, 219–223,
  229, 232
Ukrainian, 185
Navarino, 149
Navy. *See* Russian Navy
Nazism, Nazis, 211–213, 230
Near East, 8, 29, 149
Nechaev, Sergei, 181
Nekrasov, Nicholas, 158, 231, 235
Nekrylova, A. F., 87
Nepmen, 215
Neronov, Ivan, 56
Neva river, 40
Nevsky, Saint Alexander, 31, 35, 61
Nevsky, Daniel, 35
New Age movement, Russian, 235
New Economic Policy, 215, 225, 227
Newton, Sir Isaac, 196
Nezhin, 115
Nicholas I, 130–166; 125, 167, 191, 196, 231
  admiration for Peter the Great, 131, 140
  alliance between government and its educated
    public broken in regime of, 162
  as avid reader of Russian history, 139
  becoming Emperor, 126
  change in image of Russia held by other
    nationalities during reign of, 163–164
  and codification of the law, 147–148
  and the Decembrists, 126–129
  description of reign, 130–132, 143, 161–163
  difference between Alexander I's sense of
    responsible rule and that of, 131, 137–138
  and doctrine of Official Nationality, 133–137, 139,
    141–143, 148, 166
  growth of His Majesty's Own Chancery during
    reign of, 144
  ineffectiveness of committees, 143–144
  and Ministry of Education, 145–147
  Near Eastern policy, 149–150
  other nations' hatred towards regime, 164
  personality, 132, 137, 163
  and the Petrashevtsy, 145, 161–162, 165–166, 168
  position on serfdom, 147, 164
  reaction to European revolutions of 1848,
    148–149
  as representing dynastic view of nationalism,
    141–143
  and the Slavophiles and Westernizers, 156–162,
    166
Nicholas II, 167, 183, 186, 201–202, 209

Nichols, Johanna, 10

Nietzsche, Friedrich, 194

Nihilism, nihilists, 173–174, 193, 217

Nijinsky, Waslaw, 205

Nikitenko, Alexander, 142, 162

Nikon, Patriarch, 52, 84

nomads, 8, 15–16, 30, 69

Norway, Norwegians, 19, 22, 34

Notes from the House of the Dead (Dostoevsky), 193

Novgorod, 28, 31, 37, 52, 59, 71

 as East Slavic town, 10

 as home to the *strigolniki*, 53

 and its long history of warfare with neighbors, 29, 34–35

 and its tradition of placing limits on princely power, 22

 Ivan III's acquisition of, 65

 and the Judaizers, 53

 origin of Kievan state traced to linkage between Kiev and, 21

 repression by Ivan IV, the Terrible, 38, 42

 Scandinavian princes invited to govern, 18

 as site of magnificent ecclesiastical architecture in Kievan period, 20

Novgorod-Seversk, 35

Novikov, Nicholas, 105–106, 109–110

Novosiltsev, Nicholas, 113, 116, 120, 122, 125, 131, 165

Oblomov, 176, 192

obrok, 170

obshchee blago, 77

occultism, 233

October Manifesto, 202–203

October Revolution, 216, 225, 227, 229

Oder river, 8, 14

Odessa, 198

Odoevsky, Prince Vladimir, 151

Official Nationality, doctrine of,

 application in foreign policy, 148

 assessment of, 143

 and the autocracy, 144

 and Eastern Orthodoxy, 132–136

 and education, 130, 142

 and Minister of Education Uvarov, 130, 132–135, 137, 139, 142, 145–146, 148

 and nationalism, 132–143, 145–146, 148, 150, 161, 163, 165–166, 168, 197–198, 231

 and Nicholas I, 133–137, 139, 141–143, 148, 166

 opponents of, 151–161

 underlying social philosophy, 137

 widespread public support for, 161

Ogarev, Nicholas, 160

Oka river, 35

Old Belief, 57–58, 61, 72

Old Believers, Old Ritualists, 5, 29, 49, 52, 57–58, 72, 84–86, 90, 107–108, 185, 189

Old Church Slavonic, 26

Old Russian, 26

Old Testament Holy Trinity, 54

Olga, 25

On Law and Grace (Hilarion), 27

On the Eve (Turgenev, Ivan), 193

oprichniki, 42–43

oprichnina, 41–44, 61

organicism, 198

Orient, 19

Orlov, Prince Alexis, 144

Orthodoxy, Eastern, 29, 52, 130, 141, 157, 195, 233

 as a central element in Russian history and culture, 4

 and de-Byzantinization, 23–24

 and Hesychasm, 53–54

 and the Jews, 185–186

 and Nicholas I's Near Eastern policy, 149–150

 and Official Nationality, 132–136

 and the Old Believers, 72, 84–86, 90, 107–108, 185, 189

 personal importance of, for members of Russian governing elite, 107

 and Peter the Great, 80–81

 pressure on non-Orthodox denominations during regime of Alexander III, 185

 and the *raskol*, 55–58

 religious or quasi-religious nature of Muscovite tsar and tsardom, 72

 and the religious protection bill of Yeltsin, 232

 Russians regarded themselves as the defenders of, 61

 Russification and militant, 185

 and schism of 1054, 20, 53

 during Second World War, 219

 and the Slavophiles, 152

 Soviet era persecution of, 226–227

 and the *strigolniki*, 53

 See also Church, Russian

Orthodoxy, autocracy, and nationality. *See* Official Nationality, doctrine of

Osiris, 14

Ostrovsky, Alexander, 192

Ottoman empire, 65, 149, 198

 See also Turkey, Turks, Turkish

Our Disagreements (Plekhanov), 200

Pacific, 234

Padua, 104

paganism, pagans, 11–12, 15, 17, 19, 24, 28–29, 60–61, 69, 84, 92

Palaea, 26

Palaeologus, Emperor John VIII. *See* John VIII
    Palaeologus
Palaeologus, Sophia (Zoe), 65
Pale of Jewish Settlement, 185
paleolithic, 11
Pangermans, 209
Panslavism, Panslavs, 141, 155, 193, 198–199, 209
pantheon, 11–12
Paperno, Irina, 174
Paris Commune, 177
Paschalia, 65
Paskevich, Prince Ivan, 131
Pasternak, Boris, 205
Paterikon, 27
patriarch, 21, 25, 29, 45, 51–53, 56, 58, 66, 81, 219
patriarchate, 14, 23, 84, 107
patriotism, 127, 163, 222, 225, 229, 232–233
Paul I, 38, 88, 110–111, 116, 192
Pavlenko, Nicholas, 77
Pavlov, Ivan, 192
Pavlov, Michael, 150
Pavlova, Anna, 205
peasant communes. *See* communes, communal
peasants, peasantry, 5, 11–12, 52, 85, 111, 116, 124, 128,
    135–136, 139, 152, 155, 166–167, 171–174, 176,
    178–179, 181, 188–192, 194–195, 197, 203–205,
    208–209, 227, 230–231
    and Alexander I and the Unofficial Committee,
        115, 121
    in Alexander III's regime, 184
    and Bolotnikov, 46
    and Catherine the Great, 97
    during collectivization, 213, 224
    communes of, 152, 155, 166, 170, 174, 176, 178–180,
        197, 204, 216
    as cossacks, 44
    deterioration of position of, in Time of
        Troubles, 44
    and *dvoeverie*, 28–29
    and the emancipation proclamation of February
        19, 1861, 169–170
    free, 31
    as fundamental to the gathering of the Russian
        lands, 44
    insurrections of, 168, 180, 201–202, 217
    in Kievan Russia, 19, 31
    legend of Peter the Great's kindness towards, 87
    and Muscovite princes, 36
    and NEP, 215–216
    and Nicholas I's Fifth Department of His
        Majesty's Own Chancery, 144
    and Nicholas I's Ministry of Education, 145–146
    and Nicholas I's reorganization and reform of
        state, 130–131, 137, 147

    as participants in 1613 *zemskii sobor* selecting
        Michael Romanov as tsar, 48
    and the *raskol*, 57–58
    and service in Peter the Great's army, 60
    as victims of Ivan the Terrible, 42
*Peasants into Frenchman: The Modernization of
    Rural France, 1870–1914* (Weber), 4
Pechenegs, 30
Peking, 69
Perovskaia, Sophia, 182
Persia, Persians. *See* Iran
Persian Letters (Montesquieu), 104
Pestel, Colonel Paul, 125–128, 166
Peter, Metropolitan, 50
Peter I (the Great), Petrine, 74–87; 56, 58–59, 88, 92,
    98, 104, 108, 110, 131, 140, 151, 153–155, 162
    Catherine the Great's view of, 93–95
    denial of legitimacy as tsar and portrayal as the
        anti-Christ by Old Believers, 83–86
    educational and cultural achievements during
        reign, 79–80
    as enlightened despot, 77–78, 91, 93
    and Enlightenment, 76–77
    governmental reforms, 81–82
    introduction of Arabic numerals by, 80
    military reforms, 60
    period after death of, 89–90
    personality, 78, 81
    popular support of, 86–87
    reign during times of wars, 78
    reign viewed as fundamental divide in Russian
        history, 74–75
    reorganization of Russian Church, 80–81
    self image, 82
    turn to the West as comprehensive governmental
        plan, 73, 76, 79, 100
Peter III, Emperor, 88–89, 93, 98, 108
Petrashevtsy, 145, 161–162, 165–166, 168, 193
Petrovia, Petrovians, 74
Petrushka (Stravinsky), 205
philanthropy, 115, 125
Philip, Metropolitan, 42
philosophes, 76, 96–97, 99–100, 103, 106, 124, 150, 163
Philosophical Letter (Chaadaev), 151–152, 163
philosophy,
    absence in Kievan Russia of independent and
        creative theology and, 24
    evidence of widespread influence in Catherine
        the Great's reign of western Enlightenment,
        89, 101, 108–109
    influence on Russia of romanticism and German
        idealistic, 150–161
    links to modern nationalism and modern Right
        found in, 3, 197–198

philosophy, (*continued*)
  Nicholas I's suspicion of, 135, 142–143, 148
  Official Nationality's underlying social, 137
  and *philosophes*' admiration of Russia, 100
  in Russia
    and anarchism, 166, 195–197
    and emergence of modern Panslavism,
      198–199
    and the Lovers of Wisdom, 151, 161
    and Marxism, 199–201
    and nihilism, 173–177, 193–194, 217
    and panslavism, 141, 155, 193, 198–199, 209
    and the Petrashevtsy, 145, 161–162, 165–166, 168,
      193
    and populism, 19, 174, 177–181, 188, 190,
      192–196, 200–201
    and radicalism, 57, 108, 157–161, 176, 180, 209
    and the Slavophiles, 152–155, 161
    and utilitarianism, 77, 88, 150, 172–173,
      206–207, 217
    and the Westernizers, 79–80, 88, 107, 150–152,
      155–161, 166, 168, 176, 192, 197
    and the Young Hegelians, 158–159
  Russian revival of, 206–207
Philotheus, Philotheos (Filofei), Abbot, 54, 65, 71
physical traits, 8
Pisarev, Dmitri, 173–174
plague, 42
Platonov, S. F., 43
Plehve, Viacheslav, 186–187, 201
Plekhanov, G. V., 106, 199–201
Plurality of Worlds (Fontenelle), 104
Pnin, Ivan, 116
Pobedonostsev, Constantine, 172, 183, 186, 191,
  197
podestà, 71
poetry, 18, 102–103, 112, 137, 151, 165, 173, 204
Pogodin, Michael, 133, 137–142, 148, 198
pogroms, 185, 187
Poland, Poles, Polish, 19, 40, 43, 49, 51–52, 61, 63–64,
  74, 107, 123, 125–126, 131, 135, 147, 163, 190,
  193, 212, 230
  and Alexander I, 120
  acquisition with Lithuania of the western
    portion of Russia in appanage period, 35
  as a branch of Slavic language, 7
  Constitution of 1815, 113–114
  and conversion to Christianity in 966, 10
  designs on Russia by King Sigismund III, 47
  fifteen matrimonial alliances between Kievan
    Russia and, 22
  Finnish suppression of, 187
  influences of westernization on Russia by, 34, 56,
    73, 75

involvement in Russia during Time of Troubles,
  44, 48
Katkov's all-out campaign against Poland,
  197–198
migration to the West, 164
Nicholas I's posture towards, 149, 164
nongovernmental support for False Dmitri from
  some, 45, 47
partitioning of, 99
rebellion of 1863 in, 180–181
Russia's posture outside Roman Catholic Church
  seen as cause of longstanding enmity with,
  20
Russification of, 185
and serfdom, 108
Shuisky's eternal alliance with Sweden against,
  47
10th century founding as Slavic state of, 10
and the Union of Lublin of 1569 connecting
  Lithuania to, 42
Poliane, 10
Polish Diet, 120
Polish University of Vilna, 147
Polish uprising, 149
Politburo, 219–220, 222
Polotsk, 34, 40, 42
Polovtsy, 30, 60
Poltava, 75, 86, 91, 140
  battle of, 78
pomestie, 39, 44
Poor Folk (Dostoevsky), 193
Poor Liza (Karamzin), 109
Popov, Alexander, 192
popovtsy, 57
Popugaev, Basil, 116
populism, populists, 19, 174, 177–179, 181, 188, 190,
  192–196, 200–201
positivism, positivists, 172–173, 177, 206
Possessed, The (Dostoevsky), 193
Potemkin, Gregory, 107, 202
Power of Darkness, The (Tolstoy, Leo), 194
pravda-istina, 179
pravda-spravedlivost, 179
prehistory, prehistoric, 6–7, 11, 17, 19, 31
Preobrazhenskii prikaz, 85
Presniakov, Alexander, 60
Primary Chronicle, 18, 21, 27–28
Problems in Understanding History (Lavrov), 177
Prokopovich, Feofan, 81–83
proletariat, 172, 189–190, 216, 222
Protestantism, 153
proto-culture, 8
proto-language, 8
proto-Slavs, pre-Slavs. *See* Slavs

Prus, 66, 164
Prussia, 110, 112, 132, 149, 164
Pskov, 21–22, 42, 53, 59, 69, 71, 84
Pugachev, Emelian, 108
Pugachev rebellion, 107, 124, 147, 168
Pulkovo observatory, 146
pure communism. *See* anarchistic communism
purges, 42, 52, 216–222, 224–225, 227–229
Pushkin, Alexander, 23, 69, 101, 112, 117, 128–129, 135,
    139–141, 144, 158, 168, 173, 193
Putin, Vladimir, 232–233, 235

Rachmaninov, Sergei, 205
racism, 233, 235
radicalism, 57, 108, 159, 176, 180, 209
Radishchev, A. N., 104–105, 108, 110, 113, 165
rannie slavianofily, 155
Ranny Nedorosl. See *First Minor, The*
raskol, 55, 57–58
Rasmussen, Karen, 94
Rasputin, Grigory, 186, 208–209
rationalism, rationalists, 53, 114, 150, 153, 194–195
Raynal, Guillaume Thomas François, Abbé, 99
Razin, Stepan (Stenka), 49, 59, 82
Reader's Library, 135
realism, 17, 106, 172–174, 205, 215, 223
Realpolitik, 199
Realschule, 191
Rechtsstaat, 120
Red Army, 212, 215
Red Square, 38
Redkin, Peter, 156
Reformation, 57, 62, 89, 107
reforms, 61, 89, 140, 162, 175, 180,
    of Alexander I, 113–122, 124
    Alexander II's "great," 5, 160, 168, 171–172, 188, 191,
        193, 197
    of Catherine the Great, 93–98, 100
    the Decembrists' attempt for, 125–129
    and growth of labor movement, 201
    of Ivan IV, the Terrible, 38–39, 41, 43
    of Nicholas I, 130–131, 144, 146–148, 152
    of Nicholas II, 204, 207–208
    of Nikon, 56, 58
    Petrine, 5, 56–57, 75–80, 82–83, 100–101,
    to the Russian Church, 51–53, 80–82
    to serfdom, 105, 120–122, 124, 144, 147, 152, 154,
        160, 164, 168–170, 172, 182, 189,
    and the Slavophiles, 150–155
    in Soviet era, 212, 227
    and the Westernizers, 150, 152, 155–161, 166
Regensburg, 23
Renaissance, 62, 71, 89
republicans, 96, 108, 119, 201

Revolution of 1905, 5, 183, 188, 190, 204, 207
Revolution of 1917, 57, 167, 200, 209
revolutionaries, 34, 75, 89, 110, 113, 125, 135, 144, 146,
    149, 162, 172, 175–177, 180–182, 194, 196,
    200–202, 210, 212, 214, 224, 235
Riazan, 35, 46
Riga, 190
Rig-Veda, 11, 13
ritualism, rituals, 11, 17, 51, 54–59, 64–66
Riurik, 28, 66
Robinson, G. T., 167, 188
Robespierre, Maximilien, 109
Rod, 14
Roman Catholicism, Roman Catholics, 20, 24, 50,
    151–153, 185, 193, 206, 226
Romanov, Tsar Michael, 48–49, 52
Romanova, Anastasia, 38, 42
Romanovs, 4–5, 77, 99, 103–104, 186, 202, 207, 210
Romanticism, Romanticists, 3, 139, 141, 143, 150,
    153–155, 160, 165–166, 172–173, 175, 199
Rome, Romans, 20, 53, 63, 66, 70–72, 82, 115
Romme, Gilbert, 113, 116
rossiiskii, 210
Rostov, 21, 34, 52
Rousseau, Jean-Jacques, 99, 108
Rozanov, Vasily, 206
Rublev, Andrew, 54
Rudin (Turgenev, Ivan), 193
Ruge, Arnold, 158
Rumania, Rumanians, 54
Rus, 4–6, 10–11, 18–21, 27, 29, 32, 39, 61, 66, 70
Russia: People and Empire, 1552–1917 (Hosking), 167,
    209
Russia and Europe (Danilevsky), 199
Russian ballet, 205
Russian History (Ustrialov), 139
Russian Justice (Pestel), 125
Russian Navy, 91
Russian Orthodox Church. *See* Church, Russian
Russian Revolution, 176, 196, 212, 222
Russian Word, 173
Russification, 24, 141, 185, 187, 197, 208
russkaia zemlia, 32
russkii, 64, 210
Russo-Japanese War, 188–189, 201, 209
rusyi, 64
Rybakov, B. A., 8, 11, 15–17
Ryleev, Conrad, 126
Ryndziunsky, Paul, 168

Sabaoth, 14
Saint Alexis, 37
Saint Andrew, 66
Saint Anthony, 25

Saint Boris (and Saint Gleb), 25, 31
Saint Cyril, 26
Saint Dmitri, 27
Saint Gregory Palamas, 53
Saint Joseph of Volok, 53–55
Saint Methodius, 26
Saint Nil Sorsky, 54–55
Saint Olaf, 22
Saint Sergius of Radonezh, 50
Saint Stephen of Perm, 50
Saint Theodosius, 25, 28
Saint Vladimir, 18, 25, 27, 31, 63, 66
Sakharov, Andrei, 230
Saltykov (Saltykov-Shchedrin), Michael, 103, 192,
    240, 247
Samarin, Iurii (George), 152, 156, 162
samizdat, 230
Sarai, 68
Sarmatians, 9–10, 15
Savitsky, P. N., 234
Scandinavia, Scandinavians, 18, 22
Schapov, A. P., 57
Scheinkonstitutionalismus, 208
Schelling, Friedrich Wilhelm Joseph von, 142–143,
    151, 160, 166
Schiller, Friedrich von, 150, 160
School of Mathematical and Navigational Sciences,
    80
Schwartzmann, Leo. *See* Shestov, Leo
scientism, 172
Scotland, Scots, Scottish, 104, 142
Scriabin, Alexander, 205
Scythians, 8, 10, 14–17
Sechenov, Ivan, 192
Secret Expedition, 113
sejm, 120
Selected Passages from Correspondence with Friends
    (Gogol), 135
self-definition, self-identification, self-image, 17,
    29–30, 37, 49, 59, 234
Semevsky, V. I., 121, 168
Senate, 117, 119, 124, 126, 128, 143, 171
Senkovsky, Joseph (Osip), 135, 137
Serbia, Serbians, 60, 63–64, 70, 198–199
Serbo-Croatian, 7
serfdom, serfs, 5, 48–49, 63, 70, 98, 100, 130, 141, 160,
    172, 182, 189
  abolition of, 4, 116, 121, 124, 147, 152, 154, 168–170
  and Bolotnikov, 46
  and the Crimean War, 169
  and the Decembrists, 125–129
  as embarrassment to Russian government and
    society, 108

  failure to abolish in regime of Alexander I,
    118–119, 122–124
  increase of, via *pomestie* system in Muscovite
    Russia, 44, 59
  as main obstacle to progressive Russian thought
    and action, 105
  and Old Belief, 61, 85
  public opinion in favor of abolition of, 168–169
  in regime of Nicholas I, 144–147, 164–165
  in regime of Peter the Great, 74, 87
  and the Slavophiles, 152, 154
  and the Unofficial Committee, 117–121
  uprisings of, 46, 168
  Uvarov as defender of, 142
Sergei, Grand Duke, 201
service gentry. *See* gentry, Russian
Sevastopol, 194, 209
Shakhmatov, A. A., 7
Shakhovskoi, Gregory, 46–47
Shchedrin, N. *See* Saltykov-Shchedrin
Shestov, Leo, 206–207
Shevchenko, Taras, 162
Shevyrev, Stephen, 133–134, 139–142, 156
Shirinsky-Shikhmatov, Prince Plato, 148
Shostakovich, Dmitri, 223
Shuisky, Basil, 45–48
Siberia, 4, 84, 98, 123, 161, 174, 193, 196, 222
Signposts (Struve, Berdiaev, Bulgakov, *et al.*), 206
Silver Age, 204–207
Simeon, Prince, 41, 57, 63
Sipiagin, Dmitri, 186, 201
Skharia. *See* Jew Zechariah
Skopin-Shuisky, Michael, 46–48
Skuratov, Maliuta, 42
Slavdom, 9–11, 15, 17, 21, 134, 155, 198, 234
slavery, slaves, 30–31, 39, 46, 60–61, 90, 169
Slavic, Slavonic, 7–11, 13–17, 19–22, 26, 34, 40, 51, 54,
    63, 79–80, 101, 125, 162, 198–199
Slavophilism, Slavophiles, 6, 164–166, 168, 170, 172,
    176, 198, 234
  and Chaadaev, 152
  conflict with regime of Nicholas I, 135, 141, 150,
    154, 156, 161–163
  debate with the Westernizers, 156–157, 159
  description, 152–155
  and message of Solzhenitsyn, 156
  as opposed to reforms of Peter the Great, 75,
    150–151, 154
  as a part of Russian search for identity, 155
  and the peasant commune, 152–153
  revival of, 193
  and Romanticism, 150
  Schelling's and Hegel's influence on, 151

and *sobornost*, 152
views of the West of, 153–154
Slavs, 7–11, 14–17, 139, 152, 154, 198–199
    Baltic, 19
    East, 7, 10–11, 17, 20, 31
    proto-, pre-, 9, 11, 17
    South, 7, 26, 64, 66
Slitte, 40
smenovekhovstvo, 229
smerdy, 31
Smoke (Turgenev, Ivan), 193
Smolensk, 10, 21, 34, 48, 69
Smolny Institute, 98
sobor, 38, 45, 48–49, 82, 152
sobornost, 152
Social Democrats, 201–202
socialism, socialists, 160–161, 175–176, 193, 197, 200,
        205, 212–214, 216–217, 219–225, 227, 231
Socialism and the Political Struggle (Plekhanov), 200
socialist realism, 205, 223–224
Socialist Revolutionaries, 194, 201
Society of the United Slavs, 125
Solovetsky Monastery, 57
Soloviev, S., 35
Soloviev, Vladimir, 155, 206
Solzhenitsyn, Alexander, 156, 217, 230, 233
South Russia, 8
South Slavs. *See* Slavs
sovet, 202
Soviet. *See* Union of Soviet Socialist Republics
Soviet history, historians, 31, 36, 43, 121, 168, 213, 216,
        230
Soviet Union. *See* Union of Soviet Socialist
        Republics
sovkhozy, 216
Spain, Spanish, 112, 149
Speransky, Michael, 114, 117–120, 125, 131, 147–148, 165
Spinoza, Baruch, 200
Spirit of Journals, 124
Spirit of the Laws (Montesquieu), 96
Spiritual Reglament, 81, 83
St. Petersburg (Petrograd, Leningrad), 81, 109, 120,
        153–154, 160, 182, 184–185, 189, 198, 201, 208
    Alexander I founds university in, 114
    as beloved city of Pushkin, 140
    as center for those advocating dynastic view of
        Russia during Nicholas I's regime, 142
    and the Decembrists, 126–127
    as home of the Petrashevtsy, 161–162
    as one of world's most magnificent cities, 98
    as one of two centers for the Union of Salvation
        and the Union of Welfare, 125
    Peter the Great establishes naval academy, school
    of medicine, museum of science, and
        general library in, 80
    Peter the Great moves capital from Moscow to,
        75–76
    and the St. Petersburg Soviet, 202
    significant German population in, 103
    as site of Russia's first significant strikes in 1870,
        1878, and 1879, 190
    as site of strikes of 1896 and January 1897, 190
Staël, Madame de, 121
Stalin, Stalinism, 4, 211–212, 216, 218–225, 227–228
Stalin in Power: The Revolution from Above
        (Tucker), 218
Stalingrad, 228
Stanislavsky, Constantine, 205
Stankevich, Nicholas, 157–159
starovery, staroobriadtsy, 57
State Council, 143, 147, 203
State Gentry Land Bank, 184
steppe, 5–6, 9, 15–17, 21, 29–30, 34, 59–61, 70
Stepun, Fedor, 153
Stolypin, Peter, 204, 208, 210
Straits Convention, 149
Stravinsky, Igor, 205
streltsy, 39, 45, 60, 83
strigolniki, 53
Stroganov, Count Paul, 113, 116, 119, 121
Struve, Peter, 200, 206
subjective sociology, 177
Sudebnik, 39, 69
Sukhomlinov, Vladimir, 208
sultan, 99, 149
Sumarokov, Alexander, 92, 102
Supreme Secret Council, 108
Survey of the History of Materialism, A
        (Plekhanov), 200
Survey of the History of Thought, A (Lavrov), 177
Survey of the Issues in Practical Philosophy, A
        (Lavrov), 177
Survey of the Physical and Mathematical Sciences, A
        (Lavrov), 177
Suvchinsky, P. P., 234
Suzdal, 20–21, 34–35
Svarog, 14
sviataia Rus, 39
Sviatopolk, Prince, 25
Sviatoslav, Prince, 18, 35
Sweden, Swedes, Swedish, 22, 77, 83, 120, 187
    Catherine the Great's attempt to portray Russia
        as protector of freedoms and deplore their
        decline in, 97
    influence on Petrine institutional and
        administrative reforms from, 75, 104

Sweden, Swedes, Swedish (*continued*)
  as one source of Freemasonry, 109
  Peter the Great's decisive victory at Poltava over,
    74–75
  Peter the Great's desire to catch up militarily
    with, 60
  Russian defeat at Narva by, 99
  Shuisky's agreement with, 47
  and wars with Novgorod, 34
  and wars with Russia, 42–44, 49
Switzerland, 181, 196
Sylvester, 38, 41
symbolism, 12, 17, 64

Tamerlane, 35, 69
tamizdat, 230
Tartars, 41–42, 46, 60
Tartu. *See* Dorpat
Telescope, 151
Temporary Regulations, 183, 186–187
Testament (Monomakh), 26–27, 30, 53–54
Teuton, Teutonic, 154
Teutonic Knights, 27, 30
Theodore (Fedor), Tsar, 43, 45–46, 49
theology, 24, 53, 57, 135, 148, 152, 155, 206
Third Department, 144, 165
Third Estate, 100
Third Rome, 71
  See also Muscovy, Muscovites, Moscow
Thrace, 10
Tikhomirov, M. N., 10
Timasheff, Nicholas, 219
Time of Troubles, 39, 59, 61, 72, 139
  and Bolotnikov, 46–47, 49, 82
  boyars in, 45–46, 48
  decrease in foreigners' presence during, 73
  definition, 43–44
  dynastic phase, 45
  and False Dmitri, 45
  and False Dmitri the Second, 46–47
  Russian Church's standing during, 51–52
  service gentry in, 44, 48
  spread of serfdom in, 44
  struggles with Poland and Sweden during, 44, 48
  understood as end product of rise of Muscovite
    state, 44
  uprisings during, 44, 46, 49
Tiutchev, Theodore, 3, 135, 138, 141–142, 151
Tkachev, Peter, 181
tma, 69
Togliatti, Palmiro, 221
tolstovstvo, 195
Tolstoy, Dmitri, 183, 191
Tolstoy, Leo, 187, 192, 194

Tomsky, Mikhail, 218
Torzhok, 42
Total Land Repartition. *See* Land and Freedom
totalitarianism, totalitarians, 211, 230
Transcaucasia, 144, 185, 197
Treaty of Adrianople, 149
Treaty of Brest-Litovsk, 212
Treaty of London, 149
Treaty of Nystadt, 74, 103
Treaty of San Stefano, 182, 198
Treaty of Unkiar Skelessi, 149
Trediakovsky, Basil, 101
Trepov, General Fedor, 182
Tripolye, 13–14
Trubetskoi, Colonel Prince Sergei, 127
Trubetskoy, Prince N. S., 234
Tsargrad, 64–65
tsars, tsardom, 82–83, 98, 110, 163
  changes during reign of Peter the Great to
    concept of Muscovite, 77–78
  Constantinople as Russian Tsargrad, 64
  flourishing of 17th century Muscovite, 49
  hat of Monomakh of, 66
  history of evolution, 61, 63–64
  increased powers of, via the *oprichnina*, due to
    Ivan IV's demands, 41–42
  mid-16th century landlords' required service to,
    39
  Muscovite, as an integrated society with organic
    culture, 5
  Muscovite, as descendants of Kievan princes, 22
  Nicholas II, last, 186,
  and Official Nationality, 136–138
  and the Old Believers, 49, 52, 57–58, 72, 84–86,
    90, 107–108, 185, 189
  and Orthodoxy, 4
  popular belief in, 72
  possessors' and nonpossessors' differing
    conceptions of, 54
  in reign of Alexander II, 172
  in reign of Alexander III, 183–184
  reign of Ivan IV, the Terrible, first Muscovite
    ruler to be crowned, 38–42
  in reign of Nicholas I, 168–171
  religious or quasi-religious nature of Muscovite,
    72
  rise of Muscovy into powerful east European,
    35–37
  special *zemskii sobor* of 1613 elects first Romanov
    as, 48
  theory of Golden Horde as predecessors of
    Muscovite, 62–72
  views of both educated public and uneducated
    masses supported autocratic monarchy, 92

Tucker, Robert C., 218–219
Tugarin, 30
Tugor Khan, 30
Tukhachevsky, Mikhail N., 217
Tula, 46
Tulchin, 125
tumen, 69
Turgenev, Ivan, 158, 168, 173, 192–193
Turgenev, N. I., 121
Turkey, Turks, Turkish, 46, 64, 66, 74, 94, 118, 189,
    234
  as destination of Russian industrial exports, 190
  as "pagans" or "infidels" per Orthodoxy's view,
    60
  Russian wars with, 60, 99, 149, 187, 198
  as supporter of the Crimea, 39
  as threat to Russia from the south, 49, 65
  See also Ottoman empire
Turku. *See* Abo
Turov, 26
Tushino, 47–48, 52
Tver, 36–37, 65
Twentieth All-Union Communist Party Congress,
    220

udel, 33
Uglich, 45–47
Ukraine, Ukrainians, 5, 7, 17, 26, 49, 61, 73, 84, 99,
    222, 227, 232
  belief in Messianic role of, 162
  and Christianity, 20
  clergy, 56, 58
  influence of Orthodoxy on joining of Muscovy
    by Kiev and, 56, 60
  and Kievan Russia, 21–22, 34
  Lithuanian and Polish rule and influences on, 34
  as members of progressive wing of Russian
    Church during reign of Peter the Great, 83
  as one-quarter of Russian population in 1914, 5
  and Prince Sviatoslav, 35
  'proto'-Indo-Europeans' migration from South
    Russia to, 8
  site of strikes in early labor movement, 190
  and the Uniates, 56, 226
Ukrainian nationalism, 185
Ulozhenie, 49, 94, 147
Uniate Church, 51
Uniates, 56, 226
Union of Florence, 51, 66
Union of Liberation, 200
Union of Lublin, 42
Union of Salvation, 125
Union of Soviet Socialist Republics, 211–230; 5–6,
    23, 26, 28, 31, 35–36, 42–43, 50, 59, 62, 71, 102,

    105, 111, 121, 147, 163, 168–169, 186, 188, 190,
    194, 196, 202, 205, 220, 222–223, 229–235
  achievements in industrialization and education,
    224
  as based on ideology, 211–212
  and collectivization, 213–217, 224–225, 227–228
  emigration from, 214
  and Five-Year Plans, 207, 213, 216, 221, 226
  great purges of, 216–217
  and *kolkhozy* and *sovkhozy,* 216
  and NEP, 215, 225, 227
  1991 collapse of, 212
  problems of, 225
  subordinate teachings in, 213
Union of Unions, 201
Union of Welfare, 125
Union with Rome, 51
United States of America, 104
University of Kharkov, 115
University of Moscow, 98, 109, 114, 139, 150, 157, 159,
    183
University of St. Petersburg, 139, 196
University Statute of 1835, 146
University Statute of 1884, 183
Unofficial Committee, 113–114, 117–120, 124, 127, 129
Urals, 18, 70, 189
urbanization, 224
Uspensky, Gleb, 192, 194
Ustrialov, Nicholas, 139–140, 229
utilitarianism, utilitarians, 77, 88, 150, 172–173,
    206–207, 217
utopianism, utopians, 161, 214–215, 226
Uvarov, Sergei, 130, 132–135, 137, 139, 142, 145–146,
    148

vampires, 11
Varangians, 18, 21, 23
veche, vecha, 19, 71
Vedomosti, 79
Veles. *See* Volos
Velikie, Luki, 42
Venevitinov, Dmitri, 151
Vernadsky, George, 22, 62–63, 66, 68, 70, 234
Vestnik Evropy. See *Messenger of Europe, The*
Viatka, 22, 159
Viazemsky, Prince Peter A., 103, 120, 124, 131, 164
Vilna, 114
Virgin Soil (Turgenev, Ivan), 193
Vistula river, 7–8, 66
Vladimir, 21, 27, 34, 159
Vladimir, Prince, 12, 19–21, 25
Vladimir of Staritsa, Prince, 42
Vladimir-Suzdal, 20
Vlasov, Andrei, 225

Vlasovites, 225
Volga river, 19–20, 35–36, 39, 46, 54, 103
Volokolamsk, 53
Volos, 11
volost, volosti, 184
Voltaire, François-Marie Arouet de, 95, 97, 99–100, 103, 164
Volynia, 34
Vonifatiev, Stephen, 56
Vostokov, Alexander, 116
votchina, 39
Vsevolod, Grand Prince, 23
vultures, 16
Vybor guvernera. See Choice of a Tutor, The

Walicki, Andrzej, 174, 200, 214, 217
War and Peace (Tolstoy, Leo), 195
War Communism, 214–215, 225
War of 1812. *See* 1812, War of
Warsaw, 120, 131
Weber, Eugen, 4–5
Weber, Max, 208
Wenden, 42
West, the. *See* Europe, the West, Europeans, Westernization
West Slavic, 7
Western Bug, 8
Westernization. *See* Europe, the West, Europeans, Westernization
Westernizers. *See* Europe, the West, Europeans, Westernization
What Is to Be Done? (Chernyshevsky), 175
White Russians, 7, 34, 226
Will of the People, 177, 182–183, 201

Witt, Count, 131
Witte, Sergei, 189, 192, 202–203, 210
Wladyslaw of Poland, Prince, 48
Wolff, Christian, 103

xenophobia, 127

Yeltsin, Boris, 231–233
Yiddish, 222
Young Hegelians. *See* Hegel, Hegelianism, Hegelians
Yugoslavia, 17

Zagoskin, Michael, 139
Zakharina, Natalie, 160
zamechatelnoe desiatiletie, 161
Zasulich, Vera, 182
Zavalishin, Dmitri, 128
zemshchina, 41
zemskii nachalnik, 184
zemstva, 203
Zeus, 14
Zhabotin, 16–17
Zhdanov, A. A., 222
Zheliabov, Andrew, 182
Zhidovin (the Jew), 30
Zhirinovsky, Vladimir, 233–234
Zhukovsky, Basil (Vasily), 142
Zinoviev, Gregory, 217–218
Zosima, Metropolitan, 65
Zubatov, Sergei, 202
Zyriane, 50
Zyuganov, Gennady, 232